# Workbook for
# News Reporting and Writing

Seventh Edition

## Melvin Mencher
Columbia University

Madison, WI  Dubuque  Guilford, CT  Chicago  Toronto  London
Mexico City  Caracas  Buenos Aires  Madrid  Bogotá  Sydney

Copyright © 1997 by Melvin Mencher. All rights reserved

A Times Mirror Company

ISBN 0-697-28903-6

No part of this publication may be reproduced, stored in a retrieval system, or transmitted, in any form or by any means, electronic, mechanical, photocopying, recording or otherwise, without the prior written permission of the publisher.

Printed in the United States of America by Times Mirror Higher Education Group, Inc., 2460 Kerper Boulevard, Dubuque, Iowa, 52001

10 9 8 7 6 5 4 3 2 1

# Contents

**Preface** vii
    How to Use the Map, Source List and Directories *viii*

**PART ONE    The Reporter at Work   1**

1    **On the Job**   1
    Introduction   *1*
    Editing Your Copy   *1*
        Exercises I   *1*
        Skill Drill I: Spelling   *4*
        Skill Drill II: Grammar, Punctuation and Style   *4*
        Skill Drill III: Abused and Misused Words   *5*
    Developing the Story Idea   *6*
        Exercises II   *6*
        Exercises III   *8*
        Assignments   *12*
        Campus Projects   *13*
        Community Projects   *13*
        Home Assignments   *14*
        Class Discussion   *16*
        DB/CAR   *16*
        What's Wrong?: Backache   *16*

**PART TWO    The Basics   17**

2    **Components of the Story**   17
    Introduction   *17*
    Attribution   *17*
        Exercises I   *17*
    Verification   *17*
        Exercise II   *17*
    Balance and Fairness   *19*
        Exercise III   *19*
    Brevity   *19*
        Exercises IV   *19*
    Human Interest   *22*
        Exercise V   *22*
        Assignments   *22*
        Campus Project   *23*
        Community Projects   *23*
        Home Assignment   *24*
        Class Discussion   *24*
        DB/CAR   *24*
        Skill Drill: Guidelines   *25*
        Fix It: Attribution   *26*
        What's Wrong?: Jilted   *26*

**PART THREE    Writing the Story   27**

3    **What Is News?**   27
    Introduction   *27*
    Exercises   *27*
    Assignments   *30*
    Campus Project   *31*
    Community Projects   *31*
    Home Assignment   *32*
    Class Discussion   *32*
    DB/CAR   *33*
    What's Wrong?: Winner   *33*
    You Decide: Enhancement   *33*

4    **The Tools of the Trade**   34
    Introduction   *34*
    Exercises   *34*
    Assignments   *38*
    Campus Projects   *40*
    Community Project   *41*
    Home Assignment   *41*
    Class Discussion   *42*
    Skill Drill I: References   *43*
    Skill Drill II: Arithmetic   *43*
    Fix It: Usage (1)   *50*
    What's Wrong? *The New York Times* Bloopers   *50*

5    **Story Structure**   51
    Introduction   *51*
    Exercises I   *51*
    Exercises II   *52*
    Assignments   *52*
    Campus Project   *53*
    Community Projects   *53*
    Analysis   *55*
    Home Assignment   *55*
    Class Discussion   *55*
    DB/CAR   *56*
    Skill Drill: Necessities   *58*
    Fix It: Scrambled   *59*
    What's Wrong: *Newsweek*   *60*
    You Decide: Term Paper   *60*

## 6   The Lead   61
    Introduction   *61*
      Exercises   *61*
      Assignments   *63*
      Campus Project   *63*
      Community Projects   *63*
      Home Assignments   *65*
      Class Discussion   *66*
      Skill Drill I: Lead Choice   *66*
      Skill Drill II: Simplifying   *67*
      Fix It: Leads   *67*

## 7   The Writer's Art   68
    Introduction   *68*
    Fifty Common Errors   *68*
      Exercise   *72*
      Assignments   *72*
      Campus Projects   *73*
      Community Project   *74*
      Home Assignment   *74*
      Class Discussion   *74*
      DB/CAR   *75*
      Skill Drill: Tightening the Lead   *75*
      Fix It: Usage   *76*
      You Decide: Gangs   *76*

## 8   Features, Long Stories and Series   77
    Introduction   *77*
    Features   *77*
      Exercises I   *77*
      Assignments I   *79*
    Long Stories and Series   *80*
      Exercises II   *80*
      Assignments II   *81*
      Campus Project   *83*
      Community Project   *83*
      Home Assignment   *83*
      Class Discussion   *83*
      DB/CAR   *84*
      Fix It: Who-Whom   *84*
      Test I: Spelling   *84*

## 9   Broadcast Writing   85
    Introduction   *85*
      Exercises I   *85*
      Exercises II   *87*
      Assignments   *88*
      Campus Projects   *89*
      Community Project   *90*
      Home Assignment   *90*
      Class Discussion   *90*
      DB/CAR   *91*
      Skill Drill: Identify   *92*
      Fix It: Or Let It Go   *92*
      What's Wrong?: Wet   *92*

## PART FOUR   Reporting Principles   93

## 10   Digging for Information   93
    Introduction   *93*
      Exercises   *93*
      Assignments   *95*
      Campus Projects   *96*
      Community Projects   *97*
      Home Assignment   *98*
      Class Discussion   *98*
      DB/CAR   *99*
      Fix It: Fact Checking   *99*
      Test II: Error Identification   *99*

## 11   Making Sound Observations   100
    Introduction   *100*
      Exercises   *100*
      Assignments   *102*
      Campus Project   *103*
      Community Project   *103*
      Home Assignment   *104*
      Class Discussion   *104*
      DB/CAR   *104*
      Fix It: Trademarks   *105*
      What's Wrong?: Escapee   *105*
      You Decide: Johns (1)   *105*

## 12   Building and Using Background   106
    Introduction   *106*
      Exercises   *106*
      Assignments   *108*
      Campus Projects   *108*
      Community Project   *109*
      Home Assignment   *109*
      Class Discussion   *109*
      DB/CAR   *110*
      Skill Drill I: Famous Works   *110*
      Test III: Punctuation   *111*
      You Decide: Holocaust (2)   *112*

## 13   Finding, Cultivating and Using Sources   112
    Introduction   *112*
      Exercise   *113*
      Assignments   *116*
      Campus Project   *117*
      Community Project   *117*
      Home Assignment   *118*
      Class Discussion   *119*
      DB/CAR   *119*
      Skill Drill: What's Next?   *119*
      Fix It: More Trademarks   *119*

**14   Interviewing Principles   120**
   Introduction   *120*
      Exercises   *120*
      Assignments   *121*
      Campus Projects   *123*
      Community Project   *124*
      Home Assignment   *124*
      Class Discussion   *125*
      DB/CAR   *125*
      Fix It: Prepositions   *125*
      Test IV: Subject-Verb Agreement   *126*

**15   Interviewing Practices   126**
   Introduction   *126*
      Exercises   *126*
      Assignments   *130*
      Campus Project   *130*
      Community Projects   *130*
      Home Assignment   *131*
      Class Discussion   *133*
      DB/CAR   *133*
      Fix It: Count 'Em   *133*
      What's Wrong?: Vote   *133*

**16   Speeches, Meetings and News Conferences   134**
   Introduction   *134*
   Speeches   *134*
      Exercises I   *134*
   Meetings   *146*
      Exercises II   *146*
      Assignment   *148*
   News Conferences   *148*
      Exercises III   *148*
   Panel Discussions and Symposia   *150*
      Exercises IV   *150*
      Campus Project   *150*
      Community Projects   *151*
      Home Assignment   *151*
      Class Discussion   *151*
      DB/CAR   *152*
      Fix It: To the Point   *152*
      You Decide: Restrictions   *153*

**17   Hunches, Feelings and Stereotypes   153**
   Introduction   *153*
      Exercises   *153*
      Assignments   *158*
      Campus Projects   *158*
      Community Projects   *159*
      Home Assignment   *159*
      Class Discussion   *159*
      DB/CAR   *160*
      Skill Drill: Auditing Your Emotions   *160*
      What's Wrong?: Hopped Up   *161*
      You Decide: Claims   *161*

**PART FIVE   From Accidents to Education   162**

**18   Accidents and Disasters   162**
   Introduction   *162*
   Accidents   *162*
      Exercises I   *162*
      Assignments   *163*
   Disasters   *164*
      Exercises II   *164*
      Assignment   *164*
      Campus Project   *165*
      Community Projects   *165*
      Home Assignment   *165*
      Class Discussion   *166*
      DB/CAR   *166*
      Test V: Case   *167*

**19   Obituaries   167**
   Introduction   *167*
      Exercises   *167*
      Assignments   *175*
      Campus Projects   *175*
      Community Project   *176*
      Home Assignments   *176*
      Class Discussion   *177*
      DB/CAR   *178*
      Fix It: Obits   *178*
      What's Wrong? Prizewinner   *179*
      You Decide: Anti-Gay   *179*

**20   The Police Beat   179**
   Introduction   *179*
      Exercises   *180*
      Assignments   *183*
      Campus Projects   *184*
      Community Projects   *185*
      Home Assignment   *185*
      Class Discussion   *185*
      DB/CAR   *186*
      Skill Drill: Police Vocabulary   *186*
      Fix It: Tighten, Adjust   *187*

**21   The Courts   187**
   Introduction   *187*
      Exercises   *187*
      Assignments   *191*
      Campus Project   *192*
      Community Projects   *193*
      Home Assignment   *194*

    Class Discussion *194*
    DB/CAR *196*
    Skill Drill: Court Terms *196*
    Test VI: Usage *197*

**22** **Sports** **197**
   Introduction *197*
    Exercises *198*
    Assignments *205*
    Campus Project *205*
    Community Project *205*
    Home Assignment *206*
    Class Discussion *206*
    Skill Drill: Sports Vocabulary *206*
    You Decide: No English *207*

**23** **Business Reporting** **208**
   Introduction *208*
    Exercises *208*
    Assignments *210*
    Campus Project *213*
    Community Project *215*
    Home Assignment *216*
    Class Discussion *216*
    Skill Drill: Business and Labor Terms *216*
    Fix It: Match 'Em *217*
    What's Wrong?: Look Again *218*

**24** **Local Government and Education** **219**
   Introduction *219*
    Exercises *219*
    Assignments *229*
    Campus Project *235*
    Community Project *235*
    Home Assignment *236*
    Class Discussion *236*
    DB/CAR *236*
    Skill Drill: Property Assessments *237*
    Fix It: Basic Budget *238*
    Test VII: Troublesome *238*

**PART SIX Laws, Taste and Taboos,**
     **Codes and Ethics** **239**

**25** **Reporters and the Law** **239**
   Introduction *239*
    Exercises *239*
    Assignments *241*
    Campus Project *243*
    Community Project *243*
    Home Assignment *244*
    Class Discussion *244*
    DB/CAR *245*
    Skill Drill: Libel and Privacy *245*
    What's Wrong?: Arson *247*

**26** **Taste—Defining the Appropriate** **247**
   Introduction *247*
    Exercises *247*
    Assignment *251*
    Campus Project *251*
    Community Project *251*
    Home Assignment *252*
    Class Discussion *252*
    DB/CAR *253*
    Fix It: Leave or Delete *253*
    Test VIII: Define *254*
    You Decide: Rapper *254*

**27** **The Morality of Journalism** **255**
   Introduction *255*
    Exercises *255*
    Assignments *258*
    Campus and Community Project *258*
    Campus Project *258*
    Home Assignments *258*
    Class Discussion *259*
    DB/CAR *260*
    Skill Drill: Ethical *260*
    You Decide: Case Studies *262*
    You Decide: Sex Education *(2)* *264*

**Freeport City Map** **265**
**Freeport Directory** **266**
**Freeport Cross Directory** **270**
**Freeport Source List** **274**
**Index** **277**

# Preface

Like all craftspeople, journalists sharpen their skills by working with the tools and the material of their trade or profession. The *Workbook* provides the material for practice and describes the necessary tools. *Workbook* chapter titles correspond to those in the textbook, *News Reporting and Writing*.

Eleven types of work are offered:

**Exercises:** All the facts are given so that you can do these in class on deadline. The exercises are intended to develop and hone your writing skills.

**Assignments:** Story ideas are suggested for individual reporting. You will be asked to gather background material, interview sources and observe events. The assignments will help you sharpen your information-gathering competence.

**Projects:** These are reporting assignments for the class. Sometimes you will be asked to gather information about one aspect of the assignment. At other times, the individual reporting will be shared and the class members will write a wrap-up piece. Two types of projects are assigned in each chapter, one for reporting on the campus, the other for reporting in the community.

**Home Assignments:** You will do these on your own time.

**Class Discussion:** Topics are offered for study and dialogue. You are urged to make written preparation for class.

Each chapter will contain these five types of work. In addition, most chapters will contain the following:

**Database/Computer-Assisted Reporting (DB/CAR):** You will be asked to make a database search and/or to use the computer to help you develop and compile material for a story.

**Skill Drills:** Short-answer quizzes.

**Fix Its:** Material to be corrected.

**What's Wrong?:** Stories that lack essentials.

**Tests:** Material employers use to test job applicants.

**You Decide:** Situations that require journalistic decision making, often in the areas of taste and ethics.

The subject matter of the work assigned here covers the full range of journalistic activity. You will be asked to write obituaries and to write about arrests, trials, city council meetings, sports events and traffic accidents. In addition to focusing on these everyday events that are the mainstay of journalism, you will be asked to look into some of the volatile issues of our time:

- The conflict over the place of religion in our public schools.
- The failure to narrow the economic gap between the very poor and the very rich and the widening culture of poverty.
- The changing face of religion as religious groups deal with women in the clergy, abortion and sexuality.
- Racial tension on campus and in the community.
- The campaigns by gays and lesbians for acceptance.
- The role of the press in its frequent forays into private lives and in its handling of sex crimes.
- The role of women in politics.
- Sexism on college faculties as reflected in differentials in promotions and pay scales.
- The pressures on the press to entertain rather than to inform.
- The epidemic in sexually transmitted diseases.
- Sexual harassment in the workplace.
- The debate over how to improve public school education.

# How to Use the Map, Source List and City Directories

Here is how you can use these resources that are at the back of the *Workbook:*

    1.   An exercise may refer to the superintendent of schools without naming the official. Your story should include his name, which you can find by consulting the **Freeport Source List** under *Freeport School Officials.* You'll find his name is Herbert Gilkeyson.

    2.   You may be told in an exercise that Anne Downey was injured in an automobile accident. Since addresses are an essential part of a person's full identification, you would consult the **Freeport Directory** to find her address, 165 Vincent St.

    3.   Your instructor may give you an exercise about a fire located at State Highway 166 and U.S. 81 and ask you how you would handle the assignment if you were on deadline. You would, of course, call the fire department for information. You would also want an on-the-scene account if it were a big fire. Since you could not take the time to go there, you might call people who live nearby.

    The map and the **Freeport Cross Directory** allow you to locate someone. Consulting the **Freeport Map,** you would find the intersection is at the southern edge of town and that Hunter Avenue is the city continuation of U.S. 81. The map shows that a place known as Three Corners Junction is in the vicinity.

    You could use the **Freeport Cross Directory** to find an address on Hunter Avenue. The first entry, 4700 Hunter Ave., lists a Three Corners Cafe. You could call the Cafe to try to locate someone who can describe the fire for you while another reporter and a photographer are on the way.

    Unless otherwise indicated, all exercises are set in Freeport.

# PART ONE
## The Reporter at Work

# On the Job

Roy Karten, *City & State.*
**Interviewing the mayor on taxes.**

### Introduction

Journalists say that their first step before they begin writing is to think the story through, to decide what the story will say. They review the material and draft a writing plan. This helps them know how to begin their story, where they will go with it and how they will end it. The writing plan may consist of a short written outline, or it may be a mental picture of the story. Some writers number their notes in the order in which the material is to be placed in the story. Adopt whatever approach works best for you. Not all writing plans work out. On rereading their stories, writers sometimes decide to rewrite or start over.

## Editing Your Copy

Before handing in their stories, writers correct errors they may have made in grammar, punctuation, spelling and word usage. They check to see that their copy conforms to the stylebook for abbreviations, capitalizations and the like. Names, addresses and titles are double-checked for accuracy in the directories.

Stories are always given a final read before they are handed in. When possible, stories are pencil-edited in this final reading. Corrections should be printed, not written in longhand. Lines and arrows are not used to indicate changes in order.

On the next page are the copy editor's marks for almost all changes you will make in your copy. Never use proofreader's marks.

### *Exercises I*

*A. Kliff*

A 22-year-old man was chared with reclessly driving last night after a high-speed chase from Pleasant Valley road, up albright Avenue to the driveway of his home.

The man, Paul A. Kliff, 22, of 29 Tudor St., was to be arranged on district court today.

Police said a Police Cruiser gave chase when the suspect's auto was seen speeding on Valley Rd. When it was stopped finally in the driveway at Tudor St., police said, Kliff removed himself of his auto and began to struggle with officers as a crowd of people gathered.

**Copy Editing Marks**

| | | |
|---|---|---|
| capitalize | U. S. district court judge Frank | District Court Judge |
| transpose / insert word | J. Broyles will hear arguments oral Monday | oral arguments / Monday |
| delete word and close up | on a suit ~~Monday~~ filed by a woman | suit filed |
| correction | who wants to build a new Montessori | Montessori |
| new paragraph | School east of Freeport. ¶ Jane | |
| lower case / separate | Fraker Levin, President of a | president / of a |
| insert apostrophe / insert comma | childrens group filed suit last week | children's / group, filed |
| delete letter and close up | alledging that city officials illegally | alleging |
| separate / bring together | revokeda building permit she said s he | revoked a / she |
| spell out | obtained last July from the CHA for | City Housing Authority |
| abbreviate | the school at 301 Maple Avenue. | Ave. |
| abbreviate | In January, the City Housing Authority | CHA |
| use figures | said it had eleven objectives but | 11 |
| retain / addition | STET the permit<br>decided ~~to~~ issue anyway. | to / the permit |

## B. Dumped

Michael Canzian, deputy A.G., charged today that the states' menatl institutions are being used as "dumping grounds for senior citzens and alcoholocs."

Canzian estimaed that it costs the state approximately $15,000 a year for each mental patient now "incarcerated" in State institutions over the state. He said the attorney generl's affice has filed suit against sveral hospitals to call attention to the situation. He hopes that the suits will go to trial in the spring of next year.

"Too many people whose only problem is ther age have been sent to mental homes", he said in a talk to the Golden Years Club at its clubhouse at 56 Forester Road.

## C. Spring

A menu of wet snow, slush and rain—gurnished with glum and fog—was dished up to Maryland residents today as the state struggled to switch from winter to Spring.

Whereas most of the state was doused with rain, northwestern areas recieved not-unsubstantial amounts of snow. The record for the sudden return to winter was May 9, of 1977, when the regeion recieved eleven inches, an event that caused power failures and alot of traffic problems throughout the state.

State police said there was no major traffic problems state-wise. Sanding crews took care of the slush and ice that piled up on highways police said.

## D. Trees

The planing of trees on long-barren city streets will be slowed considerably this year because the amount of federal funds available for the work of planting is much less than last year, when almost 3,000 street trees were planted throughout the city.

City Forester John T. Voboril said he hopes to plant about 1,000 trees this year, but he said he is not sure that enough money will be available to reach that goal of 1000 tree plantings.

Because of this uncertainty, Voboril said he has temporarily halted work on a survey to ascertain which streets are most in need of new trees.

Last year the city used a $400 thousand dollar public works grant from the Federal Government to pay for about 2,000 trees, and planted about 1,000 more with funds provided by the Mayor's office of Community Development (MOCD).

But the Federal Government is not offering public works grants this year. So the city has to rely solely on its community development fund for tree plantings.

Voboril said he requested $200,000 from the development office for street trees, enough for about 1,000 plantings. But has not been told yet whether he will get this amount.

## E. Various

1. "You can not flaunt the will of the people", Gov. Janet Kocieniewski warned the state legislator today. Last week, she said, the democrats hung themselves when they vetoed her welfare program. In her last press conference, the governors face turned livid in response to reporters questions. She pointed out she became nauseous when she read reports that her administration was running a gauntlet of public criticism, "we are doing a good job," she said, adding that she is confident her staff is performing good.

2. The university accepted the bid of Haight & Sons Co. for the construction of a new facility to store atheletic equipment. The sight will be near the gym.

3. For desert, he not only ate the pie but also 2 bowlfuls of Jello.

4. Polce said J. Frank Pounder, 38, is wanted for the murder of Mr. and Mrs. Arthur B. Harris. The Harris's were found dead yesterday in the bedroom of their home, 123 Western Avenue. A large amount of money, between $2–$3000 dollars was taken, police said, in giving robbery as a possible motive for the mishap.

5. From the group of fifty who took the test, there were only three who received As, the professor said. They included Arthur b. Able, J. Frank Rodgers, and Roberta Redford.

## *Skill Drill I: Spelling*

The 50 words that follow are some of the most frequently misspelled. Circle the correct spelling. Put a check mark next to the words whose spelling you would usually check in a dictionary.

| | | | | | | |
|---|---|---|---|---|---|---|
| _____ | 1. (a) municipal | (b) municiple | | _____ | 26. (a) belief | (b) beleif |
| _____ | 2. (a) cemetery | (b) cemetary | | _____ | 27. (a) privilege | (b) priviledge |
| _____ | 3. (a) indispensable | (b) indispensible | | _____ | 28. (a) predjudice | (b) prejudice |
| _____ | 4. (a) occurrence | (b) occurence | | _____ | 29. (a) their | (b) thier |
| _____ | 5. (a) villain | (b) villian | | _____ | 30. (a) grammer | (b) grammar |
| _____ | 6. (a) exhillirate | (b) exhilarate | | _____ | 31. (a) accommodate | (b) accomodate |
| _____ | 7. (a) irresistible | (b) irresistable | | _____ | 32. (a) barberous | (b) barbarous |
| _____ | 8. (a) consensus | (b) concensus | | _____ | 33. (a) athelete | (b) athlete |
| _____ | 9. (a) committment | (b) commitment | | _____ | 34. (a) preceed | (b) precede |
| _____ | 10. (a) nuclear | (b) nuculear | | _____ | 35. (a) arguement | (b) argument |
| _____ | 11. (a) pronunciation | (b) pronounciation | | _____ | 36. (a) harrass | (b) harass |
| _____ | 12. (a) existance | (b) existence | | _____ | 37. (a) repetition | (b) repitition |
| _____ | 13. (a) illiterate | (b) iliterate | | _____ | 38. (a) definately | (b) definitely |
| _____ | 14. (a) liaison | (b) liason | | _____ | 39. (a) disasterous | (b) disastrous |
| _____ | 15. (a) nineth | (b) ninth | | _____ | 40. (a) exagerate | (b) exaggerate |
| _____ | 16. (a) dissention | (b) dissension | | _____ | 41. (a) achievement | (b) acheivement |
| _____ | 17. (a) develepment | (b) development | | _____ | 42. (a) vaccum | (b) vacuum |
| _____ | 18. (a) desireable | (b) desirable | | _____ | 43. (a) apparent | (b) apparant |
| _____ | 19. (a) occasion | (b) occassion | | _____ | 44. (a) conscience | (b) concience |
| _____ | 20. (a) nickle | (b) nickel | | _____ | 45. (a) dependant | (b) dependent |
| _____ | 21. (a) alot | (b) a lot | | _____ | 46. (a) forty | (b) fourty |
| _____ | 22. (a) referring | (b) refering | | _____ | 47. (a) embarrass | (b) embarass |
| _____ | 23. (a) seperate | (b) separate | | _____ | 48. (a) interpetation | (b) interpretation |
| _____ | 24. (a) similar | (b) similir | | _____ | 49. (a) assistant | (b) assisstant |
| _____ | 25. (a) receive | (b) recieve | | _____ | 50. (a) allotted | (b) alotted |

## *Skill Drill II: Grammar, Punctuation and Style*

Each of these sentences contains a writing error of some kind. Rewrite each sentence to eliminate the error in grammar, punctuation, style or usage.

### *A. Grammar*

1. Leaping on his back, the horse galloped into the circus ring to applause.
2. The cook found he had no salt, he immediately stalked out of the kitchen.
3. Oil is it's leading export.
4. All departments lost business last year. Except furnishings and hardware.
5. He shot at the fleeing man. Hoping to hit him in the leg.
6. He said he was feeling alright but was still a little dizzy from the trip.
7. He looked up at the planes. Straining to see the biplane he had been told was performing.
8. The plane went into a spin. Which thrilled everyone.
9. Its too late to help, he said.
10. Everyone hoped they could help.
11. The team played as though they wanted to win.
12. Before typing his story, the notes were arranged.

### B. Punctuation

1. The two men each of whom had a hat pulled over his eyes entered the store.
2. To confuse them the owner busied himself at the rear.
3. He asked "What do you want?"
4. "Nothing." the taller one answered.
5. The childrens', mens', and womens' departments lost money last year.
6. He took James's books and ran.
7. He asked who's book it is.
8. "Why do you want to know," he asked?
9. The question—which was shot out like a bullet, left him dazed.
10. He enjoyed daydreaming, but some people thought him a little "strange."

### C. Style, Word Usage

1. Clarity is a major principal in good writing, he said.
2. To weak writers, the proper words are often illusive.
3. Nevertheless, even weak writers like to be complemented on their work.
4. One of the marks of a weak writer is a lose style.
5. She ordered a box of monogrammed stationary.
6. Police discovered the convict's horde of bonds in a cellar.
7. Some products domineer the marketplace.
8. Milton's percentage of Anglo-Saxon words was 81, with 90 for Shakespeare, and the King James Bible runs around 94 percent.
9. This doesn't mean a writer has to consultate the dictionary.
10. Just avert jargon and colloquialisms.
11. This is excellent advise that effects us all.
12. The media is often blamed for establishing writing criteria that is copied without thinking by the public.
13. Less errors in newspapers would be helpful.
14. However, no one should imply all newspapers print poor writing.
15. Scarcely never do you see outrageously bad writing like you do in freshman compositions.
16. The true facts are sometimes difficult to face.
17. Too much writing is discursively digressive and is wordy and verbose.
18. As a freshman, I could always anticipate my instructor to literally cover my compositions with indecipherable red marks.
19. At that point in time, I thought I could write.
20. At this point, I know I can't.
21. He has his facts wrong.
22. Five bandits convinced a Brink's armed guard to open his truck door.
23. A cement block building was destroyed.
24. Three persons died in the mishap.
25. Its no fun trying to write but not knowing how.

## Skill Drill III: Abused and Misused Words

Samuel Johnson, the 18th-century lexicographer and author, was riding in a closed carriage with several other passengers on a hot, dusty and long trip. As the afternoon wore on, one of the passengers, an estimable middle-aged woman, was obviously disturbed by the odor arising from the corner where Johnson was sitting. In those days, bathing was infrequent, and Johnson's personal hygiene was minimal. Finally, unable to hold back, the woman turned to Johnson. "Sir, you smell," she said.

"No madam," Johnson said. "You smell. I stink."

Few reporters have to make these fine distinctions, although the precise use of language is one tool of the good reporter. Here are word-couples often confused and misused. Use them properly in sentences:

1. affect/effect.
2. allusion/illusion.
3. angry/mad.
4. bring/take.
5. complement/compliment.
6. council/counsel.
7. emigrate/immigrate.
8. flaunt/flout.
9. farther/further.
10. fewer/less.
11. imply/infer.
12. lay/lie.
13. lend/loan.
14. principal/principle.
15. rebut/refute.

# Developing the Story Idea

## Exercises II

In the following exercises, find the important idea or ideas in the information supplied. If you have selected one idea, make it the basis of the lead. If you have selected more than one, put the ideas in order of importance and write a lead based on the most important one or combine two for the lead. Then write the rest of the story. Make certain to check facts that you think may be questionable or need explanation.

### A. Memorial

The mayor's press secretary, Leon Roper, calls to tell you that a softball game will be played on the Horace Mann High School athletic field Sunday at 2 p.m. between teams composed of city employees and members of the local chamber of commerce. No admission will be charged, but contributions will be solicited for the Chris Hatfield Memorial Fund. Hatfield was the city manager for three years and died last August of Hodgkin's disease at the age of 31. The fund goes toward cancer research. Cliff Guzman, the president of the chamber, will pitch for his team, and Albert Heffner, the city budget director, will throw curves for the city team.

### B. Merit

Pamela Elman, 18, 3732 Palisades Ave., a senior at Dwight D. Eisenhower High School, won a National Merit Scholarship: $3,000. Will attend the University of Texas (Austin), as a premed student. The only one to win from this city; 3,500 in country. (Information from Bernard A. Meyers, principal.) Your newspaper's files have a story dated last year in which Meyers announces she is one of six students to have all A's in their first three years of high school work. In her freshman and sophomore years, she was confined to a bed while undergoing treatment of spinal birth-injury and took courses by special telephone. She has been in a wheelchair since then.

### C. Planning

The secretary of the city Zoning and Planning Board, Betty Forde, telephones to say that the regular board meeting scheduled for tomorrow night is called off because of the death this morning of the wife of the chairman, Philip Nicholson. The meeting, set for 8 o'clock in the city council chambers, will be held next Tuesday at 8 p.m. instead. Her name is Alice Nicholson. She was 42 and died of cancer.

### D. Wind

Police report: High winds last night damaged residences and businesses on State Highway 166 near Clovia. The winds were estimated at 80 miles an hour at their height, and they touched down for about two minutes at 11 p.m. Most of the damage, totaling $15,000, was to outbuildings. Largest single damage, about $5,000, was to the Crossroads Grocery at Three Corners Junction, where all the glass was blown out and merchandise shaken from shelves. Two gas pumps shattered and a storage building flattened. No injuries.

### E. Zoo

Information from Cyrus Tucek, the director of the zoo: The Newman Municipal Zoo has purchased two animals, a 6,000-pound female African elephant and a burro. After becoming accustomed to their surroundings, the animals will be put on exhibit. The elephant is named Baby and was obtained from the Brookfield Zoo in Chicago. The burro, which will be added to the Children's Zoo, is from the H. Gage Ranch in northern New Mexico and will be named by children who use the zoo. Suggested names will be put on a bulletin board and the children will vote. Names put up by zoo workers are Pancho, Rodney, Eeyore, Captain B, Secretariat, Taco, Chico, Cyrus, Mr. Cronkite and Cyrano.

Tucek also said the zoo is considering the use of birth control methods to keep its tiger population down. The female tigers have been producing litters of three to five cubs every 10 months, he said, and the zoo has no room for them. Nor will other zoos accept the young tigers. "They're full up, too, and are using a time-release contraceptive implanted under the skin for females and vasectomies for males.

"Lions, tigers and leopards are disappearing in the wild and proliferating in zoos and wildlife parks so fast there's no room for them," Tucek said.

## F. District Attorney

Paul Robinson, the district attorney, calls to say he will give a talk at a National Conference of Prosecutors convention in Chicago on July 23 where about 1,500 district attorneys will meet. His talk will be about the career-criminal tracking system that he says he has begun to use here. The system is designed to identify the frequent offender on arrest. An assistant district attorney is immediately assigned to the case and follows it, beginning with arraignment. "The purpose is to avoid plea bargaining with the resultant lenient sentences and probation for these offenders," he says. Robinson says the latest data show that career criminals commit 61 percent of all homicides, 76 percent of all rapes, 73 percent of all robberies and 65 percent of all aggravated assaults.

## G. Laundromat

Police report: Jerome Pardee, 20, 1874 Ogden St., arrested and charged with public drunkenness. Found naked in a laundromat at 402 Newell St. at 11 p.m. yesterday, Pardee told police that he planned to put his clothes back on as soon as the dryer was finished with them. Police had to wait 30 minutes for the cycle to finish before they could take him in.

## H. Weather

The weather bureau said temperatures over the past 24 hours ranged from 25 at 5 a.m. to 40, the high, at 2 p.m. This was the third straight day of unseasonably cold weather. This morning's temperature of 25 was the lowest for this time of year in 15 years. The all-time low for the date was in 1880, 15 degrees. The all-time high was 69 in 1991. The forecast for today is for lows in the 40s, highs in the 50s and an end to the sudden cold snap.

## I. Fire

The fire department reports two small fires overnight: a storeroom blaze at the IGA at 135 Kentucky Ave., 10:30 p.m., cause unknown, damage $450 in canned goods; a fire in a car in a garage at 630 Orcutt Ave., 11 p.m., cigarette ignited papers on car seat, $1,200 damage to the car. Dennis Held, car owner who lives at Orcutt address, treated for minor burns at Community Hospital and discharged. Wife saw smoke and pulled him from car. He had fallen asleep listening to a baseball game.

## J. Parade

The county volunteer fireman's association calls: It will hold its annual Kiddies Day Parade next Sunday, beginning at 1 p.m. at Massachusetts Avenue and Albany Street and running down Massachusetts through the city's business section to the grounds of the First Congregational Church, where judges will make awards for funniest costume, prettiest costume, smallest pet and best float. On display at the church grounds will be the new pumper purchased last month. Last year, some 200 children from three to eight years took part. Mayor Sam Parnass will lead the parade, carrying his 1-year-old daughter, Candy.

## K. Ombudsman

Call from the governor's office: Bruce Stroh, a former local high school basketball player who was sentenced to 15 years in the state penitentiary for armed robbery 10 years ago, has been appointed state ombudsman for prisoners in state institutions. Gov. Janet Kocieniewski made the announcement today from the state capitol. "Stroh will investigate prisoner complaints and report directly to the governor. This is a new system that is designed to make us more responsive to the needs of inmates," the governor said. Stroh was paroled five years ago and has worked as a probation officer in Freeport.

*L. Recital*

Telephone call from the parent association secretary and notes from the switchboard operator: Artur Rothstein, a French concert pianist, has donated his services for a recital in the music wing of the Horace Mann School, Friday, 8 p.m. Tickets are $5. The concert will include Chopin's mazurkas and études, Beethoven's piano version of music from "The Magic Flute" and several works of Franz Liszt. Proceeds will go toward the purchase of a high-fidelity system for the music department.

## *Exercises III*

These stories are more complex than the dozen preceding stories. Handle them in the same way. If you find more than one basic idea, again select only the most important of the ideas for the lead. Put the others in order of importance and base the body of the story on your priority list.

*A. Bus*

Here are a reporter's notes based on a call from Jack Nagel, who is the press officer for the state Public Utilities Commission:

The People's Bus Line, Inc., 1320 Torrence Ave., owner George W. Hulbert, has filed with the state Public Utilities Commission today a request for permission to operate a route into the downtown area from outlying communities, state PUC chairman Michael McKirdy announced today.

Hulbert seeks state approval to operate an unscheduled Monday through Friday service and asserts in his application that "domestic workers needing to reach downtown for trains to the suburbs where they work are not being served by present bus lines." Protests or supporting witnesses will be heard 28 days from the date of the application, at 3 p.m., in the state Executive Office Building.

Hulbert submitted with his request a petition bearing 65 signatures of local residents. The petition has a preamble reading: "We the undersigned find it costly to reach commuter lines from our section of the community and support the request of George W. Hulbert for unscheduled bus service in our area."

*B. Missing*

It is 60 minutes to deadline, and the police reporter calls in the following notes for you. Write a story:

Billy Joe Appel, 4, 1133 Madison St., was located at 12:30 p.m. at the home of Mrs. Bernice McCoy, 320 Manley St., a friend of Alice Kragler, 16, the babysitter. He disappeared from the Appel home around 9 o'clock last night when the babysitter said she fell asleep looking at TV. He is the son of Alan and Roberta Appel.

Police said that after questioning Miss Kragler this morning, she admitted she had wanted "to get even with the Appels for not letting me have my boyfriend visit me when I was babysitting with Billy Joe."

She said she called her friend, Mrs. McCoy, 20, and asked her to come and pick up the kid because she had to return home for an emergency and would pick him up in an hour. When McCoy heard the news about the missing child on the radio last night she said she was too frightened to do anything.

The Appels say they are happy to have their child back and are not going to file charges against Kragler.

Quote from Mrs. Appel: "Alice is a good girl. She just got upset. Those things happen. She loves Billy Joe and would never let anything happen to him."

The police say a full report will be turned over to juvenile authorities since there was a violation of the law. Kragler lives with her divorced mother, Bertha. About 20 volunteers turned out last night to search for the child in the woods near the Appel home where the parents thought he might be wandering.

*C. Calendar*

Here is the program of dates, times and events for next month at the Civic Auditorium. The public is invited to all events. Fees, if any, are in parentheses. Write a story.

—5, 7 p.m. "Mao as an Expression of the Chinese Political and Cultural Ethos," John Langley, Far Eastern correspondent of the *Toronto Star*. (Free to members of the Community Events Society; $3 to others.)

—10, 8 p.m. A program of chamber music presented by students of the Oberlin Conservatory of Music. Beethoven, Mozart and Ravel quartets. ($5.)

—15, 1 p.m. "The American Indian as Victim," John Dozier, professor emeritus of ethnology, of Stanford University. Sponsored by Friends of the First Citizens.

—16–20, 1–5 p.m. Exhibition of photographs of nature by the members of the Friends of the Earth.

—22, 7 p.m. Speech by Sen. Edward M. Kennedy of Massachusetts, "Making the Political System Work—A Tribute to Party Workers." Sponsored by the state Democratic Party. ($100-a-plate dinner.)

—24–27, 8 p.m. "Yerma," a play by Federico García Lorca. Directed by Francisco Perez. Players are students and faculty of the University of Florida. In Spanish. ($3.)

### D. Daredevil

Write a story based on the following information that you obtained in a check with the state highway patrol:

Had a strange one around midnight about 20 miles east of Canton. A 20-year-old short-order cook employed by Leek's Cafe was going home when his car went out of control on a bridge over the tracks of Amtrak. Broke through the guardrail, sailed through the air, hit power lines, and then fell to the tracks, landing upside down. The guy was unhurt, but it took 15 minutes to get him out of the car. His name is Alan Taylor of Freeport. We booked him for reckless and drunk driving, driving without a license and speeding. A guy following him says he must have hit that bridge at 90. Had a 1986 Chevy that he'd modified.

Kind of miraculous all around. It's a wonder he wasn't electrocuted or killed in the fall. If it'd happened a few minutes before, the eastbound Broadway Limited might have hit him and his car.

### E. Longo

An official of the B.C. Krebs Manufacturing Co. calls to tell you of the death from a heart attack in San José, Costa Rica, yesterday of Frank Longo, former personnel manager of the local company, which employs 250. He has prepared the following, which he dictates to you and which you should use as the basis for a story:

Longo was visiting his sister, Mrs. Rose Quintana, who lives in San José and is his only survivor. Longo was 78 and lived at 465 Lief St.

He went to work for the firm as a teen-ager after immigrating from Italy. Employed as a janitor, he worked up to inventory clerk within two years. As a clerk, he noticed the painstaking and cumbersome way in which inventory was kept and he devised an automatic system that was so successful it was copied by other large firms and eventually became the established procedure. Business textbooks referred to it as the Longo System, and it was in use until the introduction of the computerized inventory system.

Longo never had any formal education that we know of, but he was an omnivorous reader and donated books and funds to the local public library, which he called his high school, college and graduate school. He was made personnel manager at the age of 45 and completely changed the company's hiring system so that it became color-, sex- and age-blind two years later. He retired at 75.

He adds that the company telephoned Quintana at noon to offer assistance. Longo will be buried there tomorrow. She said her brother had been a prudent investor and had an estate of $1.5 million. He left $250,000 to her and the rest to the local public library system.

### F. Outage

On a routine check of the sheriff's office 15 minutes before deadline, you are given the following information by the dispatcher:

We got a call from one of our patrol cars about half an hour ago that a car hit a power pole northwest of town and people in the new housing subdivision out there were without electricity for about 45 minutes. I don't know any more than that. Oh, yes—no one was hurt in the accident.

You call the local office of the power and light company and the public information officer tells you:

We have just returned service. It was out from 1:02 to 1:40 p.m. It affected Arden Hills, where we have 250 meters, all residences. All of them were out.

Write a brief story based on the information. (Arden Hills is a new subdivision. It was completed last year.)

### G. Elephant

Cyrus Tucek, the director of the zoo, calls to say that they believe Baby, their new acquisition, is pregnant. He says that officials at Baby's previous home encouraged a match between her and Zoltan, a bull elephant, and that the local zoo knew of the nuptials. "Two for the price of one was our hope," Tucek says. "A more positive diagnosis will be available in a month or two. Too bad Daddy can't be here."

## H. Goals

A well-known British journalist and critic who appears on television (BBC) is giving the major address at the annual state convention of the Daily Newspaper Association, which is held in conjunction with Newspaper Day at Mallory College. The speaker is Jeffrey St. George. His topic is "Goals for Journalism Education." He will speak at 8 o'clock tonight. Here are some excerpts supplied by the campus press office from the text of his talk which you should use for a story of 300 to 350 words.

> Your experiences in this country with public events and public officials have served to develop a sense of responsibility and maturity in your press that is, I believe, unmatched anywhere in the world. This is a positive development for educators who prepare men and women for newspapers and stations. Let us try to set out some goals for the journalism educator so that he or she may respond to these responsibilities.
>
> Clearly, a professional education must give the student skills and a sense of craft. But it is not enough to prepare the student only for the first job. The education must be sufficiently broad and deep so that the underpinnings of a creative and positive life are established. There must be established a commitment to the contemplative as well as the active life, for skills without understanding become as automatic as the water pump. . . .
>
> I do not mean to imply that these aims are visionary. Journalism education in your country is clearly moving in this direction. I should only wish to reinforce the movement. I would suggest a few questions any educator might ask of the program of study he or she is adopting:
>
>> Will the curriculum or the course do the following?
>> —Will it give the student a sense of purpose and broaden his or her knowledge?
>> —Will it deepen his or her interest in ideas, give him or her sufficient materials to think about?
>> —Will it free the imagination and develop initiative?
>> Finally, the fourth question whose answer might be the most important of all of these:
>> —Will it develop a free and open mind, a journalist free of the biases of the society so that he or she can act independently, intelligently and spontaneously?
>
> In closing, let me emphasize that I do not share the disdain of some educators for the real needs of the editor for young reporters who can spell the words of their mother tongue correctly and who can use a comma and a period with precision. But I do believe that this can hardly be the goal of journalism education. Nor, for that matter, can the education be narrowly conceived as instruction in the forms and practices of current journalism, which is only a step beyond the rules of grammar, punctuation and spelling. All are essential, of course. To use the words of one of my countrymen, Alfred North Whitehead, "The major aim of education should be an understanding of the insistent present. To do this one must know a great deal of the world and must understand the past in order to know the present."

## I. Golfers

You are on the sports desk of the local newspaper when a call comes in from a stringer assigned to cover the state Women's Amateur Golf Meet in which several local women are entered.

She dictates the following:

> Here's a rundown of first-round play for the tourney. I also got their local addresses and ages:
>
> Mrs. Heidi Levy, 39, 54 Maplewood Ave., shot an 83.
> Mrs. Anne Downey, 42, 165 Vincent St., 87.
> Mrs. B. Kroeger, 32, 880 Augusta Ave., 77.
> Mary Ellen Flynn, 18, Roth Road, 77.
> Sally Grubbs, 17, Smith Farms, 71.
>
> Sally shot a hole-in-one on the seventh hole, and I went over to interview her after her first round. It was the only hole-in-one today, and they say it is the first one on this course by a woman in 20 years since a visiting pro, Sandra Haynie, did it on the same seventh.
>
> Sally is a senior at Eisenhower High and is going to go to the University of Missouri. Her mother and father were here and they were pleased as punch. Her dad, Oscar Grubbs, said he gave her a putter when she was three and "she never stopped swinging it." She sank it with a four iron on the 145-yard par-three hole.
>
> Says Sally: "The ball hit on the front of the green just to the right and the ball rolled smoothly into the cup. It looked good when I hit it, right on the line, but I never thought it would go in.
>
> "It's my first since I was seven and played on a kiddie course. My 9-year-old sister, Kay, was here today and she brings me good luck."
>
> Sally didn't compete at all last year. This is her first big tourney. The leaders: Terry Pauli, 70; Carol Trucco, 71; Sally Grubbs, 71; Carolyn Oshiro, 72; Janet Bakinski, 73; Maureen Gerson, 75; Tamara Cort, 75; Joan Bodnar, 75; Diane Stark, 76; Tess Walters, 76.
>
> The concluding round will be played tomorrow.

## J. Wedding

You are the courthouse reporter for an Albuquerque newspaper. One morning you come across this suit among a dozen on file in the courthouse. Write 150 to 200 words. (Mr. and Mrs. Lopez live at 712 Silver Ave., SW.)

---

STATE OF NEW MEXICO          COUNTY OF BERNALILLO

IN THE SECOND JUDICIAL DISTRICT COURT

TOBIAS LOPEZ and
CAROLYN LOPEZ,
his wife,
      Plaintiffs,

-VS-

MRS. L. DURRANCE and
THE WOMEN'S CLUB, INC.,

      Defendants.

No. 578749

FILED IN MY OFFICE THIS

AUG 12

*Solomon Gallegos*

CLERK DISTRICT COURT

COMPLAINT

Plaintiffs state:

I

That on or about 8 July Plaintiffs entered into a lease contract with Defendants for the purpose of leasing premises known as Women's Club Hall at 22 Gold Avenue, SW, for a wedding celebration to take place between the hours of 8:00 p.m. and 12:00 p.m., on 25 July.

II

That rental was paid therefor and accepted by Defendants.

III

That as a result of said agreement, Plaintiffs invited over 200 parties for said wedding celebration, relied upon said agreement therefor, made large and elaborate preparation, including the hiring of musical entertainment therefor, and planned a honeymoon trip immediately after the culmination of said celebration, all with knowledge to invitees and said Defendants.

IV

That on 25 July at the hour of 8:00 p.m. Plaintiffs, together with approximately 200 invitees, and their orchestra, attempted to enter said premises as per their contract and were met by another party of approximately 100 people who advised Plaintiffs and their invitees that said hall was being used by them and that Plaintiffs and their invitees could not use said hall for the purpose for which Defendants promised.

V

That the entire wedding celebration was ruined, all to the deep and everlasting and irreparable humiliation suffered by Plaintiffs and their invitees.

VI

That as a result of the ruination of said celebration, the humiliation suffered by Plaintiffs, the gross embarrassment to their reputation, Plaintiffs were forced to postpone perhaps indefinitely their honeymoon trip, Plaintiff CAROLYN LOPEZ suffered deep and excruciating shock to her nervous system, the extent of which is unknown to Plaintiffs.

WHEREFORE, Plaintiffs pray for judgment against Defendants, and each of them, in the sum of Five Thousand ($5,000.00) Dollars each plus costs herein lawfully expended.

## Assignments

Some of these assignments ask for specific information that will form the basis of your story. Others give starting points only.

### A. Charity

List all the fund drives in your community. Include the dates of the next campaign, the goal, last year's goal and the actual amount raised.

Interview the executive director of one of the organizations. Any new techniques to be used? Any general comments on generosity or parsimony of the community? Any national or local factors involved in the amounts set as the goal or actually raised?

If the city has a United Fund, write about its next fund drive; summarize the most recent campaign, using exact totals and comments.

### B. Merit Folo

Locate the names and schools of National Merit Scholars from local schools over the past five to 10 years. Call their high school principals, and try to learn where the scholars are now and how they have done in college and thereafter. If one is available locally, interview him or her.

### C. Acquisition

Visit a local or nearby museum and interview the curator or director on new acquisitions. Has he or she been able to obtain what the museum has wanted? Is the museum interested in specializing in a particular area? How much money is available for acquisitions? Is it sufficient? What is the source of the funds? Is there a plan to try to increase funds? If the museum has priorities other than acquisitions, ask about them.

### D. Tippers

Are local residents and visitors good tippers? Interview hotel bellhops, waiters, barbers, taxi drivers and others. What is considered a good tip? Who are the best tippers: men, women; young, middle-aged or elderly; local people or out-of-towners; U.S. citizens or foreigners?

### E. Meetings

For practice in covering spontaneous events, cover a meeting of one or more of the following:

1. City council or commission.
2. Service club speaker (Lions, Kiwanis, etc.).
3. Planning, zoning commission.
4. County commission, board of supervisors.

## Campus Projects

### A. Plans

What do college seniors plan to do after graduation? Interview students about their plans for work, travel, graduate study. Will those who plan to work be doing so in the area of their major? Where are the travelers bound? Ask those who intend to continue their education why they selected their field for graduate study. Are some planning marriage soon after they graduate? What are the work or study plans of people planning to marry?

### B. Involvement

A recent survey of more than 330,000 college freshmen conducted by the Higher Education Research Institute at UCLA found among the freshman class the lowest interest and involvement in politics in three decades. Fewer than a third said that "keeping up with political affairs" is an important goal for them. Thirty years before, two-thirds said it was important for them.

A similar trend was found in the numbers of those who said they have a desire to take part in community programs or in efforts to improve race relations or the environment.

These findings continue the trend noticeable in the late 1980s when a study found that one in eight young Americans defined being a good citizen meant voting and taking part in politics.

Design a poll for your school. What is the involvement factor of students on your campus?

## Community Projects

### A. Career

What do high school seniors want to do after they graduate? What affects their plans—finances, parents' wishes, high school studies and grades, friends' decisions?

### B. Prayer

One of the most angrily debated subjects in the country is whether prayers should be allowed in public schools. The American Center for Law and Justice states that there is legal ground for states challenging court rulings against school prayer.

But the American Civil Liberties Union says federal courts generally have ruled that prayer in public school is unconstitutional.

Prayers at graduation have been upheld by a federal appeals court in Texas but rejected in federal courts in Virginia and California.

What is the situation in your city and state? Are prayers offered at graduation? Are after-hours religious classes and clubs permitted? Is religious literature handed out in school, and may students wear religious emblems in class? Are any groups advocating more religious activity in the public schools and, if so, has there been opposition?

## *Home Assignments*

Under each slug are several facts about an event. Underline or circle the most important fact—the one you think best sums up the event and is of greatest reader or listener interest.

Then write a lead based on the underlined or circled material.

### *A. Dispute*

1. The Queens Mountain Rescue Squad and the Queens Mountain police chief have been in a controversy for a week.
2. Chief Lloyd Earl had ordered police officers not to stop traffic at intersections to let ambulances through.
3. The squad, made up of volunteer rescue workers, felt the chief interfered with its work.
4. The rescue squad complained to Mayor Henry Joyner and to the Queens Mountain Board of Commissioners.
5. At an executive session of the board with the mayor last night, the chief resigned.

### *B. Taxes*

1. Next year's proposed Gaston County budget calls for expenditures of $54.8 million.
2. This is $2.1 million more than the current budget.
3. Revenue collections will be about $1.4 million short of the expenditures next year.
4. David Hunscher, the county manager, supplied this information to the county board of commissioners last night in presenting his proposed budget.
5. Hunscher says that he made many cuts in budget requests from department heads and it will be difficult to make more.
6. The probability, he said, is that taxes will have to be raised.

### *C. Mail*

1. T.J. Ellingson, an assistant United States postmaster general, issued a statement at a news conference today.
2. He said that the costs of running the postal service are constantly increasing.
3. "Further attempts must be made to cut costs," he said.
4. "One of the plans under consideration is twice-weekly home mail delivery and thrice-weekly deliveries to business."
5. "Nothing is definite yet pending further examinations of the options," he said.

### *D. Shooting*

1. Mrs. Bernice Joyce, 32, of 44 Broadway, was arrested this morning at the home of her mother.
2. She was taken to criminal court and charged with shooting her husband, Coleman, last night during an argument.
3. The two had quarreled over her plans to divorce him.
4. He had been staying at a hotel and returned to the house to try to persuade her to drop the divorce.
5. A fight ensued during which he was shot.
6. He is in critical condition at Fairlawn Hospital.
7. The charge is attempted homicide.

### *E. Drive*

1. Sara F. Glasser, president of the local chapter of the American Civil Liberties Union, announces a new membership drive.
2. The chapter usually solicits members by mail and telephone.
3. Next month, the drive will be made on a person-to-person basis to gain 50 new members.
4. Members and volunteers will be asked to invite friends to their homes to acquaint them with the ACLU.
5. "The chapter hopes to increase its membership to replace those who have dropped out and moved away," she said.
6. "If we cannot do so, we must discontinue the chapter," she said.

## F. Gas

1. The supply of natural gas to Wisconsin has been going down for the past five years.
2. The state Public Service Commission has warned natural gas customers that the situation will steadily worsen.
3. Today, the Wisconsin Gas Co. announced it is halting all further commercial and industrial gas hookups.
4. It also announced it is submitting a plan to the PSC to reduce gas deliveries to some present customers during temporary shortages.
5. The utility will continue to serve its 356,000 customers in central and eastern Wisconsin.
6. The cutbacks were necessary, the firm says, because of continued natural gas shortages and an anticipated further reduction in available supplies next year.

## G. Tennis

1. The annual Freeport Tennis Clinic will be held Aug. 21 to 24 at Mallory College.
2. The clinic will feature exhibitions and instruction.
3. This is the 12th annual clinic, sponsored by six Freeport civic clubs.
4. Chris Evert Lloyd, holder of a number of tennis titles, will play Aug. 23 at 2 p.m.
5. Lloyd will play local tennis pro Marty Friedman in a singles match and then will team up with Friedman to play a mixed doubles match against Mr. and Mrs. James Wigglesworth, the state mixed-doubles champions.
6. Friedman made the announcement today.

## H. Bicycle Trip

1. Two students are going by bicycle from Boston to Seattle this summer.
2. The University of Rochester announced the project in a news release.
3. Edward A. Nelson and Kenneth Hardigan, third-year students in the university medical school, will make the trip.
4. The project is designed to test the body's ability to adapt to intensive training, the university release states.
5. "Information gained from the cross-country ride is expected to provide data of value to physiology in general and to sports medicine in particular," the release states.
6. Nelson, of Kent, Conn., will be the test subject and Hardigan, of Boston, will accompany him.
7. Nelson will be tested before and after the trip, and along the way he will conduct frequent self-tests.

## I. Guns

1. Albert Waring, of the Washington office of the National Coalition to Ban Handguns, spoke last night at a meeting sponsored by the League of Women Voters and the Business and Professional Women's Club in the Civic Auditorium.
2. About 150 persons attended.
3. He said, "415,000 Saturday Night Specials (cheap handguns) were sold last year."
4. "There are at least 40 million handguns now in private ownership in the United States, more guns than the armies of Europe possess," he told the audience.
5. He also said, "The consequence is a murder rate 200 times greater than in Great Britain, Canada, Israel, West Germany and Japan, countries where it is almost impossible for a private individual to secure a handgun."
6. "About 33,000 Americans died by the gun last year: 18,000 in suicides, 3,000 in accidents and the rest in manslaughter and murder."
7. "About three-fifths of all gun murders in the United States are committed with handguns."
8. "Our organization will make a concerted effort to defeat the local congressman, William Trenzier, who has stated he does not approve of banning assault weapons through federal legislation." Trenzier is a Republican.
9. Injuries caused by handguns cost taxpayers almost $1 billion a year in hospital and rehabilitation costs.

## J. Brush-Back

1. During the past two weeks several fights have taken place during baseball games in both leagues.
2. In most cases, the cause was the brush-back pitch, a ball that is intentionally pitched close to a batter.
3. The pitch is used to prevent hitters from taking a firm footing in the batter's box and to retaliate for similar pitches by the opposing pitcher.

4. Two days ago, managers were warned to cool off their players.

5. Sparky Anders, manager of the local team, does not like the warnings. He said today, "I think they've taken it to the point where they've made it too safe for everybody. I think you have to live a little dangerously. Without that, you take away some of the competitiveness."

## *Class Discussion*

### *Traits*

From your reading and, if possible, your observations of journalists, discuss the qualities or characteristics most important to the journalist. Give examples.

## *DB/CAR*

### *Books*

Assume that in your city a group of parents has called on the city board of education to remove several books from class use and from the high school libraries because they are "racist, immoral and subversive to family values." Your editor asks you to prepare a Sunday feature putting the local action into perspective; she wants you to see what has happened along these lines in recent years in other communities.

Presume that the books the local group has listed are *Catcher in the Rye* (Salinger), *The Adventures of Huckleberry Finn* (Twain), *Of Mice and Men* (Steinbeck), *The Merchant of Venice* (Shakespeare), *Oliver Twist* (Dickens) and *Black Boy* (Wright).

Use a database or reference materials to track down censorship attempts and successes and failures around the country. Use this material to write several background paragraphs. Make sure to look for any legal action that resulted from the attempted censorship.

## *What's Wrong? Backache*

Here is a paragraph from a news story:

> Mark Messier had other things to worry about. He stood in the locker room with an ice pack strapped to his back, which was aching and sore.
> 
> "It affects everything," Messier said. "When you're back's sore, you can't do anything."
> 
> —The New York Times

# PART TWO
## The Basics

# 2 Components of the Story

Naomi Halperin, *The Morning Call.*
**Accurate observations are essential.**

### Introduction

The news story is an accurate, clear and concise account of an event. It is also:

- **Properly attributed.** Sources are fully identified.
- **Objective.** The writer's feelings and opinions are not included.
- **Balanced.** All sides are presented on controversial issues.
- **Well written.** Clarity is achieved through short sentences, everyday language.
- **Interesting.** The story is told in human terms whenever possible.

## Attribution

### Exercises I

The following exercises have more than one source. In your stories, make sure the reader is told clearly the source for all statements and information for which attribution is necessary.

### A. Hot Line

There have been rumors in Washington, D.C., that the president was awakened by a wrong number plugged in on his hot line. This is the closely guarded private wire between the White House and the Pentagon over which the president would first be told of any enemy attack and would give the order that might mean all-out nuclear war.

The White House press secretary confirms the story and gives out the following material:

The president was awakened late one night recently when the "hot line" buzzed. He picked up the phone and heard a strange man's voice:
"Is this the animal hospital?"
"No," said the president.
"Is this South 5–6855?"
"No, this is the White House."
"Is Mr. Smathers there?"
"No, this is the president."
The caller disconnected.

At the Animal Hospital in Alexandria, Va., the switchboard operator tells you, "For the past three weeks we've had trouble with the phone. We've been hearing other conversations. Apparently there have been some crossed wires somewhere."

She says the Chesapeake and Potomac Telephone Co. has been asked to find out how a wrong number could be plugged in on the president's private hot line. The phone company says it is looking into the matter.

Write 200 words.

### B. Superintendent

Here are some notes from the pad of a reporter who has interviewed Herbert Gilkeyson, the newly appointed superintendent of the Freeport city school system. Gilkeyson came from a similar post in Carson, Calif. This is his first day on the job. He is 45; married; the father of three boys, 17, 19, and 20. His wife has been an elementary school teacher for the past 12 years. He was a high school teacher in Huntsville, Ala., and a principal in Savannah, Ga. He graduated from the University of Florida and earned a master's degree and doctorate from Teachers College, Columbia University.

> Urban education is challenging for all of us. There are 180,000 children and more than 10,000 administrators and teachers in the system and all of us must work together.
>
> I see my first job here as the education of our teaching staff and the re-establishment of public trust in the teacher, who is the carrier of the major values of civilization.
>
> Teachers seem to have forgotten their task over the past two decades. It isn't to give custodial care, to supervise the activities of their students, but to direct them toward learning. We will be stressing the fundamentals here.
>
> I like what Gilbert Highet says in one of his books. Here is the quote: "There is one particular danger in educational theory . . . the notion of education by doing instead of thinking. In practice this often means that teachers are happy when their pupils are engaged in more or less harmless social activity, and that they do not want them to sit alone, reading and learning to think, through assimilating other men's and women's thoughts and then forming their own ideas."
>
> Our teachers will have to try to instill in students the value of thinking, and the pleasure that can be derived from it. Nowadays, our teachers have surrendered to the simpler pleasures of a leisure society. I am called an educational conservative. I don't think so. I think a teacher who realizes that the poetry of Keats and the plays of Ibsen and Shakespeare make more sense and ultimately give more pleasure to people than the words of a popular song is a good teacher.
>
> Once the teacher begins to make demands on the students so that they can think for themselves, the public will begin to trust the teacher. Why should voters approve bond issues and pay raises when their children in high school can't read a fifth-grade story book and can't add a column of figures? We must return to the basics in our educational system.

In the clippings about Gilkeyson's appointment two months ago, one of the stories quotes the reaction of the head of the local unit of the National Federation of Teachers, Helen Carruthers, a fifth-grade teacher, as follows:

> We neither oppose nor endorse the appointment by the school board. Dr. Gilkeyson is a well-known administrator whose ideas are what many of our members describe as conservative. He is a believer in a return to the school of discipline. We shall see whether his ideas are workable in this community.

You call Carruthers and ask if there is any change in the NFT's attitude toward Gilkeyson. She replies:

> We will cooperate in every way with Dr. Gilkeyson in his attempts to administer a harmonious school system.

Write 300 words.

# Verification

## Exercise II

### Poetry

You are sent to the Freeport Motor Lodge to interview a visiting lecturer, James Talbot, who is a writer of fiction, a literary critic and a poet. He is English and his work appears in the *Times Literary Supplement* in England and in many quarterlies in this country. He is to lecture on modern poetry tomorrow noon at Mallory College. Your editor tells you that Talbot has recently written a book, *Melodious Frontiers,* that maintains that modern poets are as rich and varied in their work as in any period in history. Since your readers include academicians and students, he suggests you ask Talbot about his theme and some of the poets he likes. "Get some good quotes," is his final advice.

Talbot, 45, tall, thin, dressed in a gray suit, invites you to his room for "an hour only so that the good professors" can have him to lunch at the faculty club. Here are some of your notes. Write 250 to 300 words.

> Yes, it's true I like modern poetry because of the variety. You have a Ginsberg coming out of—Was it your Brooklyn?—with his political and social consciousness, and we have an Eliot whose "Love Song" is a display of bad temper at the times.
> And there is the rich lushness of a Thomas singing hymns to grass and the "muscle pools and the heron-priested shore" on his 30th birthday. And the dry, sometimes incomprehensible, lowercase Cummings with his, "how do you like your blue-eyed boy, mister death?"

He pauses for breath, and you realize you are going to need someone to find the material from which these quotes are taken. You do not trust your spelling of some of the words, nor the punctuation, and you are not sure you caught the names correctly. He resumes:

> I mean to say that, if you look back, what we have is all this mooning about—boy wants girl and then tightens bow to shoot arrow at resistant target. And in the Earl of Rochester we have the bow misfiring now and then. Good old Andy Marwell and his coy mistress, urging her on. It's good enough I suppose, for hot-blooded young men in freshman English.
> But why don't you read your own Walt Whitman with his great understanding of the democratic experience. If I were an American teacher of literature, I'd have my students read nothing but Frost, Emily Dixon, Wallace Stephens, Ted Rutkey and any two you can name.
> Sorry, time to go. As T.S. would say, "Hurry up please it's time."

## Balance and Fairness

### Exercise III

### Appreciation

Here is a handout from the local chamber of commerce. It is marked for immediate release. Write two to three takes.

> Stinson Airport will celebrate Stinson Airport Appreciation Day, Sunday, beginning 1 p.m.
> The Junior Chamber of Commerce aviation committee will sponsor the program, which will salute the local field that is one of the nation's busiest airports not handling regular commercial or military flights.
> The field was opened in 1939. Since the field has been in operation there have been more than a million landings and takeoffs without a fatality.
> The program will open with an hour of plane rides for the public. Passengers will pay for the rides at the rate of one penny a pound for their weight. State officials are expected to attend.
> Demonstrations will include crop dusting and spraying and freefall parachute jumps. The Southwest Parachute Association will sponsor the jumps. The association president, Tom Slinkard, who has made 51 safe jumps, will lead three other association members in the 4,500 foot jumps.

You call the chamber public relations man, Thomas Everingham, to ask for the names of the state officials, and he tells you that William Sullivan, the state commissioner of aeronautics, and Lt. Gov. Harry Lee Waterfield will fly in, arriving about 1:50 p.m. to start the demonstrations. You ask for Slinkard's address. Everingham says that Slinkard won't be there because he tripped off the back steps of his home and suffered a broken leg. But the demonstrations will be staged anyway. He says that the airplane rides also will be given from 3 to 6 p.m. At 4 p.m., the Sports Car Club will give an exhibition of skill driving at the southeast corner of the field. There also will be about 30 aircraft on display at the field in front of the Administration Building.

## Brevity

### Exercises IV

### A. Appointees

Figure 2.1 is a release from the Federal Trade Commission. Rewrite for:

1. A newspaper in Boston.
2. A newspaper in Lexington, Ky.
3. The Associated Press wire.

**FEDERAL TRADE COMMISSION NEWS**

WASHINGTON, D.C. 20580

FOR RELEASE 7am EDT, Friday September 5

FTC APPOINTS GERALD P. NORTON DEPUTY GENERAL COUNSEL
AND THOMAS LYNCH ADAMS, JR., ASSISTANT GENERAL COUNSEL

Federal Trade Commission Chairman Lewis A. Engman today announced the appointments of Gerald P. Norton, 35, to the newly created position of deputy general counsel, and of Thomas Lynch Adams, Jr., 33, as assistant general counsel for legislation and congressional liaison.

Norton's appointment is effective September 15, and Adams', August 4.

\* \* \*

Norton has been assistant to the Solicitor General, Department of Justice, since 1990, and in that capacity has prepared and argued Supreme Court cases on behalf of the United States.

A native of West Roxbury, Mass., he received an A.B. degree (magna cum laude in economics) from Princeton University in 1984 and an LL.B (magna cum laude) from Columbia University Law School in 1987. At Columbia he was managing and research editor of the Law Review. Following graduation from law school, Norton was a law clerk to Judge Leonard P. Moore, U.S. Court of Appeals for the Second Circuit.

He joined the Washington, D.C., law firm of Covington & Burling as an associate in 1988, handling antitrust and other litigation until he joined the staff of the Solicitor General.

In creating the new position of Deputy General Counsel, General Counsel Robert J. Lewis explained that, "Because of Mr. Norton's extremely impressive credentials as a court room lawyer we expect to apply his experience principally to that area."

Norton is married to Amanda B. Pedersen, an attorney in private practice, and they live in Washington, D.C.

\* \* \*

Adams had been legislative counsel for the Small Business Administration from early this year until his appointment to the FTC staff. From 1991 until early 1992 he was a Senate legislative assistant and minority counsel for the U.S. Senate Commerce Committee. For two years prior to that time he was an attorney with the Land and Natural Resources Division of the Department of Justice.

A native of Lexington, Ky., he received a B.A. degree in history in 1987 from the University of Virginia. He was graduated from the Vanderbilt University Law School with a J.D. degree in 1989.

Adams is married to Anne Randolph, and they live in Washington, D.C.

# # #

PRESS CONTACT: Office of Public Information, (202) 963-4325
Arthur L. Amolsch, Director

REQUESTS FOR FTC DOCUMENTS SHOULD BE MADE TO LEGAL AND PUBLIC RECORDS, ROOM 130, FEDERAL TRADE COMMISSION, WASHINGTON, D.C. 20580. TELEPHONE (202) 962-5214.

I004—APPTGC

FEDERAL TRADE COMMISSION
WASHINGTON, D.C. 20580

OFFICIAL BUSINESS
PENALTY FOR PRIVATE USE $300

POSTAGE AND FEES PAID
U. S. FEDERAL TRADE COMMISSION

**A. Appointees**

**Figure 2.1**

## B. Belmont

The city editor tosses the following three releases on your desk and asks you to rewrite them for today's paper.

Belmont Motel
7989 Airport Road
765-4321
P. Lyon, Director of Press Relations

FOR IMMEDIATE RELEASE

The Belmont Motel today announced an underwater extravaganza will be held next month in Freeport in the motel's magnificent Turquoise Pool, which is the world's largest indoor swimming area.

The festivities will include entertainment by a bevy of colorful motion picture and television stars and starlets. Beginning June 21st and running through the 23rd, the activities will include a water show to begin the gala weekend on Friday at 8 p.m. Paul Nissen's Bathing Beauties, 12 pretty and curvaceous swimming stars, will open the weekend with coordinated swimming and diving. Their home base is Miami, Fla.

Saturday will feature former Olympic swimming greats Frieda Schwartz of Berlin and Mark Switzer of Switzerland, who will combine their talents to offer a magnificent display of underwater acrobatics. Following their show at 1 p.m., competitions will be held for all hotel guests in various swimming categories: 100-yard dash (under 21 years of age; 21–35; and senior citizens); backstroke (same categories); diving from high and low platforms (open). Winners will receive all-expense weekends in the Belmont Motel.

Sunday, there will be personal appearances by Buster C. Rabbe and Holly (Kitten) Grove, a toddler's wading contest in the children's pool and other activities.

Albert Gill Associates
Public Relations Consultants
Times-Mirror Plaza
Los Angeles, Calif.

The underwater film festival scheduled for next month in Freeport will add another well-known aqua-star to its imposing list of cinematic and television greats. Buster C. Rabbe, star of the TV drama "Seafarer," will appear next month to demonstrate a new lightweight underwater movie camera made by the Hashiki Industries of Tokyo, creators of the famous Hashiki-O, the official underwater camera which will be used to film the festival.

(Radio announcers note: Rabbe is pronounced *Rab,* as in *dab.*)

Triple A Ads, Inc.
From: Barney Bishop
To: Freeport News, exclusive.

A vivacious Georgia Peach will be one of the stars at the underwater extravaganza scheduled for next month in the Belmont Motel's Turquoise Pool, the world's largest indoor swimming pool.

Holly (Kitten) Grove will attend the film festival, straight from the West Coast.

Now pursuing her career in Hollywood, Kitten has crowded a number of exciting activities into her 19 years.

Born into a Southern family that traces its lineage back to the Scotch Highlanders, Kitten began winning beauty contests at the age of 16. Among her laurels are runner-up, Athens Press Photography Beauty Queen; Athens High School Miss Cut-Up; Freshman Beauty Queen, University of Georgia; Miss Revlon; Maid of Cotton semifinalist; and Miss Salvo, Naval ROTC, University of Georgia.

Kitten, a bountiful 36-24-36, has appeared on several television shows.

## C. Rumor

You hear rumors at city hall that the mayor has cancer and recently visited a doctor for a checkup. You ask his press secretary for confirmation and he tells you that a statement will be made at noon. This is the statement:

THE CITY OF FREEPORT             OFFICE OF THE MAYOR

For Immediate Release

*Statement by Mayor Sam Parnass*

Yesterday I visited a dermatologist, Dr. Richard Green, to have five noncancerous lesions removed from my face. Three of the five are what are known as solar keratoses and, as the name suggests, are caused by exposure to the sun. The other two are seborrheic keratoses and are an inherited condition. They are common and benign lesions.

The procedure took approximately 20 minutes in Dr. Green's office and required only a local anesthetic, xylocaine. I experienced no pain or discomfort. Dr. Green told me that I could either place bandaids over the areas where the procedure had been performed or I could allow them to heal by exposure to the air. I chose the latter course. No additional medical treatment is required.

Dr. Green has placed me under no restrictions. I can wash my face with soap and water and I can swim without any risk. Not surprisingly, since this is a sun-related condition, he advised me to avoid prolonged exposure to the sun. That is good advice for anyone.

Write 150 words.

# Human Interest

## *Exercise V*

### *Changes*

School superintendent Herbert Gilkeyson announces the following personnel changes that will affect the teaching staff next year:

Adele Bartles moves from sixth-grade English to vocational adviser, Southside High School. Mrs. Bartles took courses over the past three years at Mallory College and earned her M.A. in counseling.

Daniel Fox, physical education instructor in the Horace Mann School, appointed assistant principal of the school. His teaching post has been filled by Albert Pardone, of Flagstaff, Ariz., who graduated from the university there after three years as a member of the basketball and football teams.

Ron Phealan, fourth-grade teacher at George Packer Elementary School, has resigned to become a driver for Greyhound. He had taught in the system since 1982 and submitted his resignation two months ago citing his need for higher pay.

Michael Lang, Peoria, Ill., hired to replace Phealan after three years at the American School in Warsaw, Poland, where he taught elementary school. He is a graduate of the University of Georgia and is 31. Married, two children, 7 and 3.

## *Assignments*

### *A. Safe*

Some city schools distribute maps of school areas that indicate the safe route to the school. The maps show intersections with school guards and places—such as firehouses and libraries—where students will find a "safe haven." Make a Safe Route School Map for an elementary school in the community and write a caption and 250-word story.

### *B. Low Pay*

A study of the high school class of 1972 showed that American women who graduated then had better grades in high school and college, finished their degrees faster and were happier about their education than the men. Yet they were rewarded with lower pay and suffered a higher rate of unemployment.

Talk to some women who graduated from high school and college 20 to 25 years ago and see what their experiences in the job market have been.

### *C. Inflated*

Twenty-five years ago, private colleges and universities bestowed honors to the top 3 or 4 percent of the graduating class. Today, about 20 percent of the class receives honors, which are based on grade average. This has led some graduate schools to rely on scores on standardized tests such as the Graduate Record Examination rather than on grades.

"High grades are no longer an adequate index of a student's knowledge of ability," says Paul J. Korshin of the English faculty at the University of Pennsylvania. He cites the incident of a state college student with a 2.1 grade average who falsified his transcript and was admitted to Yale where he earned a 3.0 average.

How have grade averages changed over the years at your school? What are the criteria that the graduate schools use for admission?

## *Campus Project*

### *Bias (1)*

Surveys of news sources and of public opinion show that most people consider the press negative and biased.

The Josephson Institute of Ethics in California surveyed 131 legislative leaders and their staff members in 50 states and found 87 percent believed the media focus on "critical and negative behavior and ignore positive issue-centered stories." In story selection and coverage, 62 percent said journalists are likely to reflect their ideological and personal views. And 55 percent said stories are not balanced and are unlikely to include the position of the person accused of wrongdoing.

The Times Mirror/Gallup polls showed these results in questions about press performance:

1. In presenting the news dealing with political and social issues, do you think that news organizations deal fairly with all sides, or do they tend to favor one side? **Percent**
   - (a) deal fairly with all sides — 28
   - (b) tend to favor one side — 68
   - (c) don't know — 4
2. In general, do you think news organizations are pretty independent, or are they often influenced by powerful people and organizations?
   - (a) pretty independent — 33
   - (b) often influenced by powerful organizations — 62
   - (c) don't know — 5
3. In general, do you think news organizations get the facts straight, or do you think that their stories and reports are often inaccurate?
   - (a) get the facts straight — 54
   - (b) inaccurate — 44
   - (c) don't know — 2
4. Do you think that news organizations have a willingness to admit mistakes or do they try to cover up mistakes?
   - (a) willingness to admit mistakes — 34
   - (b) try to cover up mistakes — 55
   - (c) neither/can't say — 11
5. In general, do you think news organizations pay too much attention to good news, too much attention to bad news, or do they mostly report the kinds of stories they should be covering?
   - (a) too much attention to good news — 1
   - (b) too much attention to bad news — 60
   - (c) report stories they should be covering — 35
   - (d) don't know — 4

Use these five questions for a campus poll of media confidence. You might want to study different subgroups—students, faculty members, administrators—to see whether their assessments differ significantly from each other. Compare your results with the figures in the table.

## *Community Projects*

### *A. Bias (2)*

Conduct the same poll in your community. You may, again, want to make subgroups. You can divide your sample by age group, sex, educational attainment, political party registration, ethnicity.

### *B. College Plans*

A recent College Board study of high school seniors showed these findings about the seniors' plans for majors, careers and college degrees:

**Health and Allied Services:** 19 percent planned to major in this field, which was the most popular college major; 68 percent of these students were female.
**Business and Commerce:** 14 percent planned this major, which represented less interest than seniors had in 1985 when 25 percent of the students chose it.
**Social Sciences and History:** 12 percent.
**Engineering:** 9 percent; 81 percent of these students were male.
**Education:** 8 percent.

More than half these students (53 percent) intended to go on to seek a graduate or professional degree. The percentage of women who planned to continue their education beyond the undergraduate level increased from 33 percent in 1974 to 54 percent. Of the men, 51 percent planned graduate study.

Female plans for doctoral work exceeded those of males, 25 percent to 22 percent.

Make a study of high school seniors in your community and see how their plans compare with these national figures.

## *Home Assignment*

### *Components*

Clip stories from campus and local newspapers that illustrate:

1. The two kinds of attribution:
    (a) **Statements** that are attributed to a source.
    (b) **Information** about events not witnessed by the reporter that is attributed to a source.
2. A trial balloon (see Chapter 2 in textbook for a description of the term) and a media-event or pseudo-event. What do you think the motives of the source are?
3. Unfairness that falls into these categories:
    (a) **Slanting:** Using material that is favorable to a person or a policy and ignoring contradictory, relevant information.
    (b) **Distorting:** Using material inaccurately with the intention to mislead.
    (c) **Quoting out of context:** Using quoted material to make a point the original material did not intend.
    (d) **Name-calling:** Using words that have an unpopular or unfavorable connotation.

For number 3 you may use any material you have heard or read—books, magazines, television, advertising, editorials, columns.

4. The use of human interest to make a technical or complex story more interesting and easier to understand. Also, find an example of a story that could profit from the introduction of human interest. What kinds of people, or which specific individuals, would you interview for the story?

## *Class Discussion*

### *Direct*

Clip from your college and community newspapers local stories that are based on direct observation and second- and third-hand sources. Explain your classification and indicate whether the reporter could have observed the event directly but settled for another person's account. Did the reporter fail to attribute information not obtained directly? If so, why do you think there was no attribution?

## *DB/CAR*

### *Colleges*

Some publications rate colleges and issue annual rankings. Use a database to obtain the latest rankings and write a 300-word story based on the ratings. Use this search term: *Best Colleges.*

## Skill Drill: Guidelines

Each of the following items violates at least one basic guideline for writing news stories. The guidelines are:

**Accuracy** in detail and expression.
**Attribution** of all statements and information to reliable sources.
**Verification** of assertions, charges.
**Balance** and **fairness**.
**Brevity**.
**Human interest** in stories when possible.
**News point** stressed.

Identify the errors. When possible, make corrections or indicate what should be done.

### A. Salary

He said his take-home pay from his salary of $400 a week as an elevator operator was slightly more than $300 a week. His weekly deductions included: social security, $16; federal taxes, $46; state taxes, $21; and series EE government bonds, $25. (Paragraph in story.)

### B. Fine

He was fined $25 last year for loitering near the theater. But this felony conviction did not deter him from his task. (Paragraph in story.)

### C. Resignation

Jenkins announced his resignation yesterday. He is quitting the force because of its authoritarian structure and the dictatorial attitude of Chief McCabe. (Paragraph in story.)

### D. Shots

A city plan, proposed by municipal health authorities today, would inoculate all unleashed animals and take them to the local pound where they would be given anti-rabies shots and returned to their owners after a $15 fine is paid. (Lead.)

### E. Success

Lee capped his successful 1975 season with the Red Sox by helping his teammates to win the World Series against the Cincinnati Reds, Peralta said in his talk to the Boosters' Club. (Paragraph in story.)

### F. Talk

The local chapter of the Public Relations Society said today José Lopez García, director of an advertising agency in Mexico City, will address its meeting Oct. 20 at 8 p.m. in the Chamber of Commerce boardroom.
Mr. García is on a tour of this country to gather ideas for the Mexican public relations industry. (Short item.)

### G. Noise

A special airport-sound study committee, set up at the local airfield, issued its report, Marshall Peat, airport manager, reported today.
The study was set up to determine whether there would be any problems if the undeveloped land to the northeast of the field were developed for use as a housing project.
The report stated that noise and the possibility of accidents make this area unfit for housing.
"That should kill the housing proposal of Mitchell & Co.," Peat said. More than 250 acres are involved. Half the residents of the area said they intend to move if they can find housing. (Story.)

### H. New Age

"A new age of pot is dawning," said Albert Goldman in his talk to the Rotary Club this afternoon.
Goldman, a writer, said marijuana will replace liquor and tobacco as the new middle-class social habit. Already, he said, it is used by almost all age and social groups. Since it has no known ill effects, Goldman said, it is safer than the habit-forming alcohol and cigarettes. (Story.)

*I. Adoption*

Robert G. Dowle was named head of the Interfaith Children's Agency today at the annual meeting of the board.

The agency arranges for the adoption of local youngsters through the various religious groups and the city social services department.

Dowle said he was pleased by the appointment, particularly since he was placed in the home of his adoptive parents, Mr. and Mrs. Albert Dowle, in the first year of the agency's operation in 1937. (Story.)

*J. Tour*

During his travels, he dropped off in Iceland, the world's largest island. He toured the interior, which is covered with an enormous sheet of ice. He said the island was discovered by Eric the Red almost 1,000 years ago. (Part of story.)

## *Fix It: Attribution*

The first two sentences are from AP stories and the remainder from student copy. Fix them.

**1.** The government bought advertising space in major South African newspapers to print a letter in which President P.W. Botha emphasized his commitment to draw majority blacks into decision making.

**2.** Tens of thousands of workers, most of them from independent unions, marched to the main city square to protest the burden the country's economic crisis is placing on them.

**3.** The dispatcher failed to follow the proper procedure, and the result was the Metroliner crash.

**4.** The institute, which is considered the best in the country, has turned to genetic engineering studies.

**5.** The noise, which at times is beyond human endurance, led residents to protest the location of the body shop.

## *What's Wrong?: Jilted*

CAMBRIDGE, MASS.—An Austrian college student has admitted making more than 10,000 harassing telephone calls to Harvard University students, mainly women, over the last three years.

Based on a tip, Harvard police wiretapped several phones and caught the student, who attends a Vienna institution, making the calls from Austria. Police said the student, whom they refused to identify, was angry because he felt jilted by a female Harvard student he had met in Austria.

The man has randomly called as many as 10 Harvard students a day, often making death threats. Police are deciding whether to seek to extradite him to press charges.

—*The Chronicle of Higher Education*

# PART THREE

Writing the Story

# 3 What Is News?

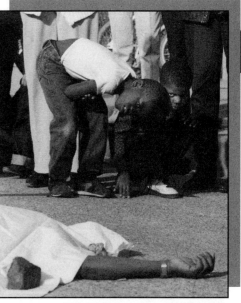

Richard Carson, *Houston Chronicle.*
**News shows us the way we live now.**

### Introduction

News is the timely account of events of importance and significance. The closer the event—psychologically or physically—to those reading or hearing about it, the greater its news value. News value is enhanced by the involvement in events of people who are well-known. We also make news out of strange and unusual situations. News values are not absolute. Decisions on what is to be used and how it is to be used depend on considerations such as the nature of the news medium and its audience and the role that the individual station or newspaper has established for itself in the community.

## Exercises

### A. Craftsman

You are working on the news desk of the newspaper in Flagstaff, Ariz., and you receive this press release in the mail. Rewrite it in less than 100 words for your newspaper.

DETROIT—Youths from Medford, Ore., and Arlington, Va., were the top winners today in the $38,000 Fisher Craftsman's Guild Scholarship Awards for Model Car Designs.

Eighteen awards were made.

Tom H. Semple, 19, Medford, Ore., won a $5,000 university scholarship for taking first place in the 16–20 age group with his original one-twelfth scale model of a black sports coupe.

Winner of a similar scholarship in the competition for boys between 11 and 15 years old was Richard R. John, 15, Arlington, Va. His entry was a blue and aqua hardtop sports car.

The awards will be made at a special luncheon for the winners, Nov. 15.

Each year hundreds of youths enter the competition for awards totaling $117,000, including the scholarships. The contest is sponsored by Fisher Body Division for General Motors. Runner-up in the senior division was Michael B. Antonick, Mount Vernon, Ohio, while John M. D'Mura, 13, Flagstaff, Ariz., took second place honors in the junior competition. Each received a $4,000 scholarship.

The other awardees:

Third Place ($3,000 scholarships): Richard L. Beck, 20, Louisville, Ky., senior division; Melvin G. Gable, 14, Ypsilanti, Mich., junior division.

Fourth place ($2,000 scholarships): Michael S. Reese, 16, Houston, Tex., senior division; Harry F. Mahe Jr., 15, Brooklyn, N.Y., junior division.

### B. Poet

You are covering the county courthouse and a court employee tells you that District Court Judge Harvey Smith has handed down a decision in rhyme and that it might make a good story. You check and find he has indeed written a poem consisting of 15 stanzas.

The decision was made in an appeal of a municipal court decision in Ridgefield Park in which Eugene T. Bohelska was fined $300 on his conviction for using profanity on the telephone, a violation of state law. Bohelska was also convicted of driving an improperly registered vehicle, although he contended he was driving someone else's car and should not have been held responsible. He appealed his conviction on the profanity charge, which grew out of an incident with the court clerk.

The incident began when, after two delays in his municipal court hearing on the driving charge, Bohelska called the court to ask for another delay. He said he was ill with a fever. The clerk refused to make a postponement and he allegedly cursed her. The clerk, Geraldine Mucella, then filed charges.

Here are the key stanzas from the judge's long poem:

DECISION:
Vulgar words transmitted by
　phone
Are not enough when standing
　alone
To land said caller in a jail cell
Where, for six months, he's
　required to dwell;
For while such words may cause
　some resentment
Their use is protected by the First
　Amendment.
Tempers then flared 'til it
　sounded the same
As a Rangers-Flyers hockey game.
"F– – – you, go f– – – yourself"
　Eugene blurted
Though use of that word should be
　averted.
Before the sentence was even
　completed
He wished that the expletive had
　been deleted.
You say things couldn't possibly
　worsen?
Well the clerk of the court was a
　female person.
Next day the cop in the hat rang
　the bell and waited.
Eugene opened the door, his fever
　had abated.
He knew that he now would be
　printed and booked.
Figured his goose was practically
　cooked.
They went to the station and
　straight to the jail.
He stayed there til mother posted his
　bail.
Title Two A, Chapter One Seventy,
　Section Twenty-nine (three)
Is the charge for which posting of
　bail set him free.
It provides that when using the
　telephone
Mere profanity standing alone
Even if stated in friendship or jest
Is a criminal act, hence the arrest.
The Ridgefield Park docket was
　busy that night
Traffic, this case and a big bar
　room fight.

Judge George A. Browne, if I may
　opine
Talks a lot like the late Gertrude
　Stein.
Justice was dispensed at a good
　rapid pace.
Next thing you know they called
　Eugene's case.
There were few facts disputed, no
　witnesses lied.
The question was "How would the
　law be applied?"
Judge George A. Browne made his
　position quite clear
He said that his clerk was shell
　pink of ear.
The words Eugene used were
　obscene and profane
And it caused her anguish and
　much mental pain.
For that telephone call with the
　curses and hollers
The fine imposed was three
　hundred dollars.
The lawyer protested and fought
　on with zeal
So now we turn to Eugene's
　appeal.
Can you swear if you hit your
　thumb with a hammer
Without risk of spending six
　months in the slammer?
When the bank computer errs and
　bounces your check
Is your language confined to aw
　gees and oh hecks?
Does the law require you to stand
　mute
While a cigarette burns a hole in
　your suit?
Is it reasonable to remain calm and
　composed
If the photograph shows your
　horse has been nosed?
Statutory attempts to regulate
　pure bluster
Can't pass what is called
　constitutional muster.
Use of vulgar words that may
　cause resentment
Is protected by the First
　Amendment.

There must be a danger of breach
    of the peace
For this near sacred right ever to
    cease.
This was no obscene call from a
    sick deranged stranger.
Of a breach of the peace there was
    no possible danger.
Eugene hurled an expletive in
    sheer exasperation

And that isn't a crime anywhere in
    this nation.
The cop in the hat and Judge
    George A. Browne
Will read this opinion and grumble
    and frown.
They may ring me up just to holler
    and curse
But I still can't affirm. I have to
    reverse.

## *C. Center*

The Zoning and Planning Board last night completed a hearing on the proposal of the Salvation Army for a community center at 740 Springfield St. A decision is expected at the next meeting, Jan. 20.

At the hearing:

The Army proposes to build a two-story center at a cost of $500,000. The Army was promised the new location as part of a land swap in a downtown urban renewal project whose planning was completed two years ago.

The present center is three blocks away. That land is part of a proposed mall.

Merchants at 740 and 742 Springfield oppose the board's granting approval. The owners are Frank Chaffee, Frank's Deli; Margaret Williams, Mayfair Fabrics; Thomas Ashkinaze, Ashkinaze's Men's Styles; and Bernzar Berents, B&D Butchers.

They ask the board not to get rid of going businesses that pay taxes. "We cannot find anything in the area," Berents said. He's the spokesman. "It would be tragic to eliminate going concerns."

The Army spokeswoman, Major Barbara Geddings, said, "We will have to eliminate our youth program at a time when the city's juvenile delinquency rate is growing. This is a part of the city where young people are without parks, without recreation of any kind, if we close our center."

Berents also told the board, which must approve a zoning change before the community center can be built: "We are taxpayers, contributing to the city treasury. What sense does it make to remove us from the city tax base and in our place put a tax-exempt operation? You are finding out that downtown businesses are fleeing every week and your tax base is eroding."

Asked by Harry Kempe, a member of the board, whether the merchants have investigated moving to the mall, Berents said that the merchants have done so but have not been assured of a date when the mall will be completed.

"We can't just close up and wait," Berents said. "For all we know, the mall won't be built for another two years. What will we do in the meantime? Go on welfare?"

## *D. Larceny*

The most common campus crime is larceny-theft, according to the FBI. Here is a list of the campuses on which more than 400 such crimes were reported in a recent year. If your campus or one nearby is listed, localize the material and obtain comments from campus and city police authorities.

Do you see any concentration of these crimes in any areas, states? If so, try to determine why.

| | | | |
|---|---|---|---|
| University of Alabama, Tuscaloosa | 575 | Irvine | 794 |
| Arizona State | 1,088 | Los Angeles | 1,078 |
| University of Arizona | 1,032 | Riverside | 569 |
| Calif. State Poly., Pomona | 412 | San Diego | 915 |
| Calif. State Poly., San Luis Obispo | 452 | San Francisco | 787 |
| California State Univ.: | | Santa Barbara | 799 |
|    Chico | 468 | San Diego State University | 917 |
|    Fresno | 477 | San Francisco State University | 500 |
|    Fullerton | 460 | University of Colorado, Boulder | 701 |
|    Long Beach | 488 | Yale | 587 |
|    Los Angeles | 434 | Florida State Univ., Tallahassee | 694 |
|    Northridge | 697 | Univ. of Florida | 1,265 |
|    Sacramento | 474 | Georgia Inst. Tech. | 844 |
|    San Jose | 408 | Georgia State Univ. | 437 |
| University of California: | | Univ. of Georgia | 439 |
|    Berkeley | 1,540 | Ball State Univ. | 690 |
|    Davis | 1,602 | Univ. of Indiana, Bloomington | 960 |

| | | | |
|---|---|---|---|
| Univ. of Indiana Indianapolis | 602 | Duke University | 1,025 |
| Purdue Univ. | 840 | North Carolina State Univ., Raleigh | 668 |
| Iowa State Univ. | 587 | Univ. of North Carolina, Chapel Hill | 722 |
| Univ. of Kentucky | 718 | Ohio State University | 1,335 |
| Louisiana State Univ. | 537 | Univ. of Akron | 506 |
| Univ. of Maryland, Baltimore City | 816 | Univ. of Cincinnati | 952 |
| Univ. of Maryland, College Park | 983 | Univ. of Oklahoma, Norman | 698 |
| Boston University | 796 | Brown Univ. | 470 |
| MIT | 787 | Medical Univ. of S. Carolina | 613 |
| Univ. of Massachusetts, Amherst | 544 | Univ. of S. Carolina, Columbia | 628 |
| Central Michigan Univ. | 406 | Univ. of Tennessee, Knoxville | 616 |
| Michigan State Univ. | 1,109 | Texas A&M, College Station | 648 |
| Univ. of Michigan | 1,631 | Texas Tech Univ., Lubbock | 410 |
| Univ. of Minnesota | 1,171 | Univ. of Houston, Central Campus | 512 |
| Univ. of Missouri, Columbia | 472 | Brigham Young Univ. | 463 |
| Univ. of Nebraska, Lincoln | 909 | Univ. of Utah | 813 |
| Rutgers Univ. | 691 | George Mason Univ. | 477 |
| Univ. of Med. and Dentistry, Newark | 640 | Univ. of Virginia | 627 |
| New Mexico State Univ. | 454 | Virginia Commonwealth Univ. | 685 |
| Cornell Univ. | 719 | Virginia Poly. Inst. and State Univ. | 452 |
| State Univ. of New York | | Univ. of Washington | 830 |
|     Buffalo | 498 | Univ. of Wisconsin, Madison | 826 |
|     Stony Brook | 770 | | |

## Assignments

### A. Restricted

Librarians are placing books that might be stolen or mutilated on restricted reserve. Years ago, the restricted section consisted of works that were considered bawdy or licentious: James Joyce's *Ulysses* and the works of Henry Miller, Havelock Ellis and the Marquis de Sade. During the 1960s the locks came off and students could find de Sade's *120 Days of Sodom* on the open shelves.

Their place on the closed shelves was taken by valuable books that brought a high price on the used and rare book markets. Also, engravings were a target: Thieves would razor out the Winslow Homer engravings in old copies of *Harper's Weekly*, for example.

In the 1990s, another group made it to the closed shelves, books deemed politically incorrect and thus likely to be mutilated. Salman Rushdie's *Satanic Verses* was isolated. De Sade's works went back in the cupboard because they depict "violence against women," as one group put it.

Interview the head librarian on the campus and in the community. What books are on the restricted shelves? (Obtain authors' names and book titles.) Why?

### B. Canines

Interview an official at the local American Society for the Prevention of Cruelty to Animals or dog shelter for a story on the dog population and its characteristics.

Do most people own mutts? What is the favorite breed? Is there a licensing regulation or leash law; if so, how is it obeyed and how is it enforced?

### C. Vox Populi

How strong is the voice of the people in your community? Interview the editor of the editorial page of the local newspaper and the station managers of local broadcast stations. How many letters and telephone calls do they receive a day, a week? What are the subjects that move people to write or call? Select a recent local issue—have there been any letters or calls about it?

### D. Emergency

Visit the emergency clinic of a local hospital. Are the doctors and nurses overwhelmed? Why? How many patients do they see on a shift? Is there a peak—weekends, late evenings? What are the most common ailments? Who uses the clinic? Are there any proposals to alter the clinic's services?

*E. Shoplifting*

Is shoplifting a problem for local merchants? If so, how do they cope with it? Is the situation better or worse than 10 or 15 years ago? Why? Are most shoplifters in one age group, of one sex? Do merchants prosecute? Consult the police and the district attorney's office to determine whether any shoplifters have gone to court; if so, learn what has happened to them. What is the usual charge (misdemeanor, felony) lodged against a shoplifter?

*F. Fans*

Interview members of one of the local teams—college or professional—about local fans. Are the fans enthusiastic, tolerant of losses, fair-weather followers? Is the team treated better on the road? Does the attitude of fans affect play? How?

Obtain attendance figures: total, season ticket holders. Up or down?

Do winning and losing affect attendance?

Do not settle for the usual quotes, but try to dig into the actual feelings of the athletes.

*G. Register*

More than 2,000 high schools participate in a program, First Vote, that gives high school seniors a chance to register to vote in their social studies classes. More than 100,000 students register a year in their schools. Some schools open the program twice a year, but most do it close to graduation. What's the situation in your city's high schools?

*H. Names*

Do a feature on last names. Does the person named Smith or Jones wish for a more distinctive name? Have those with names that are difficult to pronounce considered changing them? How does a person change his or her name? Are there any interesting examples of such changes? What are the names of the children of women who retained their own names after marriage?

Bob Thayer, *The Journal–Bulletin.*

**Hot, cold; wet, dry; winning, losing—the fan is there.**

## Campus Project

### Diet

Interview students who live off-campus about their eating habits. Try to have them recall their meals for the last two or three days. Set these findings against your background information and what the campus dietitian or a local nutritionist says is a healthy diet.

If you want to take this a step further, differentiate among students who eat at home, those who live in a cooperative arrangement and those who are on their own. Are there significant differences in their diets? Do eating habits differ between men and women?

## Community Projects

### A. Eating

In the last 20 years, consumers have made a major shift in their food consumption. Beef and eggs are consumed less often, poultry and fish more frequently. Fruits and vegetables are a major part of the diet, as are whole grains. The U.S. Department of Agriculture reports these changes in food consumption over the two decades:

What Is News? **31**

**Fruits:** up 125 percent
**Low-fat milk and yogurt:** up 202 percent
**Whole grains:** up 245 percent
**Fish:** up 39 percent
**Red meat:** up 5 percent
**Chicken:** up 105 percent
**Broccoli:** up 770 percent
**Green vegetables:** up 169 percent

Make a survey of local residents and their eating habits. Talk to shoppers in groceries and supermarkets, men shopping after business. Have shoppers changed their family's and their diets in response to concerns about cholesterol, heart disease, overweight, hypertension? Is there a difference in the dietary practices among age groups, between men and women?

### B. Outdoors

What do people do when they have spare time? A survey found that most take to the road. People were asked to list their favorite outdoor recreations, and they responded:

| | |
|---|---|
| Driving for pleasure | 40 percent |
| Swimming | 35 |
| Picnicking | 33 |
| Fishing | 26 |
| Bicycling | 21 |
| Running, jogging | 19 |
| Hiking, wildlife viewing | 18 |
| Camping (tent at campground) | 16 |
| Photography | 15 |
| Bird watching | 14 |
| Backpacking | 13 |
| Golf | 11 |
| Motorboating | 10 |

Less than 10 percent responded, in order: tennis, recreational vehicle camping, hunting, target shooting, motorcycling, water skiing, canoeing and kayaking, downhill skiing, horseback riding, mountain biking, off-road vehicle driving.

List these recreational subjects and let people check their preferences. Compare your findings locally with these national results.

## Home Assignment

### Technical

**Hauling in a muskie on the French River.**

Leaf through a technical journal to find an article that could be of general interest if rewritten. Rewrite it for a newspaper, magazine or radio broadcast. Hold the rewrite to 300 words. Some suggestions: *American Journal of Nursing, American Journal of Psychology, American Journal of Sociology, Journal of the American Medical Association, Journalism Quarterly, Lancet, Nature, Science, Public Opinion Quarterly, Foreign Affairs.*

## Class Discussion

### Front-Page Play

Select newspaper stories that have been given front-page play because of impact or significance, timeliness, prominence, proximity, conflict, the bizarre and currency. Identify the stories as such. Do you agree with the newspaper selection and the comparative play of the stories?

## DB/CAR

### Cities (1)

Since the mid-1980s *Money* magazine has been ranking the livability of the 300 largest U.S. metropolitan areas. In recent years, the magazine has given its number one spot to Provo, Utah, Sioux Falls, S.D., and Raleigh/Durham/Chapel Hill, N.C.

Use a database to find the latest survey by the magazine and write a 350- to 400-word news story on where your city or the city closest to you stands.

If your city is not mentioned, use the criteria and see how your city measures up.

Readers' top priorities: clean water, low crime, clean air, abundant medical care and strong local government.

Magazine's criteria: low unemployment, low property taxes and cost of homes, state fiscal strength, low death rates at hospitals, high public high school graduation rates.

You can use the computer in assessing your city. Assign values for the mentioned criteria, using the magazine as a guide.

For your story, use a database to obtain other stories about the livability of cities. You may find stories about the objections of some cities to their rankings.

If your city is ranked low, obtain local reaction; if ranked high, interview authorities on what is being done to keep that ranking.

### What's Wrong?: Winner

RENO—The youngest player to win a major casino jackpot walked off with $432,000 last night.

Albert Paulson of Lafayette, Ind., set off bells and whistles at Harold's when his slot machine came up with the winning combination. The youngster was on a two-week vacation with his parents, Richard and Margaret Paulson of 2244 Orchard Dr. in Lafayette.

Albert, a second grader, was overwhelmed. He said he intended to buy a full set of baseball cards of his favorite team, the Cleveland Indians, with his takings.

### You Decide: Enhancement

You are the photo editor of your newspaper and you are considering these photos for use in the Sunday newspaper:

1. The photo shows an historic old home that is being refurbished for use as a museum. The photograph is marred by telephone lines across the top portion. You cannot crop them out.

2. A color photo for page one of a couple being married on a hilltop at midnight shows the moon off in a corner. The photo would look better if the moon were over the couple.

3. You have a figure in a photo you would prefer to remove from the middle of the picture.

You can alter these easily with your equipment. Do you?

**Touch up, or leave as is?**

# 4 The Tools of the Trade

Jean Pierre Rivest, *The Gazette*.

**·A basic tool: the telephone book.**

### Introduction

The news writer uses a variety of reference materials and tools to assure the story's accuracy and thoroughness. Among these are the telephone and city directories, a dictionary, and a handbook of grammar. Names and addresses are always double-checked, allegations and charges verified whenever possible, and all mathematical calculations are checked for errors. The writer's rule is: When in doubt, check it out. The computer has become a basic tool for gathering information through the use of databases. It is also useful in sorting large quantities of material for stories and has made possible large-scale investigative projects.

## Exercises

### A. Priorities

Social scientists at Mallory College took a poll of student opinions last semester and the results were released today. The results were compared with a similar poll taken 20 years ago. Professor Margot Adler, head of the Department of Sociology, announced the results. In both polls, 600 students were questioned.

In addition to the information that follows, she says that 20 years ago 32 percent of those polled were interested in a political revolution; the figure last semester was 23 percent. Twenty years ago, 32 percent of those polled felt a religious commitment was important; last semester, the figure was 38 percent. One area remained unchanged: the importance of love relationships. The figure was 92 percent for both years.

Administrators have used the polls for clues about student attitudes and dissatisfaction. Write 350 to 450 words. (See the textbook, Appendix B, Public Opinion Polling Checklist.)

Column A refers to the poll taken 20 years ago, B to last semester's poll.

**Personal Priorities**

|  | Important | | Unimportant | |
|---|---|---|---|---|
|  | A | B | A | B |
| High Grades | 48% | 89% | 47% | 11% |
| Social Service | 49% | 75% | 44% | 24% |
| Sports | 47% | 65% | 50% | 35% |
| Personal Pleasures | 85% | 95% | 12% | 5% |
| Professional Preparation | 63% | 81% | 33% | 19% |
| Entrepreneurship | 18% | 43% | 73% | 57% |
| Satisfying Employment | 68% | 85% | 27% | 15% |

### Expectations of Mallory

|  | Expected | | Actually Found | |
|---|---|---|---|---|
|  | A | B | A | B |
| Great Teachers | 58% | 57% | 17% | 16% |
| Opportunity to Become More Humane | 20% | 12% | 19% | 10% |
| Prestige in Outside World | 26% | 35% | 21% | 31% |

### Contributes to Overall Learning

|  | Contributes | | Does Not Contribute | |
|---|---|---|---|---|
|  | A | B | A | B |
| Bull Sessions | 79% | 60% | 16% | 19% |
| Personal Contact with Faculty | 53% | 37% | 36% | 44% |

### Sources of Frustration at Mallory

|  | Frustrated | | Satisfied | |
|---|---|---|---|---|
|  | A | B | A | B |
| Immutability of System | 53% | 67% | 9% | 5% |
| Living Arrangements | 36% | 26% | 52% | 59% |
| Personal Grades | 30% | 34% | 45% | 45% |
| Competitive Atmosphere | 35% | 59% | 21% | 20% |
| Financial Aid | 22% | 34% | 31% | 26% |
| Extracurricular | 15% | 11% | 60% | 84% |

### B. Growth

The news office at Mallory College has released some figures for the current academic year and for 10 years ago:

|  | Now | 10 Years Ago |
|---|---|---|
| Students | 1,608 | 1,435 |
| Faculty | 118 | 105 |
| Holding Doctorates | 86 | 52 |
| Buildings | 40 | 33 |
| Volumes in Library | 325,000 | 245,000 |
| Annual Operating Budget | $9,709,000 | $4,695,000 |
| Endowment | | |
|   Book Value | $25,937,156 | $11,770,500 |
|   Market Value | $28,732,939 | $14,888,675 |
| Investment in Plant | $17,348,159 | $11,274,100 |
| Total Assets | $47,882,299 | $25,711,500 |
| Faculty Salary Scales | **Now** | **10 Years Ago** |
|   Instructor | $26,350–$29,500 | $16,000–$19,000 |
|   Assistant Professor | $28,870–$32,750 | $17,000–$22,000 |
|   Associate Professor | $31,500–$44,700 | $18,500–$25,000 |
|   Full Professor | $43,800–$64,500 | $21,000–$29,000 |
| Student Aid | | |
|   Number Assisted | 460 | 348 |
|   Total Awards | $1,179,000 | $650,000 |

The college president, Ruth Pitts Renaldi, described it as "a decade of progress," according to the press release accompanying the data. The release goes on, quoting Renaldi:

> In every category, there is marked improvement. We have finally, through the addition of our science center, been able to improve our offerings in the physical sciences. Our library has grown considerably.

But it would be dangerous to rest on this growth. We are faced with ever-increasing demands on our plant. Our faculty salaries are not competitive with other small, high-quality liberal arts schools. We need more money for student aid to match our tuition increase from $5,000 10 years ago to $10,000 today.

I think that our first priority will have to be to raise funds for a library addition. I foresee a fund drive of $4,500,000. This will be one of our major construction projects. . . .

Your editor suggests that, in addition to using some of the data, you make calculations of your own to derive relevant information. Write 350 words.

## C. Projection

In 1984, the consumption of soft drinks exceeded the consumption of water for the first time. The growth in soft drink consumption has not let up since. During the 1980s and 1990s, coffee consumption steadily declined, beer and milk consumption were slightly down and consumption of fruit juice slowly climbed. Here are some projected figures for U.S. per capita annual consumption of beverages in gallons released today by the Associated Beverage Industry:

|  | In Two Years | 2000 |
| --- | --- | --- |
| Soft drinks | 61 | 65 |
| Water | 43 | 41 |
| Coffee | 22 | 21 |
| Beer | 21 | 20 |
| Milk | 20 | 19 |
| Fruit juice | 14 | 15 |
| Other | 19 | 19 |

Soft drink bottlers released the following current consumption percentages:

|  | Current Year Percentage Consumption |
| --- | --- |
| Soft drinks | 25 |
| Water | 19 |
| Coffee | 11 |
| Beer | 12 |
| Milk | 15 |
| Fruit juice | 6 |
| Other | 12 |

Write 250 to 350 words.

## D. Mortality

You obtain some figures from the Freeport Health Department on deaths from infant mortality, cancer, heart disease, AIDS and homicide. Other data will be released in about a week. Your editor wants the material now in a 300-word story.

You have the **total number** of deaths for last year. You have death **rates** from the previous year. This means you will have to turn last year's totals into rates so that you can make a comparison of the death rates. Freeport's population is 654,000.

Here are the totals:

|  | Last Year (Total deaths) | Previous Year (Death rates) |
| --- | --- | --- |
| Infant Mortality | 113 | 9.7 |
| Cancer | 1,561 | 228.7 |
| Heart Disease | 3,828 | 572.0 |
| AIDS | 97 | 12.6 |
| Homicide | 116 | 14.8 |

Rates are figured as follows:

Deaths from disease: $\dfrac{\text{disease toll}}{\text{total population}} \times 100{,}000 = $ rate of death from disease

Death rate: $\dfrac{\text{total deaths}}{\text{total population}} \times 1{,}000 = $ death rate

Infant mortality rate: $\dfrac{\text{total deaths under 1 yr.}}{\text{total live births}} \times 1{,}000 = $ infant mortality rate

As you can see, you will need to know the number of live births last year in order to figure the infant mortality rate for last year. That number was 10,598 live births. Here is how to figure last year's cancer death rates.

Cancer: $\dfrac{1{,}561}{654{,}000} \times 100{,}000 = 238.68$ or $238.7$

Using these guides, figure the rates for last year in all the categories and write the story.

## E. Infant

You work for the major newspaper in your state and the editor asks you to compare these sets of figures for infant mortality rates. Pay special attention to your state, but give the readers an overall sense of the data. Write 500 words for a Sunday feature.

| State | Two Years Ago | | | Last Year | | |
|---|---|---|---|---|---|---|
| | **Average** | **White** | **Black** | **Average** | **White** | **Black** |
| Alabama | 13.3 | 9.8 | 20.0 | 10.86 | 7.99 | 16.50 |
| Alaska | 10.8 | 10.1 | 11.0 | 9.34 | 7.66 | 13.17 |
| Arizona | 8.6 | 9.0 | 14.7 | 8.60 | 7.90 | 19.24 |
| Arkansas | 10.3 | 8.9 | 15.3 | 9.92 | 8.32 | 15.47 |
| California | 8.9 | 8.6 | 16.2 | 7.49 | 6.92 | 16.76 |
| Colorado | 8.6 | 8.3 | 17.2 | 8.25 | 7.73 | 17.37 |
| Connecticut | 9.1 | 7.8 | 18.4 | 7.64 | 6.33 | 16.50 |
| Delaware | 11.5 | 9.6 | 17.6 | 10.19 | 7.59 | 18.78 |
| District of Columbia | 20.9 | 13.3 | 24.0 | 20.44 | 10.91 | 24.00 |
| Florida | 11.0 | 8.8 | 18.2 | 9.14 | 7.07 | 16.13 |
| Georgia | 12.5 | 9.4 | 18.4 | 11.35 | 7.87 | 17.55 |
| Hawaii | 9.3 | 8.6 | 11.9 | 6.82 | 4.38 | 18.72 |
| Idaho | 11.3 | 11.3 | 26.3 | 8.71 | 8.65 | ## |
| Illinois | 12.1 | 9.3 | 22.3 | 10.52 | 7.60 | 21.16 |
| Indiana | 11.3 | 10.1 | 21.5 | 9.39 | 8.24 | 19.01 |
| Iowa | 8.5 | 8.3 | 13.9 | 8.05 | 7.77 | 18.29 |
| Kansas | 8.9 | 8.4 | 15.0 | 8.67 | 7.67 | 19.76 |
| Kentucky | 9.8 | 9.6 | 12.7 | 8.58 | 8.02 | 14.20 |
| Louisiana | 11.9 | 8.7 | 17.0 | 10.36 | 7.40 | 14.62 |
| Maine | 8.8 | 9.0 | ## | 6.20 | 6.11 | ## |
| Maryland | 11.7 | 9.5 | 17.3 | 9.50 | 6.60 | 16.08 |
| Massachusetts | 8.5 | 7.7 | 18.5 | 6.71 | 6.15 | 12.53 |
| Michigan | 11.4 | 9.0 | 22.8 | 10.40 | 7.41 | 21.77 |
| Minnesota | 9.2 | 8.9 | 16.4 | 7.28 | 6.50 | 20.97 |
| Mississippi | 12.4 | 9.0 | 16.2 | 11.83 | 7.95 | 15.93 |
| Missouri | 10.7 | 9.3 | 18.5 | 9.40 | 7.53 | 18.57 |
| Montana | 9.6 | 8.7 | ## | 7.86 | 6.99 | ## |
| Nebraska | 10.1 | 9.2 | 20.3 | 7.74 | 6.90 | 18.86 |
| Nevada | 9.1 | 8.6 | 15.9 | 8.09 | 7.30 | 17.44 |
| New Hampshire | 9.1 | 9.1 | 16.1 | 6.37 | 6.33 | ## |

| State | Two Years Ago | | | Last Year | | |
|---|---|---|---|---|---|---|
| | Average | White | Black | Average | White | Black |
| New Jersey | 9.8 | 7.8 | 18.5 | 8.69 | 6.31 | 18.47 |
| New Mexico | 9.5 | 9.0 | 17.4 | 8.20 | 7.79 | 23.38 |
| New York | 10.7 | 9.2 | 16.7 | 9.27 | 7.35 | 17.16 |
| North Carolina | 11.5 | 9.2 | 17.4 | 10.46 | 7.79 | 16.70 |
| North Dakota | 8.4 | 8.3 | ## | 7.98 | 7.47 | ## |
| Ohio | 10.6 | 9.5 | 17.4 | 9.55 | 7.92 | 18.43 |
| Oklahoma | 10.4 | 10.1 | 17.3 | 9.20 | 8.59 | 16.21 |
| Oregon | 10.2 | 9.3 | 18.8 | 7.54 | 7.22 | 21.46 |
| Pennsylvania | 10.2 | 8.6 | 19.8 | 9.23 | 7.32 | 20.08 |
| Rhode Island | 9.4 | 8.8 | 16.7 | 7.83 | 7.39 | 14.92 |
| South Carolina | 13.2 | 10.1 | 18.1 | 11.13 | 7.82 | 16.58 |
| South Dakota | 13.3 | 10.4 | 25.2 | 9.59 | 8.03 | ## |
| Tennessee | 11.0 | 8.7 | 18.6 | 9.91 | 7.42 | 17.99 |
| Texas | 9.5 | 8.6 | 15.9 | 7.84 | 6.86 | 14.49 |
| Utah | 8.6 | 8.6 | 9.3 | 6.49 | 6.43 | ## |
| Vermont | 10.0 | 9.7 | 38.5 | 6.47 | 6.54 | ## |
| Virginia | 11.1 | 9.0 | 18.0 | 9.86 | 7.22 | 18.49 |
| Washington | 9.8 | 9.8 | 13.5 | 7.38 | 7.00 | 16.86 |
| West Virginia | 10.2 | 9.6 | 25.9 | 9.08 | 8.88 | 14.90 |
| Wisconsin | 9.2 | 8.5 | 17.3 | 7.91 | 7.08 | 15.53 |
| Wyoming | 10.9 | 10.8 | ## | 8.48 | 8.38 | ## |
| **Average** | **8.9** | **8.6** | **15.5** | **8.3** | **7.7** | **14.8** |

## = Number of infant deaths is fewer than 20.

## Assignments

### A. Checks

Find out where the following information may be obtained and then do so and write tight stories—no more than 300 words each—with the information.

1. What was the per capita federal aid to your state last year, and how does it compare with the highest and lowest state rates of per capita aid and the median for the nation?
2. What is the birth rate for your city and state, compared with previous years?
3. What was the amount of financial aid to students last year—total and per student, in the institution as a whole and by schools?
4. What is the income of families by race in your city and state?
5. What were the expense account expenditures by the mayor and members of the mayor's staff over the past month, the past six months, the past year?

### B. High-Low

Here are some indicators used to determine how well or poorly a state stands in relation to other states. The list includes only those at the top and at the bottom of the rankings.

1. Write a 750-word feature story for a Sunday magazine section on these findings.
2. Find out where your state stands in these categories by consulting the *Statistical Abstract of the United States* and other references. Write a 750-word story on how your state compares with the others nationally and regionally.

|  | Ranking | |
|---|---|---|
|  | High | Low |
| Percent of population under the poverty level | Mississippi (24.5%) | Delaware (7.6%) |
| Percent of the population with annual income greater than $75,000 | Arkansas (18.6%) | North and South Dakota (3.5%) |
| Personal income (per capita) | Connecticut ($26,099) | Mississippi ($11,709) |
| Household income | Hawaii ($42,171) | South Dakota ($24,339) |
| Store sales per household | New Hampshire ($27,831) | West Virginia ($15,229) |
| Average annual paycheck | Connecticut ($32,587) | South Dakota ($18,016) |
| Automobile insurance/vehicle cost | New Jersey ($957) | Wyoming ($366) |
| Motor vehicle deaths (per 100 million vehicle miles) | New Mexico (2.7) | Massachusetts (1.0) |
| Percentage of voting age population registered to vote | North Dakota (90.8%) | California (57.6%) |
| Percentage of those of voting age who voted in the last election | Wisconsin (75.3%) | California (52.8%) |
| Divorces per 1,000 population | Oklahoma (7.3) | Massachusetts (2.8) |
| Ratio of abortions to 1,000 live births | New York (694) | Wyoming (74) |
| Suicide rate | Nevada (24.8) | New Jersey (6.6) |
| Death rate from cirrhosis of the liver | New Mexico (15.3) | Idaho (5.1) |
| AIDS infection rate | South Dakota (2.6) | New York (82.3) |
| Physicians per 100,000 population | Massachusetts (353) | Idaho (129) |
| Nurses per 100,000 population | Massachusetts (1,066) | Texas (528) |
| Infant mortality rate (Average) | Mississippi (11.83) | Maine (6.20) |
| (White) | Idaho (8.65) | Maine (6.11) |
| (Black) | Oregon (21.46) | Massachusetts (12.53) |
| Average teacher salaries | Alaska ($46,581) | South Dakota ($25,199) |
| Beginning teacher salaries | Alaska ($33,408) | Idaho ($17,086) |
| Dropouts as a percentage of youth population | Nevada (15.2%) | North Dakota (4.6%) |
| Less than a ninth grade education | Mississippi (15.6%) | Utah (3.4%) |
| Holders of a bachelor's degree | Colorado (18%) | West Virginia (7.5%) |
| Holders of a graduate degree | Connecticut (11%) | West Virginia (4.8%) |
| Percentage of state and local government expenditures for elementary and high school education | Utah (42.2%) | Arkansas (23.4%) |
| Percent of state and local government expenditures for higher education | Utah (15.1%) | New York (4.9%) |
| Reading proficiency of fourth graders in public schools as measured by the National Assessment of Educational Progress test | Iowa and Massachusetts (228) | Mississippi (200) |
| Mathematics proficiency of fourth graders as measured by NAEP test | Maine (231) | Alabama (207) |
| Percent of residents receiving public aid | West Virginia (9.7%) | New Hampshire (3.4%) |
| Percent of murders involving handguns | Louisiana (72.12%) | Iowa (22.2%) |
| Births to unmarried women as a percent of all births | Mississippi (42.9%) | Utah (15.1%) |

*C. No Phone*

Almost all polls are based on a random sampling of telephone numbers. This leaves out of consideration people who do not have telephones, usually people in the low-income group. How many people is that in your city and state? Try to obtain data and then question pollsters and others who may be able to tell you how this affects polling results.

*D. TV Viewing*

The National Assessment of Educational Progress test measured student performance in a number of areas. In one area, the NAEP checked the proficiency in reading of fourth graders and compared it with reading and television watching habits.

Children who read almost every day scored 223, whereas those who never or hardly read scored 199. Children who watched television six or more hours a day scored 198, whereas those who watched TV one hour or less a day scored 220.

Interview authorities in childhood education for a feature article on these and related findings.

*E. High Scorers*

A study of the Scholastic Aptitude Test results shows the following:

• Students who took the most academic subjects in high school had by far the highest SAT scores. Those who took 20 or more academic years in six subjects scored 200 points higher in their total test scores than those who took 15 academic years in subjects.

• High school rank and grades directly correlated with test scores. Students in the top tenth of their classes who were A+ students scored several hundred points higher than those at the bottom of the classes.

• The highest scorers in the verbal portion of the SAT were those with four or more years of study in foreign languages. The highest scorers on the mathematics section were those with four or more years of study of natural sciences (not mathematics).

• Students with plans for advanced placement in social studies and physics had the highest verbal scores; and students with plans for advanced studies in mathematics, chemistry and physics had the highest mathematics scores.

• Parental income correlates exactly with scores: Students whose parents had an annual income of less than $10,000 scored a total of 766, whereas those whose parents earned more than $70,000 scored 1,000.

Interview an administrator in your college admissions office for comments on how these and other factors affect admissions.

## Campus Projects

*A. Weight*

More than half of all female college students are overly concerned about their weight, health officials report, and 20 percent of them have severe eating disorders. Thousands suffer from anorexia and bulimia.

By age 13, 53 percent of the girls surveyed in a national report said they were unhappy with their bodies. This unhappiness lasts through college, studies show.

A study of 682 women enrolled in a Midwestern university showed two-thirds of them admitted being so concerned about their body image they resorted to unhealthy behavior to control their weight. Laurie Mintz, a psychologist at the University of Southern California who did the study, said 17 percent reported taking appetite control pills, 10 percent used self-induced vomiting or laxatives to control weight and many engaged "in other unhealthy behavior such as chronic dieting and meal skipping."

The data, she said, suggest a widespread, damaging effect of American society's "pervasive preoccupation" with female weight and appearance. She said that advertisers for clothes and other commodities "often set up an unattainable body image for women by hiring adolescent models and dressing them up to look older."

A generation ago, a fashion model weighed 8 percent less than the average woman; today, models weigh 23 percent less. The average model, actress or dancer is thinner than 95 percent of the female population.

Devise a plan for a study on your campus that will result in a story about women and weight. For additional background, use a database.

*B. Spending*

What does it cost students to attend your college or university, and how do they raise the money? Make a survey and obtain plenty of anecdotal information. Include in the cost side of the ledger tuition, room and board, entertainment, travel, payment of debts, laundry, etc.

On the income side include savings, jobs, loans, grants and scholarships, assistance from home, etc.

Reach some general conclusions: Do students have to skimp to get by? Do they consider entertainment (movies, tapes, video equipment) part of their necessities? What have they had to eliminate? Do they find they will be able to graduate without taking an extended period away from school to earn money?

## *Community Project*

### *Bodies*

Every year, 150,000 women die from complications associated with anorexia and bulimia. The National Association of Anorexia Nervosa and Associated Disorders says 7 million American women suffer from the two diseases associated with the female desire to be thin.

A survey of 33,000 women by *Glamour* magazine shows that women value being thin more than they value success or love.

"More women than ever before are dissatisfied with their bodies." This is the beginning of a story in a Midwestern newspaper that covers surveys of American women "varying in age, occupation, marital status, race, ethnic background and social class."

A story in *The Wall Street Journal* reports that many "outwardly healthy teen-agers think of these drugs (appetite suppressants) as a standard way to diet. An astonishing 49% of teen-age girls responding to a recent survey by *Sassy* magazine reported using diet pills, while 13% of the magazine's young readers have tried laxatives or diuretics for weight loss."

These pills are "neither effective nor safe," says the *Journal* story, but they are easily available and their use continues despite articles about their dangers.

*The New York Times* reports that "poor body image is the most common cause of depression among adolescent girls," and a survey of 10-year-old girls shows that a majority reported being afraid of becoming too fat.

Among adult women, complaints center on anxiety over specific body parts. One physician said women view their bodies as "an enemy." Surveys have found:

- One out of two women diets most of her life.
- Two out of three have mixed or depressed feelings looking at their nude bodies in the mirror.
- Fewer than half agreed with the statement, "I like my looks the way they are."
- Almost half said they would consider cosmetic surgery.

Using this information, and any other you may obtain through a database search, devise a survey of girls, teen-agers and women in the community on the subject of body image and diet.

## *Home Assignment*

### *STD (1)*

Here are tables of the 10 states and 10 major cities with the highest rates of gonorrhea for five years ago, two years ago and last year. Rates are based on the number of cases per 100,000 population. The figures are from the Centers for Disease Control and Prevention.

Select from the tables the city or state in which you live or attend school, or use a city or state nearby, and write a 450-word story based on the material. Last year's figures have just been released and are included in the tables that follow.

Place the material in some perspective by obtaining background about sexually transmitted diseases, which officials with the Centers have described as epidemic.

**Note:** Health authorities say that only one of three to five cases of STD is reported to the Centers.

# Gonorrhea

## States

| | Five Years Ago | | | Two Years Ago | | | Last Year | |
|---|---|---|---|---|---|---|---|---|
| Rank | State | Rate | | State | Rate | | State | Rate |
| 1 | Georgia | 756.7 | | Georgia | 664.9 | | Mississippi | 439.3 |
| 2 | Mississippi | 555.8 | | Mississippi | 556.8 | | North Carolina | 424.3 |
| 3 | Alabama | 533.7 | | Alabama | 516.7 | | Alabama | 385.4 |
| 4 | Delaware | 506.3 | | North Carolina | 513.0 | | South Carolina | 361.8 |
| 5 | Maryland | 489.7 | | Delaware | 460.1 | | Tennessee | 314.8 |
| 6 | North Carolina | 483.9 | | Maryland | 456.6 | | Maryland | 306.7 |
| 7 | Tennessee | 408.6 | | Tennessee | 434.9 | | Georgia | 299.6 |
| 8 | South Carolina | 402.2 | | South Carolina | 408.2 | | Delaware | 295.0 |
| 9 | Missouri | 391.2 | | Louisiana | 349.6 | | Arkansas | 288.7 |
| 10 | Arkansas | 362.1 | | Missouri | 342.3 | | Louisiana | 280.2 |
| **Average** | | **278.0** | | | **272.4** | | | **169.3** |

## Cities

| | Five Years Ago | | | Two Years Ago | | | Last Year | |
|---|---|---|---|---|---|---|---|---|
| Rank | City | Rate | | City | Rate | | City | Rate |
| 1 | Atlanta | 2,921.8 | | Atlanta | 2,281.1 | | St. Louis | 1,456.9 |
| 2 | Washington, D.C. | 2,441.7 | | St. Louis | 2,080.2 | | Baltimore | 1,165.2 |
| 3 | St. Louis | 2,179.1 | | Baltimore | 1,768.1 | | Washington, D.C. | 1,026.3 |
| 4 | Kansas City, Mo. | 1,737.4 | | Rochester, N.Y. | 1,636.6 | | New York | 1,011.8 |
| 5 | Rochester, N.Y. | 1,631.4 | | Washington, D.C. | 1,628.7 | | Rochester, N.Y. | 999.4 |
| 6 | Detroit | 1,533.7 | | Norfolk, Va. | 1,316.8 | | Richmond, Va. | 991.4 |
| 7 | Baltimore | 1,471.5 | | Memphis | 1,311.8 | | Norfolk, Va. | 973.6 |
| 8 | Newark | 1,261.1 | | Richmond, Va. | 1,263.6 | | Detroit | 826.8 |
| 9 | Philadelphia | 1,259.4 | | Birmingham | 1,259.3 | | Birmingham | 827.0 |
| 10 | New Orleans | 1,239.9 | | Detroit | 1,1173.3 | | Memphis | 826.8 |
| **Average** | | **594.1** | | | **477.3** | | | **322.6** |

## *Class Discussion*

### *Figures*

Arthur M. Ross, a former federal commissioner of labor statistics, made these points, among others, in an article, "The Data Game," in *The Washington Monthly:*

If you are measuring the number of cows in Nevada, nothing more is reported or implied than what has been counted: 6,000,000 cows. A cow exists in a state of nature and is directly observable. But suppose you administer an intelligence test to a group of children. The test is one thing, a mechanical instrument; intelligence is something else altogether, an abstraction devised by psychologists. While the scores of a test can be calculated, that which is measured remains an abstraction. Educators have been learning the painful lesson that great care must be used in drawing inferences from one to another.

When government officials call for statistics, they seldom want anything as palpable as the cows of Nevada. They want measures of inflation, or poverty, or hard-core unemployment, or criminal activity, or American prestige abroad, or the progress of the Vietnam war. These are man-made concepts, *socially defined.* It is man who invents the categories; it is man who decides to characterize them in terms of one or two measurable dimensions. But as in the case of I.Q. tests, the people who read government statistics—the press, the public, and the officials—are prone to regard partial or statistical truths as objective realities.

Thus shadow is confused with substance. Essentially this is how public officials deceive themselves with statistics of impeccable quality. The officials are vulnerable because they are searching desperately for ways to clarify and simplify the protean problems of government. Statistics enable them to do this at the cost of heroic oversimplification: one or two dimensions, which happen to be measurable, serve to symbolize an elusive, many-sided phenomenon.

The trouble is that the unmeasured, or unmeasurable, aspects of a problem may be vastly more important than those which have been, or can be, measured. And even with measurements that are known to reflect on the core of a problem, the rate of change in the United States has become so swift that "good" statistics, intelligently used in decision-making, may be rendered irrelevant or obsolete by the time action results from an official's decision. . . .

Charles Murray, senior fellow at the Manhattan Institute for Policy Research, said in a study:

> Dollars fail to capture the real difference between Manhattan and Denison, Iowa, in the cost of living a decent life. What the average rent does not tell you is how big the rooms are, whether there is a yard for the children to play in, what the place looks like and smells like and how many rats inhabit it. Perhaps even more importantly, the average rent does not tell you what the street outside the front door is like, what the neighbors are like, what the schools are like, and whether you can safely go for a stroll after nightfall.

How can journalists tell their readers and viewers the real story of people's lives?

## *Skill Drill I: References*

Which reference works would you consult to obtain the following information?

1. The name of the senior U.S. senator from Nevada.
2. Background about a corporation president.
3. The name of the author of a book published last year.
4. The National FBI crime figures for each of the past five years.
5. Background for an article on professional sports as a big business.
6. A good quote from "*Hamlet*" to start a story on the local theater's production of the play.
7. An explanation of how the steam engine developed.
8. The names of all African countries.
9. The names of cities in the United States with populations of more than 1 million.
10. The vote for president in the past 10 elections in three neighboring states.
11. The occupation of a man, while a local resident, who left town five years ago.
12. The states and the ZIP codes of cities in the country named Mt. Pleasant.
13. Details about the toxic waste problem—the Love Canal disaster—near Buffalo, N.Y., several years ago.
14. The content of any bills introduced in the last session of the state legislature regulating optometrists.
15. The highway distance between the state capital and Washington, D.C.

## *Skill Drill II: Arithmetic*

Arithmetic is a useful tool in reporting and writing. When tax revenues increase from $1,653,000 to $1,812,000, the reporter who can do percentages can state in his or her lead that tax collections jumped 10 percent. The reporter unable to use this useful tool must be content with an array of figures that will not tell the reader at a glance the extent of the increase. Reporters often have to compute percentages, fractions and rates. The figures below were all supplied by sources. The reporters did the computing. Try your hand.

### *A. Percentages*

1. The number of bankruptcy cases went from 1,300 to 1,600 in a year. This is an increase of _____ percent.
2. In the city, arrests increased by _____ percent. Police said last year that there were 18,725 arrests, and in the preceding year the total was 15,025.
3. His weight jumped from 145 to 265 pounds while he was visiting his grandmother, a _____ percent increase.
4. The faculty contributions reached $1,450 this year, a _____ percent increase over the $1,050 donated last year.

5. The average textbook now runs about 200 pages, he said, compared to about 350 a decade ago. Today's texts are _____ percent of the size of those 10 years ago, but the price has gone up about 100 percent.

## B. Fractions

1. During the Depression, milk consumption by children was _____ of what it had been previously, going from 15 quarts a month to four.

2. About _____ of the students had grades of B or better, and _____ failed. Of the 850 students, 265 had A's and B's and 165 failed.

3. _____ times as many children were in the school lunch program last year as five years ago, she said. Last year, there were 1,390, and five years ago, around 450.

4. The United Fund Drive is _____ of the way done, having raised $59,000 toward its $80,000 goal.

5. If any more than _____ of the felonies were prosecuted as felonies, the courts would be overwhelmed. There were 15,270 felony arrests, and officials estimate the criminal courts can handle up to 1,500 cases a year without breaking down.

## C. Rates

1. If the state were to put $1 million of its surplus in 8-percent government bonds, it would realize a return of $ _____ a year.

2. The power company said its rate of return under the new rate structure would not be as high as its critics fear. Actually, the new rates are projected to earn $500,000 a year on a total plant investment of $5,500,000, which would be a _____ percent rate of return.

3. He said he chose the new savings bank for its higher rate of interest. The old bank gave him 6 percent on his $60,000 in deposits, or $3,600 the first year. The bank he chose pays 6.5 percent and would return $ _____ the first year.

4. The city hopes to sell the $2,000,000 auditorium-construction bond issue at an interest rate of no more than 7 percent, but some officials say it would be more likely to go at 7.5 percent, which would mean $ _____ a year more in interest payments over the 20-year life of the bonds, or $ _____ more in interest over the life of the bond issue.

5. Police said the vehicle was seen at the Freeport toll station at 10:15 p.m., and at 10:45 p.m. it passed through the Roxborough exit, 47 miles away. That means the vehicle was averaging _____ miles an hour.

## D. Math Test

After you have done percentages, fractions and rates, try these more general questions.

1. The meter stick has been broken at the 12 cm mark. A rug is as long as 3 lengths of the broken meter stick. About how long is the rug?

   a. 236 cm
   b. 264 cm
   c. 270 cm
   d. 276 cm
   e. 300 cm

2. A stereo tape plays for ¾ of an hour on each side, so 1½ hours can be recorded on a single tape. How many tapes are needed to record a 5-hour concert?

   a. 1
   b. 4
   c. 2
   d. 3
   e. 5

3. The circle graph shows how the town of Littleburg spent its money last year. $50,000 was spent on X, and $25,000 was spent on Y. About how much was spent on Z, and how much was spent on W?

a. $20,000 on Z, and $42,000 on W
b. $20,000 on Z, and $85,000 on W
c. $40,000 on Z, and $85,000 on W
d. $40,000 on Z, and $42,000 on W
e. $30,000 on Z, and $65,000 on W

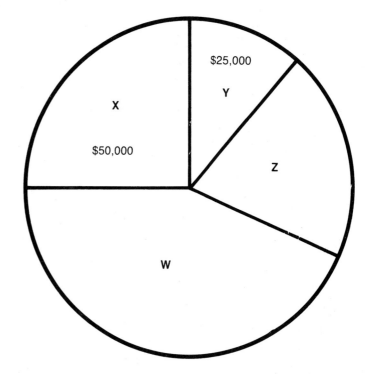

4. The information on a package of rice cakes says each rice cake contains:
   Protein .7 gram
   Carbohydrates 7.6 grams
   Fat .28 gram

Each rice cake contains:
   a. More fat than carbohydrates
   b. More protein than carbohydrates
   c. 17.4 grams of protein, carbohydrates and fat altogether
   d. 4 times as much fat as protein
   e. $2\frac{1}{2}$ times as much protein as fat

5. Mary began a trip at 10:30 a.m. and finished at 6:45 p.m. the same day. How many hours did the trip last?

   a. $8\frac{1}{4}$
   b. $9\frac{1}{2}$
   c. $17\frac{1}{4}$
   d. $4\frac{3}{4}$
   e. $3\frac{3}{4}$

6. Somebody has spilled ink on this problem, covering one digit in each number. Which of the following answers is correct?

   a. 218
   b. 718
   c. 2,218
   d. 22,718
   e. 202,718

The Tools of the Trade    45

7. A restaurant bill is $60.00. The service charge is to be 15% of the bill. How much is the service charge?

   a. $1.50
   b. $15.00
   c. $7.50
   d. $75.00
   e. $9.00

8. The list price of a radio is $50. The radio is on sale for $40. What percent discount is that?

   a. 90%
   b. 10%
   c. 40%
   d. 20%
   e. 15%

9. Jean wants to cut strips of cardboard 1.5 cm long. How many of these strips can be cut from a strip of cardboard 10 cm long?

   a. 15
   b. 1
   c. 9
   d. 7
   e. 6

10. In triangle ABC, angle A measures 25° and angle C measures 90°. What is the measure of angle B?

    a. 115°
    b. 65°
    c. 85°
    d. 40°
    e. 100°

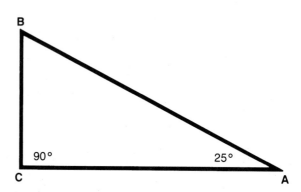

11. At 6 p.m. the temperature was 3°. By 8 p.m. the temperature had gone down 9°. What was the temperature at 8 p.m.?

    a. 34°
    b. 4°
    c. 0°
    d. 3° below 0
    e. 6° below 0

12. In triangle PQR, angle R measures 90°, PR measures 4 cm and QR measures 3 cm. How long is PQ?

   a. 3 cm
   b. 4 cm
   c. 5 cm
   d. 6 cm
   e. 7 cm

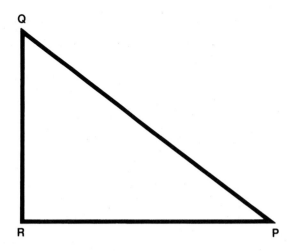

13. If I toss a coin, the probability is 1/2 that it will land heads. If I toss the coin 3 times, what is the probability that it will land heads all 3 times?

   a. $1/8$
   b. $1/6$
   c. $1/4$
   d. $1/2$
   e. $3/2$

14. According to a heart specialist, effective exercise makes the heart beat at about 80% of the number found by subtracting your age from 220 times per minute. That is: 80% of (220–A) times per minute, where A is your age. About how many times per minute should the heart of a 15-year-old beat for effective exercise?

   a. 164
   b. 176
   c. 246
   d. 315
   e. 188

15. Ms. Scott's lawn is about 20.2 meters wide and 30.5 meters long. A bag of fertilizer will cover about 400 square meters of lawn. How many bags of fertilizer must she buy to cover her lawn?

   a. 5
   b. 1
   c. 2
   d. 4
   e. 3

The Tools of the Trade    47

16. In figure ABCDE, angles B, C and D are right angles. The lengths of AB, BC, CD and EA are, in order, 6 cm, 10 cm, 10 cm and 5 cm. What is the area inside figure ABCDE?

a. 100 square cm
b. 94 square cm
c. 88 square cm
d. 97 square cm
e. 91 square cm

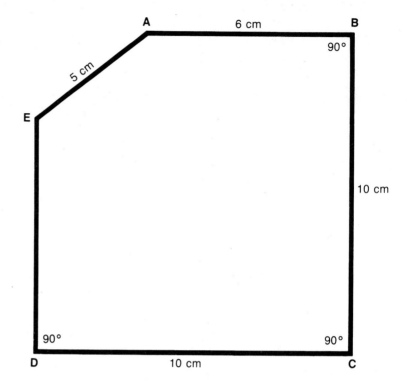

17. In the rule $y = 3x + 5$, the value of $x$ is multiplied by 3 and then 5 is added. So, if $x = 2$, then $y = (3 \times 2) + 5 = 11$. What value of $x$ will make $y = 25$?

a. $6^2/_3$
b. $8^1/_2$
c. $15^1/_4$
d. 75
e. 4

18. On her first four tests this year, Wendy's average score was 90. On her first five tests, her average score was 80. What score did Wendy earn on her fifth test?

a. 20
b. 40
c. 60
d. 80
e. 100

19. The distance from Northburg to Westburg is 40 km. Use the map to estimate how far it is from Northburg to Eastburg.

a. 100 km
b. 20 km
c. 80 km
d. 60 km
e. 40 km

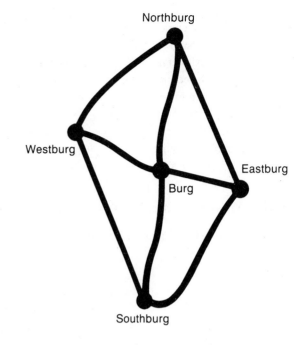

20. The coordinates of four points that are on the straight line of the graph are (1,0), (3,3), (5,6) and (15,y). What is the value of y?

a. 12
b. 15
c. 21
d. 18
e. 14

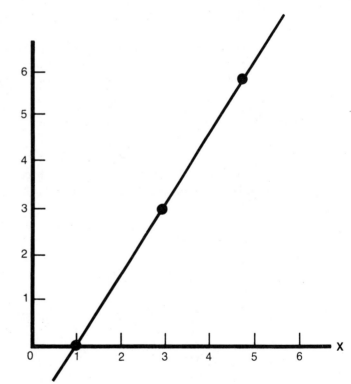

The Tools of the Trade   49

## Fix It: Usage (1)

These sentences were taken from newspapers and broadcast news accounts. Indicate the problems.

1. In a random poll of a dozen patrons in the Belmont Park grandstand, horseplayers said the most moving moment in their race-going was the death of the gallant filly Ruffian.
2. Although polls show Noonan with a 24-point lead over Vercini, no poll of only 1,500 people can represent the country's voters.
3. An informal and random poll at the convention showed that the party's anti-abortion stand was hurting it among younger women.
4. The *News* poll showed that if the election were held today, Trevor would win. With 615 persons polled, Trevor had 314 votes, Peterson 301, a 51-49 percent lead for Trevor.
5. New York is the country's murder capital, with six murders a day.

## What's Wrong?: The New York Times *Bloopers*

1. Here is an item from *Winners & Sinners,* the in-house critique of *The New York Times:*

> *Mean average item.* The story spoke of the "average scores" of high school graduates in the scholastic aptitude test, but the table with the story referred to the "mean scores" (Dec. 16). Which was it? The "average" is the sum divided by the number of components (i.e., students), while the "mean" is a figure midway between the highest and the lowest scores.

What do you think of the explanation of *average* and *mean?*

2. The following paragraphs appeared in a roundup on population control that was printed in *The New York Times.* Can you see the flaw in the reasoning used by the researcher?

> At the extreme, militants charge that efforts to persuade black women to use contraceptives or to have abortions—where they are legally available—are really aimed at achieving black genocide.
>
> A recent report by a black researcher, Dr. William A. Darity of Amherst, Mass., suggests that these sentiments have large support in the black community. In one New England city, Dr. Darity found that 88 percent of the black males under 30 were opposed to abortion. Almost half of them felt that encouragement of the use of birth control methods "is comparable to trying to eliminate (blacks) from society."

3. The lead story on page one of *The New York Times* reported that the U.S. Senate had approved the lowering of tariffs by a "wide margin, 76 to 24." It continued, "The House of Representatives approved the agreement on Tuesday by an even wider margin, 288 to 146."

# Story Structure

### Introduction

The news story moves logically and smoothly from the lead through the body of the story to the ending. Each part of this structure serves a distinct purpose:

- **Lead:** Gives the reader the crux of the story. It is written to invite the reader into the story.
- **Body:** Amplifies the lead with supporting documentation; includes secondary material.
- **Ending:** Carries the least important material. For features, it provides the punch line or kicker and sometimes is used to summarize the material in the story.

Michel du Cille.

**Structured notes, structured story.**

## *Exercises I*

Write 150 words at most for each.

### A. *Opening*

Information called in by campus stringer:

The College Food Cooperative opened with flying banners and rock music yesterday. Provost Thomas Palmer and a college alum, Louis Truett, '34, founder and president of the ShopRite supermarket chain, were on hand to send off the manager, David Green, and his staff of a dozen students in their program to bring students a low-cost campus grocery. The school turned over a basement room in the F.L. McCoy dormitory to the student entrepreneurs after Green complained that students were paying exorbitant prices for basics in town.

### B. *Lobby*

Call from Mildred Cahan:

The League of Women Voters will send a 10-person delegation to the state capitol, leaving 8 a.m., Monday, to talk to members of the state legislature about a minimum wage bill, introduced last month and now in the Senate Labor Committee, that would exempt several types of workers from the state minimum wage law. To be exempted: hotel, restaurant and laundry workers, hospital aides, domestic workers, nonclassified municipal and state clerical workers. The local league last week endorsed the stand of the state organization opposing the bill. Mildred Cahan, chairwoman of the local chapter, said, "The bill clearly is aimed at the low-income female worker who now barely makes $5 an hour, a wage enabling her to bob up and down in a sea of poverty."

### C. Trip

Peter Hay, BPOE secretary, press release:

The local Elks Club announces that 42 of its members and their wives have signed up for a trip this summer to Russia, and 16 will be going to China. The Russian contingent leaves July 15 for two weeks; the Chinese group leaves Aug. 15 for 15 days. One couple, Mr. and Mrs. Dale L. Himmelstein, will make both trips. "These will be our 21st and 22d countries since Dale retired three years ago," Mrs. Himmelstein says. He was a clerk at United Airlines in Freeport for 30 years "and never left the state until his retirement," she adds.

## Exercises II

Write a story of 200 words for each of these exercises.

### A. Gun

Last night there was an armed robbery of a drug store at 450 Stanley St. Two men wearing ski masks entered the store, and while one held a gun on the owner, Barney G. Joseph, 43, 1625 Tennessee Ave., the other removed $382.65 from the cash register. Time, about 8:30 p.m. The men left in a car that was parked with its motor running at the curb in front of the store.

One of the desk sergeants says Joseph kept a pistol under the counter near the register but decided not to use it. He told the police it was over in less than a minute. He could have reached for the gun, he told the police, but he felt it unwise.

Back at office in clips under Joseph's name: His father was killed in a holdup at the same store 25 years ago. Call to Joseph to ask if he remembered that incident during the holdup: "Yes. Dad resisted, I guess. Anyway, they found him shot to death, his own gun in his hand, and a bullet in the store ceiling. I'd rather part with my money than my life."

### B. Park

Handout from the city parks and recreation department:

There's a new joy ride for local kiddies coming soon.

The city parks and recreation department announced today that it has purchased a series of "educational rides" for children to use for a total of $11,000 for placement in three city parks. Among them is the Hanging Gate, which is an iron pole embedded in the ground with a gate hanging from it. The children push themselves in a circle.

Another is the Super Slide for tiny toddlers, which lets preschoolers have the thrill of a slide without the fear of climbing way up.

The money was made available six weeks ago by Robert T.F. Ho, a local merchant who owned the Quick Stop Laundry, 39 Millbank Rd., and whose gift was until today anonymous. Since his death two days ago, the department decided to reveal his beneficence. His widow approved. Mrs. Ho said, "Robert always enjoyed watching the kids play in the park across the street. He felt sorry for the kids who had to wait to use the equipment, especially the little ones."

### C. Quicksand

Write a short feature from the following material:

John Baily, 7, and Porter Smyth, took a hike with John's six-month-old puppy, Peppie, along the Tallapoosa River near Tallassee, Ala., last night. Smyth, 19, got stuck in quicksand and could not extricate himself.

John tied a rope to a tree and put it under Smyth's arms and set out for Tallassee for help. They had hiked 10 miles from home and John had difficulty finding his way in the growing darkness. He said Peppie guided him home, which they reached at 7 p.m.

Smyth's father, Raynold Smyth, Peppie and John went out to try to find Porter Smyth and two hours later, led by Peppie, they found him. The mud was up to Porter's shoulders and it took 20 minutes to dig the young man out.

"Without Peppie," said Raynold, "we never would have found my son. That dog is a hero, first class."

## Assignments

### A. Trail (1)

Reporters talk about following the "paper trail" of a person they are checking or investigating. They obtain documents about the person that include birth certificate, court records, divorce filing, and school documents. First, make a list of documents you think would make up part of the paper trail; then, see which of these is available to the public.

*B. Trail (2)*

Make a paper trail on someone in the community: a politician, school official, lawyer, physician, police official, business person.

*C. Admissions*

A rash of fabricated applications for admissions has hit colleges in recent years, and some schools have reviewed their admissions process. Students who submitted excellent essays were discovered to have had low grades in high school English. Some applicants falsified membership in student organizations. Transfer students doctored their grades, and some did not submit all SAT test scores despite being required to do so.

"We're all vulnerable," said the dean of admissions at the University of Pennsylvania. "The system is based on trust. There are no metal detectors in this business."

Has your school's admission office had trouble with admissions and, if so, how has it handled the problem?

## Campus Project

*Tatters*

A study by the Carnegie Foundation for the Advancement of Teaching said the campus has been the scene of a breakdown in civility and that traditional academic and social values on campus have been undermined.

It also found that many students were unprepared for college work and that, while on campus, most did only enough studying "to get by."

Racial and other tensions have undermined a sense of community in academic life, the foundation found. "The idyllic visions that are routinely portrayed in college promotional materials often mask disturbing realities of student life," said Ernest L. Boyer, president of the foundation, in the prologue to the study.

The study found that "words are used not as the key to understanding but as weapons of assault. . . . Equally disturbing is the fact that abusive language is revealed most strikingly in racial, ethnic and sexual slurs."

The problems were most acute at large institutions, where more than 60 percent of the students said sexual harassment was a problem and half complained of "racial intimidation and harassment." At smaller liberal arts colleges, the study found the percentages were 30 and 15 percent, respectively.

The foundation criticized the academic system that encourages faculty members to pursue research at the expense of teaching. "Faculty, because of their reward system, are often not able to spend time with students, especially undergraduates," the foundation reported. "Teaching frequently is not well rewarded, especially for young teachers seeking tenure. . . ." The report stated that young instructors find "it's much safer to present a paper at the national convention than it is to spend time with undergraduates back home."

It also reported that 23 percent of the students spent more than 16 hours a week studying outside the classroom, down from 33 percent in 1985.

Organize a campus study that includes students, admissions officers, nontenured and tenured faculty members and administrators. Paint a portrait of campus life.

## Community Projects

*A. Polite*

How polite are people in your city? Some cities have the reputation of being cold and indifferent, and others are known for warmth and courtesy. New York City is considered by residents and visitors alike to be harsh and rude. Cheyenne, Wyo., says Marjabelle Young-Stewart, who runs etiquette classes for executives, is the most polite city in the country.

Young-Stewart, who has been compiling lists of the country's most polite cities for 15 years, says the Wyoming city encourages residents to greet visitors with a friendly "howdy," and out-of-towners are given tongue-in-cheek parking tickets that state that hanging is the usual punishment for such infractions.

Among the other cities she lists as polite are Charleston, S.C.; Portland, Ore.; Seattle; Mobile; Pensacola, Fla.; San Diego; Denver; Pittsburgh; Washington, D.C.

Washington? One of her clients, Young-Stewart said, told her, "When they hold someone up there they say, 'Excuse me, but can I have your wallet?' "

Conduct a politeness survey of your community.

## B. Concern

What's bothering people in town? Here is a list of problems most commonly cited in many polls. Draw up a survey plan and write a story that blends data with comments by individuals:

| Problem | % Very Highly Concerned | % Highly Concerned | % Moderately Concerned | % Not Concerned |
|---|---|---|---|---|
| Federal deficit | | | | |
| Quality of education | | | | |
| Pollution | | | | |
| Poverty and homelessness | | | | |
| Availability of quality health care | | | | |
| Drug abuse | | | | |
| Crime | | | | |
| Decline of U.S. economic competitiveness | | | | |
| Racism | | | | |

Add any other concerns you feel relevant.

Rodger Mallison, *Forth Worth Star-Telegram.*

**Crime scene—home burglary.**

# Analysis

## *Home Assignment*

### Cemetery

The news story structure is:

> **Lead** that contains the most important fact or facts.
> **Body** that contains:
> - Material that amplifies and buttresses the lead.
> - Background information.
> - Secondary facts or information.

Clip a local news story from the most recent issue of the newspaper you read and break it down into its basic structure. Here is an example of how you might do it with the use of a lettering system.

| | |
|---|---|
| The city zoning board yesterday approved the construction of a 10-foot-high chain link fence around the Temple B'nai Shalom cemetery to keep out vandals. | Lead—A |
| But the board denied the congregation's request for a barbed wire at the top of the fence because the cemetery, at 1282 Airport Road, is in a residential zone. | Amplification of lead—$A_1$ |
| "The fence is not worth anything to us without the barbed wire," William Gamm, a lawyer for the congregation, said last night. | Amplification of lead—$A_2$ |
| Mr. Gamm said that young people are using the cemetery as a shortcut to the GoldMart Shopping Center at 1300 Airport Road and that unless an impenetrable fence is erected graves will be desecrated. | Amplification of lead—$A_3$ |
| The temple made its request for the fence last month following the discovery by members of the congregation of several overturned grave markers. | Background |
| In other actions, the zoning board acted on the following requests: | Secondary material |
| Barry Tobin, 112 Bismark St., use of first and second floors as massage parlor—postponed. | Secondary fact—B |
| Raymond Feeney, 167 Kentucky Ave., remove one-story rear addition and erect three-story rear addition—approved. | Secondary fact—C |
| Daniel Snead, 481 Yale Ave., use of first floor as private club—disapproved. | Secondary fact—D |

## *Class Discussion*

### Bids

Analyze this story, using the sample analysis of *Cemetery* as a model:

Apparent low bids totaling $216,000 were submitted today for the renovation of the former Scott Building, 526 Broadway, for use by the local police and traffic engineering departments as a garage.

The bids were referred by the city purchasing agent to the city engineer for review.

A total of 41 bids were received for four separate contracts involved in the renovation. The city council had appropriated $350,000 for the renovation project. The city has already spent $423,000 for the purchase of the property.

The board also received bids for the purchase of 15 police vehicles, for the purchase of two pickup trucks for the water department and for the paving of a portion of Elm Street.

Apparent low bidders for the garage renovation, the amount bid and the number of bidders for each contract were:

—General construction: Hesch Construction Corp., of Albany, $111,958, 13 bidders.

—Heating and ventilation: Brown Plumbing and Heating, Inc., of Clovia, $44,492, 10 bidders.

—Plumbing: J.N. Hunsley Co., of Piedmont, $33,332, eight bidders.

—Electrical work: McCall Electric Co., of Albany, $25,980, 10 bidders.

Freeport Dodge, Inc., the sole bidder in each instance, was awarded three contracts to provide 15 police vehicles for a total cost of $120,237.

Freeport Dodge offered the apparent low bid of $15,400 each for two pickup trucks. The only other bid of $19,554 was from Simpson Motors Co.

Wrightson Industries Inc., of Freeport, submitted the apparent low bid of $67,986 for the improvement of 1,500 feet of Madison Street. The council had appropriated $120,000 for the job. There were five other bidders.

In a final action, E.W. Grimes Co., of Freeport, was awarded $15,605 for fireproofing the city-owned Mohawk Brush Building on Blue Ridge Road.

## *DB/CAR*

### *A. Mothers*

The percentage of women in the labor force with children under 6 has steadily increased from under 30 percent 25 years ago to around 60 percent today. The educational background of the working mothers is as follows:

| | |
|---|---|
| College, four or more years: | 68.0 percent |
| College, one to three years: | 62.8 percent |
| High school, four years: | 52.0 percent |
| Less than high school: | 30.0 percent |

Gather information about working mothers from newspapers and magazines and through local interviews and write a 500-word story.

Use your computer to design graphs and tables to accompany your article.

### *B. STD (2)*

Examine the rates in the following table for your city or one nearby. Then rank all cities to determine where your city stands. Indicate the trends in the data. Interview local and state health officials to find out the reasons for your city's standings for the three periods. Obtain sufficient background about the changes in rates.

**Syphilis Rates in Selected Cities of Greater Than 200,000 Population**

| City | 1989 | 1990 | Last Year |
|---|---|---|---|
| Akron, Ohio | 2.3 | 3.9 | 2.5 |
| Albuquerque, N.M. | 12.0 | 18.3 | 16.9 |
| Atlanta, Ga. | 369.4 | 418.6 | 183.8 |
| Austin, Texas | 19.7 | 24.5 | 47.9 |
| Baltimore, Md. | 81.4 | 100.0 | 68.8 |
| Birmingham, Ala. | 98.9 | 136.0 | 116.4 |
| Boston, Mass. | 63.3 | 123.0 | 59.6 |
| Buffalo, N.Y. | 32.7 | 35.6 | 35.6 |
| Charlotte, N.C. | 116.1 | 164.2 | 99.6 |
| Chicago, Ill. | 71.6 | 117.3 | 113.7 |
| Cincinnati, Ohio | 7.0 | 11.2 | 76.3 |
| Cleveland, Ohio | 8.8 | 28.4 | 107.7 |
| Columbus, Ohio | 5.5 | 21.4 | 7.1 |
| Corpus Christi, Texas | 28.0 | 24.5 | 16.4 |
| Dallas, Texas | 124.8 | 132.5 | 68.8 |
| Dayton, Ohio | 2.3 | 5.6 | 22.3 |
| Denver, Colo. | 17.0 | 15.4 | 30.4 |

**Syphilis Rates in Selected Cities of Greater Than 200,000 Population**

| City | 1989 | 1990 | Last Year |
|---|---|---|---|
| Des Moines, Iowa | 4.9 | 12.2 | 22.9 |
| Detroit, Mich. | 106.9 | 182.1 | 110.5 |
| El Paso, Texas | 43.4 | 49.2 | 35.6 |
| Fort Worth, Texas | 42.7 | 48.4 | 67.7 |
| Honolulu, Hawaii | 5.9 | 3.5 | 4.6 |
| Houston, Texas | 111.4 | 161.0 | 117.1 |
| Indianapolis, Ind. | 9.9 | 13.3 | 34.7 |
| Jacksonville, Fla. | 171.3 | 128.7 | 30.9 |
| Jersey City, N.J. | 139.1 | 155.5 | 94.8 |
| Kansas City, Mo. | 35.7 | 50.6 | 65.2 |
| Los Angeles, Calif. | 127.9 | 108.5 | 65.7 |
| Louisville, Ky. | 13.2 | 13.4 | 64.8 |
| Memphis, Tenn. | 279.2 | 368.7 | 224.4 |
| Miami, Fla. | 228.7 | 188.0 | 101.4 |
| Milwaukee, Wis. | 25.6 | 55.4 | 98.6 |
| Minneapolis, Minn. | 22.5 | 39.2 | 34.4 |
| Nashville, Tenn. | 41.7 | 93.7 | 73.3 |
| New Orleans, La. | 256.8 | 319.2 | 226.5 |
| New York City, N.Y. | 184.7 | 218.1 | 142.4 |
| Newark, N.J. | 217.9 | 345.6 | 192.0 |
| Norfolk, Va. | 44.4 | 57.5 | 91.0 |
| Oakland, Calif. | 94.3 | 85.6 | 36.9 |
| Oklahoma City, Okla. | 25.9 | 53.6 | 91.6 |
| Omaha, Neb. | 15.5 | 6.0 | 5.6 |
| Philadelphia, Pa. | 285.6 | 407.7 | 237.8 |
| Phoenix, Ariz. | 29.5 | 48.7 | 14.6 |
| Pittsburgh, Pa. | 12.3 | 10.7 | 4.3 |
| Portland, Ore. | 69.1 | 37.1 | 22.4 |
| Richmond, Va. | 160.3 | 148.3 | 99.2 |
| Rochester, N.Y. | 156.5 | 152.1 | 98.7 |
| Sacramento, Calif. | 16.3 | 17.5 | 11.2 |
| San Antonio, Texas | 55.1 | 41.3 | 42.2 |
| San Diego, Calif. | 29.6 | 30.5 | 20.5 |
| San Francisco, Calif. | 86.2 | 129.4 | 21.5 |
| San Jose, Calif. | 14.3 | 14.3 | 8.6 |
| Seattle, Wash. | 20.1 | 21.1 | 388.0 |
| St Louis, Mo. | 19.5 | 35.1 | 13.2 |
| St Paul, Minn. | 9.0 | 7.2 | 47.7 |
| St Petersburg, Fla. | 87.1 | 89.2 | 60.5 |
| Tampa, Fla. | 161.6 | 139.3 | 44.8 |
| Toledo, Ohio | 7.8 | 26.0 | 22.0 |
| Tucson, Ariz. | 13.7 | 18.7 | 40.5 |
| Tulsa, Okla. | 19.9 | 29.8 | 275.1 |
| Washington, D.C. | 324.5 | 477.3 | 8.9 |
| Wichita, Kan. | 10.7 | 9.2 | 41.7 |
| Yonkers, N.Y. | 41.3 | 65.8 | 0.0 |
| **U.S. City Total** | **98.4** | **114.5** | **78.8** |

## Skill Drill: Necessities

Every story may be said to demand certain necessary information. It is the reporter's task to include the information in the story. List the information that would be required in the following stories:

Jeff W. Henderson.

**A. Royalty.** The election of the school homecoming king and queen.

### B. Fatal

A traffic accident in which a person died.

### C. Lieutenant

Promotion of a local serviceman.

### D. Project

Announcement of a new construction project.

### E. Blaze

A fire that destroys a building in town.

### F. New

Appointment of a new teacher, clergyman, city official.

### G. Game

The result of a football or basketball game.

*H. Verdict*

The verdict in a trial.

*I. Death*

The obituary of a former city official.

*J. Clinic*

Proposed closing of a neighborhood public health clinic.

*K. Zone*

Request for a change in zoning classification from residential to commercial.

*L. Crime*

The annual citywide crime report.

*M. Split*

A divorce filing.

*N. Damage*

Suit alleging $250,000 damages for injuries in an auto accident.

*O. Meters*

Introduction of an ordinance to get rid of parking meters downtown.

## *Fix It: Scrambled*

The sentences in the following news stories have been rearranged. Put them in correct order.

**A.**

    (1) Clarence Barton, 58, of 452 Johnston St., was listed in stable condition at Mercy Hospital.
    (2) State police said a pickup truck driven by Barton collided with a truck driven by Harry Belford, 85 Roe Ave., at State Route 45 and U.S. Highway 1.
    (3) A collision of two trucks west of the city yesterday left one man hospitalized with face and chest injuries.
    (4) Police said Belford was driving north on U.S. 1 when Barton's truck turned onto the highway. Belford was not hurt.
    (5) Belford was ticketed for failure to yield.

**B.**

    (1) Charles Lee Bieder, of 7 Kondo Lane, was scheduled to be arraigned Thursday to face the charges.
    (2) Local police were called to the apartment after a telephone call from a resident of the building.
    (3) Police officer Fred Christopher said Bieder was found in a hallway with a pistol that had an empty chamber.
    (4) A 22-year-old unemployed baker was arrested last night and charged with reckless conduct after he allegedly fired six shots into the door of an apartment at 76 Tanner St.
    (5) Six people were in the apartment at the time of the incident. No one was injured, but one man broke his leg when he leaped from a third-story window of the apartment.
    (6) Police gave no motive for the incident.

*C.*

(1) The 30-year-old exhibition hall has exhibited $250,000 necklaces and dollar vegetable cutters. All sorts of goods were pedaled.

(2) Outside the building, workmen loaded the last exhibits on waiting trucks.

(3) An exhibitor, Rudolph Klas, owner of the Annalee's Beauty Salon at 150 Rapp Ave., said he would be effected by the closing because he could not afford the new exhibition rates at the Jurvis Center.

(4) The Center will be raized to make way for a high-rise apartment building.

(5) Rents in the new apartment building will be higher, too. They are expected to start at $1,500 a month for a one-room apartment, which is about $3 a square foot. "Closet life," said a prospective tenant who looked at the floor plans.

(6) The show closed at Franklin Center today.

(7) One of the reasons given for closing the Center was that there was insufficient space for large exhibitions.

(8) The Center was hardly commodious either. Built before the pursuit of luxury became a necessity, it was broken into small cubicles for exhibiting kitchen items, clothing and such.

### *What's Wrong?:* Newsweek

In a full-page advertisement about its cover article—"TechnoMania"—*Newsweek* stated:

> The technological revolution has started. But where is it going? . . . How will computers effect the way we do business, conduct politics, protect our privacy and create jobs.

### *You Decide: Term Paper*

Your beat for the local newspaper is the university. Your editor tells you that he has heard that fraternities and sororities on the campus have extensive files that their members use as the basis for assignments in many classes. He wants you to do a story on the situation.

You are a graduate of the university and were a member of one of the fraternities on the campus. You know from personal experience that such files exist and that members still use them. Does this personal experience disqualify you from accepting the assignment?

# 6 The Lead

## Introduction

Because the lead is the first part of the story the reader sees or the listener hears, it must be crafted with particular care. Generally, it is short—25 to 35 words—and encapsulates the most important or interesting aspect of the event being described. The lead follows the subject-verb-object sentence pattern for quick comprehension. The two types of leads are the direct lead, which is used for breaking news events, and the delayed lead, which is used for feature stories. Increasingly, the delayed lead, with its emphasis on an interesting incident or anecdote, is being used on straight news stories.

Rich Turner, *The Stockton Record.*
**Making 25 words do the work of 50.**

## Exercises

### A. Shotgun

This is Saturday night and you are working on a large newspaper that serves Lawrence, some 40 miles away. Your city editor hands you the following story that appeared in the Lawrence newspaper Saturday afternoon. He tells you to put a second-day lead on the story and to rewrite it for the regional news page of the Sunday newspaper. Give it 150 words.

    A 71-year-old Lawrence man died instantly about 8:30 a.m. today from what the county coroner called self-inflicted gunshot wounds.
    The victim, Leslie Hartman, of 267 Tennessee St., was found on the ground between the house and the garage. The 12-gauge shotgun was lying near the body. County Coroner Dr. Albert Parsons termed the death a suicide.
    The victim apparently placed the muzzle of the gun against his throat and then used a cleaning rod to pull the trigger. He was alone at the time of his death. Police said that Hartman had been in ill health recently.
    Before shooting himself, Hartman had contacted the Lewis Funeral Home telling it what he planned to do. Undersheriff Bernard Paddock and Deputy Sheriff Marvin Weiner, of Douglas County, arrived at the scene just minutes after the shooting.
    Services will be at 2 p.m., Monday, at the Lewis Funeral Home with the Rev. Wallace Baehr in charge. Burial will be in Memorial Park Cemetery.
    Hartman was a member of the Masonic Lodge No. 9. He formerly operated a meat market at 840 Massachusetts St., and later a liquor store at the same site.
    Survivors include his wife, Mrs. Alice Hartman, of the home; a son, Robert, of the home; a daughter, Mrs. Roberta Stone, of Wichita; and two grandsons.

### B. Dickens

This story appears in the Mallory College newspaper. You are on rewrite in an AP bureau, and your editor has circled it and asked you to put 150 or 200 words on the state wire.

    Charles Dickens is often thought of as a creative giant whose novels are required reading in high school (*A Tale of Two Cities*) and in college (*Bleak House* or *Hard Times*). He is less often understood as a radical reformer with a social purpose who put his zeal not only into his novels but also into journalism.
    Professor Merle Rubens, of the English Department at Mallory College, has just completed and has had accepted for publication by the Mallory College University Press his book, *Dickens: The Crusader.*

In his book, Professor Rubens says that Dickens' crusades included campaigns against the workhouse, which mistreated and starved paupers, and the working conditions in factories. Dickens wrote many articles about the deaths and mutilations in factories and the attempts by manufacturers to defy the laws designed to protect workers. "He pointed out that there were many fewer thefts, murders and other crimes than there were deaths from factory accidents," Professor Rubens said.

In the pages of his weekly magazine *Household Words,* Dickens said of public health in London that it "was the tragedy of 'Hamlet' with nothing in it but the gravedigger." He campaigned for clean air, water fit to drink and sewers for the poor in the slums, the English professor said.

Dickens also lauded the Ragged Schools, which consisted of volunteers who gave the poor children free instruction. There were no government-supported public schools then.

"There is no one like him today, this whirlwind of energy, decency and genius. He oversaw charities and devised slum-clearing projects that included cheap housing for the poor with libraries, playgrounds and schools nearby," Professor Rubens says in the introduction to his book, which he says took five years to research and write.

"Dickens," he said, "was one of society's great activists—a tough-minded, hard-headed man who worked for reform in his novels, his journalism, his personal life."

## C. Delayed

Review the exercises in the *Workbook* and find three to five stories you wrote with direct leads. Examine them and see whether they could just as well have had delayed leads.

Here are some stories that could have taken delayed leads: ***Zoo, Longo, Goals, Poet, Violence, Gun, Undergrad.***

Make sure that you avoid the most common failing of the delayed lead: the selection of a theme that does not move the reader directly into the relevant material. Sometimes, reporters will be so entranced by a fact or a quote that they will use it for the delayed lead and then find that they have written themselves into a corner.

## D. New Voices

Alice Fahr-Johnstone, a professor of political science on leave from the City University of New York to study the role of women in politics, was in Freeport last night to address students at Mallory College. She spoke at the invitation of the College Political Science and Politics Club. Prepare a 350-word story based on her talk. Here are excerpts:

In the 1992 election, the number of women in the U.S. Senate went from two to six, and in the House it went from 28 to 47. In state legislatures, the number of women increased as well. In 1994, in the Senate the number increased to eight, and in the House it increased to 49.

In the presidential election, Bill Clinton received 46 percent of the women's vote, Bush received 37 percent and Perot 17 percent. This indicates a strong ideological tie among women.

Lyn Kathlene of Purdue University says that the fact that "women were more likely than men to vote Democratic and the fact that two-thirds of the female candidates at national and state levels were Democrats may demonstrate just such an ideological or partisan tie."

Debra Dodson and Susan Carroll at the Center for Women and Politics found that female state legislators were more liberal than male legislators.

It is possible that as women increasingly become involved in political decision making they will engage in what Professor Kathlene describes as a "different type of politics."

Carol Gilligan in her book *In a Different Voice* says that while men are concerned with people's interfering with each other's rights, women are concerned with seeing that all possibilities of helping someone are explored.

Studies of the behavior of legislators seem to indicate gender differences in the kinds of legislation introduced and how bills are acted upon. Professor Kathlene's studies of the Colorado State Legislature show women are more likely to sponsor innovative legislation, "new solutions to old problems, and new programs for the state, whereas men were more likely than women to sponsor bills that modified existing laws or updated old laws."

In crime and prison issues, Professor Kathlene's research shows, "women emphasized the societal link to crime, seeing criminal problems as part of lifelong issues, stemming from early-childhood experiences, poor education and a lack of opportunities in adulthood. This conceptualization of crime led women to sponsor crime bills that included long-term preventative strategies as well as intervention measures."

The male legislators, on the other hand, did "not talk about criminals as products of society but rather as individuals responsible for their choices." The result was "reactive policy recommendations and legislative proposals based on stricter sentencing, longer terms and rehabilitation in prison."

Women are interested in issues such as education, family and children. Women tend to believe that action can be accomplished by removing barriers, whereas the male legislators acted on the belief coercion is necessary.

It is clear women will practice a different type of politics in office. They will be more compassionate and less punitive, more interested in general solutions than piecemeal legislation.

## Assignments

### A. Unsafe

Small cars are more dangerous than larger models, reports the Insurance Institute for Highway Safety. Small cars are more prone to rollovers and to damage that can injure occupants, the Institute finds. The death rate in the smallest cars on the market is more than double the rate in the largest cars: three deaths per 10,000 registered cars for the smallest, 1.3 for the largest, a recent annual report states.

Yet people buy small cars. Interview small-car owners and automobile dealers to find out why. (Fuel economy, low cost are obvious reasons. Be specific about these; give figures for all information. Give names of manufacturers and models.)

### B. Investment

What do investment authorities advise their clients to buy these days? What are they saying are good ways to put money away that may appreciate considerably and that combine safety and good return? High return usually involves some risks; what are they?

Compare investments such as mutual and other funds, U.S. Savings Bonds, treasury notes and bonds, municipal bonds and stocks.

## Campus Project

### Marriage

About a fifth of all women surveyed say they do not plan to marry. What do women students on the campus say of their marital plans? The Census Bureau says that of women in their peak childbearing age (18–34), most plan on two children. The figures:

    No children—10 percent
    One child—13 percent
    Two children—47 percent
    Three or more—30 percent

What size family do women on your campus plan and why? How many of the women you survey plan on careers after graduation? How will those who plan careers and marriage blend the two?

## Community Projects

### A. Broken

What doesn't work in town? What do people complain about: traffic lights, potholes, traffic jams, poor city services, crowded schools, lack of certain kinds of stores, high prices, lack of opportunities for young people? See whether the complaints form a pattern.

### B. Scores

Here is a listing of SAT scores for 10 years ago and for the most recent year. Has your state done better or worse? How far is it from the national average? Interview school authorities for comments on student performance. Presume that adjustments have been made for the scores of 10 years ago so that they are comparable to last year's scores. (The SAT scores were upped in 1995 to reflect new averages, a 420 verbal becoming a 500, for example.

| State | 10 Years Ago | | Last Year | | % Graduates Taking SAT |
|---|---|---|---|---|---|
| | V | M | V | M | |
| Alabama | 467 | 503 | 482 | 529 | 8 |
| Alaska | 443 | 471 | 434 | 477 | 49 |
| Arizona | 469 | 509 | 443 | 496 | 26 |
| Arkansas | 482 | 521 | 477 | 518 | 6 |
| California | 421 | 476 | 413 | 482 | 46 |
| Colorado | 468 | 514 | 456 | 513 | 28 |
| Connecticut | 436 | 468 | 426 | 472 | 80 |
| Delaware | 433 | 469 | 428 | 464 | 68 |
| Dist. of Columbia | 397 | 426 | 406 | 443 | 53 |
| Florida | 423 | 467 | 413 | 466 | 49 |
| Georgia | 392 | 430 | 398 | 446 | 65 |
| Hawaii | 395 | 474 | 401 | 480 | 58 |
| Idaho | 480 | 512 | 461 | 508 | 16 |
| Illinois | 463 | 518 | 478 | 546 | 14 |
| Indiana | 410 | 454 | 410 | 466 | 60 |
| Iowa | 519 | 570 | 506 | 574 | 5 |
| Kansas | 502 | 549 | 494 | 550 | 10 |
| Kentucky | 479 | 518 | 474 | 523 | 11 |
| Louisiana | 472 | 508 | 481 | 530 | 9 |
| Maine | 429 | 463 | 420 | 463 | 68 |
| Maryland | 429 | 468 | 429 | 479 | 64 |
| Massachusetts | 429 | 467 | 426 | 475 | 79 |
| Michigan | 461 | 515 | 472 | 537 | 11 |
| Minnesota | 481 | 539 | 495 | 562 | 9 |
| Mississippi | 480 | 512 | 485 | 528 | 4 |
| Missouri | 469 | 512 | 485 | 537 | 10 |
| Montana | 490 | 544 | 463 | 523 | 21 |
| Nebraska | 493 | 548 | 482 | 543 | 9 |
| Nevada | 442 | 489 | 429 | 484 | 30 |
| New Hampshire | 448 | 483 | 438 | 486 | 69 |
| New Jersey | 418 | 458 | 418 | 475 | 71 |
| New Mexico | 487 | 527 | 475 | 528 | 12 |
| New York | 424 | 470 | 416 | 472 | 76 |
| North Carolina | 395 | 432 | 405 | 455 | 60 |
| North Dakota | 500 | 554 | 497 | 559 | 5 |
| Ohio | 460 | 508 | 456 | 510 | 24 |
| Oklahoma | 484 | 525 | 482 | 537 | 9 |
| Oregon | 435 | 472 | 436 | 491 | 53 |
| Pennsylvania | 425 | 462 | 417 | 462 | 70 |
| Rhode Island | 424 | 461 | 420 | 462 | 68 |
| South Carolina | 384 | 419 | 395 | 443 | 60 |
| South Dakota | 520 | 566 | 483 | 548 | 5 |
| Tennessee | 486 | 523 | 488 | 535 | 12 |
| Texas | 413 | 453 | 412 | 474 | 48 |
| Utah | 503 | 542 | 509 | 558 | 4 |
| Vermont | 437 | 470 | 427 | 472 | 68 |
| Virginia | 428 | 466 | 424 | 469 | 65 |
| Washington | 463 | 505 | 434 | 488 | 49 |
| West Virginia | 466 | 510 | 439 | 482 | 17 |
| Wisconsin | 475 | 532 | 487 | 557 | 9 |
| Wyoming | 489 | 545 | 459 | 521 | 12 |
| **National** | **426** | **471** | **423** | **479** | **42** |

*Source:* College Board

## Home Assignments

### A. Leads

Clip from a recent newspaper five local stories for a study of their leads.

1. Classify them as direct or delayed leads.
2. Are they all denotative leads, or is there an interpretative lead among the five?
3. Do any of the five stories back into the lead, or is the lead buried? If not, locate a local or wire service story with a buried lead.
4. Make a readability study of the leads. Here are the guides:
   One idea to a sentence.
   Subject-verb-object sentence order.
   Concrete nouns and action verbs.

### B. STD (3)

Here are tables with the annual rates of the 10 states and 10 major cities with the highest rates of syphilis last year and five years ago. Rates are based on the number of cases per 100,000 population. The figures are from the Centers for Disease Control and Prevention.

Select from the tables a city or state in which you live or attend school, or use a nearby city or state, and write a 350-word story based on the material. Last year's figures have just been released.

Place the material in perspective by obtaining background about sexually transmitted diseases, which officials with the Centers have described as epidemic.

**Note:** Health authorities say that only one of three to five cases of STD is reported to the Centers.

## Syphilis

### States

| | Last Year | | | Five Years Ago | |
|---|---|---|---|---|---|
| Rank | State | Rate | Rank | State | Rate |
| 1 | Mississippi | 174.4 | 1 | Georgia | 142.2 |
| 2 | Louisiana | 126.7 | 2 | Louisiana | 125.1 |
| 3 | Tennessee | 59.5 | 3 | Florida | 115.9 |
| 4 | North Carolina | 59.0 | 4 | New York | 107.3 |
| 5 | Arkansas | 55.6 | 5 | Mississippi | 96.5 |
| 6 | South Carolina | 53.8 | 6 | Tennessee | 89.1 |
| 7 | New York | 51.7 | 7 | Alabama | 77.6 |
| 8 | Texas | 51.2 | 8 | Texas | 77.5 |
| 9 | Georgia | 47.2 | 9 | Maryland | 66.4 |
| 10 | Alabama | 46.9 | 10 | Pennsylvania | 64.7 |
| | **Average** | **32.0** | | **Average** | **54.3** |

### Major Cities

| | Last Year | | | Five Years Ago | |
|---|---|---|---|---|---|
| Rank | City | Rate | Rank | City | Rate |
| 1 | St. Louis | 388.0 | 1 | Washington, D.C. | 477.3 |
| 2 | Washington, D.C. | 275.1 | 2 | Atlanta | 418.6 |
| 3 | Philadelphia | 237.8 | 3 | Philadelphia | 407.7 |
| 4 | New Orleans | 226.5 | 4 | Memphis | 368.7 |
| 5 | Memphis | 224.4 | 5 | Newark | 345.6 |
| 6 | Newark | 192.0 | 6 | New Orleans | 319.2 |
| 7 | Atlanta | 183.6 | 7 | New York City | 218.1 |
| 8 | New York City | 142.4 | 8 | Miami | 188.0 |
| 9 | Houston | 117.1 | 9 | Detroit | 182.1 |
| 10 | Baltimore | 116.4 | 10 | Charlotte | 164.2 |
| | **Average** | **78.8** | | **Average** | **113.7** |

## Class Discussion

### A. Second Day

Here is the beginning of a story in the regional morning daily newspaper in your area:

> The Freeport Chamber of Commerce announced last night that it will launch an investigation into complaints that merchants along U.S. 81 are gouging tourists.
>
> The chamber's board of directors approved the inquiry after a four-hour closed-door discussion that was marked by heated debate. The vote was 8-7, Fred Graham, secretary of the Chamber said.
>
> The matter was forwarded to the chamber by the U.S. Highway Users Assn., which said its members had complained of "outrageous prices, discourteous service, and unsanitary conditions" along U.S. 81 approaching and in Freeport. . . .

Make a list of story ideas for a folo in the local afternoon newspaper. Give specifics for those you would contact.

U.S. 81 begins at the southwest corner of the city near Three Corners Junction, enters on Hunter Avenue, goes up Vermont Avenue to Concord Street and then turns northeast on Oregon Avenue and exits the city.

### B. Purpose

In his essay "Why I Write," George Orwell says there are

> ". . . four great motives for writing, at any rate for writing prose. They exist in different degrees in every writer, and in any one writer the proportions will vary from time to time, according to the atmosphere in which he is living. They are:
>
> "1. Sheer egoism. Desire to seem clever, to be talked about, to be remembered after death, to get your own back on grown-ups who snubbed you in childhood, etc., etc. It is humbug to pretend that this is not a motive, and a strong one. . . .
>
> "2. Aesthetic enthusiasm. Perception of beauty in the external world, or, on the other hand, in words and their right arrangement. Pleasure in the impact of one sound on another, in the firmness of good prose or the rhythm of a good story. Desire to share an experience which one feels is valuable and ought not to be missed. . . .
>
> "3. Historical impulse. Desire to see things as they are, to find out true facts and store them up for the use of posterity.
>
> "4. Political purpose—using the word *political* in the widest possible sense. Desire to push the world in a certain direction, to alter other people's idea of the kind of society that they should strive after. Once again, no book is genuinely free from political bias. The opinion that art should have nothing to do with politics is itself a political attitude."

In this essay, Orwell said that when he sits down to write it is "because there is some lie that I want to expose, some fact to which I want to draw attention, and my initial concern is to get a hearing. But I could not do the work of writing a book, or even a long magazine article, if it were not also an aesthetic experience. . . ."

Do you think Orwell's motives apply to journalism and journalists? Where do you find yourself in his list? Or have you still another motive?

## Skill Drill I: Lead Choice

Indicate whether a direct or a delayed lead would be appropriate for these events:

1. Adoption of the city budget. _____
2. Announcement of a performance next month of "Trial by Jury" by the local Gilbert and Sullivan Society. _____
3. Introduction of calculators into grade school arithmetic classes. _____
4. Election of officers of the county medical society. _____
5. Award of fellowship to a faculty member. _____
6. Arrival of Barnum & Bailey Circus in town. _____
7. Preparations of Doina Melinte for metric-mile race in Olympics. _____
8. Teaching innovations by modern language department. _____
9. Total employment in the United States for past year. _____
10. Background of candidate for U.S. Senate. _____
11. Approval by FCC of interstate telephone rate increase. _____
12. Jury verdict. _____

13. Survey of consumer complaints on automobile repairs. _____
14. Arrest of Utah congressman on charge of soliciting for prostitution. _____
15. Curtis Strange's dropping out of college to become golf pro. _____

## Skill Drill II: Simplifying

Some editors demand short leads, under 30 words whenever possible. This requires reporters to stress single-element and summary leads in their stories. Rewrite the following leads, making them single-element or summary with fewer than 30 words.

1. The city planning department plans to make repairs this coming summer on Ogden, Concord and Vincent Streets at an estimated cost of $18,000, $22,000 and $78,000, respectively, it was announced by City Engineer O.M. Shelton.

2. After a three-day search, police today reported the arrest of Eileen McCoy, 19, in a Chicago bus depot on a charge of arson in connection with the fire that left Kmart Eastview a burned-out hulk last week at an estimated loss of $2 million.

3. The state purchasing agent will open bids Dec. 10 for the purchase of electronic equipment for the state university, including calculators for the mathematics department, audiovisual projectors and tape recorders for the modern language department, and installation of an all-electronic newsroom for the school of journalism. The newsroom installation is expected to cost at least $250,000 and will enable students to write and edit copy without typewriters or pencils.

4. A last-quarter scoring spree by Connie Hawkins, the newly arrived forward, enabled the Bullets to erase a seemingly insurmountable 22-point halftime lead by the Warriors in a come-from-behind win, 88-87.

5. "The defendant's crime may not have caused physical harm, but the hardship he inflicted on those who trusted him with their savings cannot be ignored," said District Judge Marvin Hurley yesterday in sentencing Norris Josephson to a minimum of five years in the state penitentiary on a fraudulent investment scheme that bilked local residents of more than a half million dollars.

6. The weather bureau today offered little hope to corn and wheat growers across a wide belt of Minnesota with a prediction of no rain for the next week to relieve the month-long drought that has cut crops by an estimated 5 percent to date.

7. F.W. Walkenhorst, a university regent, said at a meeting of the regents today that the teaching staff at the state university works an average of fewer than 20 hours a week and that, unless this is remedied by a larger course load, the state legislature could not be expected to approve the university's current budget request.

8. The Crested Butte Dam burst last night and a wall of water 12 feet high swept through small towns, farms and ranches in eastern Idaho leaving an unknown number of dead and injured and millions of dollars in destruction.

9. In a talk last night to the local press club, Russell Cooper, a political reporter based in Washington, D.C., said that the traditional role of the political reporter has been superseded by modern advertising techniques, which allow a candidate to project the image the candidate desires in "the picture-hungry, simplicity-oriented media that are unwilling or unable to deal with complexities."

10. The use of publicly employed teachers in religious schools has come under constitutional challenge in a suit filed in federal court here today by the National Coalition for Public Education and Religious Liberty (PEARL). The organization contends that the United States Commission on Education has violated the Constitution by ignoring Supreme Court rulings barring the assignment of public school teachers to religious schools during regular school hours.

## Fix It: Leads

Look over the following leads, identify the problems and rewrite them:

1. MANILA, Philippines (AP)—A government commission created to recover wealth allegedly plundered from the Philippines by Ferdinand E. Marcos has discovered an $800 million Swiss bank account held by the ousted ruler, a commission official said today.

2. More than 50 angry parents showed up last night at the monthly board of education meeting to protest the action of the school superintendent on physical education classes.

The superintendent, Ruth Passenger, had ordered a halt in interscholastic high school basketball games. She said recent brawls at the games "endangered safety and damaged the school system's reputation."

Parents urged the board to take other means to cope with the situation, and after an hour's discussion, the board voted unanimously to rescind Passenger's decision.

3. Have you ever tried to walk for 24 straight hours?

4. Hoping to end speculation that he would seek the Republican nomination for governor, Ralph Rappaport said today he is "delighted" to stay on as a member of the city council and has no intention to seek the nomination.

5. The special election to fill the city council vacancy caused by the death of George Grumble will be held Nov. 28, City Clerk Ruth Farrell announced today.

# 7 The Writer's Art

Jim Peppler, *Newsday*.

**Quotes, incidents pace the piece.**

### Introduction

The well-written story is clear and convincing. Quotes, anecdotes and actions involve the reader and listener in the event. Their use and the inclusion of specific details serve to convince the reader and viewer that the account is truthful. To keep the reader glued to the piece, sentences are short, an everyday vocabulary is used and transitions are used to keep the separate elements and themes tightly structured. The well-written story has a pace and a rhythm that match the nature of the event. Writers read widely to learn the writing trade, and they are not reluctant to rewrite their work.

## Fifty Common Errors

This list of errors in word usage, spelling and grammar was compiled by a writing/editorial committee of the Associated Press Managing Editors organization. The committee based the list on the work of Richard C. Reid of the *Minneapolis Tribune*. A few changes and additions have been made in the APME list.

1. **Affect, effect.** Generally, *affect* is the verb; *effect* is the noun. "The letter did not *affect* the outcome." "The letter had a significant *effect*." *Effect* is also a verb meaning *to bring about:* "It is almost impossible to *effect* change."

2. **Afterward, afterwards.** Use *afterward*. The dictionary allows use of *afterwards* only as a second form. The same applies to *toward* and *towards;* use *toward*.

3. **All right.** Two words. The dictionary may list *alright* as a legitimate word, but it is not acceptable in standard usage.

4. **Allude, elude.** You *allude* to (or mention) a book. You *elude* (or escape) a pursuer.

5. **Annual.** Do not use *first* with it. The first time is not an *annual* (yearly) event.

68

6. **Averse, adverse.** If you do not like something, you are *averse* (or opposed) to it. *Adverse* (bad) is an adjective, as in *adverse* weather, *adverse* conditions.

7. **Bloc, block.** A *bloc* is a coalition of persons or a group with the same purpose or goal. Do not call it a *block,* which has some 40 dictionary definitions.

8. **Compose, comprise.** Remember that you *compose* things by putting them together. Once the parts are put together, the object *comprises* (includes or embraces) the parts.

9. **Couple of.** You need the *of.* It is never "a *couple* tomatoes"; it is "a *couple of* tomatoes."

10. **Demolish, destroy.** To do away with *completely.* You cannot *partially* demolish or destroy something, nor is there any need to say *totally* destroyed.

11. **Different from.** Things and people are *different from* each other. Do not write that they are different *than* each other.

12. **Drowned.** Do not say someone *was drowned* unless an assailant held the victim's head under water. Just say the victim *drowned.*

13. **Due to, owing to, because of.** We prefer *because of.*
Wrong: "The game was canceled due to rain."
Stilted: "Owing to rain, the game was canceled."
Right: "The game was canceled *because of* rain."

14. **Ecology, environment.** They are not synonymous. *Ecology* is the study of the relationship between organisms and their *environment.*
Wrong: "Even so simple an undertaking as maintaining a lawn affects our ecology." (Use *environment.*)
Right: "There is much interest in animal *ecology* these days."

15. **Either, each.** *Either* means one *or* the other, not both. *Each* means both (one by one).
Wrong: "There were lions on either side of the door."
Right: "There were lions on *each* side of the door."

16. **Fliers, flyers.** Pilots are *fliers.* Handbills are *flyers.*

17. **Flout, flaunt.** They are not the same words. *Flout* means to mock, to scoff or to show disdain for; *flaunt* means to display ostentatiously.

18. **Funeral service.** A redundant expression. A funeral *is* a service.

19. **Head up.** People do not head up committees. They *head* committees.

20. **Hopefully.** One of the most commonly misused words, in spite of what the dictionary may say. *Hopefully* should describe the way the subject feels. For instance: "I shall hopefully present the plan to the president." (This means I will be hopeful when I do it.) But it is something else again when you attribute hope to a nonperson. You may write, "Hopefully, the war will end soon." You mean you hope the war will end soon, but it is not what you are writing. Write, "I hope the war will end soon."

21. **Imply, infer.** The speaker *implies.* The hearer *infers.*

22. **In advance of, prior to.** Use *before;* it sounds more natural.

23. **Its, it's.** *Its* is the possessive; *it's* is the contraction of *it is.*

24. **Lay, lie.** *Lay* is the action word; *lie* is the state of being.
Wrong: The body will *lay* in state until Wednesday.
Right: The body will *lie* in state until Wednesday.
Right: The prosecutor tried to *lay* the blame on him.

However, the past tense of *lie* is *lay.*
Right: The body *lay* in state from Tuesday until Wednesday.

The past participle and the plain past tense of *lay* is *laid.*
Right: He *laid* the pencil on the pad.
Right: He had *laid* the pencil on the pad.
Right: The hen *laid* an egg.
Wrong: The body *laid* in state from Tuesday until Wednesday.

25. **Leave, let.** To *leave* alone means to depart from or cause to be in solitude. To be *let* alone means to be undisturbed.

Wrong: "Mr. Jones talked him into *leaving* her alone."
Right: "Mr. Jones talked him into *letting* her alone."
Right: "When I entered the room I saw that Jim and Mary were sleeping, so I decided to *leave* them alone."

26. **Less, fewer.** If you can separate items in the quantities being compared, use *fewer*. If not, use *less*.

Wrong: "The Rams are inferior to the Vikings because they have *less* good linemen."
Right: "The Rams are inferior to the Vikings because they have *fewer* good linemen."
Right: "The Rams are inferior to the Vikings because they have *less* experience."

27. **Like, as.** Do not use *like* for *as* or *as if*. In general, use *like* to compare phrases and clauses with nouns and pronouns; use *as* when comparing phrases and clauses that contain a verb.

Wrong: "Jim blocks the linebacker *like* he should."
Right: "Jim blocks the linebacker *as* he should."
Right: "Jim blocks *like* a pro."

28. **Marshall, marshal.** Generally, the first form is correct only when the word is a proper noun: John *Marshall*. The second form is a verb form: Marilyn will *marshal* her forces. And the second form is the one to use for a title. Fire *Marshal* Stan Anderson. Field *Marshal* Erwin Rommel.

29. **Mean, average, median.** Use *mean* as synonymous with *average*. "The *mean* is the sum of all components divided by the number of components." *Median* is the number that has as many components above as it has below it. *Mode* is the number that appears most frequently in a distribution.

30. **Nouns.** There is a growing trend toward using nouns as verbs. Resist it. "Host," "headquarters," and "author" are *nouns* even though the dictionary may acknowledge they can be used as verbs.

31. **Oral, verbal.** Use *oral* when use of the mouth is central to the thought; the word emphasizes the idea of human utterance. *Verbal* may apply to spoken or written words; it connotes the process of putting ideas into writing.

32. **Over, more than.** They are not interchangeable. *Over* refers to spatial relationships: "The plane flew *over* the city." *More than* is used with figures: "In the crowd were *more than* 1,000 fans."

33. **Parallel construction.** Thoughts in a series in the same sentence require parallel construction.

Wrong: "The union delivered demands for an increase of 10 percent in wages and to cut the work week to 30 hours."
Right: "The union delivered demands for an increase of 10 percent in wages and for a reduction in the work week to 30 hours."

34. **Peddle, pedal.** When selling something, you *peddle* it. When riding a bicycle or similar form of locomotion, you *pedal* it.

35. **Pretense, pretext.** They are different, but it is a tough distinction. A *pretext* is that which is put forward to conceal a truth: "He was discharged for tardiness, but this was only a *pretext* for his general incompetence." A *pretense* is a "false show," a more overt act intended to conceal personal feelings: "My profuse compliments were all *pretense*."

36. **Principle, principal.** A guiding rule or basic truth is a *principle*. The first, dominant or leading thing is *principal*. *Principle* is a noun; *principal* may be a noun or an adjective.

37. **Redundancies:**

Easter Sunday: *Easter.*
Incumbent congressman: *congressman.*
Owns his own home: *owns his home.*
The company will close down: *the company will close.*
Jones, Smith, Johnson and Reid were all convicted: *Jones, Smith, Johnson and Reid were convicted.*
Jewish rabbi: *rabbi.*
During the winter months: *During the winter.*
Both Reid and Jones were denied pardons: *Reid and Jones were denied pardons.*
I read three different books: *I read three books.*

I am currently tired: *I am tired.*

Autopsy to determine the cause of death: *autopsy.*

38. **Refute, rebut.** *Refute* connotes success in argument and almost always implies an editorial judgment. *Rebut* means answering an argument.

Wrong: Father Bury *refuted* the arguments of the pro-abortion faction.

Right: Father Bury *rebutted* the arguments of the pro-abortion faction.

39. **Reluctant, reticent.** If she does not want to act, she is *reluctant*. If he does not want to speak, he is *reticent*.

40. **Say, said.** The most serviceable words in the journalist's language are the forms of the verb *to say*. Let a person *say* something, rather than *declare* or *admit* or *point out*. And never let a person grin, smile, frown or giggle something.

41. **Slang.** Do not try to use "with-it" slang.

42. **Spelling.** It is basic. Some frequent misspellings:

*consensus,* not concensus.

*restaurateur,* not restauranteur.

*dietitian,* not dietician.

43. **Temperatures.** They may get higher or lower, but they do not get warmer or cooler.

Wrong: Temperatures are expected to *warm up* in the area Friday.

Right: Temperatures are expected to *rise* in the area Friday.

44. **That, which.** *That* tends to restrict the reader's thought and direct it the way you want it to go; *which* is nonrestrictive, introducing a bit of subsidiary information. For instance:

"The lawnmower *that* is in the garage needs sharpening." (Meaning: We have more than one lawnmower. The one in the garage needs sharpening.)

"The lawnmower, *which* is in the garage, needs sharpening." (Meaning: Our lawnmower needs sharpening. It is in the garage.)

"The statue *that* graces our entry hall is on loan from the museum." (Meaning: Of all the statues around here, the one in the entry hall is on loan.)

"The statue, *which* graces our entry hall, is on loan." (Meaning: Our statue is on loan. It happens to be in the entry hall.)

**Note:** *Which* clauses take commas, signaling they are not essential to the meaning of the sentence.

45. **Under way.** Two words. But do not say something got under way. Say it *started* or *began*.

46. **Unique.** Something that is *unique* is the only one of its kind. It cannot be *very* unique or *quite* unique or *somewhat* unique or *rather* unique. Do not use it unless you really mean *unique*, the only one of its kind.

47. **Up.** Do not use it as a verb.

Wrong: The manager said he would *up* the price next week.

Right: The manager said he would *raise* the price next week.

48. **Who, whom.** Generally, you are safe to use *whom* to refer to someone who has been the object of an action. *Who* is the word when the somebody has been the actor.

"A 19-year-old woman, to *whom* the room was rented, left the window open."

"A 19-year-old woman, *who* rented the room, left the window open."

49. **Who's, whose.** Though it incorporates an apostrophe, *who's* is not a possessive. It is a contraction for *who is*. *Whose* is the possessive.

Wrong: I don't know *who's* coat it is.

Right: I don't know *whose* coat it is.

Right: Find out *who's* there.

50. **Would.** Be careful about using *would* when constructing a conditional past tense.

Wrong: If Soderholm *would* not have had an injured foot, Thompson *would* not have been in the lineup.

Right: If Soderholm *had* not *had* an injured foot, Thompson *would* not have been in the lineup.

## Exercise

### A. Coach

> WANTED RIGHT AWAY—a baseball coach for 14 eight- to eleven-year-olds who want to compete in the Little League. Ask for Joe Pretz, 569-9884, or leave a message.

You work in Denver, Colo. Your editor shows you this classified advertisement from the *Clear Creek Courant* and suggests you call Joe Pretz and try to develop a story. You do. Mrs. Pretz calls Joe to the phone. He is 10 years old, and he tells you, "We can't play in the Little League when the games start June 14 unless we have a coach. There are 14 of us, 8 to 11 years old. We are all ready. Except for a coach. We have been practicing anyway. Everyone we ask is busy. No one has the time." You ask Joe Pretz, "What's the best reason someone should coach your team?" He answers, "Because we need a coach."

He tells you a friend, Bill Geiger, offered to help by placing the advertisement, and you call Geiger, who tells you, "The boys are in the same pickle as Charlie Brown, you know. But there's no girls or beagles on the team." You have a roster for the team, the Georgetown Red Sox, and you notice there is a name, Stacy Bartels, which could be that of a girl. You check. Stacy is indeed a girl.

Write a story with a Georgetown, Colo. dateline.

## Assignments

### A. Inflation

The senior research scientist at the College Board, Howard Everson, made the following observation about grades and SAT scores:

> Between 1987 and 1994, the percentage of students reporting "A" grade averages rose from 28 to 32 percent, but their average SAT scores fell 6 to 15 points. Overall, average grades were lowest in mathematics and natural science, and highest in arts/music and social science/history.

Interview campus sources for an explanation of Everson's observation.

### B. Librarian

Among the 850,000 high school students who took the Scholastic Aptitude test, fewer than 300 indicated that they intended to study library science in college. That's a tiny fraction of 1 percent and by far the smallest intended college major. Why? Interview librarians on campus and in town.

### C. Camera

Interview the head of a local photography club or organization. Discuss recent developments in photography such as the digital camera. What seems to interest photographers who, in the past, seemed to prefer the grab shot, candid pictures taken with the 35-mm camera? Is there any tendency to salon or scenic photography, toward larger cameras? What do they think of photo enhancement?

### D. Architecture

Have a local architect or a member of the art or architecture department accompany you on a walking tour of the city center for an assessment of the architectural value of the buildings there.

### E. Jailed

Visit a city jail and ask the person in charge for an inventory of crime. That is, for what offenses are the men and women behind bars? Does this vary with the day of the week, time of month, part of year? Are totals from the past week or the past month significantly different from previous periods?

### F. Deposits

Obtain from local banks, or other reliable sources, total amounts in savings and checking (time and demand) accounts for the last period for which new figures are available—quarter, half-year or annual. Is there a marked change from previous periods? What is the significance of these figures? What do they usually reflect? Note the Christmas Club totals.

*G. Grades*

Is there a correlation between the Scholastic Aptitude Test (SAT) or American College Test (ACT) scores of entering students and their success in your school? The subject is frequently studied on campuses. Compare with national data and other schools, if your source has such information. (At the University of New Mexico, of 2,147 students entering with ACT scores of 15 and under, 388 graduated; of 1,649 students entering with ACT scores of 26 and above, 1,237 graduated.)

*H. Health Stats*

Interview local health authorities and examine statistics to identify some of the major health problems in the city.

## Campus Projects

*A. Cheating*

College authorities report that cheating is increasing on the campus. Instructors say they are finding more cases of plagiarism than ever before. A journalism instructor tells this story:

> I assigned students to select a well-known person to interview, and this student handed me a well-written piece. The trouble is he didn't know the man had died three years ago. I went to NEXIS and found that he picked up an interview story from a Chicago newspaper, then apparently didn't look further.

The student was dismissed from the program.

Student newspapers at the Naval Academy and MIT report unprecedented cheating. A study by Donald McCabe of the Rutgers University business faculty of 6,000 students found that two-thirds of the students admitted cheating. His follow-up study in 1993 of 18,000 students concluded nine of 10 students admitted cheating at least once.

Cheating varies from putting notes on handkerchiefs to stealing examinations before they are given. It includes providing false footnotes on a paper, using fraternity term papers for a course, submitting papers written by another.

How does your school define cheating, and what is its frequency?

*B. Recruit*

Make an inventory of your college's or university's recruiting efforts. Examine its efforts to recruit bright high school students, athletes, students with special abilities (musicians, artists, actors) and faculty members.

**Scholars:** Is anyone in the admissions office assigned to reach out to bright students? How? Is there a special fund for such recruiting? What inducements are offered these students: scholarships, special placement, jobs? How does the school describe the kind of student it is looking for? Is there alumni participation in this area of recruiting? Do any particular high schools have a reputation for graduating bright students?

Interview administrators, students, faculty members and high school college placement officers. Dig for particulars, examples, specifics.

**Athletes:** What kind of recruiting is done for intercollegiate athletics? Do coaches make trips to high schools? What is the budget for this? What sports are emphasized in recruiting athletes? What inducements are offered these athletes: special classes for remedial work, special eating facilities, athletic dormitory, scholarships? Describe these in detail.

What is the contribution of alumni and booster clubs in financial assistance and recruiting? How is this formalized? Do local merchants contribute? Has the school been involved in any problems with the NCAA? Explain.

In both areas, make sure to interview those involved: students who have been recruited, administrators, faculty members, people in the community.

*C. Interfaith*

The rate of interfaith marriages has steadily increased over the past 25 years. About 40 percent of the Catholics who marry each year do so outside their faith. The 1973 figure was 23 percent. Among Jews, the percentage of interfaith marriages went from 30 percent in 1970 to 52 percent in a recent year.

How much of a factor is religion in campus dating? Ask students and chaplains assigned to student religious organizations.

## Community Project

### Bottlenecks

Make a traffic inventory of the community. Do commuters complain of delays? Are there dangerous intersections, poorly marked corners, pockmarked streets?

Interview commuters; listen to radio traffic reports for trouble spots and talk to those who gather information for the traffic reports. Talk to school safety patrol personnel, city street department employees and their superiors. Interview police, sheriff's officers and highway patrol officers who deal with traffic. Have the city highway or traffic engineer conduct a tour of known trouble spots.

Obtain the master plan for road repair, reconstruction, rerouting and new construction.

## Home Assignment

### Fog

One way to check the readability of a story is to use the following formula:

1. Find the average number of words per sentence by counting the words in each sentence and dividing by the number of sentences. Use seven or eight sentences.
2. Add to the average sentence length the number of three-syllable words. Don't count easy words.
3. Multiply by 0.4.

The result will give you the grade level of the material.

The seven sentences and five three-syllable words I just used make for a sixth-grade reading level.

Test the daily newspaper you read and at least one of the magazines you read for their reading levels. Write a brief assessment of each, and indicate whether the material is written so that readers of the publication can understand it.

Background: About 25 million adults read below the fifth-grade level. Half the high school seniors cannot read at grade level. Mike Royko's columns read at the eighth-grade level. *The Washington Post* news columns tested at 14.5, *New York Times* at 12.6 and *USA Today* at 10.6.

## Class Discussion

### Syracuse

Here is a handout from a sports publicity office. List all the clichés and trite expressions. Rewrite.

SYRACUSE, N.Y.—Syracuse University has 10 sophomore newcomers who may play more than a little football, but four of the young men could climb well up the ladder of success by December.

The athletes in question are halfback Ernie Davis, and Ken Ericson, center Bob Stem and quarterback Dave Sarette. The authority is Orange head coach Floyd (Ben) Schwartzwalder.

Top man among the rookie group is Ernie Davis, the fleet 6-2, 205-pound speedster from Elmira, N.Y., who was a world-beater with the SU frosh last fall and an All-American in high school. As the expression goes, Davis has all the tools.

"Ernie is our top prospect, no question about that," offers Schwartzwalder. "He'll be in our starting lineup against Kansas this Saturday and he's going to become a great football player. I'd like to have about 10 more like Ernie."

Ericson, a 6-2, 190-pound end from Weymouth, Mass., became an even more important factor in Schwartzwalder's plans last week when knee injuries sidelined starting left end Dave Baker and slowed up reserve flanker Tom Gilburg.

Ericson got a chance to scrimmage with the Syracuse starting team, due to the mishaps, and was very impressive. He is regarded as an outstanding pass receiver.

Stem, a fire-plug 5-11, 195-pound pivot from Phillipsburg, N.J., has improved by leaps and bounds and is pressing veterans Dave Applehof and Al Bemiller at center. Bob has drawn raves for his linebacking.

## DB/CAR

### Census

You are told to write a story about the population changes in your city and state over the last 30 years. You know that the census reports contain not only the population figures but also details on the population such as racial composition, age groupings and income.

For your story, first, make a list of the various factors that you want to track over the last three census counts. Then decide how you will go about gathering this information. Last, write a story or a series of articles that covers the changes in your city and/or state.

## Skill Drill: Tightening the Lead

Reporters usually try to make their leads as short as possible. Here are some leads that contain unnecessary attribution, redundancies, opinions of the reporter, excess wordage, unimportant quotes, unnecessarily specific information. Use the subject-verb-object sentence structure for most of the leads.

### A. Pollute

In looking for pollution along the city's lakeshore, investigators for the state Environmental Protection Commission said today they have discovered what they described as "high levels of beach and waterfront pollution."

### B. Contract

The city today awarded a contract to Polly Plumbing Inc., of Roanoke, for the construction of 35 "necessary houses," also known as outhouses, along the state's roads and highways. The successful low bid by the firm was $89,565.

### C. Year-End

The office of the police department today released year-end crime figures for the city that show homicides were down from 139 the previous year to 124 last year, but all other types of violent crime increased, 896 to 1,086.

### D. Women

In a talk entitled "Whither Women," Hortense Hillerbrandt, an assistant state attorney general, and vice president of the caucus, told some 450 delegates to the annual convention of the Women's Caucus meeting here not to "put aside family responsibilities when you hang up the apron."

### E. Kids

Benjamin Brown, the well-known child psychologist and author, said today in a speech to state educators that his studies and those of others indicate young children spend more time in front of TV sets than in bed asleep.

### F. Fatal

Two cars collided at the intersection of Elm and Johnson Streets last night at 10:45 p.m. and took the lives of a local couple, Herbert and Helen Oliver, 56 Fairmont Blvd., and injured the passengers in the second car, Dwight Tanner and Beatrice Honer, both of Topeka.

### G. Retire

When the church bells strike 12 noon tomorrow, the Rev. Frederick Malabee, who has retired, will walk down the main isle of St. John's for the last time as the church's pastor. He has presided over 542 Sunday services without missing one since he came here more than 10 years ago.

### H. Concert

The community concert of the Philadelphia Symphony Orchestra, which had been scheduled for tomorrow evening at 8 p.m., has been indefinitely postponed because of the sudden illness of the conductor, Mrs. Ellen Klein, secretary of the concert association, said today.

*I. Aspirin*

Although we do not know much about why it works wonders, the most common household medicine, aspirin, has added stroke prevention to its powers, a report by a team of researchers at the Southwestern Community Hospital reported today. One or two aspirin a day is the recommended dosage.

*J. Tax*

Good news for taxpayers: Rep. Harmon C. Connally, of Texas, told members of the local Lions Club at their luncheon today at the Belmont Motel that big federal spending programs will face tough sledding in the money-parched Congress next season.

## *Fix It: Usage*

These sentences and sections from news stories contain various errors in usage. Identify them and rewrite.

1. Friedman was liable to vote against any bills that Haffner favored.
2. Senior captain of the school's math team with hobbies including photography and chemistry, his project involved algebraic number theory and developing different representations for a class of numbers.
3. Aware of the "willingness and ability of pregnant women to continue to serve," the Navy plans to relax its policy governing ship assignments for pregnant female sailors and officers.
4. Cuomo evoked the names of two recent Democratic presidents.
5. He acted to insure that the door was closed.
6. A bill to create a $10 million indemnity fund to back troubled Iowa grain farmers is being pushed by members of the Senate Agriculture Committee. (Lead.)
7. Thanks to his mistake, Potter lost the fight in the last two rounds.

## *You Decide: Gangs*

You are a reporter for a local radio station and learn that the police have arrested four youths, aged 14 and 15. They are charged with a variety of crimes ranging from burglary to weapons possession. The police tell you that they are members of a gang known as the Disciples that has caused considerable trouble in the city. You have the names of those arrested.

Your station has a policy of not using the names of juvenile offenders. But your news director says that a number of newspapers and stations are using the names of gang members. The media contend they have no right to censor the news. Those who keep the names confidential contend this helps the youngsters with their rehabilitation.

What do you recommend the station do?

# 8 Features, Long Stories and Series

Stephan Savoia, *The Associated Press.*
**Happily muddied Woodstockers.**

**Introduction**

• **Features.** Written to entertain. When people are involved, the writer lets the personalities carry the story. People are made to talk, act, and interact.

• **Long story.** Structured to keep the reader committed to staying with the story to the end. Sidebars are used to keep story length within readable bounds.

• **Series.** Written when the subject is too complex for a single story. Each part makes a specific point.

These story types rely for effectiveness on revealing details, meaningful quotes, and incidents that symbolize the thrust of the event or personality.

## Features

### Exercises I

#### A. Opening React

A local merchant, Russell Rothkrug, owner of Russ's Market, which is across the street from the Mallory College campus, calls the city editor with a complaint. The editor turns the call over to you. He says it is a complaint about the new campus grocery store whose opening was recently described in the newspaper. (See Chapter 5, Exercise I, **B. Opening.**)

"No, it's not the story I don't like," says Rothkrug. "It's the college encouraging the kids to compete with private merchants. We have to operate at a profit, but these kids don't have families to support or rent to pay. I think it's unfair."

You ask if his business has been affected.

"Sure it has. Since that store opened 10 days ago, my business has fallen off about 20 percent."

Has he done anything?

"Yeah, I called the provost, Thomas Palmer, and complained, but all he would say is that he would look into it. He wasn't very encouraging."

You check with another merchant near the campus, Aaron Elston, owner of A-1 Shopping Center, and he says that he, too, has been disturbed, but that he has not yet noticed any appreciable downturn.

"Maybe 10 percent. But I am worried what it may be like when word spreads around the campus. They certainly don't have any costs, like hiring a guard here to keep those college kids from stealing everything off the shelves.

"They won't do that to the campus store. Well, maybe they will. Maybe those junior businessmen will learn what it's like to be a small merchant. Oh, the worries and the taxes and the rip-offs and the lousy quality of goods. You know, now that I think of it, I hope they stick around for a while. Those kids who talk so much about how private enterprise is exploitative may learn something.

"Tell that kid running the store I'll be happy to give him the name of my doctor. He has some good stuff for the nerves."

Write a story of 300 words.

## B. Waiter

A Freeport woman, Mrs. Arthur Katzen, telephones the newsroom to say she wants to describe a pleasant experience she had in New York City on a recent trip. She had read a piece in your newspaper about a honeymooning couple whose luggage was stolen by a taxi driver on their arrival in New York. She says:

> I was staying at the Waldorf Astoria this weekend and had breakfast in the Peacock Alley. I left what I thought was a $1 tip. During the day I noticed that I was short of money and couldn't figure out why.
>
> The next morning I went back for breakfast in the Peacock Alley. A waiter came over to me and handed me a $20 bill. He said I'd left it as a tip.
>
> So you see, not everyone there is a thief. He was such a pleasant young man. I gave him a reward of $5 for returning the $20.

Write a brief story.

## C. Santa

It is three days before Christmas and you are sent to Stranger's department store to interview a Santa Claus on his experiences. The Santa Claus is Alfred York, 43, of 15 Templeton Ave., who had been a shipping clerk in a warehouse until last month.

> I got tired of hauling 80-pound crates around and when I saw the ad for a Santa Claus I figured lifting three-year-old kids would be a lot easier.
>
> I have four of my own, a little older now, but I could pick one up with each hand when they were little. I like kids, too. I mean, they give you a fresh way of looking at the world. They are so innocent, most of them, that is. But you can't believe some of them.
>
> They not only want everything they can think of, but they let you know if they don't get it there's going to be hell to pay. The other day I had this kid who whispered in my ear what he wanted, and then said to me, "And if I don't get it, you old bastard, I'm going to kick your ass."
>
> I used to hear that language in the Army. Maybe I hear a couple like that a day. Some of them don't know that their language is unusual. They hear it all day long and they think it's as normal as please and thank you.
>
> I wish all kids could have the innocence of youth that I had. But they grow up with violence, hookers on streetcorners, porno films everywhere. That's progress.
>
> Most of the boys still ask for basketballs, helmets and guns, and the girls want dolls and other feminine things. I guess liberation hasn't seeped down to the younger generation.

York is 6′2″, weighs 195, needs a little padding around the stomach. He sits in a high chair in the toy department on the third floor and usually has a line of four or five children waiting to talk to him. Each child is given a minute or two. He continues:

> Most of them are decent kids. If their parents could hear what they ask for they might be ashamed of themselves—some for pampering the heck out of their children and spoiling them, some for having such narrow goals for themselves and their children. Many of these kids just want love, and they'll ask me if I can tell their parents to be kind to them. One little boy said to me, "Santa, I want peace and love for everyone, that's all I want."

Write a story of 300 words.

## D. Astrology

Albert Sherman, professor of physics at Mallory College, is a speaker at the luncheon of the annual meeting of the college science club. As the newspaper's science reporter, you decide to attend because the topic sounds intriguing: "Astrology Is Bunk."

Here are some of your notes. Write a 250 to 300 word story for today's newspaper.

> Astrology has millions of followers in this country. Generally, no harm is done by it. Reading the daily charts in the newspapers is as harmless as following Dick Tracy or Peanuts.
>
> But some people do take astrology seriously. They make business decisions, marry and mate on the principles of the solar stirrings as interpreted by the astrologer. . . .
>
> Astrologers defend their field vigorously, but it is really quasi-scientific occultism. They talk about scientific research, but they pay only lip service to the search for scientific validation of evidence. . . .
>
> What distinguishes science from pseudoscience is its method. Some of these principles are:
>
> Falsibility—if the hypothesis is not true, you will get a negative result.

Replicability—different researchers will derive the same results.

Intersubjective verifiability—agreement between the advocate and his critic on the standards for verifying claims.

Astrology does not subject itself to these tests.

Finally, one of the simplest tests we use in science is a logical principle known as Occam's Razor. This says that when given two equally satisfactory explanations of an event, you take the simplest.

Incidentally, students ought to think of that when they do their own research. Nature is not complex. It loves order and simplicity.

But in the case of the astrologers, their work is a complex of signs, conjunctions and couplings whose interpretations no one agrees on.

Divining the fate and future of human beings from the positions of the stars and other heavenly bodies is ancient man's way of understanding the universe, not modern man's way.

### *E. No Baby*

You are looking at some old clips and your eye catches a story about Baby, an African elephant in the local zoo whose pregnancy was reported by the zoo director, Cyrus Tucek, five months ago. You wonder how Baby is faring and you call the zoo.

Tucek is not there but his assistant, Bayard Parker, fills you in with a few words.

"She isn't," he tells you.

"Isn't what?" you ask.

"Pregnant," he replies.

"What happened?" you ask.

"False pregnancy, I guess," he says.

Sensing that Parker is a man of few words, but hoping to draw him out, you say you never heard of such a thing.

"Well, you have now," he says.

"How's she doing generally?" you ask.

"OK."

"When did you find out about Baby's false pregnancy?"

"Two days ago."

"When will Mr. Tucek be back?"

"Two weeks."

You decide you can't wait that long. Anyway, you see that you have the basic information, and you decide to write a short.

## *Assignments I*

### *A. IRS*

The FBI says that most threats and almost half of all assaults on federal workers are directed at employees of the Internal Revenue Service. Interview an IRS worker and find out what his or her life is like. 350 words.

### *B. Pets*

Write a short feature on one of these topics:

1. What are some of the pets students keep on campus? Are there restrictions?

2. Snakes and monkeys are supposedly bad risks for those seeking exotic pets. Why? What are the best bets for someone who wants an offbeat pet at home?

3. Breeds of dogs ebb and flow in popularity. Cocker spaniels were the favorites a couple of decades ago and then German shepherds, poodles and a variety of small dogs. What's the latest favorite? How expensive are these animals?

4. Is raising saltwater fish in the home aquarium as expensive and difficult as it once was? How popular is this hobby?

5. The lure of the cat, to some, is that it is mysterious. Unlike dogs, cats usually cannot be trained. Is this why people keep cats? Interview cat lovers.

6. Do people keep birds as pets? Canaries used to be popular but are no longer. Why? Can exotic birds be kept in the average home?

*C. Lunch Box*

What do manual workers eat for lunch? Go to construction sites where workers take lunch boxes and see what is inside. Write 300 words.

*D. Dining*

A third to a half of all meals are supposedly eaten outside the home. Interview family heads and single people about their dining habits. Why do they prefer to eat out? Write 350 words.

*E. Genealogy*

Interview local genealogists who help people do the research that enables them to find their roots.

*F. Portrait*

Write profiles of no more than 350 words on the following people:

1. A couple recently celebrating their 50th wedding anniversary.
2. A person born on February 29.
3. A fry cook at a fast food outlet.
4. A maid in a local motel.
5. A rookie police officer. The police officer with the longest service record. An officer who works with juvenile offenders, with rape victims.
6. A disc jockey on an all-night radio program.
7. The winner of an award for academic achievement: National Merit Scholar, Westinghouse prize, Phi Beta Kappa, etc.
8. An athlete recruited from a distant city or country.
9. The night clerk in a local hotel or motel.
10. A faculty member recently returned from a trip abroad.

*G. Holiday*

Write a precede with as much local material as possible on one of these holidays: New Year's Day, Chinese New Year, Lincoln's Birthday, St. Valentine's Day, Washington's Birthday, Ash Wednesday, Purim, St. Patrick's Day, Palm Sunday, first day of Passover, Good Friday, Easter, May Day, Memorial Day, Pentecost, Flag Day, Independence Day, Labor Day, Martin Luther King's Birthday, first day of Rosh Hashana, Yom Kippur, Columbus Day, Halloween, All Saints' Day, Veterans Day, Thanksgiving, first Sunday of Advent, first day of Hanukkah, Christmas.

Also, check your local ethnic, religious and racial groups for any special observances, parades, services. Write 300 to 350 words.

## Long Stories and Series

### Exercises II

*A. Museum*

You are sent to interview Thomas Chamberlain, who has recently joined the staff of the Chicago Art Institute as an assistant to the director. He is visiting colleges and universities around the country to learn about new techniques in the management of art museums. He is 29, has graduate degrees (M.A. and Ph.D.) from Brown University and his B.A. from the University of New Mexico. He was born in Grand Junction, Colo., is married, has no children.

Your editor wants a piece for the Sunday Leisure section on his opinions about museums. Chamberlain has been abroad on a study tour of museums and is just about finished with his U.S. tour, the editor says, and should have strong opinions about art. You interview him and you find he does have such opinions. Here are some quotes:

One of the key questions in art museum work today is whether to maintain the museum for the discerning person or to reach out to the masses. That may be a crude way to put it, but if you go to some museums you will see what I mean. In some, children are everywhere. Hordes of them. Sitting, bored out of their skulls, in front of a Rembrandt while some poor soul lectures these seven-year-olds on his use of somber colors.

The art student, or the person who wants to look at the genius of a Rembrandt that day, simply hasn't a chance to contemplate the work. Nor can he or she find quiet refuge anywhere in the museum most days.

But let's look at the other side. Museums are public institutions—many of them anyway. People are entitled to make use of what their money is paying for. More important, isn't the function of art in a democracy to uplift people, to take them from their daily pursuits of money, prestige, power, material possessions and the like?

Why shouldn't Rembrandt be for them? Why shouldn't his genius, his incredible humanity reach all of us? That outreach was the belief of Thomas Hoving at the Met in New York, and it was one of the many reasons for his stormy tenure there.

Ah, but that's only the beginning, and you people are going to have to face the problem here when your local art museum board or curator or director makes policy. By emphasizing the museum as "art accessible to all," do you take a small but definite step toward the majority culture of entertainment? Do you start to entice the crowds in with tricks; do you spiffy up the exhibits; do you somehow make your artists "relevant"?

Is there something to be said for high culture, that it should be kept from popular culture's lowering hand? Everything today in art and culture has become marketable, even the museum. The bottom line is all-important. Move in that direction in high art and it becomes lowbrow.

You interrupt Chamberlain and ask him what his own feelings are about the subject. Should the local art museum—any art museum, for that matter—be administered for those who seek education, inspiration, edification or should it consciously reach out with programs, tours for children, large-scale exhibits and the like?

What worries me is that when you reach out for the many you end up with a leveling process, and although the low may come up, the high goes down. Exhibits are geared for the person who has never heard a Mozart quintet or seen an El Greco. I know this sounds old-fashioned, even undemocratic. I like what Robert Brustein, the theater critic, says about how the traditional lines between culture and show business broke down. "Something happened in the Fifties," Brustein says, "something symbolized by the marriage of Arthur Miller and Marilyn Monroe. . . . "

Everyone wants culture with a capital C delivered in easy and digestible bites. Well, why not put the "Polish Rider" on the back of a cereal box? Or have a Renoir doll in every nursery? That doll would really sell, and it would take culture into every little girl's playroom.

Great works of art should not be inaccessible to people. But they cannot be mass marketed with the idea that they are as easily reached as some situation comedy on television. Hard work is involved in reaching out to the artist. Effort that makes the understanding all the more enjoyable. It's not that hard to understand.

Read *The Great Gatsby* or *Wuthering Heights* slowly. The language, the emotion open up to you. You cannot get it on television or in the movies—not the splendor of the creation, the beauty of the language and the depth of meaning. Those books are to be read, reread, to have people stop in the middle of a paragraph and look up and wonder. The same with art. You should certainly have all the guidance and help you need to meet the artist on his terms. But finally, it's as they say in football—or is it basketball?—it's one on one. You and the artist. And the museum should make that confrontation possible.

Use the schools, use the lecture halls for education in art. But keep museums for those confronting the artist's work.

Write 750 to 900 words. Include background from research and interviews with members of the fine arts department, museum specialists.

## *Assignments II*

### *A. Diseases*

Draw or obtain a map of your city by health district. Chart changes in each district by cause of death for the past year, the year before and appropriate other years. Can you find any correlations between income and the mortality rates? Any other correlations? Pay special attention to infant mortality and to deaths from pneumonia and influenza, AIDS, drugs, diabetes, tuberculosis, cirrhosis of the liver, homicide. These usually are associated with socioeconomic factors. Write a long piece or plan a series.

## B. Catholic

Interest in the papacy and the changes in the Roman Catholic Church have grown since the pontificate of John XXIII in 1958. A historian, J.M. Cameron, said in *The New York Review of Books* in 1979:

> Papal authority is today scrutinized in a new way. The authority of authorities is less compelling and less evidently justifiable than it used to be . . . that particular authorities stand in need of justification, that no claims on their part are to be taken as self-justifying, as we might think the authority of a musician or an actor is justified in the performance, these things are accepted, even by theologians.
>
> In the past 15 years Roman Catholic theologians have become increasingly nervous over their performances, especially where the question of authority has been touched upon. . . .

Since the pontificate of John Paul II in 1978, some observers of the church see a countermovement to preserve the power of the church with its own followers and in countries that have enacted laws that directly violate some of the church's sacrosanct teachings. They saw John Paul II as a conservative force, unyielding in the face of liberalizing efforts by U.S. and western European bishops. His refusal to recognize the state of Israel—church policy for more than 15 years—and his welcome to Austrian President Kurt Waldheim, a former Nazi whom many nations shunned, were seen as impediments to ecumenism.

Some say the church's turn away from Vatican II and toward more conservative values, a turn away from what some describe as the American virtues of democracy and pluralism, a toleration of differences, began in 1968 with the encyclical *Humanae Vitae*. In it, Pope Paul VI solemnly reaffirmed the church's condemnation of "artificial birth control." This, said many outside the church and some liberals inside it, was an historic mistake.

Bob Thayer, *The Journal–Bulletin*.

**Religious news interests readers.**

As the critics of the encyclical predicted, in Europe and North America the prohibition is ignored. Birth rates reveal that Catholics use contraception as frequently as non-Catholics.

This rejection, say students of the church, also indicates a rejection of the authority of the papacy and it has weakened the doctrine of papal infallibility. (The doctrine is relatively new in the church's history; it was issued by the First Vatican Council in 1870.)

One church observer, James Carroll, a former Paulist priest, says, "The increased willingness of Catholics to trust their own consciences, even in grave violation of official teaching, represents the long overdue beginning of a new era in the life of the church, one that builds on earlier, unrealized impulses. . . ."

John Miller, a British neurologist who was a member of the Papal Commission on Birth Control of Pope John XXIII, said that around 85 percent of Catholics use some form of artificial birth control and do not think it is morally wrong to do so. He argues that this high number of practicing Catholics who do not abide by the church's instructions leads to questions by Catholics about the church's credibility on larger matters of faith.

But Pope John Paul II has not retreated from his strong position on many social issues, particularly on abortion.

In his encyclical *Evangelium Vitae* in 1995, the pope called on Catholics to resist laws that violate the "original inalienable right to life." He said that despite legislation that permits abortion and euthanasia, there is "no obligation in conscience to obey such laws. Instead, there is a grave and clear obligation to oppose them by conscientious objection."

He warned of a "profound crisis of culture" that is the result of exalting individual freedom at the expense of personal responsibility. This freedom has created, the pope said, "a veritable structure of sin."

For women who have had abortions, the pope offered hope for redemption: "The wound in your heart may not yet have healed. Certainly what happened was and remains terribly wrong. But do not give into discouragement and do not lose hope."

The pope's message was offered at a time, the Vatican reported, that 40 million abortions are performed around the world each year. An aide commented, "This is a pope who wants to say 'no' to aspects of what is known as modernity. It doesn't upset him in the least to be against society."

To remove legal protection from life at any stage, even by majority vote, the pope wrote, introduces moral relativism that undermines democracy.

Conor Cruise O'Brien, a former U.N. official and international commentator, wrote in his book *Passion and Cunning and Other Essays* that John Paul's purpose is to rehabilitate the doctrinal authority of the papacy and revert to pre-Vatican II moral dogma. Although in public the pope appears to endorse Vatican II, O'Brien concludes, he is in reality reasserting the conservative doctrines of Vatican I.

For a long Sunday feature or a two- or three-part series, write about the changes in the Roman Catholic Church and the direction in which it seems headed in the areas of doctrine, the celibate clergy, women priests, abortion, birth control and other issues. Use local and campus authorities and consult reference works and databases for background.

## *Campus Project*

### *Educated*

What are the most important books ever written? Interview members of the faculty, department heads, deans and distinguished professors for a list of books that they think a person must have read before he or she can be described as an educated person.

Compile a list of no more than 10 of the most frequently mentioned books and then visit the college library and the local public library to see whether they are available and how frequently they circulate.

You might ask your sources about the latest additions to their lists.

Finally, survey students and try to determine how many of the books they have read.

This can be a two-part series: (1) the list of books and (2) the students' reading.

## *Community Project*

### *Schoolhouse*

What is this generation of primary-grade schoolchildren being taught? Go into classrooms in the community to find out whether there are new techniques in teaching reading, writing and arithmetic. Are pupils being taught how to work computers? Are they made aware of pollution and other threats to the environment and of the dangers of drugs, smoking, alcohol and AIDS?

What is unchanged from their parents' and grandparents' days?

## *Home Assignment*

### *Writer*

Select a writer whose work you enjoy and admire. Give some reasons for your preference. Guides to good writing include accuracy of description; clarity of expression; conviction through simple and forceful language; use of illustrations, examples and human interest; appropriateness of language, a style befitting the nature of the event. You can choose a novelist, poet, playwright, short story writer or author of nonfiction. Can you apply some of the author's techniques to journalism? Discuss.

## *Class Discussion*

### *Top Five*

In every reporter's experience there are stories that should be covered but somehow never are. Most of the time, the stories go unreported because there is insufficient time to dig into them. For a class project, select three to five subjects, on or off campus, that should be but have not been covered. How would you turn the ideas into journalism? Why did you select these stories? Your story ideas should be added to those of the other students, and then the list should be reduced to five stories. You can select one of the five to write, or the whole class can decide on which one has the highest priority and do that one. Write 750 words.

## DB/CAR

### Offenders

Write a long piece or a two-part series on new programs for lawbreakers. As a means of coping with the overcrowding of jails and prisons, cities and states have adopted tactics for keeping some types of criminals under control but outside of incarceration. Imaginative programs have been adopted to cut down on the heavy costs of imprisonment—estimated at $45,000 a year per convict.

A survey by the National Council on Crime and Delinquency found that 80 percent of those in prison are guilty of low-level offenses: minor parole violations, property crime, drug and public disorder offenses. Critics of the penal system call the imprisonment of these people "warehousing," and they say the cost is half the $16 billion a year spent on prison and jail inmates.

Has your city adopted any innovative programs? See how your city's and state's conviction rates have changed with the years and also see how costs have risen.

Check references and/or make a database search to find out what is happening around the country. Are any of these solutions applicable to your city and state?

## Fix It: Who-Whom

If incorrect, change and explain.

1. The painting on the album cover is a kind of statement, showing a fiddler who she sees as being his own man.
2. Who do you call to fix your satellite dish?
3. Archbishop Whealon, whom an aide said was not available for further comment yesterday, did not say in his column whether he planned to join the Republican Party.
4. Investigators have also ruled out any involvement by three local law enforcement officials who the Brawley family and its advisers have repeatedly implicated.

## Test I: Spelling

In each of the three-word sets below, choose the word that is NOT spelled correctly. Note that "all correct" or "all wrong" are also options.

1. (a) fiery   (b) judgement   (c) exceed   (d) all correct   (e) all wrong
2. (a) desireable   (b) recieve   (c) truely   (d) all correct   (e) all wrong
3. (a) siege   (b) sheik   (c) disappearance   (d) all correct   (e) all wrong
4. (a) cemetery   (b) calendar   (c) valuable   (d) all correct   (e) all wrong
5. (a) describe   (b) proffession   (c) awkward   (d) all correct   (e) all wrong
6. (a) alot   (b) rythm   (c) marvellous   (d) all correct   (e) all wrong
7. (a) category   (b) picnicking   (c) forty   (d) all correct   (e) all wrong
8. (a) liesure   (b) usable   (c) assassin   (d) all correct   (e) all wrong
9. (a) religious   (b) pursue   (c) dilemna   (d) all correct   (e) all wrong
10. (a) harrass   (b) Fahrenheit   (c) tomatoes   (d) all correct   (e) all wrong
11. (a) suprise   (b) analysis   (c) sheriff   (d) all correct   (e) all wrong
12. (a) souvenir   (b) beginner   (c) bureaucrat   (d) all correct   (e) all wrong
13. (a) yeild   (b) committed   (c) attendance   (d) all correct   (e) all wrong
14. (a) support   (b) connoisseur   (c) fulfill   (d) all correct   (e) all wrong
15. (a) acknowledgement   (b) developement   (c) advertising   (d) all correct   (e) all wrong

# 9 Broadcast Writing

Who's interviewing whom here?

## Introduction

Broadcast copy is written for comprehension at its first and only hearing. To accomplish this, the writer uses simple language and short sentences that consist of a single idea and conform to the subject-verb-object structure. The present tense is used whenever possible to give the listener a sense of the immediacy of the report. Action verbs are preferred, adjectives and adverbs avoided. Attribution is placed at the beginning of the sentence so the listener knows the source of the information. The active voice is preferred to the passive. For complex stories, introductory phrases and sentences may be used.

## Exercises I

Rewrite for radio the following stories taken from the news wires of the AP and UPI. Keep the copy under 100 words.

### A. Solitary

SAGINAW, Mich. (AP)—Unruly students will again be placed in solitary confinement, in a decision by the Carrollton School District that is being protested by some parents and a school board member.

Under the program, names of students who misbehave are written on a chalkboard. After the fourth incident, students may be confined to one of three rooms—one 9 by 12 feet and two others 6 by 9 feet—for a six-and-a-half-hour school day, with two restroom breaks and with lunch brought in.

David Pawley, a high school principal, said 21 of the school's 486 students had gone into solitary confinement since the policy went into effect at the beginning of the school year. The infractions covered by the policy include talking out of turn, walking around the classroom without permission and forgetting books for class.

The policy was scrapped last month after several parents complained. But the school board, in a 6-1 vote Monday, decided to reinstate it.

### B. Edison

NEW YORK (AP)—In a ruling that could affect scores of other cases, a civil jury in the Bronx has found Consolidated Edison Co. guilty of gross negligence in connection with last year's city blackout.

The jury of one woman and five men returned a damage award of $40,500 to a chain of supermarkets Wednesday after deliberating three hours following an eight-day trial in state Supreme Court.

Con Edison, which had won all other blackout damage decisions in higher courts, said it would immediately appeal the decision.

The latest ruling differs from earlier ones in that it is the first involving a commercial establishment and also in that a different section of the law was argued in this case.

The award went to Pageant Food Co., Inc., a chain of seven supermarkets. The company had sought $75,000, alleging spoilage and loss of business due to the blackout, which darkened the city for more than 24 hours in July.

In what had been considered the most significant ruling on the matter to date, a three-judge appeals panel found last December that Con Edison could not be held liable for damages incurred by residential customers during the blackout.

The judges threw out seven damage awards ranging from $45 to $972 that had been granted by a lower court.

The judges noted in that ruling that the lower court judge had incorrectly overruled a state Public Service Commission regulation that exempts Con Edison from ordinary negligence claims.

But the appeals panel ruled that Con Edison could be found liable if gross negligence was demonstrated.

A Bronx jury found the utility guilty of gross negligence following the trial.

Con Edison spokesman Irv Levine said the company was confident the state exemption clause would be upheld in this case on appeal, as it has been on the previous occasions involving residential customers.

In the case of a finding of gross negligence, Con Edison claims its tariff exempts damage claims when service is interrupted "from causes beyond its control."

Scores of other cases against Con Edison are pending in state Supreme Court throughout the city and parts of Westchester County. The only action thus far on those suits has been the denial of class-action status for them, thereby forcing individual firms to file their own suits.

—AP-NY-05-09 23:20 EDT

## C. Twins

CINCINNATI (UPI)—On Aug. 19, 1939, a 14-year-old unwed girl gave birth to identical twin boys in Piqua, Ohio.

A few weeks later, the twins were put up for adoption and taken in by different families—the Ernest Springer family in Piqua, and the Jess Lewis family in Lima, Ohio, 45 miles away.

Apparently through bureaucratic misinformation, neither family knew at the time that their adopted son had a twin brother.

About a year later, the Lewis family discovered through final adoption papers their adopted son had a twin, but they couldn't find out who had adopted him.

So, the twins grew up in different homes 45 miles away, not knowing the other, and went on to lead separate adult lives.

But the Lewis twin, who learned from his adoptive family that he had a brother, kept searching for his look-alike.

Finally, 50 years after birth, he found probate court records that led him to his brother, now living in Dayton, Ohio.

When the twins got together, they discovered some amazing coincidences about their separate lives.

The Springer family named their adopted son "Jim." The Lewis family named their adopted son "Jim."

Both boys had had pet dogs. Both named their dogs "Toy."

After school, both took law enforcement training. Both enjoyed similar hobbies: blueprinting, drafting and carpentry.

Jim Lewis had been married three times, Jim Springer twice. Both their first wives were named "Linda." Both their second wives were named "Betty." Both named their first sons "James Allan."

University of Minnesota researchers who specialize in studying twins recently examined the two for a week to study similarities and differences in twins who had grown up separately. Similarities were the rule.

"They found out that our brainwaves and heartbeat patterns are the same," Springer said. "Our handwriting is similar. We have virtually identical fingerprints. Our eye and ear structures are exactly the same, which is the real test of twins.

"And," he added, "the results of all the tests we took looked like one person had taken the same tests twice."

—UPI 05-10 01:09 AED

## D. Hoofer

NEW YORK (AP)—A horse and a taxicab tried to negotiate the same Manhattan corner at the same time early today and the horse lost.

The horse pulling a hansom cab was about to turn left from Seventh Avenue onto 52nd Street when the taxi, making the same turn, cut the horse off, leaving the high stepper's right front hoof stuck fast in the taxi's rear bumper, police said.

A fire rescue unit came and extricated the horse, who stood patiently by, according to John Driscoll of the rescue company. "He was a good horse," said Driscoll, who didn't get the horse's name.

Police didn't have it either, or the name of the cab and hansom drivers. It was just one of those unusual street occurrences, they said.

The horse did sustain a bad cut just above his hoof, but not bad enough to warrant a horse ambulance, Driscoll said.

The rescue team bandaged him up "just like a human" and sent him on his way.

"He just drove—or I should say rode—off into the sunset," Driscoll said.

—AP-NY-05-10 05:16 EDT

## E. Lakes

ORLANDO, Fla. (AP)—The 82 lakes that give Orlando its picture-card look will die without the infusion of millions of dollars and stringent drainage and pollution-control ordinances, a consulting group says.

The lakes, which get their water from rainfall and runoff, are victims of pollution washed from the city's growing expanse of roofs, driveways, parking lots and streets, according to a report released this week by the firm of Dyer, Riddle, Mills & Precourt.

Every lake in Orlando "has been degraded by storm-water and other pollutants to the extent that favorable conditions exist for excessive aquatic weed growth, large-scale algae blooms, possible fish kills and loss of recreational use," the report said.

## Exercises II

Here are some news stories that are to be tightened up for an evening television newscast. Give each tell story 20 seconds.

### A. Heart

CHICAGO (UPI)—Some smokers think that after they have been diagnosed with heart disease, it's too late to give up the cigarettes that caused their disease.

"It's never too late," counters Dr. Ronald Vliestra, author of a study published today in a special anti-smoking issue of the Journal of the American Medical Association.

Vliestra, a cardiologist with the Mayo Clinic, reported that heart disease patients who refuse to quit smoking are nearly twice as likely to die of heart attacks as those who kick the habit. He said the study should have a major impact on how much emphasis physicians place on quitting smoking as part of the treatment of heart disease.

"The issue for physicians is made a lot more clear," he said in a telephone interview. "This is in contrast to the situation with lung cancer, where once the cancer which is related to the cigarette smoking has been caused, it's too late to give up (smoking). The same is not true for coronary heart disease—it's not too late."

Vliestra and his colleagues at the University of Washington in Seattle studied the smoking behavior and survival of 4,165 smokers who had been diagnosed as having coronary heart disease, a blockage of arteries to the heart.

The five-year survival rate for the 1,490 patients who quit smoking was 85 percent, compared to a 78 percent survival rate for smokers. Patients who never smoked had an 87 percent survival rate.

The difference in mortality was almost entirely attributable to differences in the heart attack rates between the two groups, the researchers said, with 7.9 percent of the smokers dying from heart attacks compared to only 4.4 percent of the quitters.

But despite this finding and earlier similar studies, 57 percent of the smokers in the study continued to smoke even after being diagnosed with heart disease.

"A consistently effective method of enabling patients with coronary artery disease to quit smoking would have a major impact on health care," the researchers concluded.

### B. Cyanide

NASHVILLE, Tenn.—Tests revealed cyanide in a Tylenol capsule found near the body of a man who died from the poison, but the cyanide was different than the kind that killed a New York woman this month, officials said today.

"Nothing was found that indicates any connection between the Nashville death and that of Diane Elsroth," who died Feb. 8 after swallowing a cyanide-laced Tylenol, Food and Drug Administration commissioner Frank E. Young said.

Young said the FDA's Cincinnati lab had determined that the lone Extra-Strength Tylenol capsule found Sunday under the deathbed of Timothy Green, 32, contained 91 percent sodium cyanide.

"This is a different kind of cyanide from the potassium cyanide found in the capsules associated" with Elsroth's death or the deaths of seven people in the Chicago area in 1982, he said.

Young also said the cyanide in the Nashville capsule is different from any used in the laboratories of Johnson & Johnson, manufacturer of Tylenol, and that the FDA has "no evidence that this is not an isolated incident."

The capsule and a Tylenol container were found Sunday under the bed where Green's body lay. The FDA tested the capsule, and the container was released to the FBI and sent to Washington for analysis.

Green, a bachelor who moved to Nashville about a year ago to become a songwriter and join a Jehovah's Witness congregation, was poisoned by cyanide. Police said they don't know if his death was suicide, murder or an accident.

Medical Examiner Charles Harlan said Green ingested 20 times a lethal dose of cyanide, and an autopsy found no evidence of the active ingredient in Extra-Strength Tylenol—acetaminophen—in Green's body.

That could mean Green "did not take a Tylenol, or the Tylenol could have been removed from the capsule and replaced with cyanide," Harlan said.

Green had been dead for four or five days, police said.

### C. Children

HOFFMAN ESTATES, Ill. (AP)—Six of ten children in a family for whom police had started a Christmas collection died in a fire that engulfed their home in this Chicago suburb, authorities said Sunday.

A teen-age brother of the victims escaped the blaze and had to be restrained by firefighters when he tried to re-enter the house to help his brother and sisters.

In Southfield, Mich., a brief, smoky fire killed six elderly residents of a hospice and rehabilitation center Sunday and forced the evacuation of about 30 people, some of them bedridden, according to authorities in that Detroit suburb.

The house here was engulfed in flames and smoke when firefighters and police arrived late Saturday, police Sgt. Robert Syre said.

"From what I understand, when they got there, the heat was so intense that they couldn't do anything and everything just started to break apart," he said. "This is the worst fire in our history. I've been here 15 years and I would have heard of something worse."

"There was fire coming out of the living room window. Smoke was coming out of everywhere," said neighbor Charles Durec.

The victims, five sisters and a brother ranging in age from 8 to 15, were among 10 children living in the home with their divorced mother, Patricia Krawczyk, who had recently suffered a heart attack, Syre said.

"They were having a hard time. You know how it is with 10 kids," Syre said. Officers in the police department, where one of the Krawczyk youngsters had worked for two summers, had recently begun a Christmas collection for the family.

The mother and three children were not home at the time of the blaze, police and a neighbor said.

The eldest son, Kevin, 18, was awakened by a smoke detector and yelled "Fire!" then kicked his way out a window to escape, Syre said. Police had to restrain him from trying to get back into the burning house, he said.

"They were good kids," said Durec, who added that the family had lived in the house for about six years.

Syre said it appeared the blaze may have started near a fireplace adjacent to a garage. He said it had not been determined if the fireplace had been used in Saturday night's freezing temperatures.

### D. Sting

WASHINGTON (AP)—Using free Washington Redskins tickets as bait, authorities arrested 100 fugitives who showed up Sunday at a pregame brunch where police and federal marshals posed as waiters and served warrants.

U.S. marshals called it the largest mass arrest of fugitives in recent memory.

"It was like an assembly line," said Herbert M. Rutherford III, U.S. marshal for the District of Columbia. "It was party time, and they fell for it, hook, line and sinker."

"This ain't fair, this just ain't fair," said one prisoner who was led in handcuffs from one of two large buses that carried the prisoners to a local jail.

"They said they was takin' us to a football game, and that's wrong," said another man. "That's false advertising."

"I came to see Boomer, I came to see Boomer," said a third, referring to New York Jets quarterback Boomer Esiason.

U.S. marshals, working with the Metropolitan Police Department, sent out invitations to 3,000 wanted persons. The invitations said that as a promotion for a new sports television station, Flagship International Sports Television, they were winners of two free tickets to the National Football League game Sunday between the Redskins and the Bengals.

The invitation said 10 of the "lucky winners" would receive season tickets to the Redskins' games and that a grand prize drawing would be held for an all-expenses paid trip to the upcoming Super Bowl XX in New Orleans.

The initials for the TV enterprise, F.I.S.T., also stand for the Fugitive Investigative Strike Team, a special U.S. Marshals force.

About 100 fugitives responded to the invitation and appeared at the D.C. Convention Center for the special brunch. The building was decorated with signs saying, "Let's party" and "Let's all be there."

Some of the fugitives showed up wearing the bright burgundy and gold wool Redskins hats as well as Redskins buttons, while others were attired in suits and ties for the pregame feast.

One marshal was dressed in a large yellow chicken suit with oversized red boots while another turned up as an Indian chief complete with large headdress.

Other marshals wearing tuxedos handed small name stickers to each of the fugitives.

Buses that were to take them to the game, however, took them to the police department's central cellblock several blocks away instead.

"When we verified their identity, we escorted them in small groups to a party room, where officers moved in from concealed positions and placed them under arrest," said Stanley Morris, head of the U.S. Marshals Service.

The sting netted 100 fugitives by 11 a.m., marshals said.

Arrested were two people wanted for murder, five for robbery, 15 for assault, six for burglary, 19 for bond or bail violations, 18 for narcotics violations, officials said. Others were arrested on charges of rape, arson and forgery. Two of those arrested were on the D.C. police department's 10 most wanted list.

A similar scam in Hartford, Conn., last November invited people to attend a luncheon with pop singer Boy George. Fifteen were picked up by a limousine and arrested. Marshals said they used job offers as the bait to arrest about 90 people in Brooklyn last year.

"Redskin tickets are valuable. And when you're trying to get a person, you play on their greed," said Toby Roche, chief deputy U.S. marshal for Washington, who coordinated the operation.

The cost of the project was estimated to be $22,100, or about $225 dollars per arrest.

One man who got into the Convention Center before apparently being spooked by the circumstances was arrested on the street, still wearing his "Hello, my name is . . ." sticker.

## Assignments

### A. Hope

Prepare a feature of at least three minutes on the dreams and aspirations of children in grade school. Obtain permission to interview in school, or seek out youngsters after class. Talk to them without their parents or other adults listening in, and try to conduct your interviews one-on-one, not in a group of youngsters. Discuss their plans for school, jobs, marriage, family. Let them take the interview where they will.

### B. Parents

Prepare a companion feature to *A. Hope* by interviewing parents of grade-school children on the same subjects. Do they believe their children will have the opportunities children require to develop their dreams and aspirations? If not, what are the obstacles?

### C. Ceremonial

Many groups celebrate important stages in a person's life, from birth to death. Christians have baptismal celebrations, and Jewish boys are circumcised in a ceremony shortly after birth known as the *bris*. Confirmation is an important occasion in the lives of Catholic boys and girls.

The passage to adulthood for Mexican girls, which is celebrated with lavish parties in many Mexican-American communities, is known as the *quinceañera*. Navajo, Apache and other Native American tribes also celebrate the beginning of adult life.

Among Jews, the bar and bat mitzvah mark the beginning of religious duty and responsibility.

Do a feature on one of these celebrations or another that occurs in your community.

Sweet 16 parties are common, and in some cities there are lavish coming-out parties for young women described as *debutantes*.

Later in life, couples who have been married for 50 years sometimes ask a priest to conduct another church wedding ceremony.

Do a feature on one of these celebrations or on another that occurs in your community.

Betty Tichich, *Houston Chronicle*.

**Enjoying the quinceañera cake.**

## Campus Projects

### A. Ivory Tower

An article in *The New York Times* about college students says, "Students used to leave behind the world of television when they went to college. Twenty years ago, TV sets tended to be found in dormitory lounges and fraternity and sorority houses, not so much in individual rooms. Now televisions are nearly as common as stereos. . . ."

The article quotes Todd Gitlin, professor of sociology at the University of California at Berkeley: "It's as if they're carrying their pews with them. They've always watched 'L.A. Law.' They can't imagine a world without it. . . ."

Some college living quarters are wired for cable. The University of Southern California has cable in all student apartments and dormitories.

Gitlin doesn't think this is all for the good, but a USC official says the university has not seen a drop in grade-point averages despite the increased use of TV.

    1. What do students take to their campus housing from home: TV, microwave, VCR, tape deck? How has this changed over the years?
    2. Survey TV viewing: hours of viewing, daytime, evening; favorite programs.
    3. Interview local faculty members and administrators on the effect of student TV viewing.

You are to gather the material for a radio or television documentary or a series of three- to five-minute broadcasts.

*B. Population*

A national organization, Zero Population Growth, has initiated a campaign to urge "lawmakers to make a contract with future generations by adopting measures that encourage a sustainable balance of people, resources and the environment." It predicts that, unless efforts are made to curb world population growth, today's population of 5.7 billion could become 19.2 billion at the end of the next century. The group urges:

- Universal access to a full range of reproductive health care services.
- Stronger environmental protection and an end to government subsidies that promote wasteful consumption.
- U.S. policies that reduce global migration pressures.
- A comprehensive and compassionate national adolescent pregnancy prevention program.
- Education, employment and training to improve women's status.
- School-based programs that raise awareness of population and environmental issues.
- Increased funding for international population and sustainable development programs.

Interview authorities on the campus to find out what they think of the goals of the campaign, how feasible population control is politically, who the proponents and opponents of the campaign would be.

## Community Project

### At Risk

A study by the Centers for Disease Control and Prevention found "a substantial proportion of students engage in behaviors that place them at risk for HIV infection." By their senior year, 29 percent of high school seniors have had four or more sex partners, and less than half of the students are protecting themselves against AIDS and other sexually transmitted diseases, the CDC reported.

In fact, says the federal agency, condom use falls off as students advance in high school.

"The best way to explain it to kids is that it's like playing Russian roulette and not knowing how many live bullets are in the chambers," says Dr. Lloyd Kolbe, director of the CDC's Division of Adolescent and School Health. "If you pull the trigger once it can cause you to become infected."

Male high school students are more likely than female students to be sexually active, 27 percent to 12 percent. By age 19, 54 percent of females have experienced sexual intercourse. A similar study 20 years ago among females 15 to 19 found 29 percent had engaged in sexual intercourse.

The New Jersey Governor's Advisory Council on AIDS recommended that condoms be made available to all students beginning in the ninth grade. It also recommended that a sexual education program be statewide and mandatory. "H.I.V./AIDS education should *not* be left entirely up to local school boards," the Council stated. For a documentary or a series of programs, gather information locally on AIDS education programs and blend this in with any data you gather about sexual activities of high school students.

## Home Assignment

### Choices

Select three *Workbook* exercises that you have written in newspaper style. Rewrite for radio, giving no more than 100 words to each item. Compare the two versions: Are all the facts given in the broadcast account? What was eliminated and why? Is there some validity to the observation that broadcast news is a headline service?

## Class Discussion

### A. Time

Time each item on a half-hour evening TV newscast. Make a log of subject matter, the placement of items in the newscast and the amount of time given each item.

Then compare the space given these items in the next day's newspaper.

Also, compare the play in the newspaper with the placement on the TV newscast. Was the lead item on the newscast given major play by the newspaper?

With whose decisions on time-space and play do you find you agree? Why?

### B. Wasteland Revisited

Here are excerpts from an article by Newton Minow, who as chairman of the Federal Communications Commission in the early '60s described television as a "vast wasteland." This article, "How Vast the Wasteland Now?," was written 30 years after he made that assessment:

> One evening as I watched, with my remote control in hand, I flipped through the channels and saw a man loading his gun on one channel, a different man aiming a gun on a second, and another man shooting a gun on a third. And if you don't believe me, try it yourself. I think the most troubling change over the past 30 years is the rise in the quantity and quality of violence on television. In 1961 I worried that my children would not benefit much from television, but now I worry that my grandchildren will actually be harmed by it. One recent study shows that by the time a child is 18 he has seen 25,000 murders on television. In 1961 they didn't make PG-13 movies, much less NC-17. Now a 6-year-old can watch them on cable. . . .
>
> In the last 30 years, the television marketplace has become a severely distorting influence in at least four important public areas. We have failed 1) to use television for education; 2) to use television for children; 3) to finance public television properly; and 4) to use television properly in political campaigns. . . .
>
> . . . Bob Keeshan, our Captain Kangaroo for life, has seen how television for children all over the world is designed to be part of the nurturing and educational system. But "in America," he says, "television is not a tool for nurturing. It is a tool for selling."
>
> . . . Studies of political campaigns show that the average block of uninterrupted speech by a presidential candidate on network newscasts was 9.8 seconds; in 1968 it was 42.3 seconds. As Walter Cronkite observed, this means that "issues can be avoided rather than confronted." And David Halberstam adds, "Once the politicians begin to talk in such brief bites . . . they begin to think in them."
>
> A United States senator must now raise $12,000 to $16,000 every week to pay for a political campaign, mostly to buy time for television commercials. A recent United Nations study revealed that only two countries, Norway and Sri Lanka (in addition to the United States), do not provide free airtime to their political parties. If we are to preserve the democratic process without corrupting, unhealthy influences, we must find a bipartisan way to provide free time for our candidates and stop them from getting deeply in hock to special interests in order to pay for television commercials.

Do you agree with this assessment? Why?

### C. TV News

Neil Postman, head of the Communication Arts Department at New York University, says that television news is "fatally hampered" by television's need to keep people entertained. When people turn on the set, they are waiting to be entertained, whatever the program, even when it is news.

Do you agree? Watch the evening news for a few days. Can you detect techniques and content used to keep the audience glued to the set?

## DB/CAR

### Readers

Only half the nation's adults say they read a newspaper every day. In 1967, three-fourths said they read a newspaper daily. The greatest nonreadership occurs among teen-agers and young adults, most of whom prefer radio and television for news.

In response, newspapers have adopted a variety of measures: shorter stories, more color illustrations, lifestyle stories. The Gannett chain has a special program for its newspapers, called the News 2000 Project, and Knight-Ridder adopted the 25/43 Project to win back readers.

Make a computer search of articles relevant to what newspapers are doing to attract readers and summarize your findings in 350 to 500 words. If there are results of these projects, include them. If you can find criticisms and assessments in your search, make these the subject of a second article.

In one of your articles, address the question: Can radio and television news substitute for newspaper news?

## Skill Drill: Identify

Briefly describe these people:

1. Al Neuharth
2. Jesse Jackson
3. Sandra Day O'Connor
4. Jimmy Carter
5. James Hoffa
6. Nelson Mandela
7. Harriet Beecher Stowe
8. James Baldwin
9. Eleanor Roosevelt
10. Martha Graham

## Fix It: Or Let It Go

If the sentence needs correcting, do so. If not, put a check at the end.

1. I imply from your comments you consider me guilty.
2. This jacket has one of it's buttons missing.
3. Can I be excused to attend class?
4. She has less clothing than she did a year ago.
5. He has less shoes than he did a year ago.

## What's Wrong?: Wet

Sioux Falls picked up another half-inch of rain Saturday, but is still more than one inch away from a record monthly rainfall.

The city has had 8.05 inches for the month—.59 fell Saturday—making it the second wettest July on record, said Bill Behrend, meteorologist with the National Weather Service in Sioux Falls.

The record for July is 9.11 inches.

Today should be partly cloudy with a high near 80. No rain is forecast, but some areas may be foggy, Behrend said.

# PART FOUR
## Reporting Principles

## 10 Digging for Information

Lois Bernstein, *The Sacramento Bee*.
**Digging reporters get their story.**

### Introduction

The reporter's task is to make the story come as close to the truth of the event as his or her reporting and writing skills allow. In reporting, the deeper journalists dig, the closer they come to the underlying truth, which is often covered by layers of material constructed from self-serving sources. Perspective on the event is best served through the observations of several sources; the single-source story can cause trouble. Background, causes and consequences are an important part of the account, and when reporters are allowed to provide interpretation, this, too, helps to give a rounded picture of the event.

## Exercises

### A. Commencement

You are covering the commencement ceremonies at St. Mary's University. The commencement address is to be delivered by Patrick Kelley of Washington, D.C., who has held several government posts, including positions abroad in Africa and the Middle East and a post as domestic advisor to the Health, Education and Welfare Department. The board of trustees voted 7-2 to give him an honorary doctorate of law. The two no votes said he was "too controversial." Kelley is an outspoken public servant and has served in Democratic and Republican administrations. He is on leave to write a book.

His speech, entitled "Facing Realities Here and Abroad," starts at 2 p.m. at the college amphitheater. As he begins to talk, 10 graduating seniors walk out and about 25 stand and turn their backs to him. Half the protesters are black, half are white. A few minutes later, about 50 spectators walk out quietly in single file. You manage to interview a few of the seniors who leave:

Jack Kelp, 22, major in English literature: Kelley is a racist. His advice to HEW on the problems of minorities clearly revealed a racist mentality. He advocates benign neglect for blacks, for example.

Jean Gogelman, 21, major in chemistry: His statements all have a bravado about them, a sexist and chauvinistic undertone. He believes in the idea that if you're poor, it's your own fault. He is a believer in the discredited idea of blaming the victim.

Philip Moffitt, 21, psychology major: He represents the machismo complex that almost had us in a nuclear confrontation with Russia during Kennedy's presidency, that put us into the Bay of Pigs fiasco and had us in Vietnam. It's a tragedy we have become so conservative at the university that we recognize this kind of foreign policy.

93

The president, N. Francis Simms, has no comment. Nor do any of the trustees. The remaining audience did not seem unusually disturbed, and Kelley went through his talk without a pause.

Parts of the text as provided by the college news bureau:

> No longer can this country tolerate assaults on its integrity from the self-righteous national leaders abroad who condemn every minor act of discrimination here while ignoring the tyrannies of their rule. It is time for us to tell truths to the world.
>
> We have dictators of left and right lecturing us, the freest large nation in the world. The left dictators say we ignore the problems of our people, that we are a colonialist power. Yet in this country no one is in jail for his or her beliefs, and our history is replete with a generosity unparalleled since the city-states. . . .
>
> We must recognize that any national policy that doles out grants, welfare or any kind of assistance without seeking to find long-range solutions for poverty, ill-health, unemployment and undereducation will eventually be bankrupt and worse, condemned perpetually to a welfare state mentality. . . .
>
> On the campus, we find intolerance gaining a stranglehold in the guise of tolerance. We have intrusions on the freedom of expression in the guise of preventing racism and sexism. We have developed political correctness to a point just short of totalitarianism, again in disguise.
>
> Administrators surrender to the threat and the mob. They abjectly give in to those who refuse to allow the university to perform its traditional function as the marketplace of ideas.

A total of 1,378 undergraduate degrees were awarded and 432 graduate degrees. Author Kurt Vonnegut Jr. received an honorary doctorate of letters at the ceremony. The president gave a welcoming talk. The degrees were awarded by Mrs. Dorothy M. Seaver, one of the two trustees who voted against Kelley's honorary degree. She had no comment.

Write 350 to 400 words for tomorrow's newspaper.

**An honorary degree for the author Kurt Vonnegut.**

Bob Thayer, *The Journal-Bulletin.*

*B. Interpret*

Here is a table distributed by the College Board of those who took the Scholastic Aptitude Test in a recent year. Use it as the basis of a news story.

| Income | Number of SAT Takers | Percent | % Male/Female | SAT-V Mean | SAT-M Mean |
| --- | --- | --- | --- | --- | --- |
| Less than $10,000 | 49,649 | 6 | 38/62 | 350 | 416 |
| $10,000–$20,000 | 92,912 | 11 | 42/58 | 377 | 435 |
| $20,000–$30,000 | 116,562 | 13 | 44/56 | 402 | 454 |
| $30,000–$40,000 | 138,850 | 16 | 46/54 | 416 | 469 |
| $40,000–$50,000 | 109,982 | 13 | 48/52 | 429 | 482 |
| $50,000–$60,000 | 95,861 | 11 | 49/51 | 437 | 492 |
| $60,000–$70,000 | 71,482 | 8 | 49/51 | 446 | 502 |
| $70,000 or more | 200,262 | 23 | 50/50 | 469 | 531 |
| No response | 174,826 | | | | |

## *Assignments*

### *A. Issue*

Select an issue of national, regional or local significance that is before the U.S. Senate or House of Representatives and write to one or more of the senators or the congressperson from your area asking for the senator's or representative's opinion on the matter.

Your letter should include specific questions. Base the questions on research, and include this background material in the article that you write.

### *B. Barometers*

Interview city officials and businesspeople about data they use to measure the community's economic health. Some of these figures include bank clearings, sales tax receipts, building permits, unemployment payments. Obtain the most recent data.

What do these figures tell you about present economic conditions?

### *C. Feet*

A San Diego podiatrist, Brian A. Rothbart, is quoted in a wire service story from that city as saying that, although long distance runners may have the cardiovascular fitness of teen-agers, they have the feet of old men. "Runners are putting more stress on their feet in one year than the average person does in 10 years," he said. "I can look at a runner who is 20 and who is in superb condition, except for his feet, which are those of a 60-year-old." He suggests runners practice on sawdust tracks, sand or grass. Concrete can be a foot killer, he said. Athletes may suffer mild to serious injuries of the foot, he said.

Interview joggers about their foot problems. Interview the runners at the local college or university about their foot problems. How do they practice? Is there a team podiatrist? What is the track coach's attitude?

### *D. Payroll*

Make a study of the number of people on public payrolls, city, county or state, whichever is most accessible to you. How many are there now compared with last year and five years ago?

How many are appointive, civil service or merit system employees? What is the total cost of public employees in salaries, retirement, other benefits?

Obtain comments from the heads of various bureaus, departments and agencies whose payrolls have increased or decreased the most sharply. What are the reasons?

### *E. Sterile*

The president of the California Veterinary Medical Association, Dr. Dan R. Evans, advocates birth control for animals, a wire service story datelined Escondido, Calif., reports. He says there is an overpopulation of dogs and cats, and the result is that each year more and more animals are destroyed by humane societies. He says researchers are working on a sterilization drug, necessary because most people cannot pay to have their pets neutered.

Do a local follow-up. Does your city or county veterinary group have a voluntary sterilization program, as Dr. Evans says his county does? Is there a pet overpopulation in your area? Consult the humane society, the dog shelter, police, veterinaries, citizens. How many pets are destroyed each year? The exact figures are available, if you can dig them out.

### F. Foreign

Sunday editions of newspapers and the editorial pages of the regular editions often carry long interpretative pieces. Prepare such a piece of 750 to 1,000 words on one of the following subjects in the field of international affairs:

1. Africa: hope or despair?
2. The continuing revolution in Mexico: real or spurious?
3. China: changes over the past decade.
4. The Palestinian battle for a homeland.
5. The perils of overpopulation: a case study—India. (Or any country of your choice.)
6. Can the two Canadas coexist? (This refers to the continuing strife between French- and English-speaking Canadians.)

Consult the library and databases for background. You should be able to bring in current events by consulting *The New York Times Index*. If these governments have offices in your community or if there are faculty members or local residents from these countries, interview them.

### G. Carols

The holding of Christmas assemblies, including the singing of carols, in the public schools; prayers at athletic contests; the posting of the Ten Commandments in classrooms; the beginning of the school day with a prayer—these are some of the activities the American Civil Liberties Union and other groups have attacked as violating the constitutional separation of church and state. Write an interpretative story of 750 words on the current policy of the local school system and blend in background from a database search or use of the *Reader's Guide* and/or *The New York Times Index*.

### H. Interpret

Gather material and write an interpretative story on one of these subjects:

1. The need to protect the identity of juvenile offenders.
2. The necessity to hold the line on salary increases for city workers.
3. The establishment of a required core curriculum for all candidates for the bachelor's degree to include a year of college mathematics, three years of a foreign language, one year of a physical science, three years of humanities.
4. The end to subsidies of athletes in the major sports and a more equitable distribution of funds to all college sports.
5. Elimination of compulsory schooling at age 14 or 16.
6. The pros and cons of the strong mayor system for local government.
7. A reassessment of local residential and commercial properties to bring them into a more balanced relationship.
8. The debate over the place of multiculturalism in the curriculum.

## Campus Projects

### A. Evaluation

More than four of five colleges and universities (86 percent) use student evaluations to measure teaching effectiveness. In some schools, they are a major, and sometimes the only, source of faculty performance evaluation. But Peter Seldin, professor of management at Pace University in Pleasantville, N.Y., contends that student ratings should never be the sole determinant of teaching effectiveness.

Seldin recommends a wider approach that includes evidence of student learning, observations of teaching by colleagues and reviews of instructional material.

Also, he recommends that the evaluation form have 20 to 30 questions on teaching behavior, including:

- Are tests and papers graded and returned promptly?
- Is the instructor well-prepared?

He says that the results of the evaluations are mixed, that they do not automatically lead to better teaching. An instructor new to being evaluated takes them seriously, as does the instructor who is given information on how to improve performance.

Interview faculty members, administrators and students about the effectiveness of student evaluations. How does your administration use the results of the evaluations?

## B. Admission

Colleges and universities have been changing their requirements for admission to accommodate some groups. Traditionally, colleges have used academic records—high school grades, scores on the ACT and SAT tests, ranking in the senior class, letters from teachers—as the major criteria for admission.

Exceptions have been made for the sons and daughters of alumni, athletes and those with special talents, such as musicians. In the last two decades, the doors have been widened to accept members of racial and ethnic groups that have traditionally not attended college.

Investigate the changes in your school's admission policies. Look at admission guidelines. Have they changed the nature of students who were admitted last year as compared to 10 years ago, 25 years ago?

Has the change in admission policies affected academic work and the curriculum? Has the school added remedial courses for the less-prepared students?

Have students in minority groups found that the school meets their needs?

The admissions office keeps records on how students in various categories fare in college. Obtain dropout and graduation rates for students in minority groups, students with high and low SAT or ACT scores, athletes, etc.

Has there been any controversy about admission standards in the last few years?

# Community Projects

## A. Aged

How is your community meeting the special needs of the aged? Identify the problems; then see whether solutions have been found. For example, a growing number of the aged use walkers and small vehicles to get around. They have trouble negotiating curbs, and many cities have rebuilt curbs at intersections to eliminate the rise.

Is there a housing project for the aged, a recreation center, food programs for the shut-ins? Learn what the city, church groups and civic organizations are doing for this growing segment of the population.

## B. Gay-Lesbian

A study by the U.S. Department of Health and Human Services found that gay and lesbian adolescents make up almost a third of all teen-age suicides. One of the reasons, counselors say, is the anti-gay atmosphere in high schools. While racial and religious slurs are no longer acceptable, anti-gay comments are part of the school culture.

At some schools, gay students are advised to stay in the closet. A Boston high school teacher said, "They'd get killed if they came out. At our school, male students get harassed just for being in drama or chorus."

But at others, administrators are trying to open the closet. At the Phillips Exeter private school in New Hampshire, a gay/straight alliance was formed, and gay and lesbian students are permitted to hold dances. A number of other private schools have similar organizations. Much of the effort to open up high schools has come from gay teachers.

Opposition is powerful. A minister in Mattapan, Mass., the Rev. Earl W. Jackson, advocates firing gay and lesbian teachers who are open about their sexual orientation.

"We are not going to let anyone stand up and say, 'I'm lesbian,'" he said.

In Washington and Oregon, anti-gay initiatives have been aimed at introducing legislation that would prohibit gays and lesbians from teaching. While the situation is easing for gay students at boarding schools, gays and lesbians say little progress has been made in public high schools. Examine the situation in your local high schools. Has the board of education taken any steps to include treatment of gay issues in the curriculum; are there any gay/straight clubs in any high schools? Interview gay and lesbian students about their experiences in school.

You might post a notice about your interest in talking to these students, after you obtain permission from the school.

### C. Big Dough

At the kickoff of his campaign for the Republican presidential nomination, Senator Phil Gramm of Texas announced, "I have the most reliable friend that you can have in American politics, and that is ready money." Information about political donations to candidates in your state is available to the public. For a recent election, check the names and affiliations of donors. Interview some donors; find out their reasons for donating.

## Home Assignment

### Layers

Layer I stories are source originated.
Layer II stories consist of coverage of spontaneous events, reporter-checked or reporter-originated stories.
Layer III stories emphasize interpretative and explanatory material.

1. Clip examples of each type.
2. Do you think the Layer I stories could have been better handled, or were there obvious factors that made it unnecessary or impossible for the reporters to dig deeper?
3. Do any of the Layer II and Layer III stories contain opinions and judgments of the reporters? Are they legitimate? Explain.

## Class Discussion

### A. Pseudo-Events

There are several names given to events that are planned or planted for press coverage. They have been called *staged events, orchestrated events, media happenings* or *media events* and *pseudo-events*. They have in common the intent of the planner to entice press coverage for the benefit of the planner or the person or group represented.

1. Find an example of such an event.
2. Assess the way the reporter handled it. Did the reporter simply pass on information from the source, or was there independent reportorial checking and backgrounding?
3. One study indicates that in some newspapers as much as 80 percent of the stories originate with sources and are untouched by reporters. That is, reporters serve merely a stenographic function. Can you make an educated guess about the content of your local newspaper? Does it have a reputation for its staff-originated stories, as differentiated from source-originated stories?

### B. New News

*Rolling Stone* magazine says that the "Old News is pooped, confused and broke," and in its place the New News is evolving, "a heady concoction, part Hollywood film and TV, part pop music and pop art, mixed with popular culture and celebrity magazines, tabloid telecasts, cable and home video."

The New News, says the magazine, sets the subjects of conversation and will establish the country's social and political agenda.

In response, the television journalist Bill Moyers says:

> People want to know what is happening to them, and what they can do about it. Listening to America you realize that millions of Americans are not apathetic. They will respond to a press that stimulates the community without pandering to it, that inspires people to embrace their responsibilities without lecturing or hectoring them, that engages their better natures without sugarcoating ugly realities or patronizing their foibles.

In which direction do you think journalism is heading?

## DB/CAR

### RSI

Repetitive strain injury (RSI) is said to be the leading occupational illness in the nation. After years of denying that the newspaper industry had problems with RSI, newspapers have been struggling to adjust to the reality that a significant percentage of their employees suffer from the debilitating condition that makes it difficult for them to work at their video display terminals.

The painful and disabling injury is associated with repetitive hand work. It often begins with a tingling sensation in fingers and hands. The pain travels from the wrist through the arms and into shoulders and the neck. Reports say 200 employees of *The Los Angeles Times* have the condition.

Make a search to locate the latest material on RSI. How is the newspaper industry coping with the problem?

## *Fix It: Fact Checking*

Check facts in the following material that seem to need verification or that you would ordinarily check. Some material is accurate, some inaccurate.

1. TEGUCIGALPA, El Salvador—Nicaraguan families streamed across the border this past week to avoid their sons' conscription in the armed forces, government officials reported today.
2. Boston University, a Catholic institution, today reported it would increase tuition by 15 percent.
3. The first civil rights bill for blacks since Reconstruction was approved by Congress in 1957. The bill was designed to protect the rights of black voters.
4. How-to books and advice on how to make money and how to lead a successful sex life dominate the best-seller lists.
5. After the record drop in the New York Stock Exchange, police held a suicide watch on the Golden Gate Bridge in San Francisco which many ruined investors leaped from after the market crash of 1929.
6. Proctor & Gamble Co. is the subject of a new book published by Simon and Schuster.
7. The study asked 200 students their opinions of the quality of teaching. The result—55 percent said it was unsatisfactory—was a clear-cut victory for students who are seeking to put an end to the system of tenure.
8. From an article about Ray Bradbury, the author: Bradbury began writing at an early age and had his first success in the pulp magazines with short stories. His first story was published in 1940.
9. "No one cares to hear what Hogan calls the short and simple scandals of the poor," Finley Peter Dunne wrote in his Chicago newspaper column.
10. In 1934, Franklin D. Roosevelt ordered the banks closed to prevent their being bankrupted by worried depositors.

## *Test II: Error Identification*

Choose the answer that best describes the problem in the sentence. Note that some examples may be correct.

1. A career change is in his future plans.
   (a) lack of parallelism   (b) redundancy   (c) agreement   (d) over-subordination   (e) example is correct
2. People who run quickly lose weight.
   (a) punctuation problem   (b) fragment   (c) ambiguity   (d) split verb   (e) example is correct
3. Running to catch the bus, his hat flew off.
   (a) ambiguity   (b) dangling modifier   (c) passive voice   (d) mixed metaphor   (e) example is correct
4. He likes neither studying nor to party all night.
   (a) agreement   (b) redundant   (c) lack of parallelism   (d) dead construction   (e) example is correct
5. The ball was hit by him over the fence.
   (a) unnecessary passive voice   (b) error in agreement   (c) cliché   (d) wrong case   (e) fragment

6. Drenched in frustration, the crowd exploded with anger.
    (a) run-on sentence  (b) dangling modifier  (c) redundancy  (d) mixed metaphor  (e) example is correct
7. The jury returned its verdict in record time.
    (a) case problem  (b) agreement problem  (c) fragment  (d) cliché  (e) example is correct
8. They have a problem; we must find an answer.
    (a) fragment  (b) mixed metaphor  (c) lack of parallelism  (d) run-on sentence  (e) example is correct
9. Both of us grabbed for the egg carton, but it fell between her and I.
    (a) case problem  (b) agreement problem  (c) dead construction  (d) cliché  (e) example is correct
10. There was a bank robbery today in which three robbers took $300,000.
    (a) case problem  (b) fragment  (c) dead construction  (d) passive voice  (e) example is correct

# 11 Making Sound Observations

### Introduction

The public relies on the reporter's eyes and ears for an understanding of events and their meaning in the community and the world. Reporters station themselves at key surveillance points—called *beats*—in order to make observations of the important events that unfold. They have sufficient background to understand the events they cover, and they have a solid grasp of the subjects of their beat so that they are able to ask the questions that elicit relevant information. The journalist understands that he or she can never completely reflect the truth of the event but always seeks to move as close to truth as possible.

Joel Strasser.

**Count the firefighters, the trucks.**

## Exercises

### A. Newsstand

The circulation manager of your newspaper tells you that a newsstand operator is in his office with a "crazy story about how some sanitation workers carted off his newsstand and its contents." He suggests you talk to the man, Rosario Marvello. You go downstairs, and Marvello says that the men swept down on him yesterday and, without a word, leveled his stand.

"I've been there for 12 years," he says, "trying to make a living to support my family. And now I have nothing."

You sense a story and suggest he show you his location. You go with him to Albany and Massachusetts and, sure enough, his stand is gone. You note it was on the northwestern corner.

You call the Sanitation Department and a public affairs officer tells you that the commissioner, William Applegate, is out of town but that the stand was torn down because it violated the city code by (1) obstructing pedestrian traffic, (2) being too far from the building line, (3) not conforming to the architectural code. He says you can't quote him, just the department.

Marvello, who is 62, says six men took 15 minutes to do the job and all he could do was stand by and watch. He says he is thinking of hiring a lawyer but hasn't much money.

"That's not a way to get rich," he says. "I make enough to get by week by week, and that's it."

You call around and learn that the City Planning Department is conducting a study of the design and location of newsstands. A source in the department tells you on a not-for-attribution basis that the department wants to cut down on the number of newsstands and limit their locations. "It's all hush-hush, but word got out and somehow these guys at Sanitation jumped the gun. The idea is to get him out of there."

1. Write a story for today's newspaper with the information you have; 300 words.
2. Marvello's plight now has been on television and people are calling the mayor, who issues the following press release. Write a second-day story with the new information; 350 words.

THE CITY OF FREEPORT                    OFFICE OF THE MAYOR

For Release: Immediate

STATEMENT BY MAYOR SAM PARNASS

I was upset to learn that a newsstand operated by Rosario Marvello was demolished in error by the Sanitation Department. This should not have happened.

Everyone makes mistakes, including those of us in government. The important thing is to right those mistakes. I have ordered that the newsstand be rebuilt or replaced and turned over to Mr. Marvello immediately without cost to him. The work has already begun and it will be on the same site he has had for 12 years.

Deputy Mayor Stan Brezen talked with Ruth Marvello, expressing the city's regrets about this unfortunate incident and assuring her that any property taken by the Sanitation Department would be returned or the department's community funds would pay for any property destroyed.

While we are restoring Mr. Marvello's business, it is important to remember that the Department of City Planning and an interagency task force are engaged in a long-term study of the rules for location and design of newsstands. Our aim is to rationalize decision making on this issue so that the distribution of newspapers and magazines flourishes while legitimate community concerns, chiefly about impediments to pedestrian flow on the sidewalks, are addressed.

In a reaction to preliminary recommendations, publishers, editorial commentators and columnists have suggested that the city wants to eliminate newsstands. Nothing could be further from the truth. Newsstands are an essential part of the city and provide valuable service to people.

It is absolutely not our intention to diminish the sale of newspapers. On the contrary, we believe more news and editorial coverage of matters of public interest benefits the city and its people.

At the end of this process, it is my hope that we will have developed sensible criteria that encourage the creation of attractive newsstands in busy locations that people in neighborhoods around the city will welcome.

It is conceivable that at some future date Mr. Marvello will be asked to move, but if that happens it will be part of a city-wide reorganization plan. It will not be as the result of a demolition raid.

## B. Provost

St. Mary's University has appointed a new provost, Stanley Stiga, 42, who was a professor of chemistry at Michigan State University. The announcement was made today by university president, N. Francis Simms. You attend a news conference at which the announcement is made. In answers to questions, Stiga advances this list of actions he intends to initiate:

- Greater emphasis on research by the faculty. "We must make this university stand out, and the way to accomplish this is through research and publication of the research of our faculty. I will be stressing to all department heads that advancement depends on such activity."
- A fund for tutoring all students having difficulty in a course. "Our task is to teach students, and some learn slower than others or can see better with direction from someone with another perspective."
- More self-government among students. "A student judicial council could take over all disciplinary matters outside of the academic area. College students are just a few years away from taking on responsibilities in the real world. Why not train them here? In fact, you might say that I look at college students as adults. The days of in loco parentis are gone."
- A meaningful advisory system. Every student should have a student advisor in the freshman year as well as a faculty advisor. "We want to be able to anticipate any problems. When a student is having trouble in class, in

a dormitory or with parents or a friend, we want to be able to be in a position to offer help. Students sometimes are better able to help than faculty members."

• Coeducational housing should extend to most of the campus. "Again, this is part of the business of treating college students as adults. At Colby, the fraternities began to show an interest in such living arrangements, and one did welcome several women as residents. No one should be forced to live in a coeducational facility. Indeed, some students are much happier and productive in a single-sex housing facility. But the option should be there. This is the reality of life students will face. Anyway, the arguments in its favor are well known, and the issue now is hardly earthshaking."

Write 300 words.

## C. Heir

Wilbur Catton, 77, 1525 Brattle Ave., died 25 years ago, left $50,000 in his will to four daughters and one stepdaughter: Sylvia, $10,000; Beth, $10,000; Marianne, $15,000; Zelda, $10,000; Charleyne, the stepdaughter, $5,000. The stepdaughter had disappeared before his death. Only Marianne remains in Freeport. She says she used the money to help buy the house in which she still lives.

An officer at the First National Bank who is a friend calls to say that the stepdaughter, now Mrs. Albert Fogel of Denver, Colo., has been located and the full amount will be turned over to her soon. He thinks it will make a good story. The Freeport bank advertised in a banking publication, and a bank in Denver spotted the ad and notified the woman.

You ask the banker what Charleyne will receive, and he laughingly tells you to figure it out yourself and call back so he can check your arithmetic. You do compound interest based on the 5 percent interest rate your source told you to use. When you have the figure, you call him back and he congratulates you on your mathematical ability.

Write a story of 200 words.

## *Assignments*

### A. Bidding

Newspapers report the bidding on major contracts awarded by the city, county or state. These contracts include large construction projects such as schools, office buildings and jails; highway construction; improvements such as sewers, street lighting and sidewalks.

Here are the items usually included in a story on bid openings for public works projects:

**Bid Openings Checklist**
- Low bidder (or apparent low bidder).
- Amount of bid.
- Character of project.
- Engineer's estimates.
- Next-lowest bid, or all other bids and bidders.
- Experience of low bidder; previous contracts; reputation.
- Open or closed shop (particularly in industrial regions).
- Date for award.
- Starting date for construction.
- Source of funding for project.
- Date, location of bid opening.

Here is the beginning of a bid-opening story by Mike Hiltzik that appeared in the *Courier-Express* of Buffalo, N.Y.:

Two area construction firms were apparent low bidders Monday on an estimated $9.8 million in sewer construction contracts in Amherst, with combined bids 40 percent lower than the engineer's estimates.

The firms, Cimato Bros., Inc., of 165 Hartford Road, Amherst, and Wm. W. Kimmins and Sons, Inc., of 1300 Military Road, Kenmore, submitted bids lower than those of eight other firms, including two from out-of-state. They were on three contracts to construct an interceptor sewer along a former railroad right-of-way—known as the "Peanut Line"—that cuts across the town from east to west.

The project is part of a more than $30 million phase of the town's massive $136 million sewer plant project, one of the largest public works projects in Erie County.

The Cimato firm was apparent low bidder on two of three contracts. On one, for construction of the interceptor from Campbell Boulevard to Hopkins Road, the firm bid $1,974,655, as against the $2,902,557 estimate provided by Amherst's consulting engineer firm of Nussbaumer and Clarke, Inc.

Attend a bid opening for a local project or obtain information about such an opening and write a news story.

*B. Family*

Each year, the Department of Labor announces the annual poverty level. This is the line separating poverty and subsistence. The poverty level recently was about $14,800 for an urban family of four. Just what does this figure mean in terms of what the department considers essentials for a family of four: food, clothing, shelter, entertainment and the like? With these figures and the explanation, arrange a live in with such a family and observe not only what poverty means in terms of dollars and cents, but also in attitudes, expectations and experiences.

*C. Subsidy*

A study by the Consortium on Financing Higher Education has found that a group of private colleges is using revenue from tuition to subsidize scholarships for poor students. The study of 31 prestigious schools found that an average of 20 percent of tuition (which averaged $19,110) goes to help less affluent students. The subsidies ranged from 43.7 percent at Mount Holyoke to 1 percent at Princeton, which is low, say officials there, because the university has a $450 million endowment devoted to scholarships.

What is the situation at your school?

*D. Unobtrusive*

There are many opportunities to carry out unobtrusive observations. Try to find an inconspicuous spot in a restaurant, a laundromat, a bus, a park where mothers walk or sun their babies, a ball game, a hotel lobby, a department store, a tourist attraction, a fishing pier, a driving range, a bird walk or a hike. The possibilities are unlimited. Take notes carefully or use your memory. Do a piece that could be part of a series: "What Freeport Residents Are Talking About" or "The Talk of the Town." If there is a solid news story in what you overhear, follow that up also.

## *Campus Project*

### *Live In (1)*

The Live In, described in the textbook, usually takes about 10 hours of observation. Select someone on campus willing to let you spend some time with him or her, and over the next few weeks do your reporting. The work will be in the nature of a long feature story or a series.

Here are some possible subjects: a handicapped student; an older man or woman trying to balance studies with a job and/or family responsibilities; a student preparing for a role in a campus production; an athlete balancing practice and studies; a science student carrying out an experiment for a graduate degree; an instructor preparing for a dissertation defense; an admissions officer deciding on the next freshman class; the provost or budget officer preparing next year's budget; the official responsible for fund raising preparing to launch a new fund drive; a foreign student adjusting to the campus; a new instructor coping with his/her first classes; an instructor preparing materials for a tenure committee; an alumni officer putting together a class reunion; a student balancing jobs and classes; sorority or fraternity members screening potential new members; the organization of a new campus group—gay and lesbian, minority, political, etc.

## *Community Project*

### *Live In (2)*

Some suggestions: working people—a letter carrier, police officer, postal worker, ambulance driver, bus driver, long-distance truck driver, grade school teacher, public defender preparing a case, welfare or social worker, public health nurse, doctor, dentist, judge. A newly retired man or woman, a man or woman on probation, a local journalist, librarian, foster mother or father, any member of a family on welfare, a die-hard fan.

Usually, the live in works best when the reporter becomes involved in an ongoing situation that engages the subject. For example, a live in with a judge could involve the reporter's watching the judge try a case or observing the judge reach a decision on a sentence after conviction. Show the person doing something.

## Home Assignment

*Observe*

Gustave Flaubert advised the young Guy de Maupassant to observe one person in a group so closely that the significant details and individual characteristics of that person would clearly separate him or her from other police officers, teachers, passers-by.

Try this with a class member. Observe physical characteristics, listen to the person's speech, watch his or her actions.

Do not name the person in your description. See how quickly other students can identify your subject. Or try it with a faculty member or administrator known to classmates.

## Class Discussion

*A. Interests*

Compile a list of the special interests and the demographics of local people that influence coverage and play in local newspapers and broadcast stations. For example, in a region whose economy is based on farming, the media would emphasize crop reports, market prices for produce and animals, weather, government price supports and state and federal legislation on farm issues.

Note any large numbers of religious, ethnic or national groups and give examples of coverage of interest to those groups.

*B. Reporters*

Studies of how journalists identify themselves politically were made in 1971, 1983 and 1992. Here are the findings:

|             | '71  | '83  | '92  |
|-------------|------|------|------|
|             | (Percentages) | | |
| Democrat    | 35.5 | 36.5 | 44.4 |
| Republican  | 25.7 | 18.6 | 16.3 |
| Independent | 32.5 | 39.1 | 34.4 |

The 1992 survey, sponsored by The Freedom Forum, questioned 1,400 journalists nationwide. It was directed by David Weaver and G. Cleveland Wilhoit of the School of Journalism at Indiana University. They say they believe few reporters allow their political views to influence their reporting. But the sharp changes in political patterns, they add, do raise the question of bias.

The chairman of a conservative Media Research Center, L. Brent Bozell III, says the findings show "The media are becoming a safe haven for the left in this country."

Mary Matalin, deputy manager of the 1992 Bush presidential campaign, commented that reporters "have attitudes of political correctness toward Democratic policies and political incorrectness toward Republican policies."

Caryl Rivers of the Boston University journalism school contends that a journalist's party registration does not affect his or her reporting. Reporters are more interested in candidates who are newsworthy and generate good stories than they are in promoting a political agenda, she says.

Can you find any recent polls of journalists and commentaries that shed light on this issue?

What do you think of these findings and the trends they reveal? Have you seen any bias in political coverage?

## DB/CAR

*Tactile*

How has the computer affected writing? Some people say that the ease with which writing can be done has led to written work that is not tightly organized. Stories, these critics say, run longer than those written on the typewriter. In an article, "Do you love your VDT?" by Dominique Wolton in the July/August 1979 *Columbia Journalism Review,* the author writes:

> The fact that the transition from paper to computers is bound to modify the process of intellectual creation was never mentioned. Yet the new technology makes this creative process more abstract, involving an essentially visual, rather than material or tactile, relationship to writing, which now occurs within the fixed space of the display screen. Who can deny that here we have the seeds of change in the journalist's relation to his work?

More recently, the humor columnist Russell Baker commented in *The New York Times* on mail he has been receiving that was turned out by writers on a computer:

Just look at this letter: Writing it required several thousand dollars' worth of electronic machinery, not to mention a supply of electricity provided by vast corporations whose hot wiry tentacles stretched across thousands of miles.

With all these resources, what emerged? . . . a poorly written letter—not a graceful phrase in it, too much stiffness in the prose joints, and twice as long as it needed to be.

Such gassiness is characteristic of writing done on computers. Computers make the physical toil of writing so negligible that the writer can write on forever, and often does, now.

Many books worth only 290 pages routinely wheeze on nowadays to 800, 900, 999.

My second-rate letter with the junk-mail look is a typical child of progress. With a goose quill, Thomas Jefferson could have written a letter at a fraction of the cost. . . . It would have been better not only because Jefferson had the more interesting mind, but also because writing with goose feathers is such messy work that a writer has to put his mind in order before starting. With a computer, he merely flips a switch, then lets his brain mosey around in the fog on the chance it may bump into an idea. . . .

Write 250 to 350 words for a feature on writing with computers.

## *Fix It: Trademarks*

Give the generic name for the following names of trademark products:

1. Band-Aid _____
2. Baggies _____
3. Jockey _____
4. Alka-Seltzer _____
5. Chap Stick _____

## *What's Wrong?: Escapee*

What's missing in this story?

FARGO, N.D.—An escaped convict being sought by North Dakota and Minnesota authorities was captured Wednesday while darting through tall weeds south of the Casselton airport.

David Sterling, 47, was running near a railroad track, occasionally stopping and ducking, said Richard Sellars, who works for the Aircraft Investment Co. at the airport.

Sellars said a secretary for the company called the Cass County sheriff's department after spotting the man late in the afternoon. Casselton is about 20 miles west of Fargo.

"A citizen called in, just like we were asking (them) to do," said Budd Warren, a detective with the sheriff's department. "Like clockwork, it worked out just fine."

Duane McIntyre, an area farmer and pilot who was at the airport, joined two law enforcement officials and Sellars in the search for Sterling.

## *You Decide: Johns (1)*

The city council has voted to buy advertisements in the local newspaper for the display of photos of men arrested for soliciting prostitutes. Your newspaper also has been under pressure from a local organization, Protect Our Neighborhoods, to publicize such arrests.

In the community, there has been a significant increase in aggressive solicitation, and residents in several neighborhoods are pressuring the city to step up law enforcement.

**Neighborhoods want arrested Johns publicized.**

Scott Martin, *The Blade.*

You are the editor of the *Freeport News*. How would you respond to Protect Our Neighborhoods' request to buy advertising space for publishing photos of men arrested for soliciting?

# 12 Building and Using Background

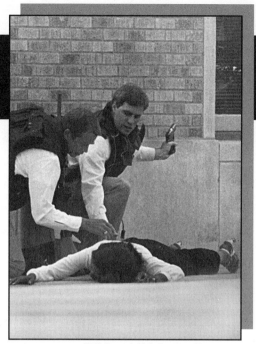

Phil Sears, *Tallahassee Democrat*.
**Background gives the event depth.**

### Introduction

Without an understanding of the subject of the beat and the particular story being covered, the reporter is handcuffed. General knowledge helps the journalist understand the context of the event. Specific information guides the reporter to the newsworthiness of the event. Reporters are always at work adding to their storehouses of knowledge and information bank. This is accomplished through wide and diverse reading—from newspapers and magazines to novels and nonfiction—and diverse experience. The good reporter is open to ideas that contradict his or her beliefs and convictions.

## *Exercises*

### A. Essays

The public relations office of the city school system calls to announce the winners of the Peter Gallagher Memorial Day Essay Contest. They are:

    1st: Beatrice Skinner, 17, Eisenhower H.S., daughter of Mr. and Mrs. Vernon Skinner.
    2nd: Michael Nelley, 18, Southside H.S., son of Margaret Nelley.
    3rd: Gretchen Young, 16, Horace Mann H.S., daughter of William Young.

The announcement is made by Rodney Addison, chairman of the city board of education. The 1st prize is a $100 savings bond; 2nd, $50 bond; 3rd, $25 bond. Each high school in the city sends what it considers to be the best essays submitted for the contest. The judges were Samuel Ward, head of the English department at Mallory College; Billy Jo Barber, juvenile fiction writer; F.W. Stern, coordinator of high school English in the city school system.

You call Addison in hopes of getting some kind of angle on the story. You wonder how many entries there were and what the quality of the writing was.

Addison tells you:

    There were only a dozen entries, the smallest number since the contest started in 1971 to honor young Gallagher, a local high school graduate of great talent who died in the Vietnam War. You know, his classmates started the prize then and they have kept it funded ever since. When we started, we would get maybe 30 or 40 fine essays.

Professor Ward tells you:

    Except for the winners, the essays were dull, poorly written and had a paucity of ideas. Received ideas, you might call them. You wonder what the younger generation has on its mind, if anything. You don't expect any startling revelations, but you hope to see young minds trying to handle subjects important to them in a fresh way.

Barber says:

> I graduated from the local school system only 20 years ago, but if these essays are an example of the best, I think something funny has been going on down there in the classes. The three winners were clearly outstanding, and then nothing. I think we're developing a meritocracy based on literacy. If you can read, write and think these days, the world is yours. But maybe the world belongs to the visual generation. Still, who is going to read manuals to repair our cars and TV sets, or will there just be deliverymen who show up with a replacement for the set when the wire is disconnected or a new car when the distributor conks out?

You begin to think that these quotes are going to make what you thought would be a routine story into a good feature, perhaps even a page-one story. You talk it over with the city editor, and he encourages you to keep going, to try to interview some of the winners, too.

"We'll make this into a Sunday feature. Let the parents know what their charming children are learning in this school system," he says.

You call the school office back and ask for the titles of the winning essays. They are:

1st: "Humanity's Hope—World Government."
2nd: "Life on an Island!"
3rd: "Meaningless Competition."

Then you call Skinner and ask what she wrote about. She replies:

> Ever since the discovery of atomic energy, we've had the power to destroy ourselves. A world government movement started then, but it disappeared in the Cold War because of the rise of nationalism, for example, among the Third World countries. The United Nations tried, but it has no teeth. I did a lot of research on world government as a hope for human survival.
>
> I hope to go into government myself. I consider that as much a public service as being a doctor. I'm putting the bond aside for college.

The editor tells you to write at least a column for a spread in the Sunday paper.

## B. Diversity

William Lennox, the president of a consulting firm, Lennox and Associates of Chicago, is in town to address local executives on "Diversity in the Workplace." You interview him for a story in tomorrow's newspaper. Here are excerpts from the interview. Write 250 words:

> Diversity in the workplace is here to stay. Companies that devote their time and money to building and managing a diverse work force—members of minority groups, immigrants and women—find that diversity is good for business. It makes for a more tolerant and innovative working group, to say nothing of eliminating discrimination suits.
>
> Employers used to think that the idea of a multicultural work force had no relevance to making money. Moreover, they felt that establishing a diverse employee group would antagonize their mostly white, male employees. This is no longer a major obstacle.
>
> Managing this new group has created some problems, and a new industry has grown up that meets the need to establish diversity and to smooth out any problems created by blending race and gender into the work force.
>
> Studies indicate that by the year 2005 the work force will have 26 million new workers, 85 percent of whom will be made up of women, minority group members and immigrants. These new workers must be blended smoothly into the workplace without disruption and antagonisms arising.
>
> The problems arise at the top as well as among employees. It takes some effort to break down stereotypes based on race and gender. We find most of these attitudes are based on personality characteristics.
>
> Placing diversity as a priority has helped some companies make money. Avon Products was faced with a declining inner-city market and put black and Hispanic managers in authority in these areas. The result was marked improvement in profits. Burger King has made diversity a major priority, with good results.
>
> A major problem in many firms is bias among middle managers. But, as we move into a global economy, we find that things are changing. Also, there is a growing belief that diverse employee groups outperform homogeneous groups. The diverse groups generate new approaches, new ways to solve problems because of the many ways they look at a situation.
>
> Lennox said his firm is part of a growing group of management consultants that make use of psychologists, anthropologists and businesspeople to advise clients on how to make multiculturalism work.

## Assignments

### A. B Copy

*B copy* consists mostly of background culled from clippings. When newspapers expect an event to occur, such as the death of a prominent person who is critically ill, B copy will be prepared ahead of time so that, should the event occur close to deadline, the story can go into print quickly with only the addition of the lead. Prepare B copy for one of the following situations:

1. The death of the president of your college or university.
2. The confirmation of the attorney general of the state as a justice of the U.S. Supreme Court.
3. The retirement of the senior U.S. senator for health reasons, to be formally announced in Washington in two days.
4. The appointment of the chairman of the board of Du Pont Co., of Delaware, as distinguished professor for one year at your college or university.

### B. Degrees

The following figures represent the percentages of the given ethnic groups that hold bachelor's degrees or higher:

| | |
|---|---|
| White | 21.5 |
| Black | 11.4 |
| Hispanic | 9.2 |
| Asian/Pacific Islander | 36.6 |
| American Indian | 9.3 |

Conduct interviews with educational authorities and consult appropriate references for an article that explains the wide variations in these figures.

### C. Periodicals

Select a subject area from the following subject list: business, computers, home construction and repair, journalism, music, psychology, religion, international affairs. Gather from library resources the titles of all periodicals that specialize in the subject.

### D. Commentary

Select an article from one of the library's publications on journalism and summarize the article in 350 words. Then comment on the article in 250 words.

## Campus Projects

### A. Unwed

Teen-age pregnancy is increasing, and many young women decide to raise their children themselves. Some experts see this as an alarming development that leads to poverty and neglect in these households. But other observers, to quote Francis A.J. Ianni, who has studied thousands of American adolescents, see it as a measure of both the increased "acceptability of single motherhood" and an inclination for "pregnant teens to avoid marriages that have little chance of success."

Interview members of the sociology, psychology and other faculties who may have some expertise in this area for their observations about the phenomenon. Obtain national and local data for background.

### B. Tension

The Carnegie Foundation reports that one-fourth of university and college presidents say that racial tension is a moderate to major campus problem. The National Institute Against Prejudice and Violence of Baltimore estimates that one in four minority students experiences a physical or psychological attack motivated by prejudice.

Make a reading of the racial situation on your campus.

## Community Project

### Deadbeat Dads

Many men walk away from court-ordered child-support payments, and little is done to make them conform to the orders. Some men owe $15,000 and more, and state governments report they are collecting on less than 20 percent of 13 million cases. The case rate is growing at a rate of tens of thousands a month.

Examine the situation in your area. Obtain the names of women who have tried to collect child-support funds without success and interview them. What are they doing to try to collect?

Some states have enacted tough child-support laws that allow officials to attach to child support everything from lottery winnings of parents behind in payments to settlements in court suits. Federal and state income tax refunds have been intercepted in some states.

In New Jersey, which has some of the toughest child-support laws in the country, the state can withhold child-support payments from paychecks, and the state notifies credit agencies about parents who are delinquent.

Look over your state's laws and see whether they are sufficiently effective. Talk to lawyers for women owed payments to see how successful they have been and whether they think your state needs tougher laws.

You can make a database search for background.

## Home Assignment

### Compute

The 13 employees of the father-and-son business of Adam Williams Repairs are on strike. Mr. Williams, who runs the electronics repair shop, puts a sign in his window saying that the strike is for higher pay and that the average pay in his shop is $24,900. He says the strike is, as anyone can see, unnecessary.

You work for a weekly and your editor suggests you do a piece on the walkout. The sign strikes your interest and you ask for a rundown of the salaries. Mr. Williams provides them as follows:

$62,500 (1) Mr. Williams
49,600 (1) Son Theodore
26,500 (4) Master Craftsmen
18,200 (6) Repairmen
15,600 (3) Laborers

You strike some averages of your own. What do you learn and what would you write?

## Class Discussion

### Educated Journalists

In the end, the educated city room betrayed its promise. When the quick but unschooled working-class reporters were displaced and the well-educated took over the work, that social dislocation might have been justifiable if the news media were going to serve democracy more effectively, if the educated reporters were using their professional skills to enhance citizens' ability to cope with power in a more complicated world. The educated reporters instead secured a comfortable place for themselves among the other governing elites. The transformation looks more like a nasty episode of social usurpation, a power shift freighted with class privilege.

What do you think of Grieder's analysis?

If the promise was not fulfilled, then what was the point of turning a craft into a profession? Aside from personal glory, what was really gained from all the journalists with college degrees, if they decline to use their skills to challenge power on behalf of their readers? Those of us who prospered from the transformation of the city room are burdened with those questions and naturally reluctant to face them. Educated journalists, it turns out, are strong on the facts and weak on the truth.

—William Grieder (*Who Will Tell the People;* New York: Simon & Schuster, 1992)

## DB/CAR

### Holocaust (1)

After the revelation of Nazi death camps in 1945, a small group of people sought to prove that Hitler and the Nazis did not try to exterminate the Jews. The theme of this movement is that there was no Holocaust. In recent years, it has been aggressive in presenting its beliefs to the public.

The so-called Holocaust revisionists have published material questioning the existence of gas chambers, the death toll of Jews and other aspects of the Holocaust story.

A clearinghouse called the Institute for Historical Review was set up several years ago to organize the work of these revisionists. Unsuccessful in placing their material in the mainline media, they turned to campus publications. Paying from $400 to $900 for full-page ads, the Institute was successful in placing its message in newspapers on the campuses of Vanderbilt, Ohio State, Northwestern, Rutgers, Duke, Louisiana State, Cornell and the University of Georgia, among others.

The ads were turned down by Yale, Harvard, Brown, Pennsylvania, Wisconsin, Georgetown, the University of Tennessee, the University of California at Berkeley and the University of Texas. A second ad submitted to Duke was refused.

Most of the campus newspapers that used the advertisement did so on the ground that they did not want to censor advertisers. Some ran the advertisement with countering comments.

Presume that *The Spectator* at Mallory College has received the advertisement and the student publications board is considering whether to run it. You are to write a story for the local newspaper about the controversy. Conduct a database search for material about the Institute for Historical Review and the controversy stirred up on campuses when the advertisements were sent to these school newspapers.

You might want to interview members of the history department on campus and to consult material about the period, such as *The Anatomy of the Nuremberg Trials, A Personal Memoir* by Teflord Taylor (New York: Alfred A. Knopf, 1992). Taylor was the chief American counsel at the trials.

### Skill Drill I: Famous Works

Who wrote, painted, composed or otherwise created or devised the following?

1. "The Republic"
2. *The Iliad*
3. "Measure for Measure"
4. *War and Peace*
5. *Ulysses* (Novel)
6. "Under Milk Wood"
7. *The Waste Land*
8. "A Hard Day's Night"
9. "A Doll's House"
10. "Kubla Khan"
11. *Miss Lonelyhearts*
12. *The Aeneid*
13. *The Catcher in the Rye*
14. *Lord of the Rings*
15. *Citizen Kane*
16. *The Brothers Karamazov*
17. *Uncle Tom's Cabin*
18. "The Magic Flute"
19. "La Traviata"
20. *La Dolce Vita*
21. "The Night of the Iguana"
22. *The Return of the Native*
23. *The Decline of the West*
24. *The Great Gatsby*
25. *The Magic Mountain*
26. *Pride and Prejudice*
27. *The Gulag Archipelago*
28. *The Sound and the Fury*
29. *The Sun Also Rises*
30. *Sister Carrie*
31. "The Cherry Orchard"
32. *Candide*
33. *The Scarlet Letter*
34. *Wuthering Heights*
35. "The Mikado"
36. *Bartleby, the Scrivener*
37. *Winesburg, Ohio*
38. *Leaves of Grass*
39. *On the Origin of Species*
40. *Bleak House*
41. *Of Human Bondage*
42. *The Turn of the Screw*
43. "Blowin' in the Wind"
44. "To His Coy Mistress"
45. *Through the Looking Glass*
46. *Don Quixote*
47. *Madame Bovary*
48. "Mona Lisa"
49. "Guernica"
50. *Birth of a Nation*

51. *Mein Kampf*
52. "Love Me Tender"
53. *Ten Little Indians*
54. "La Belle Dame sans Merci"
55. *Invisible Man*
56. *Tom Jones*
57. "Richard III"
58. *My Ántonia*
59. "The Emperor Jones"
60. *Walden*
61. The Model T
62. *The Interpretation of Dreams*
63. *The Education of Henry Adams*
64. "Die Meistersinger"
65. *Sonnets from the Portuguese*
66. "Faust"
67. "The Gettysburg Address"
68. *Annie Hall*
69. *Das Kapital*
70. The steam engine
71. "Swan Lake"
72. *The Metamorphosis*
73. "First Epistle to Corinthians"
74. *West Side Story*
75. "Swann's Way"
76. *The Shame of the Cities*
77. "Essay Concerning Human Understanding"
78. *Germinal*
79. "The 95 Theses"
80. *Black Boy*
81. "The Trout Quintet"
82. *Silent Spring*
83. *The City of God*
84. "Le Sacre du Printemps"
85. *Discourse on Method*
86. *Death in the Afternoon*
87. *Time* Magazine
88. The cotton gin
89. "Pygmalion"
90. "A Streetcar Named Desire"
91. *Point Counter Point*
92. *Coming of Age in Samoa*
93. "Mrs. Robinson"
94. *The Grapes of Wrath*
95. "The Sermon on the Mount"
96. "Letter from Birmingham City Jail"
97. *The Jungle*
98. *Jane Eyre*
99. *The Wealth of Nations*
100. "Fidelio"

## Test III: Punctuation

Place the proper punctuation in the blank.

1. She praised the students _____ and they completed the assignment.
    (a) ,    (b) -(dash)    (c) :    (d) no punctuation needed
2. He asked her, "Have you seen 'The Wizard of Oz _____
    (a) ?'"    (b) '?"    (c) "'?    (d) ."'
3. I was late _____ because the car had a flat tire.
    (a) ,    (b) :    (c) ;    (d) no punctuation needed
4. She usually doesn't give speeches _____ however, this time she will make an exception.
    (a) ,    (b) :    (c) ;    (d) no punctuation needed
5. Curtis _____ and Hilda's house is for sale.
    (a) '    (b) 's    (c) s'    (d) no punctuation needed
6. We plan to use Frank Jones _____ canoe on our camping trip.
    (a) es'    (b) 's    (c) '    (d) no punctuation needed
7. The forecast calls for light showers, morning fog _____ and late afternoon clearing.
    (a) ,    (b) -(dash)    (c) :    (d) no punctuation needed.
8. Arriving this afternoon are Martha Washington, 37, of Ashland; George Washington, 45, of Medford _____ and their three nephews, Max, 12; Harry, 8; and Tom, 3.
    (a) ,    (b) - (dash)    (c) ;    (d) no punctuation needed
9. He took the plane _____ she drove the car.
    (a) ,    (b) - (dash)    (c) ;    (d) no punctuation needed
10. She asked, "How would you feel _____
    (a) ."    (b) ?"    (c) "?    (d) ?".

Building and Using Background    111

11. "We must begin at the end _____ she said.
    (a) ."   (b) ",   (c) ,"   (d) "
12. You need to go to the library _____ and look that word up.
    (a) ;   (b) ,   (c) - (dash)   (d) no punctuation needed
13. The police describe the fugitive as _____ "armed and extremely dangerous."
    (a) - (dash)   (b) :   (c) ,   (d) no punctuation needed
14. The bells rang from all the churches in all the villages _____ and the people rejoiced.
    (a) ;   (b) ,   (c) :   (d) no punctuation needed
15. Before you arrived _____ all was peaceful.
    (a) ,   (b) - (dash)   (c) .   (d) no punctuation needed

## *You Decide: Holocaust (2)*

You are the editor of a campus newspaper, and the advertising manager shows you an advertisement accompanied by a large check. The advertisement is headed, "The Holocaust Controversy: The Case for Open Debate," and it bears the byline of Bradley R. Smith. The advertisement is from the Committee for Open Debate on the Holocaust.

You know that this is a highly charged ad by an organization that some people have described as anti-Semitic.

What do you do?

See in this chapter of the *Workbook* **DB/CAR *A. Holocaust.***

# 13 Finding, Cultivating and Using Sources

Axel Schulz-Eppers, The Associated Press.
**Good sources = Good stories.**

### Introduction

The time-honored journalism adage states: A reporter can be no better than his or her sources. Reporters depend on their sources for background, tips and corroborating information. The reporter looks for the best-qualified in terms of background and position to supply information. Reporters have techniques for testing their sources' reliability, and when a source fails the test, that source is dropped. The journalist also uses a variety of physical sources: records, documents, clippings, databases. An understanding of how systems work points the reporter to useful physical sources.

## Exercise

### A. Ignorance

You are thumbing through an old copy of a magazine and you come across a familiar name, Jorge Luis Borges. He was an Argentine writer who visited Mallory College on a national tour of five colleges 15 years ago. On his return to Argentina, he made a statement from which the magazine quotes. This is the quote that catches your eye:

> American college students are extraordinarily ignorant. They read only what they must to pass or what the professors choose. Otherwise, they are totally dedicated to television, to baseball and football.
> The United States has lost the literary tradition that produced such writers as Emerson, Thoreau, Melville and Frost.

You check the clips and find a brief story about his speaking to English classes at Mallory. You then call the English department, and the chairman, Samuel Ward, tells you the department was the host for Sr. Borges' visit. In answer to your question about the writer's reactions, Ward says:

> Yes, I saw the article containing that material. Like all generalizations, there was truth and untruth in it, and there still is.
> I've been teaching here and elsewhere in colleges for 28 years and clearly students are not as well read today as their parents were.
> Class discussions are not as lively. Sometimes you feel as though you are striking a hollow object. All you hear is your own thumping.
> You know, I find something fascinating happening now in the written work I receive. The imagery is from television and movie characters. Whereas we used to have references to the Bible, Shakespeare and mythology, or characters in fairy tales or from Hemingway, we now have these entertainment personalities.
> As someone who doesn't watch television much, I'm unable to cope with these compositions. Not much has changed since Borges made his observations.
> Each year, we go into class hoping it will be different. I'm not a pessimist. It may be wishful thinking, but I have to think we will return to our tradition of Emerson, Thoreau and the other great writers of our past.

Write 250 to 300 words.

### B. Acne

Assume this article is from the current issue of the *Journal of the American Medical Association*. Summarize in a paragraph of no more than three sentences of your own language the purpose and conclusion of the article. Then write a story of 350 to 400 words.

**Note:** As a conscientious reporter, you wonder about the sponsorship of the study, which is mentioned in small type at the end of the article. Your editor suggests you write to the foundation that made the grant and ask if it has any connection with the chocolate manufacturing industry. You receive a letter from F.L. Handy, administrative assistant, who states:

> In response to your recent inquiry, the John A. Hartford Foundation, Inc. has no connection with the chocolate industry.
> The foundation was established in 1929 by John A. Hartford and incorporated in New York State in 1932. Its capital funds came from bequests by John A. Hartford and his brother, George L., both deceased, whose father founded the Great Atlantic & Pacific Tea Co.
> The foundation's area of interest is biochemical research conducted mainly in medical schools and teaching hospitals.
> Among some 300 medical research projects currently being funded is one at the Hospital of the University of Pennsylvania for a study of the causes and treatment of acne, being directed by an eminent dermatologist. His investigations are wide ranging and, among other things, he once sought to determine whether chocolate was indeed a causative factor. But may we assure you that this was but a small and passing phase in several years of sophisticated biochemical studies that have contributed much new medical knowledge on the etiology of acne and a new clinically tested treatment which is the most effective of any developed to date. For a brief report on this see the item on page 2 of the enclosed bulletin.

Here is the article from the *Journal*. It is by James E. Fulton Jr., M.D.; Gerd Plewig, M.D.; and Albert M. Kligman, M.D., Ph.D. All are members of the Department of Dermatology, University of Pennsylvania School of Medicine, Philadelphia.

# Effect of Chocolate on Acne Vulgaris*

To test the widespread idea that chocolate is harmful in instances of acne vulgaris, 65 subjects with moderate acne ate either a bar containing ten times the amount of chocolate in a typical bar or an identical-appearing bar which contained no chocolate. Counting of all the lesions on one side of the face before and after each ingestion period indicated no difference between the bars. Five normal subjects ingested two enriched chocolate bars daily for one month; this represented a daily addition of the diet of 1,200 calories, of which about half was vegetable fat. This excessive intake of chocolate and fat did not alter the composition or output of sebum. A review of studies purporting to show that diets high in carbohydrate or fat stimulate sebaceous secretion and adversely affect acne vulgaris indicates that these claims are unproved.

Throughout history, foods have been reviled or favored in accordance with whether they were thought to be baleful or beneficial in disease. The strength of these beliefs has been proportionate to ignorance regarding etiology. Some recondite psychology has decreed that in serious, killing diseases, special foods tend to be prescribed, whereas in lesser afflictions, proscription is the rule. Acne vulgaris is a sovereign example of the latter. No foods are favored for acne victims, but many are inveighed against with holy furor. The list of forbidden foods has one remarkable feature: all of the blacklisted items are delicious and delectable to the adolescent taste. High on the list are such desiderata as nuts, candy, carbonated beverages, shellfish, cheese, and malted milk. While certain of these are deprecated more than others, none is more universally condemned than chocolate. It is a rare general practitioner and an odd dermatologist who is not persuaded that chocolate aggravates acne. We could find but one publication, from Missouri, which following the skeptical traditions of that state, questions the harmfulness of chocolate.

The prevalent beliefs concerning the influence of chocolate or any foodstuff on acne are no more than personal credos which cannot be put before the scientific assembly for evaluation. Controlled investigation is entirely lacking.

Whether foods influence acne is a matter of prime importance in theory and in practice. The disease is enough of a curse without gustatory deprivation. Moreover, if a food can really alter a disease, when there is no metabolic or nutritional deficiency, that finding alone would set into motion a wholesale attack on the effects of foods on normal physiologic functions.

We decided therefore to undertake a controlled investigation of the effect of chocolate on the course of acne vulgaris.

## Materials and Methods

**Clinical Evaluation.** The study commenced with 71 subjects, of whom 65 completed the test. The subjects were drawn from two populations: (1) 30 adolescents (14 girls and 16 boys) attending a special acne clinic at the University Hospital, Philadelphia, and (2) 35 young adult male prisoner volunteers. Most of the subjects believed that chocolate was bad for acne. Some "knew" with certainty that eating a chocolate bar a day would be disastrous. Whites predominated in both groups.

Attempts were made to minimize error by incorporating the following controls.

1. Only subjects with mild to moderate acne were included, so as to enhance the possibility of detecting worsening. The clinical state was evaluated by counting all the comedones, papules, and pustules on the left side of the face, on a weekly basis, at the beginning, middle, and end of the test period. A bland, nonmedicated lotion was the sole treatment.

2. A blind study was made possible through the Chocolate Manufacturers Association of the USA. Two bars, a control bar (A), and an enriched chocolate bar (B), identical in size, shape, color, and wrapping were supplied. To our astonishment, these were remarkably similar in taste, although the control bar contained no chocolate. The test bars were quite similar with respect to calories and percentage of fat. Both weighed 112 to 114 gm; bar A contained slightly more calories, 592 compared with 557 for bar B. The placebo bar A contained 28% vegetable fat to mimic the lipids contained in chocolate liquor and cocoa butter. Bar B was of bittersweet chocolate.

We deliberately contrived to have the subjects ingest high quantities of chocolate daily, greatly in excess of what is likely to be consumed by even the passionate lover of chocolate. Bar B actually contained more than ten times the amount of chocolate liquor of a typical 10-cent milk chocolate bar weighing 45 gm.

3. A crossover, single-blind format was followed. The subjects ate one bar of either A or B type once daily for four weeks and, after a three-week rest period, the alternate bar for another month. To simplify interpretation, a subject was considered worse if the lesion count increased 30% at the end of a test period; improved if lesion count decreased 30%; and unaffected if there was less than a 30% change. Complaints of gastrointestinal discomfort were common but irregular with both bars. Five subjects gave this discomfort as the reason for quitting the test.

**Measuring the Effect of Excessive Chocolate Ingestion.** Five healthy, adult male prisoners volunteered for this portion of the study. Each ingested two of the bittersweet chocolate bars daily for one month. It is reemphasized that this amounts to 20 times more chocolate liquor than is contained in a 10-cent bar of milk chocolate. The volunteers ate the regular prison diet ad lib. Four of the five gained 2.3 to 4.5 kg (5 to 10 lb) during the test period.

*From the Department of Dermatology, University of Pennsylvania School of Medicine, Philadelphia. Reprint requests to 3600 Spruce St., Philadelphia, Pa. 19104 (Dr. Kligman).

Sebum Production—Sebum production was assayed by the method of Strauss and Pochi, in which sebum is collected in cigarette papers fastened to the forehead for three hours. Sebum output was determined on three consecutive days before the test period; on two consecutive days midway; and on days 30, 31, and 32 at the end.

Sebum Composition—The composition of sebum was determined by photodensitometric thin-layer chromatography at the beginning of the study, after two weeks, at the end, and 14 days after ingestion of the bars. Sebum was collected in the morning, before the prisoners washed, by placing 10 ml of redistilled ethyl ether in a glass cup and holding it to the cheek for two minutes. The samples were shipped in aluminum-capped glass tubes to the laboratory of Don Downing, PhD, in Boston, who performed the sebum analysis. Rubber and plastic caps could not be used, since ether extracts contaminating compounds.

Comedogenic Potency—Comedogenic potency was assayed in the external ear canal of the rabbit after the method of Kligman and Katz. Scalp sebum was collected before and after the ingestion period by having each subject dip his head into a basin of ethyl ether on three consecutive days. After volatilization, the residue was inuncted into the rabbit ear canal once daily, five days a week, for two weeks. The amount of comedo formation was assessed at the end of this time, from horizontally sectioned biopsies.

## Results

**Clinical.** With the bittersweet chocolate bar, the conditions of 46 of the 65 subjects remained the same, 10 were better, and 9 worse. With the control bar, conditions of 53 remained the same, 5 were better, and 7 worsened. These differences are insignificant, though it is hard to resist pointing out that conditions of twice as many subjects improved after they had eaten chocolate. The adolescent patients and the slightly older prisoners did not materially differ in their responses; hence, the data are not further subdivided. After a rest period of two months, four of the inmates who had previously experienced acne flare-ups after eating chocolate were given the bittersweet chocolate bar again. One defected at the end of two weeks because of gastrointestinal upset. However, in no case did the acne flare again.

**Effect on Sebum of Ingesting Two Enriched Chocolate Bars Daily.** Sebum Production—No clear trend is discernible. In three there was an apparent increase, and in two an apparent decrease. Although the sample size is small and the method imprecise, it seems likely that forced feeding of chocolate does not importantly affect the output of sebum.

Sebum Composition—Again, no trend is discernible. Throughout, the values for the fatty acids tend to be higher than usual. Downing suggests that this results from continued lipolysis during transit of the specimens. However, the sum of the glycerides and free fatty acids is in the usual range. It is well known that there is an inverse relationship between the two, as must be the case since the fatty acids derive hydrolytically from the glycerides. Although excessive chocolate consumption did not affect the general composition of sebum, we cannot categorically assert that there was no change, since individual fatty acids were not assayed.

Comedogenic Potency—The sebum of all five subjects was moderately to strongly comedogenic before treatment. This did not change after the ingestion of chocolate. This is consistent with the lack of chemical change of the sebum.

## Comment

The key finding in this study can be reduced to a simple statement: ingestion of high amounts of chocolate did not materially affect the course of acne vulgaris or the output or composition of sebum. Actually, since the bittersweet bars contain about one-third fat, we may also infer that a diet rich in vegetable fat probably does not alter sebaceous secretion. The literature on the effect of dietary fats and carbohydrates on acne and sebaceous secretion is singularly confusing, contradictory, and controversial. Yet the belief that foods adversely influence skin disease is ancient and deeply rooted. More proof than we have supplied will doubtless be necessary before long-held clinical prejudices will yield gracefully to experimentation.

In reviewing an extensive experimental literature, mainly about animals, one becomes keenly aware of a remarkably consistent outcome. It is almost always found that high fat or carbohydrate levels increase either the quantity or quality of lipids excreted by the skin. If true, this would provide a plausible explanation for the exacerbating effects of such diets. For example, forced feeding of fats has not only been found to increase sebaceous output, but—perhaps even more remarkable—the fed lipid was excreted unchanged. Somekawa's observations on rats fed whale oil are perhaps typical of the wish to believe that high-fat diets affect lipid excretion. While there is no doubt that the skin of these animals dripped with oil, this was clearly not due to excretion via the skin, but to the spreading out of unabsorbed oil from the anus.

Another experimental limitation relates to the difficulty of accurately determining sebum output in hairy animals. Investigators who found increases in sebaceous secretion after fat feeding usually did not take the trouble to establish the reliability of their methods. Such a criticism applies notably to the oft-quoted work of Suzuki who, with excessive feeding of fats to rabbits, obtained increase of 70% to 111% of sebaceous secretion in two weeks. As a matter of fact, there has been only one critical study of the influence of dietary fats, and the conclusion clearly refutes the prevailing dogma. Nikkari fed rats diets containing 20% stearic, oleic, or linoleic acids, or cholesterol. He measured sebum output by collecting the total surface lipids four days after a previous removal of the fats, and analyzed the components by chemical and chromatographic methods. Neither the quality nor quantity of the surface lipids was affected. Nikkari states categorically that the sebaceous glands cannot serve as an excretory pathway for lipids. When C stearate was given, only a tiny fraction (0.4%) of the radioactivity appeared in the sebum, and this was no longer present as stearate but had been incorporated in all major lipid fractions of sebum.

Similarly, those who experiment on humans generally find that diet may change the amount and composition of the lipids excreted. Serrati found increases in forehead lipids when either excess carbohydrates or fats were given. MacDonald gave healthy men a low-fat diet, augmented either with 500 gm a day of starch or sucrose, for 25 days. Both caused some increase in the straight-chain C monounsaturated fatty acid; only starch increased the saturated C acid. He also gave 28 gm/kg of chocolate to 29 adolescents for five days. This increased the cholesterol content of the surface lipids, and the triglyceride in the surface lipids diminished in men, but not in women!

Lipkin et al have begun to attack the problem of finding out whether fats can pass unchanged from the blood via the sebaceous gland to the surface of the body. They perfused radioactive palmitic acid, triolein, cholesterol, and cholesteryl esters through a skin flap in dogs. Less than 1% of each of these substances could be recovered from the anatomical portion representing the epidermis and sebaceous glands. This is hardly conclusive and probably reflects contamination, since much higher amounts were found in underlying dermis.

The question is not whether circulating substances such as drugs can enter the gland; they almost certainly can. We have found that tetracycline reaches the body surface partly via sebum. The key point is whether circulating lipids can be excreted without being metabolized. We think not.

One must be cautioned not to compare sebaceous gland to adipose tissue. This latter is essentially a fat-storing, not a fat-elaborating, organ. The lipids of the subcutaneous tissue are vastly simpler: more than 99% is triglyceride, practically all of which is accounted for by a few fatty acids. Excess dietary fats unquestionably do alter the composition of subcutaneous fat after prolonged intake. Thus, with a diet rich in corn oil, the adipose lipids may slowly come to resemble corn oil.

On the other hand, there is considerable circumstantial evidence that blood lipids are not excreted by the sebaceous glands. The likelihood is that these are hydrolyzed to simple carbon fragments from which all the multifarious sebaceous lipids are synthesized by the gland. If this were not so, the lipids present in serum would also occur in sebum. There are a number of ready examples to show that such is not the case. For instance, the unsaturated C fatty acid in sebum is not linoleic, as in serum. Of the 18:1 fatty acid in serum, more than 95% is $\Delta^9$, whereas in sebum 20% is $\Delta^9$. All of the 16:1 acid in serum is $\Delta^9$ and all in sebum is $\Delta^6$, as noted by Don Downing, PhD (written communication Feb. 8, 1969). An even more extraordinary case in point is that in animal species, the sebum contains little or no triglycerides, though these are abundant in the serum.

As regards clinical studies of the influence of diet on acne, perhaps the less said the better. An egregious example of unwarranted assertions is afforded by Hoehn's tract, "Acne and Diet." Although we do not know the true prevalence of acne in any land, Hoehn compared supposedly low-incidence countries such as Korea, Spain, Turkey, and Eskimo villages where the principal source of fats is vegetable oils, fish, and fowl, with high-incidence locations like Pakistan, the United States, and Mombasa, Kenya, where the main source is saturated animal fat. Thus furnished with data as wide as the world itself, Hoehn instituted a diet low in unsaturated vegetable fats, avoiding animal fats. Not unexpectedly, the beneficial effects in instances of acne were dramatic.

Though much more critical work is required, present knowledge suggests that the sebaceous gland has a high degree of autonomy. Neither the intensity nor quality of its activity is very sensitive to the internal or external milieu. The principle of homeostasis doubtlessly applies to tissues as well as to fluids. It would be remarkable if skin functions were easily influenced by the vagaries of the diverse diets which have evolved in human populations.

This investigation was supported by a grant from the John A. Hartford Foundation.

## Assignments

### A. Government

Take any branch of local government and write a public service piece on how a department or an agency within that branch functions.

1. **Executive:** mayor's office; city manager; departments and bureaus. You might pick the head of a department and show the work done, the pressures on the executive, the rewards and frustrations. You may select a midlevel person from among the civil servants whose activities keep city government functioning.

2. **Legislative:** city council or city commission. You can focus on the body as a whole or on an individual. If the former, you might examine its changing functions through the years, its accomplishments and failures. If you select an individual, you might follow a particular piece of legislation under consideration by the council and watch the person reach a decision on the matter.

3. **Judicial:** court system, judges, prosecutors, legal aid. Is the system functioning well? If so, describe the people who make it work. If not, why not, and what will have to be done? If you focus on the individual, show that person at work.

*B. Ignorance React*

Interview members of the local college or university English department about Borges' assessment of college students. See *A. Ignorance.*

*C. Statistics*

Consult the appropriate references to find out the following about your state and nearby states and see whether your state ranks high or low in these categories. Find out why your state ranks where it does by interviewing authorities in the area concerned.

1. Physicians, dentists and nurses.
2. Motor vehicle deaths.
3. Average salary of public elementary and secondary school teachers.
4. Years of school completed, by race.
5. Median family income.
6. Life insurance in force.
7. Infant mortality rate.
8. Crime rate: homicide, robbery.
9. Suicide.
10. Infectious diseases: tuberculosis, syphilis, measles, mumps.

*D. Requirements*

A national panel recommended better science education in the schools in response to studies in the 1990s that showed American students consistently score below European and Asian students. The panel suggested science education begin in the elementary grades. It stated, for example, that fourth graders should know that the sun appears to make the same trek every day but that its path gradually changes during the four seasons. Similar findings and recommendations have been made about the study of mathematics.

Most high schools require only two years of science and two years of mathematics for high school graduation. Among those that require three years of each for all students are Florida, Georgia, Hawaii, Louisiana and Pennsylvania. To graduate with academic honors, students in Indiana and Florida are required to take four years of science and mathematics.

What is the situation in your city's high schools? Are grade and high schools emphasizing science and math? Does the state have any requirements in these study areas?

## Campus Project

### Gender

Examine the status of female faculty members on your campus. What percentage of the total faculty are women? What percentage do they make up of the ranks—instructor, assistant professor, associate professor, professor? Examine their salary levels and compare with those of their male counterparts.

Break down the totals into various schools and departments on the campus.

Interview male and female faculty members for their comments on the situation, and talk to department heads and deans.

## Community Project

### Sweet Stuff

A study of grocery and supermarket shelves has shown that children's cereals, which contain about 45 percent sugar, are displayed at eye level to attract children whereas so-called adult cereals, which contain about 10 percent sugar, are placed higher.

The study was made by the Center for Science in the Public Trust, which also listed the percentages of sugar found in various cereals:

| Cereal | Maker | % Sugar |
|---|---|---|
| Ghostbusters | Ralston | 64 |
| Apple Jacks | Kellogg | 49 |
| Froot Loops | Kellogg | 45 |
| Cap'n Crunch | Quaker | 42 |
| Cocoa Pebbles | Post | 42 |
| Trix | General Mills | 42 |
| Corn Pops | Kellogg | 42 |
| Cocoa Puffs | General Mills | 39 |
| Lucky Charms | General Mills | 39 |
| Frosted Flakes | Kellogg | 39 |

Check local grocery and supermarket shelves to see where children's breakfast cereal is kept. Talk to the store manager to see whether this is a standard practice. Examine the packaging of these cereals and compare it with so-called adult cereal packaging.

Ask nutritionists about the sugar percentages listed for children's cereals. What is an acceptable sugar level and what is wrong with the high levels? Did you notice any other sweets at a child's grab level?

Bob Thayer, *The Journal-Bulletin.*

**He shopped and shopped, and then he dropped.**

## Home Assignment

### Sources

1. Go through the local newspaper and clip at least two examples of stories that rely on human sources and two that rely on physical sources for information.

2. What are the physical sources on which articles are based?

3. Do you notice any stories that could have been strengthened with the addition of one or the other type of source? For example, does a story using physical sources lack human interest because no people were interviewed?

## Class Discussion

### Lists

Compile a list of the major news sources in your community and on your campus. Each list should contain a minimum of a dozen names that will include not only the obvious sources—mayor, police chief, university president and deans—but the so-called movers and shakers in the community and on the campus.

## DB/CAR

### Contraceptive

Your editor shows you a press release from Mallory College. The College has appointed a new dean of students, William Sharman, whose previous post was dean of students at Colby College in Waterville, Maine. One of his publicized achievements at Colby, the editor says, was a successful campaign to provide birth control and disease prevention counseling and birth control prescriptions at the student health center. A clipping about Sharman quotes him as saying, "There were many criticisms of this step, and there still are. But it seems to me that it is both responsible and appropriate for the educational and health needs of students in college today."

The editor wants you to prepare some background on birth control and disease prevention services of universities and colleges around the country so that when Sharman arrives you can interview him.

Make a database and reference search of what universities and colleges around the country offer. Is there any AIDS counseling as well? Check other schools in your state. Prepare a background story of at least 300 words.

## Skill Drill: What's Next?

1. You hear a rumor that the Democratic State Committee is planning an important meeting next week at the Freeport Motor Lodge and that it may speak out about presidential candidates. You have two hours to deadline. You call the lodge and ask for next week's events, but the desk clerk finds no party meeting on the calendar. You ask for the manager, and he replies that she is not in. Where is she? "At home, next door," he says, and in answer to your request for her name and phone number, he says he's too busy and hangs up. What do you do?

2. The manager of the Freeport Kiwanis Club, John F. Berlin, is in Atlanta attending a national convention. A source calls and says he died of a heart attack there this morning. How will you get information for a local story?

3. The Freeport Civic Society's president, Lawrence Berry, says the group will meet next month to add to the list of "objectionable" books it drew up last year. Your editor tells you he wants you to do a precede on the activities of such groups and the response to their activities. Where do you start looking?

4. You hear on the police radio that a man is holding his infant daughter outside an apartment building window on Springfield Street and is threatening to drop her. You do not have time to go there before your noon local news broadcast. The police are giving you only the barest details. How do you gather more information?

## Fix It: More Trademarks

Give the generic name for these trademark products:

1. Caterpillar _____
2. Windex _____
3. Walkman _____
4. Q-Tips _____
5. Mace _____

# 14 Interviewing Principles

### Introduction

Journalists rely for most of their information on interviews with sources. The two types of interviews are:

**News interview:** Material is gathered from sources to explain and to document the event a reporter is covering. Sometimes the source is used for explanatory background. The focus is the event.
**Profile:** The individual is the focus of the story.

Effective interviews follow the reporter's careful preparations. The reporter has a good grasp of the event or situation for the news interview. For the profile, the reporter has checked the individual's background in the files.

National Broadcasting Co., Inc.
**Getting close to the subject.**

## Exercises

### A. Flies

Roger Alexander, a biochemist who is chairman of the Friends of Nature, a national conservation organization, is in town to organize a state chapter. You are sent to interview him. He is 38, a graduate of Syracuse University, where he took his bachelor's and master's degrees, and Indiana University, where he received his Ph.D. He is married, father of two children, boy, 6, girl, 9. He is easygoing, smiles often, lives in Minneapolis, pays his own way to do organizational work. He says:

Actually, I try to combine my vacation and any other work with organizing. I think conservation is perhaps our greatest domestic priority.
Not that it isn't of worldwide concern. Everywhere, people seem intent on pillaging nature. The story of Eastern Europe's industrialization is well known. Air so polluted life span is cut a dozen years.
Instead of seeking the mastery of nature with unnatural means, we should learn to live with it in harmony and thereby derive pleasure from our niche on this planet. I mean by this that there are natural ways man can coexist. Take control of insects. We drop insecticides on our planet, poisoning the earth and ourselves in the process. But insects are developing a resistance to pesticides. We have a better way of coping with harmful pests—to use their natural enemies.
An entomologist, Philip B. Morgan, of Gainesville, Fla., has shown that the use of a parasitic wasp can control flies on the farm. He releases hundreds of thousands of these wasps—the technical name is *Spalangia endius*—near the fly breeding grounds. The female wasp lays her eggs in fly pupae. They grow and eventually kill their host.
In a month, the entire local fly population is destroyed. The wasps generally do not bother large animals or humans.
On a larger scale, several varieties of stingless wasps were imported from Europe and Asia to fight the alfalfa weevil. From 1959 to 1980, the wasps were used in 11 Northwestern states. Spraying of chemical pesticides was reduced 73 percent, at a savings of $8 million a year. Since 1981, about 15 million wasps have been released in 25 other states in the Southeast and Midwest. Savings have been in the millions here as well. Eventually, wasps will be released in all states where alfalfa is grown.
We have a membership of 16,000 nationally, which is small. But we are not a mass organization. Our people are the doers. They influence legislation, give speeches. Of course, we are happy to have anyone. But we're not trying to overwhelm Congress

with numbers but with the quality of our presentation. . . . Look, it's clear enough, isn't it? Dump sewage in the ocean, chemicals into rivers; dig holes in the deserts; pave over farmland; send deadly fumes into the air—we'll have destroyed ourselves by the end of the century. We can see disaster on the horizon.

## B. Cars

The office of financial aid at St. Mary's University calls and says it has a release of great importance. You go there and C.L. Braverman, the director of the office, says there is a new policy on the use of cars by students receiving aid. He tells you:

> We've had nothing but trouble with cars here. Students ask us for help and when we get a financial statement from them, we find they have a new Chevy or a Porsche.
> How can we justify aid to students whose college money goes not for tuition, room, board or books, but for car payments and oil and gas?
> We now have $250,000 a year for aid and about twice that amount in low-interest loans. Last year, 220 of the 600 freshmen sought help. Well, that averages to a little more than $1,000 a student for scholarships; and we estimate costs per year are $11,000, minimum.
> Then we'd hear about these students with cars. The system was not equitable.

He describes the new policy, adopted unanimously by the student aid committee:

> The following regulation, to take effect next fall, pertaining to the use of motor vehicles by financial-aid recipients, reflects the concern of the committee that limited aid resources might be awarded to students who would utilize these funds for the maintenance of a vehicle for personal convenience, rather than for educational expenses. The regulation, however, is designed to give financial aid recipients the opportunity to have at their disposal a motor vehicle if they are willing to experience a reduction in gift scholarship.

The regulation is as follows:

> Students receiving financial aid may have a motor vehicle at their disposal while attending college provided they register the vehicle or vehicles in their names at the Buildings and Grounds office, and provided that they accept a reduction in their financial aid at a rate of $200 per semester per vehicle.
> Failure to register a vehicle may result in the loss of all financial aid and/or revocation of the privilege of college vehicle registration and/or operating privileges and suspension from college.
> Any attempt, plan, device, combination or conspiracy, such as registering a vehicle in another's name, arranging a temporary sale, parking a vehicle off campus, designed to circumvent or that results in the circumvention of the above regulation may result in the loss of all financial aid and/or revocation of the privilege of college vehicle registration and/or operating privileges and suspension from college for all others involved in the combination or conspiracy.
> The Director of Financial Aid may grant exemption from the above for financial-aid recipients who (1) have necessary employment off campus requiring the use of a personal vehicle; (2) have academic assignment, such as the off-campus Teaching Practicum; (3) have physical disability; or (4) are commuters who reside at their homes with no other available transportation.

Write 250 to 300 words.

## Assignments

In the following assignments, several questions are suggested. These should not limit you. Nor should they necessarily be the thrust of the interview. All interviews should be preceded by research. Remember: Always ask the source to give specific answers and to illustrate with an anecdote or an example some of the points being made. Good interviews let us see and hear the person—use descriptions and quotations.

### A. Prospects

Interview two or three of the major automobile dealers in town about prospects for the coming year and sales during the past year. Any significant changes in purchasing patterns? Any models that are locally popular? Have the proportions of new and used vehicles sold changed in recent years?

### B. Postal

What is the life of a postal worker like—what are its rewards, discouragements? Why did the person go into the work? Would he or she advise young people to enter the field? Any interesting experiences while delivering the mail?

*C. Behavior*

Interview the dean of students about changing patterns in student behavior and in teaching:

1. Are students more mature?
2. Has racial tension increased/decreased among students?
3. Is there less concern by administrators over student off-campus behavior?
4. Is there any sentiment on campus for a more demanding curriculum?
5. Is there an indication of grade inflation, and, if so, what is being done about it?

*D. Religion*

Interview religious leaders in the community for a roundup on changes in number and types of members, attendance at services and Sunday school, shifts in doctrine or policies of the parent church. Is the church attracting young members? Why?

*E. Accountant*

Most people presume the life of an accountant is tedious and boring. Interview a local accountant about his or her work.

*F. Music*

Interview the leader of one of the local popular music groups. What kind of music do people prefer these days? Is this a shift from past preferences? Do people prefer listening, dancing or both? Is the audience growing? Are there any all-female groups, female lead musicians?

*G. Union*

Attitudes toward unions and union leaders rise and dip with the times. Lately, unions have been losing membership. Interview the head of a local union and ask for his or her assessment of public sentiment. Has this made the work of the union easier, more difficult? What is the history of a local union: when founded, membership totals, accomplishments, failures? What are its immediate and long-range goals?

*H. Donations*

Interview the school's director of fund raising, or whoever on the campus is in charge of raising money from private sources. How successful has the past year, half year or quarter been? What is the money being used for? Any plans for future fund drives for special purposes? Who, what are the big givers? Any change in giving patterns over the past few years?

*I. Lawyer*

One of the problems criminal defendants with modest income face is their inability to hire a lawyer. Legal commentators say most lawyers turn away from trial law, preferring the more lucrative practice of corporate or business law. Locate a trial lawyer and discuss his or her work, its rewards, its liabilities.

*J. Law Students*

Check the opinions and intentions of students in a law school or seniors in prelaw about the desirability of careers as trial lawyers. If a student is planning such a career, why? Those who say no, why not? Focus on two students, each representing different choices.

*K. GP*

The general practitioner in medicine seems to be another rare species among professionals. Locate one and interview him or her. What are the rewards for such an arduous life? What does the doctor think of the future of general practice? Will it be overwhelmed by the trend toward medical specialties?

*L. Med Students*

Interview several medical students about their career plans. Do any plan a small-town or general practice? Do their aspirations bear out the fear that the general practitioner and the small-town doctor will disappear? If so, do the students think that this is bad? What new fields of medicine do they see opening up for them in the future?

*M. Cars React*

What is done, if anything, on your campus to students who own cars and receive financial aid? Are there any limitations on their activities; any proposals for limitations? Do any regents, trustees or workers in the financial aid office think there should be? Interview those who are involved in making financial aid policies.

*N. Suspension React*

Interview school officials on the policies for suspension, hearings and appeal in use in the local school system. Have they changed in recent years? What is the school administration's reaction to the policies? Teachers' reactions? Obtain data.

*O. Styles*

Short skirts are back, says a headline of a trade newspaper. Interview local clothing merchants for the latest style trends in men's and women's clothing. Where will hems be next year at this time? Are stubby or pointed toes back for men's shoes? Is formal dress making a comeback?

*P. Divorce Rate*

Class project: Here are the number of divorces per 1,000 population:

| | | |
|---|---|---|
| 1962: 2.2 | 1983: 5.0 | 1990: 4.7 |
| 1969: 3.2 | 1985: 5.0 | 1991: 4.6 |
| 1979: 5.3 | 1987: 4.8 | 1994: 4.7 |

Check your state and bring the figures up-to-date. Interview religious leaders, sociologists, psychiatrists, psychologists, marriage counselors and young married couples to find out why the number of divorces is increasing or declining in your state. (Figures are from the Bureau of the Census.)

## Campus Projects

*A. Racial*

Make a study of the racial composition of the faculty and the administration and staff on your campus. How have these changed in the past decade?

Colleges and universities are making a determined effort to hire minority faculty members, but a major impediment is the scarcity of blacks, Hispanics and Native Americans with advanced degrees in a number of fields. Half the Ph.D. degrees received by blacks in a recent year, for example, were in education, and almost none were received in mathematics, astronomy, physics and allied scientific areas.

Interview faculty members, administrators, staff employees. Obtain data for your campus, and with material from a database search or other research, blend the local and national figures.

*B. Incidents*

Campus incidents of bigotry have increased in recent years. Black groups report increased harassment of students, and the Anti-Defamation League says anti-Semitic campus incidents are up more than 150 percent since 1988. Anti-Semitic acts were reported at the University of Miami, San Francisco State University and Howard University and at Bates, Colby and Bowdoin Colleges in 1994.

What is the situation on your campus? Has your campus been involved in any incidents in recent years? If there have been any acts of racism, religious persecution or homophobia, what has been the administration's reaction? How would you describe the campus attitude toward minority groups? Would a poll ascertain that attitude?

Material about homophobic incidents on campus is available from GLAAD, the Gay and Lesbian Alliance Against Defamation (8455 Beverly Blvd. Ste. 305, Los Angeles, CA 90048–9886). Anti-Semitism is tracked by the Anti-Defamation League (823 U.N. Plaza, New York, NY 10017, 212/490–2525). Local and regional chapters of the National Association for the Advancement of Colored People (NAACP) can provide information about racist incidents.

Distribution of hate literature would not fall under the category of bias crime. Nor would the uttering of slurs. However, many colleges and universities have rules about biased behavior. Some university codes about hate speech have been altered because of court challenges of their constitutionality. Does your campus have a speech code; has it been revised?

## Community Project

### Arms

Almost half of all American adults (46 percent) keep a gun in their homes, a poll has revealed. Make a determination of local gun ownership. In your survey, differentiate among hunting guns, target guns and revolvers kept for protection.

Ask if anyone has had to use a gun of any type in self-defense. Check local police to see whether guns in the home have been responsible for accidents or deaths. What do the police think of home ownership of guns for protective purposes? How do your representatives and senators stand on gun-control legislation? What are the city and state laws on the possession of guns? Has the National Rifle Association donated funds to your legislative or congressional representatives, and have they issued any statements explaining their votes on legislation?

## Home Assignment

### Scapegoat

Your editor gives you a press release from the mayor's office about a parade along Massachusetts Avenue sponsored by the Jewish Community Council. The parade is in response to the coming appearance, next Monday, in Freeport of Louis Farrakhan, head of the Nation of Islam, who is to speak at 8 p.m. in the Civic Auditorium.

Write a 350-word story that includes the mayor's release, background on Farrakhan and the following statement by Arthur Hoch, director of the Jewish Community Relations Council:

> We hope that all Freeport residents will join us in this parade tomorrow at 1 p.m. to show that Freeport does not approve the kind of religious hatred espoused by Mr. Farrakhan. In his attempt to scapegoat one religious group for the misfortunes of another group, he is espousing the bigotry he says he seeks to eliminate. We, too, know the consequences of such scapegoating. He has every right to speak, but we do not have to listen. We shall be at the Auditorium with material about Mr. Farrakhan.
>
> Freeport citizens should know that Mr. Farrakhan has attacked Judaism as "a gutter religion," and he has rewritten history to make Jews slave traders.
>
> No one disputes the real grievances of blacks and other minorities in this country, but Mr. Farrakhan serves no good purpose in espousing hatred and bigotry among the people he says he is trying to help.

THE CITY OF FREEPORT                                          OFFICE OF THE MAYOR

For Immediate Release

*Statement by Mayor Sam Parnass
on Anti-Semitism March and Rally*

Tomorrow the Jewish Community Council is holding an important march and rally to protest anti-Semitism. I add my voice to the chorus in once again condemning this odious form of bigotry.

People of good will everywhere must work to eliminate anti-Semitism, racism and prejudice whenever and wherever they occur—be it on our streets, in our workplaces, from the pulpits of houses of worship, from classroom lecterns or from the offices of political officials in America or abroad. I will continue to criticize all acts of anti-Semitism and hatred—from off-color jokes to drawings of swastikas and the desecration of cemeteries.

I hope everyone will join me in seeking passage of the hate crimes legislation now pending in the state legislature. The bill will put the force of law behind the voices of morality and justice. I know that silence is never acceptable in the face of acts of prejudice, and thus I have lent my voice for decades to the fight against prejudice: in combating the oppression of Jews in the Soviet Union, in protesting in 1975 the enactment of the Zionism equals racism resolution at the United Nations, in criticizing the comments of Louis Farrakhan at Madison Square Garden in 1985 and in memorializing the victims of the Holocaust in 1985 at Dachau. As the mayor of a city with a large Jewish population, my voice will continue to be heard and I will continue to do everything necessary to ensure that our Jewish residents, and all Freeport residents, can lead happy and productive lives free of crime and incidents of hatred. I will take part in the parade.

African-American veterans of the then-segregated U.S. Armed Forces in World War II were recently reunited with Jewish Holocaust survivors whom they had liberated in 1945 from the Nazi death camps of Buchenwald and Dachau. They shared the common pain of having been victims of discrimination and of having witnessed and survived the result of horrific hatred. They shed tears and renewed bonds of friendship in a pledge to combat prejudice.

Let all of us, of every color and every faith, draw inspiration from their example and unite to fight anti-Semitism, racism and hatred today and everyday.

## Class Discussion

### A. Profile

If you were assigned to interview the following people for profiles, how would you prepare for the interview, and what specific questions would you ask?

1. A new member of the English department.
2. A candidate for the city council.
3. The newly elected president of the League of Women Voters.
4. A local businessman who has been appointed to a newly authorized state Reorganization Commission to study the possibility of fewer elective offices and greater centralization of administration.
5. An organizer for a union of campus clerical workers.

## DB/CAR

### Priesthood

One of the most controversial issues facing Christianity is the admission of women to the priesthood. One side says that to deny half the members of the church the priesthood injures the church. The other maintains that the male priesthood was ordained when Jesus Christ summoned 12 men as his Apostles.

The Roman Catholic Church has resisted efforts made for years, mostly by its American bishops, to lift restrictions against women. The Vatican has stated, "The problem of the admission of women to the ministerial priesthood touches the very nature of the sacrament of priestly orders." The Church of England in a close vote discarded the rule that only men may serve as priests.

The Anglican church in the United States, Australia, Canada and New Zealand allows women priests, and most Protestant denominations do also. The large Southern Baptist Convention has a few women pastors, mostly in small parishes. Fundamentalists within the Convention oppose the practice.

After a lengthy study of the issue, American Catholic bishops decided not to take a position on the matter. Rembert G. Weakland, Archbishop of Milwaukee, said the decision "undermines the church's credibility and jeopardizes its ability to attract the next generation of worshippers." He said that if the door remains closed to discussion, the consequences will include "preparing to live in a church of reduced size, for many women and men would say goodbye to a church they feel is out of touch with the world. . . . The church would be seen as hypocritical."

He called for the church to "keep the doors open to further discussion and continue the important, even if painful, dialogue between the church's tradition and modern insights."

One of the opponents of ordaining women, Women for Faith and Family in St. Louis, says that the ordination of women would disregard tradition and cause dissension within the church. Advocates of women in the priesthood take issue with the concept that Jesus and the church are bridegroom and bride, and thus only men can represent Jesus in the mass.

Using the same logic, say supporters of women as priests, the Church should ordain only Jews as priests since all Jesus' disciples were Jews.

Make a search to provide recent background for an article on what various denominations are doing and blend it with how local churches treat the issue. Do any Protestant denominations have women pastors? What is the situation in local synagogues?

## *Fix It: Prepositions*

Find the error and correct the sentence:

1. He was angered with the dean's dismissal.
2. Pearl said the insurgents showered shells into the city.
3. Robinson said he was overwhelmed with the reaction.
4. Cahan gave her strongest criticism against Rep. Trenzier.
5. Addison expressed his dismay and said the heat would have to be turned up against the board.

## Test IV: Subject-Verb Agreement

Select the right answer:

1. Either Richard or Carla **(a) is (b) are** responsible.
2. The company failed to notify **(a) its (b) their** employees.
3. The rose, as well as other flowers, **(a) is (b) are** frequently exhibited.
4. The candidate's politics **(a) is (b) are** offensive.
5. Each of the cars **(a) has its (b) have their** strengths.
6. History is one of the subjects that **(a) interest (b) interests** her.
7. The trumpet, together with the bugle, **(a) is (b) are** a brass instrument.
8. The president and commander in chief **(a) is (b) are** Bill Clinton.
9. Most of the news media **(a) is (b) are** controlled by large corporations.
10. Neither of the houses **(a) was (b) were** sold last weekend.
11. The number of arrests **(a) was (b) were** shocking.
12. Twenty-five thousand dollars **(a) is (b) are** a lot of money to pay for a car.
13. The box of books **(a) is (b) are** his.
14. The alumni **(a) is (b) are** planning to attend the graduation.
15. Measles **(a) is (b) are** a disease many of us have had.

# 15 Interviewing Practices

### Introduction

Successful interviews depend upon incisive questions, accurate observations and a comfortable relationship between the reporter and the source. Occasionally, the reporter will adopt a personality to be more effective in establishing this relationship: friend, confidante, authority figure. Generally, the reporter keeps a low profile in the interview. Regardless of what the source says, no matter how much the source's opinions and comments may irk the reporter, the reporter maintains a neutral mask. Questions are kept short and relevant to the topic, although there may be a prior warming-up period of general chitchat.

Jack Rendulich, *The Duluth News-Tribune.*

**"Make sure you get it down right."**

## Exercises

### A. Criticism

You are told that Frederick Cole, a retired editor of newspapers in Florida, California and Michigan, is in the city to serve as an adviser to the local newspaper, which plans to revamp its makeup and coverage. Your editor tells you that Cole has strong feelings about journalism education and he tells you to interview Cole for a 350- to 450-word piece.

Cole is 68, never went to college, was a successful city hall, legislative and White House reporter by the time he was 30 and then became city editor of *The Chicago Sun*. He went on to the *Houston Chronicle* and then the *San Francisco Examiner*, and he was executive editor of a group of newspapers in the Chicago area, the Atlas Newspapers, since absorbed by other newspapers in the area. He retired a year ago. He had a reputation as a tough editor.

Your editor tells you that it would be a good idea to find out as much as you can about journalism education before seeing Cole, and you first make a list of material you want to dig up in references: the number of students now enrolled in journalism schools and their majors (advertising, broadcast, communications, news-editorial, public relations); the number enrolled in past years; the number of accredited schools; recent articles about journalism education.

You next make up a list of questions for Cole. You have heard that he thinks journalism students are not well prepared for their jobs. You list questions along those lines. You won't read them to him, but you want to familiarize yourself with the subjects you want to bring up.

You then interview Cole at his hotel. He is white-haired, has a ruddy complexion, is thin and of medium height, is wearing a dark blue suit. He has a strong grip when you shake hands and he often smiles, as if to reassure you that he is not really the ogre he is made out to be.

Here are some of the quotes you note for your story:

I still think of myself as an editor, and I talk that way. Can't get the business out of my system. I was a copy boy when I was 16 and I never graduated from high school. But in my day, eighth grade was terminal. A high school boy studied Latin, algebra and read the plays of Shakespeare.

Anyway, the newsroom was an education. We had sports reporters who knew the archaeology of Greece, and city editors who could recite French poetry. Not many. But enough to tell a kid that there was more to this business than fires and murders. I learned it all.

I'm not sure that youngsters take to learning the way we did, and this is showing up in the young men and women who come into the newsroom as beginners. Editors and educators have a common objective: We want to strive for optimum quality in our newspapers. And to do that we need each other.

What we need to do is candidly appraise the weaknesses of today's journalism education—and then do something about it.

Too many applicants lack a working knowledge of the English language. Some can't even type. Others can't spell.

Half of the aspirants who come into my office think a board of supervisors is plural. And they see nothing wrong with a sentence such as "The Chamber of Commerce will hold their annual meeting tomorrow night."

Many of them are hunt-and-peckers, and most of them can't type 30 words a minute. Their spelling is atrocious. I've found that fewer than half of them can spell such commonly used words as *accommodate, commitment* and *judgment*.

They are still being taught that a good lead includes the Five W's and an H. There's little evidence they ever were taught that a reader's degree of understanding drops off dramatically for each word over 20 in a sentence.

We're getting too many hopefuls who lack a background in economics, literature, philosophy, sociology and the natural sciences. They know little of local government. And they can't even report to the office on time.

Are the applicants we're getting imaginative? They think they are because, when using words of attribution, they come up with every word they can think of but the one that usually is the best to use: *said*.

That's not the kind of creative thinking we're looking for. We want young reporters who have enough imagination to go after the stories that are not usually done and to write them with a style and flair that will excite our readers.

And none of them can cope with the pressure of deadlines. When they must write fast, they tie up.

Sure, we expect a lot because we don't label our stories—written by a beginner, intermediate or advanced reporter. Our readers pay for a professionally done product.

How important is spelling to today's editors? We wouldn't even consider hiring a reporter who can't pass our spelling test. If he can't spell, we don't care how many prizes he won in college.

My advice to journalism educators is:

• You should be turning out graduates who want jobs in the general practice of newspapering rather than specialization. That will come later.
• If your students can't dig, write or spell, counsel them—or flunk them out. You'll be doing them a favor, for we don't want them.

Maybe it's time to be more demanding about applicants for the journalism major. I'd make all students who want to study journalism take spelling, punctuation and grammar tests as well as force them to write an essay from a set of facts so that we can see whether they can use the right word in the right place.

Many students are going to be terribly disappointed because they simply are in the wrong field. Journalism requires an outlook, a mental discipline, a curiosity and, above all, a willingness to work hard day and night.

## B. Galloway

You have been sent to interview a foreign correspondent, Joseph L. Galloway Jr., who will be speaking tomorrow night to journalism students at the local college. You have been given his background and have quotes from your interview. Galloway is well built and of medium height, has close-cropped hair. Write 400 words.

*Background*

Joseph L. Galloway Jr. became a UPI correspondent in 1961. Before going to Moscow as a bureau manager, he was manager for Southeast Asia with headquarters in Singapore. He also has served in New Delhi, Jakarta and Tokyo. Before going to Asia, he worked for UPI in Kansas City and Topeka, Kansas.

He was a combat correspondent in Vietnam, about which he has written a book, and was nominated for the Pulitzer Prize for his war coverage in 1965. He was among the last American correspondents in Saigon before it fell to the North Vietnamese in 1975.

He was born Nov. 13, 1941, in Bryan, Tex., and attended Victoria College in his native state. He now works for *U.S. News & World Report*. His quotes:

Given the time and material, a person who has learned the basics of bricklaying can build a grand cathedral. Without those basics his structures will turn out to be hollow and dangerous shells.

It is no different for the reporter.

A good police-beat reporter can cover the White House, and perhaps more of them should.

The basics for the reporter from station house to White House are accuracy and fairness—honest information honestly conveyed.

The reporter owes a lifelong debt to his editor, his readers and, above all, to himself. The ledger on that debt is updated and balanced every time he touches a typewriter or a VDT or a microphone.

He owes all parties the debt of full, fair, balanced coverage of a story which he should approach with personal interest, personal knowledge and a personal commitment to the truth.

There are no routine stories, only stories that have been covered routinely.

Beginning reporters are traditionally "broken in" with a tour of writing obituaries, considered a small, ho-hum, back-row operation of no seeming consequence.

What nonsense. What an opportunity.

The obits are probably read by more people with greater attention to detail than any other section of a newspaper. Nowhere else is error or omission more likely to be noticed.

A good reporter gives each obit careful, accurate handling and searches in the stack for the one or two that can be brought to life.

"Veteran of WWII," the funeral-home sheet says. Did he make the D-Day landing on the beaches of Normandy? "Taught junior high English for 43 years." Find some former pupils who can still quote entire pages of Longfellow because somehow she made it live and sing for them.

Look around. See who's likely to go before long and interview him. Few people can resist the opportunity to tell of their life and times. The good reporter finds them, listens to them, and learns from them.

Whatever the assignment, look for the people, listen to their stories, study them—and in your copy let them move, speak, act naturally. Put no high-flown words in mouths that never spoke them. You write of real people, not puppets to be yanked around from paragraph to paragraph, and you owe them their reality.

Check your facts. The more startling the claim, statement or allegation, the more attention should be given to double or triple checking for error or misinterpretation.

A good reporter is a student all his life. Each new assignment demands a crash course in the theory and practice of yet another profession or system. From station house to courthouse to state house or White House, you have to find out what the official sitting in the chair knows, and you cannot recognize the truth from a position of blind ignorance.

Reporting involves long hours of listening to those who do know the ins and outs of the story, digging in the morgue files, filling up another shelf in the bookcase at home.

Then there is always the continuing study of your job as a reporter and writer whose challenging subject is the changing and unchanging conditions of mankind. For that study, you must read.

The prescription "to read" by itself does not convey what I mean.

If in this electronic era you are not accustomed to it, then you must train yourself to gulp down the printed word with the true thirst of someone who has covered the last 15 miles of Death Valley on his belly.

Read for your life.

Read every newspaper that comes under your eye for style, for content, for ideas, for pleasure. And the books, my God, the books. The world of modern publishing has a 500-year head start on you and it is pulling further ahead every year.

Never mind your transcript or your résumé. Let me see your bookshelves at home and your library card.

In a long career, a reporter's assignments may change radically and often, or he may spend his lifetime on a single beat in one town. That is a matter of personal choice, opportunity and chance. What never changes is the basic debt owed and the only way to settle it.

I served my apprenticeship on a small Texas daily, sitting at the left hand of a fine, conscientious reporter who handled the city government beat. He had been there for years then and today—35 years later—he is still there. In amazement, I heard him turn down job offers from big city dailies. He knew and encouraged my own ambitions, but his ambition was simply to continue providing honest, informative coverage of his beat.

His explanation:

"You may go and cover the great capitals of the world and the great conflicts, and that's an important job. But unless the people of this town, and all the other towns like it, know and understand the workings of their own city hall, how can you expect them to understand what is happening 6,000 miles away? Unless there's someone doing my job right, your job is hopeless."

## C. Journalism

The personnel committee of the Associated Press Managing Editors' Association interviewed 30 top journalism students who graduated in the past five years from two dozen colleges and universities and who were working in newsrooms across the country. These recent graduates were interviewed first, and then their immediate supervisors were interviewed.

Here are some of the comments of several of those interviewed. Presume you are writing a Sunday feature for your newspaper. Your editor tells you that the school of journalism at the local state university is reassessing its curriculum and that this study might be newsworthy. She tells you not to bother about localizing the story but to go ahead and just write what the APME has found. (For the purposes of this exercise, presume that the study was published last week in the *APME News*.)

### Reporters

A police reporter: I remember my first assignment, a spot news story. I didn't know what to ask. The city editor had me on the phone and asked the questions and I acted as a conduit.

Another young graduate: I didn't learn the actual mechanics in gathering the news. I was equipped to be a rewrite man. The first couple of years after graduation were spent in learning where to look for news and how to harvest it.

Another former student: The solution would be to gear the courses so that the student would gain practical experience in all types of writing—interviewing techniques, makeup and news judgment and photo assessment—by actually performing these in a simulated professional setting. . . .

Another student: Lack of knowledge about courts and government. I never entered a courtroom and I never even had to look at a complaint.

Another student: If I hadn't spent two summers on this newspaper I wouldn't have had any idea how newspapers operated, the physical limitations. Why didn't J School teach us a little about what you can and cannot do—economically, politically, philosophically—under some managements?

Another student: Why didn't they make us write so much we'd need a new ribbon every week?

Another student: Thanks to the tough professor who taught us never to take statements, quotes, or statistics at face value. . . . This was more useful than the constant stress on style and mechanics which some professors value almost to the exclusion of training on finding information.

Another student: College gave me an exposure to city problems, both inside and outside the classroom. The curriculum put me on the street on a beat where I wrote about these problems.

Summaries of other comments: Good preparation on ethics and philosophy, but inadequate on techniques of journalism. Lack of deadline pressure. Inadequate training in reporting. Lack of knowledge of beats—courts, government, economics. Inadequate knowledge of what newspapers do in their coverage.

Many students praised the professor who "demanded rewriting, who criticized and criticized—in short who developed the love-hate relationship a reporter gets with his first city editor, if she's good," the *APME News* reports.

### Editors

An editor: The reporter brought an inquisitiveness and a social awareness above and beyond what a lot of editors had. But at first, he lacked a sense of perspective. There were no gray areas, all was black and white.

Another editor: Beginning staffers often have problems with reporting skills and ease of expression. One would expect J programs to impart these. Often they don't. I mean the ability to gather information, deal with people, spot the gaps in the things sources tell you. I mean an ability to organize and write in a lucid, concrete, structured and interesting way.

Many of the editors criticized the neophytes for poor organization of stories. One said a reporter wrote a term paper instead of a depth story. "The one weakness common to all is what I would call 'street sense.' How to develop their own news contacts; where various public buildings are; how to research a story; investigative techniques; and how to interview on a professional, penetrating level. At least one such course would give students a running start at developing street sense."

## Assignments

### A. Applicants

Interview the editors of local broadcast stations and newspapers to see what they think of applicants for reporting jobs. Use some of the material from **Exercise A. Criticism** and **C. Journalism** in this chapter as the basis of questions. Are there many applicants, more than in past years? How are they weeded out? If tests are given, how have the applicants fared?

### B. Ratings

Schools and departments of colleges and universities are accredited by various agencies called accrediting groups or accrediting agencies. Some organizations or individuals also rank professional schools. Dig out accreditation reports (which often cite areas for improvement) and ratings for your college or university. Interview students within the departments and schools, the deans or directors, faculty members and others for comments on the latest report.

### C. Dates

Valentine's Day brings out some strange stories in newspapers. One that is often plucked from the city editor's file sends out reporters to ask people, "What was your worst-ever date? What happened?" Try the questions on a few men and women.

### D. Fantasies

What do people eat when they want to indulge themselves? Some nominees: ice cream, candy, pie. Separate men and women and see whether there is a difference in selections.

### E. Class Based

A speaker on your campus has said that admissions and scholarships should not be given on a racial basis but on a class basis in order to foster diversity on the campus. In his talk, he made the following point:

> It makes no sense to use an affirmative-action program that is based on race, for that will give us the sons of doctors and accountants simply because of race, but deny admission to the white daughter of a coal miner or the white son of a single mother working in a supermarket as a bagger.
> 
> We are supposed to be furthering multicultural contacts on the campus with the racially based admission and scholarship policy. But the reality on many campuses is that blacks and Hispanics, and even Native Americans, have been allowed to self-segregate in dormitories of their own. They eat with their own, and usually congregate in classes devoted to studies of their own culture.

What is the situation on your campus regarding the admission of minorities and scholarships for minority students? What is the extent of self-segregation on your campus? What do administrators and faculty members think of shifting from race-based admissions and to class-based assistance?

## Campus Project

### Dating

Among black college students, there were 785,000 women and 495,000 men enrolled during a recent year. This presents a series of problems, and one is dating. "Some black women who are seniors say they have gone four years without a date," writes Emily Nelson in an article in *The New York Times*. "Black women will not ever have the luxury of limiting themselves to black men if they want a partner," says Audrey B. Chapman, a family therapist at the Howard University Counseling Service. "The numbers don't support that."

What is the situation on your campus? Interview students.

## Community Projects

### A. Satisfaction

The Regional Plan Association asked residents of five metropolitan areas how satisfied they were with the quality of life in their communities. Their findings in percentages:

| Area | Very Satisfied | Somewhat Satisfied | Dissatisfied |
|---|---|---|---|
| New York | 35 | 48 | 17 |
| Atlanta | 49 | 42 | 9 |
| Dallas/Forth Worth | 47 | 40 | 13 |
| Los Angeles | 43 | 43 | 14 |
| Seattle | 52 | 42 | 6 |

Residents were also asked if they would stay in the area, if they were not sure whether they would stay or move or if they would move if possible:

| Area | Would Stay | Not Sure | Would Move |
|---|---|---|---|
| New York | 54 | 4 | 42 |
| Atlanta | 61 | 4 | 35 |
| Dallas/Fort Worth | 61 | 3 | 36 |
| Los Angeles | 57 | 2 | 41 |
| Seattle | 66 | 3 | 31 |

Also, the residents of these areas were asked what they most liked or disliked about their communities. They were given a list that included taxes, crime, schools, job opportunities, affordable housing, clean air and water, public transportation, race relations.

Devise and conduct a poll of your own in your community and compare the findings with those shown here.

## B. Inhale

After years of declining cigarette smoking by high school seniors, a survey found that teen smoking is on the rise. The Centers for Disease Control and Prevention reported that 22 percent of high school students were smoking in 1994. This counters the steady drop in adult smoking. Michael Ericksen, director of the Centers Office on Smoking and Health, says:

> Over the past decade, adult smoking has declined by about 20%, while teenage smoking has actually increased. It's alarming that, despite a decade of unprecedented attention to the health dangers of smoking, there are more teenagers smoking now then there were ten years ago. Tobacco Industry opposition has hindered our ability to use the three most powerful weapons we have to reduce adolescent smoking, namely eliminating advertising, increasing price and enforcing access laws.

Vern Herschberger, *Waco Tribune-Herald.*

Conduct a survey among high school seniors to see what percentage smoke. When did they start smoking and what influenced their taking up smoking? Were they able to buy cigarettes despite the law against sales to minors? Explore the causes and ask whether they know the consequences of smoking.

## Home Assignment

### A. Farrakhan

You cover the talk given last night in the Civic Auditorium by Louis Farrakhan, leader of the Nation of Islam, a Black Muslim sect. Here are some portions of his address to some 350 persons:

> Our leaders are maligned and falsely accused by those in this society who hate to see strong black men exercising a leadership over our poor people.

> I talked to about 70 reporters, black reporters, this week in New York City. Many of our young reporters are so sick they've forgotten how they got where they are.
>
> Don't tell me nothing about you are a reporter. You're a nigger in the eyes of white people.
>
> So you got this sick condition that you must be objective. You're the only fool that there is. White people have a point of view. Such a damn fool like you should be taken and horsewhipped.
>
> You already know what you want to write of me so it don't really make any difference what I say. Your editors have a picture of what they want Farrakhan to look like, especially your Jewish editors and Jewish writers.
>
> I'm saying that our preacher-politician-education class of people are the worst crop of black people that we have ever had in our history. And we are going to make examples of them so that our people will know, the politicians, educators, clergymen and others will know that you cannot stand in front of black people and sell out our aspirations for personal aggrandizement. We are not going to permit it. We are already half dead so we might as well die all the way and take a bunch of you with us to make sure we set an example.
>
> Here come the Jews don't like Farrakhan, so they call me Hitler. Well, that's a good name. Hitler was a very great man. He wasn't great for me as a black person, but he was a great German. Now, I'm not proud of Hitler's evil against Jewish people, but that's a matter of record. He rose Germany up from nothing. Well, in a sense you could say there's similarity in that we are rising our people up from nothing. But don't compare me with your wicked killers.
>
> Listen, Jews: This little black boy is your last chance because the Scriptures charge your people with killing the prophets of God. I am not one of the prophets of God. But if you rise up to try to kill me, then Allah promises you that he will bring on this generation the blood of the righteous. All of you will be killed outright.

Farrakhan then describes a reporter's news story that quoted Jesse Jackson's disparaging remarks about New York City and Jews, and he says he was asked what he intended "to do to" the reporter.

> At this point, no physical harm. But at this point we're going to keep on going until we make it so that he cannot enter in on any black people. For now I'm going to try to get every church in Washington, D.C., to put him out. Whenever he hits the door, tell him he's not wanted. If he brings his wife she can come in if she leaves him. But if she won't leave him, then you go to hell with your husband.
>
> One day soon we will punish you with death. You're saying, when is that? In sufficient time. We will come to power inside this country one day soon. And the white man is not going to stop us from executing the law of God on all you who fall under our jurisdiction.
>
> What did Elijah Muhammad offer you from God? He said, "Separate." Thirty million black people cannot go on like this. We can't go on like this another 10 years. We can't go on like this another five years.
>
> As black people we are in a terrible condition. Black children are suffering. The black male is done in, making it difficult for black females to find a suitable mate.
>
> While white men are in college earning medical and engineering degrees, black men are playing basketball and football. The black male is being decimated.
>
> I'm not a hater of Jews. But Jews were involved in the slave trade. They made money in the distribution of blacks.
>
> Every time I am invited to speak it seems as though it causes a stir. I don't understand. I'm just a little fella with a trumpet and evidently my people are listening.

Aware that he has been accused of racism and anti-Semitism, Farrakhan added:

> Whether you like it or not, God brought the idea through me, and he didn't bring it through me because my heart was dark with hatred and anti-Semitism. . . . If my heart were that dark, how is the message so bright, the message so clear, the response so magnificent?

You ask some black members of the audience for comments. Here are some:

> "His message is one of self-pride, love, mutual respect and determination, not hate."—L.D. Parlez.
>
> "The media are clouding his message and trying to divide the black community. He is a peaceful man." —Anita Harrison.
>
> "People should buy his records or tapes to get the real material, not what the press reports."—Albert Gerard.

The audience was about a fourth white, the rest black. Farrakhan was interrupted several times with applause and with remarks: "That's right. . . . You tell 'em. . . . Isn't it the truth. . . ." At the end, the applause lasted 30 seconds.

Write 450 words. Include background from *Scapegoat* in the previous chapter.

## Class Discussion

### *Fly-Participant*

In the usual reporter-source relationship the source is aware of the reporter's presence, and the reporter is an uninvolved observer. Walter Lippmann characterizes the reporter as a "fly on the wall," present but not the center of observation.

There are two other forms of reportorial work: unobtrusive observation and participant observation. The unobtrusive observer looks on while the source is unaware of his or her presence. The participant observer becomes involved in the event—an education reporter who sits in a sixth-grade class and takes part, a sports reporter who scrimmages with the Chicago Bears or who boxes with a Golden Gloves champion.

In your reading, find examples of both types, and be prepared to discuss the advantages and disadvantages of the techniques.

## *DB/CAR*

### A. Cheating

Considerable attention is being paid to cheating in high schools and colleges. A midwestern high school teacher gave his students the answers to questions on a national tournament, and they finished first. The students remained silent about the cheating for months until one young woman said her conscience bothered her, and she revealed that the contestants had been given the answers. Her schoolmates criticized her for talking.

Two-thirds of high school seniors say they would lie to achieve business objectives, and a third said they would plagiarize to pass a certification test.

Only 21 percent of elementary students say they would look at another student's test paper; 65 percent of high school students said they would.

The models may not be much better. *The Wall Street Journal* revealed that many colleges and universities inflate the SAT scores they provide to *Money* magazine for its annual college guide.

Conduct a database search for material about cheating in schools and colleges and use this as background for interviewing and polling on your campus.

## *Fix It: Count 'Em*

John Lindsay, editor of the *Santa Cruz* (Calif.) *Sentinel,* tests job applicants to weed out the "language and spelling weaklings." Test your strength by underlining the spelling errors in this passage:

In my judgement, he said, the cemetary proposal came as a suprise to the city counsel members. We did not think it

desireable, and some of us truely believed it was made to pave the way for the new development proposed last week. But I am

willing to yeild my bill to build a liesure park out there and we can put his bill in the catagory of matters to act on at once.

Total spelling errors_____.

## *What's Wrong?: Vote*

PLEASANTON—Growers in the area conservancy district approved by a two to one majority opposition to proposed crop controls.

Ralph Barnton, a Vadalia farmer, said the limits were "set too low. Alot of us consider the limits will put us below the break-even point."

The growers will send their opposition to the state's congressional delegation, Barnton said.

# 16 Speeches, Meetings and News Conferences

Bob Thayer, *The Journal-Bulletin.*
**Watch for mannerisms, gestures.**

### Introduction

The reporter's task in covering events based on the spoken word is to select from the welter of words those that best summarize the heart of the event. These key quotes are usually paraphrased in the lead and then directly quoted high in the story. The nature of the event is conveyed through spoken words; therefore, the story will consist mostly of quotations of the speaker(s). For meetings, panel discussions and symposia, the story theme usually is the consensus reached, though sharp disagreement can form the lead, too. Audience reaction, if significant, should be part of the story. Location and sponsor are secondary.

## Speeches

### Exercises I

#### A. In-Depth

Here are excerpts from a talk by Eugene Roberts Jr., when he was the editor of *The Philadelphia Inquirer* that he gave at the University of Southern California School of Journalism. Write 350 to 400 words:

> *USA Today* celebrated its fifth birthday this year. That prompted, in some magazines and newspapers, a celebration of the colorful, readable simplification that is the paper's trademark.
>
> We were assured that the route to the reader's heart, if not his mind, is the short paragraph; the clever graphic; the weather; the sports; and avoidance, whenever possible, of any detailed governmental coverage.
>
> I go into this today not to disparage *USA Today,* or short stories, or graphics, and certainly not sports or the weather. But I must argue that in journalistic circles in recent years—and especially since the birth of *USA Today*—we have not talked enough about in-depth journalism, investigative reporting, and the art of writing understandably about complex subjects in an increasingly complicated world.
>
> These days, almost every editor's meeting I go to seems to have a group of panelists who either imply—or say head on—that the survival of Western journalism depends on the quick adoption of a three-part formula:
>
> - Drastically increasing the number of stories we run.
> - Writing shorter and shorter stories.
> - And making our front pages look like transcripts of the six o'clock television news with color graphics.
>
> It is not that I don't believe in short stories and news briefs. Indeed, we recast *The Philadelphia Inquirer* so that it bristled each day with short summaries and news digests. . . .

So I'm not saying that brevity is bad. What I am saying is that as government gets bigger and more unwieldy, as society gets more complex, as science and technology explode, as issues get more opaque and overwhelming, the old-fashioned, time-honored, inverted-pyramid, one-column-or-less, wire-service-style news story becomes more inadequate.

Let me emphasize that I used the word "inadequate"—and not the words "obsolete" or "unimportant"—in describing this kind of story. The conventional story will work most of the time, perhaps as much as 80 or 90 percent of the time.

Obviously, the major reason for the existence of daily newspapers is that they, in fact, report the news daily, as it happens.

But I am suggesting that for the other 10 or 20 percent of the time, the conventional story doesn't work. Sometimes with important and complex stories, newspapers confuse the reader by giving him or her daily dribs and drabs—punchy little shorts that stimulate but don't slake the appetite for information. People are prepared for a short-hand version of events on radio and television—but not, to the exclusion of all else, in their daily paper.

And it is to this remaining 10 or 20 percent of news coverage that I turn my attention today. I am not sure that it is always what everyone would call investigative reporting, but it is almost always difficult and hard-to-do and time-consuming reporting.

And when it is done well, it explains to readers things they should know and will find important to their lives. On *The Inquirer*, we stayed away from the term "investigative stories" or "explanatory journalism" in favor of terms like "take-outs" or "project pieces" or "enterprise stories."

The finest reporting—whether short or long—is always investigative in that it digs, and digs, and digs. And the finest writing is almost by definition explanatory in that it puts things so vividly, so compellingly, that readers can see and understand and comprehend.

One of the reasons I don't much use the term "investigative reporting" is that it misleads and it confuses. To many people investigative reporting means nailing a crook or catching a politician with his pants down. This, I think, is too narrow a definition. And, these days, catching a politician with his pants down does not require a great deal of investigating.

And while *The Philadelphia Inquirer* is reputed to do quite a bit of investigative reporting, we didn't put a heavy premium on the catch-a-crook variety, or the exposure of the sexual secrets of politicians. I couldn't, for example, imagine assigning an investigative team to explore Pat Robertson's premarital sex or to determine whether a would-be Supreme Court Justice smoked pot twenty years ago.

At *The Inquirer,* investigative reporting meant freeing a reporter from the normal constraints of time and space and letting the reporter really inform the public about a situation of vital importance. It meant coming to grips with a society grown far too complex to be covered merely with news briefs or a snappy color graphic.

Some papers fail their readers by refusing to do any investigative reporting at all. Still other papers try to do investigative reporting but go astray by narrowly defining it as unearthing a wrong-doer. This immediately casts reporters as cops rather than as gatherers of information.

Think, for a moment, about tax coverage. A paper distorts if it only covers the revenue department's press conferences and never looks into how the department decides which tax returns it will audit.

But suppose a paper grants that investigative reporting is desirable, how does the paper go about getting it? The short answer is commitment.

To do in-depth reporting on a sustained basis of more than a couple of stories a year requires that the highest levels of a paper be concerned and committed. You especially need commitment on space.

It also is important for a paper to provide reporters with time, although a reporter all by himself can sometimes scrounge the time—an hour here, a day there. He can scrimp on travel. I once knew a reporter—a dedicated man named Charlie Black—who badgered his paper to send him to cover the war in Vietnam. The paper, I am told, finally agreed, gave him $100 in expense money and told him to return when the money was gone.

Charlie came back more than six months later and gave the editors something like $22 in change. He never saw the inside of a hotel room. He simply moved into the field with the troops and slept on the ground. He produced some of the most interesting reporting of the war because he reported first hand on the life and problems of the combat soldier.

But a reporter all by himself, even if he has scrounged the time and gotten the story, has real problems if his or her newspaper will not deliver the space. You simply cannot do an in-depth job in a standard one or two column newspaper hole.

The right reason for a newspaper to provide space for project reporting is that it opens windows into society, into government, into problems and opportunities. Windows that, chances are, will never be opened if the newspaper doesn't open them.

The wrong reasons are for mere shock value, or impact or to win awards. And if you seek awards for awards' sake, they probably will not come. At *The Inquirer,* we won a good number of major journalism prizes—but those awards came only as a byproduct of our coverage. We asked ourselves constantly if we were really getting to the guts of a story. And if the answer was no, we redoubled our efforts.

The result was at the end of the year, we often had a dozen or so things we were proud of. . . .

Don Bartlett and Jim Steele of *The Inquirer* wrote an exhaustive series on the failed federal policies for disposal of nuclear waste. The story was a blistering indictment of mismanagement and neglect within the nuclear industry and the government. It warned of dire consequences and real health hazards. The series did not win one major award, possibly because it was ahead of the news, as the best of investigative series almost always are. But almost every month that passes sees the validation of yet another warning raised by the series. . . .

. . . a newspaper that contains nothing more than shorts and briefs and colorful graphics may be the easy way to attract readers, but it isn't the right way. Nor, often, the most effective way.

My first paying newspaper job more than thirty years ago was on what was then a daily of only 9,000 circulation—the *News-Argus* in Goldsboro, North Carolina, as a farm reporter.

Even then, perhaps especially then, we worried about brevity. The editor, Henry Belk, even wrote his editorials without articles, no *a*'s or *the*'s—space was too precious. But Henry and his successor, Eugene Price, knew when enough wasn't enough. Their readers were mostly tobacco farmers or merchants whose business depended on tobacco.

And because Henry and Gene understood their readers and because they understood impact journalism—which is what grabs your readers and holds them—there was never any talk at the *News-Argus* about writing short, or not jumping stories where tobacco was concerned. If I had had it in me to write the *War and Peace* of tobacco, it would have been published, and it would have been read.

I know this because I was out in the fields with these farmers every day and despite what the surveys tell you, I never ever heard a single farmer complain because he had to jump to another page of the *News-Argus* to follow a tobacco story. But I heard them complain a lot when we weren't on top of a tobacco story, or didn't dig or didn't investigate or when they heard a snatch of a story on the radio that was inadequately explained in the next issue of the *News-Argus*. They were prepared for brevity and a short-hand version of events on radio and television—but not in their daily paper. . . .

A newspaper should be a cohesive force, a constant that can hold its coverage area together. An editor's task is to make a newspaper more meaningful and relevant and readable. And sometimes the best way to do that is short, and sometimes it is long. Sometimes it is simple, and sometimes it is complex.

Just like American society. Just like the cities and countries we live in. Just like life itself. Which, after all, is what we are supposed to be reporting.

(Used with the permission of Eugene Roberts.)

## B. Health

Here are excerpts from a talk by David Satcher, M.D., director of the Centers for Disease Control and Prevention, to a journalism conference in your city. The title of his talk is "Health Communication and the Media, a Partnership for Better Health for the American People."

The significance of health communication in dealing with the leading health problems of today cannot be ignored. We're working with different perceptions. In its fight with infectious diseases, CDC can find almost universal support and respect for its position. Today's seemingly intractable ills demand that we break into the newer territory of convincing people to change behavior patterns in exchange for a promise of better health. It is here that our professions working together, mine in producing the science, yours in communicating it, can do a much better job than we have done in presenting matters of health concern to the American people.

I bring to this discussion a perspective shaped during some of the benchmark social upheavals of recent American history. My perspective is that the media help to protect democracy by assuring a voice for the minority and/or underdog.

Public health and the efforts to prevent disease are the underdog in America's health system. Only 1.3 percent of the Nation's health expenditures are earmarked for population-based prevention.

America has the most sophisticated and expensive health care system in the world with costs approaching $1 trillion a year.

Other than South Africa, America is the only industrialized nation that does not provide universal access to health care.

As we discuss and debate health care reform, the need to strengthen and reform the public health system in this country has received far too little attention from the media and others. Treatment of public health by the media reflects our major concern of the media's role in health communication.

When I look at the media coverage of the health care reform debate, I find a tidal wave of coverage. But, when I look at the substance, rather than the volume, of this health coverage, I honestly don't find much about health. Somehow in our fascination with costs and payment mechanisms—and I'm not in any way denigrating their importance—we've lost track of the reasons why reform is necessary.

We are missing what Paul Harvey calls "the rest of the story."

We are being allowed to forget that literally millions of people in the most bountiful country in the world are being denied access to the health service they desperately need because they cannot produce the magic ticket of insurance coverage.

We are being allowed to forget that this systemic failure is a direct cause of the fact that the United States, for all our wealth and concern for health, cannot achieve a ranking among the leading ten countries in the world in such indices as life expectancy at birth, maternal death rates, infant death rates. This story isn't being told. I hope we can figure ways whereby both you, and we as health officers, can be part of the solution.

There is a rather striking contrast between many of the stories that do get told and those that do not. The following are examples—others could equally well be cited—of stories that got a lot of ink recently at the expense of much more meaningful fare.

This past June a scary new phrase began appearing in the newspaper headlines: Flesh-Eating Virus. This is a combination of words guaranteed to get attention in what a colleague of mine once called the Anxiety Society. And attention, of course, is what it got. Whether or not it originated in the supermarket tabloids I'm not sure, but they predictably gave it a wonderful ride.

"I Watched Killer Bug Eat My Body," one headline announced while another—our favorite in Atlanta—read "NO AMERICAN IS SAFE says national Centers for Disease Control." This lighted up our switchboard for a week.

Once the facts were put into perspective the story went away. There is an organism—a form of Strep—which can with some poetic license be called "flesh-eating." An outbreak had been reported in England, an outbreak of a few cases. There is no indication anywhere that we are on the brink of an epidemic of a disease we've been aware of for many years. It took some good solid science reporting based on questions asked at a congressional hearing to lay it to rest.

If this had been only a flurry in the tabloids it would scarcely be worth mentioning. But before it was laid to rest, the story had infiltrated normally responsible publications and caused a lot of needless worry to a lot of people. More important to me, this kind of story distracts people from legitimate health concerns. If indeed "no American is safe" from a growing list of menacing mystery-diseases, why bother to take arms against the sea of troubles we can do something about?

I have one more example of this sort of distraction. Two years ago, in July 1992, a report came out of a major international meeting on AIDS to the effect that AIDS-like illness or severe immunosuppression was occurring in persons not infected by the HIV virus. This immediately made big-headline news. Not only did it light up switchboards, but it completely obscured everything else that came out of that major scientific session in Amsterdam. And more to our point here, it struck a chill note of fear and a sense of futility. If you do everything they say to protect yourself against HIV infection and can get AIDS anyway, why bother.

As in the case of the so-called flesh-eater, fuller presentation of the facts placed this story in perspective. We at CDC and our colleagues and counterparts in other countries took a searching look at all the data we could put together and found a total of fewer than 100 cases of this phenomenon worldwide in the past six years. As Dr. Michael Merson, director of WHO's Global AIDS Programme put it, "Despite a lot of looking in a lot of places, we found less than 100 cases, and compared with the 10,000 new HIV infections that developed in the world during just the two days of the meeting, it is a relatively rare syndrome."

These issues tend to distract the public from the real health issues in need of attention.

In contrast, some major accomplishments/successes in health enhancement receive very little media attention and, thus, very little support. When months go by without a significant outbreak of water-borne or food-borne disease, a lot of people are doing a lot of things right. When 17 years go by without a single case of smallpox reported anywhere in the world—a disease that probably caused more death and disfigurement than any other of man's ancient enemies—the success of prevention, when "nothing" happens, is impressive indeed.

When zero cases of wild-virus-borne polio occur in the entire western hemisphere in four years, parents are freed from a dread that I remember well from my own childhood years, and something really dramatic has happened.

Who knows about this accomplishment? Health officers do, but we don't seem to be communicating very effectively, either directly or indirectly through folks like you.

Who knows, for example, that the death rates for heart disease and stroke in the U.S. declined, respectively, by 51 percent and 60 percent between 1972 and 1992? This is a rather well-kept secret that, if better known, might ease some anxieties and encourage people to go on doing some of the things they have been doing right . . . like quitting smoking, decreasing dietary intake of cholesterol, increasing physical activity.

Another success story: There has been a dramatic decrease in blood lead levels in the United States because of public health efforts, leading to policy decisions which decreased the lead content of gasoline. The result: a decrease in childhood neurological problems.

It needs to be added to this story, as an important caveat, that this battle is by no means won. There remain 1.5 to 2 million children who are exposed to lead levels that are potentially hazardous, and the remaining sources of exposure will be difficult to eliminate. We are now working with two of our Federal partners, HUD and EPA, to address this remaining challenge. Health issues that are covered only in part neglect the significant "rest of the story."

High risk sexual behavior and tobacco use are prevalent among many of America's teen-agers and youth. Journalists and public health professionals must work together to be sure that the prevention side of the story is told. We need to continue talking about the benefits of abstinence among teen-agers. We need to provide information and resources to sexually active teen-agers to prevent unplanned pregnancies, sexually transmitted diseases and the spread of HIV/AIDS.

Violence is a public health problem. Violence is the single leading cause of death for large demographic segments of our population, and unlike most of the leading causes it is growing from year to year among our youth. In one recent year, firearm-related deaths alone—homicides and suicides—cost 35,000 lives, most of them young lives. The lifetime cost of firearm-related injuries occurring in a single year is estimated at $14.4 billion.

America's fascination with guns and the glamorization of violence are as old as our nation itself. Recent studies of suicide and homicide in the home have shown that the presence of a handgun in a household greatly increases the odds of a fatal episode—either self-inflicted or as a result of domestic violence. Guns purchased in good faith for protection against intruders are far more likely to be used against a member of a household. This is not surprising: The presence of a loaded gun makes it all too easy to turn a fight into a killing or a suicidal whim into reality.

The rising tide of information being communicated through the media must in the long run contribute to fuller public understanding and wiser community and individual health-related decisions. But the very fact of its increasing prominence and significance makes it doubly important that we—and here again I'm referring to journalists and health officials alike—do some soul-searching about what is being communicated. The politics of the issue are important. I recognize that when you are covering the health care reform debate, your primary job is to report what the debaters say. That's exactly what you've been doing. I want us to find vehicles for communicating "the rest of the story" as well. There is a lot of exciting and important material waiting to be told.

Among the major problems suffering from some neglect are:

- The uninsured and the impact on access.
- Problems with Medicaid.
- Runaway costs even in the face of inadequate care.
- The abuse of those committed to care for the poor.
- The plight of women and children.
- The lack of incentives for prevention in our health care system which leads to runaway cost.

CDC has some specific goals in health communication. Important among these are:

- A productive working relationship with the media.
- In dealing with health problems that are related to lifestyle (50 percent), we hope to gain better recognition of the role of behavioral science research in providing valid answers to social problems.
  - To target messages to communities most severely affected by health problems.
  - And to conduct research to continually improve health communication and media relations.

In conclusion, let me express heartfelt thanks to the professional journalists who are doing a better and better job of covering health responsibly and effectively. The *Atlanta Journal-Constitution*'s Mike Toner received a well-deserved Pulitzer Prize last year for his series on infectious diseases—new and re-emerging and drug resistant. *The New York Times Magazine* recently did an excellent job of communicating and educating about smallpox and the issues surrounding a scientific debate about whether to destroy the smallpox virus.

I mentioned earlier that some of the triumphs of public health have been regrettably unsung. Now, underdogs are accustomed to being, or to feel that they are, unsung heroes. We in public health are no exception.

We feel we have an important story to tell that needs to be included in the national dialogue about health care reform. In spite of the small amount of the total health expenditure devoted to public health in this country, the quiet, effective performance of our essential services keeps the country going its basically healthy way. State and especially local health officers have the responsibility for backstopping health care delivery, community by community.

Please come and talk with us at whatever level—and especially again I would recommend getting to know your local health departments. As we get to know each other better, we can reduce the adversarial, the controversial and the sensational contexts of our conversations and begin to tell, together, "the rest of the story."

## *C. Professions*

Here are some quotations from the keynote address, "Women and the Professions," given last night by Professor Donald L. Richards, dean of the School of Library Science of Mallory College, at the annual convention of the Tri-State Library Association held on your campus. Some 150 public and school librarians are attending. Write at least 300 words.

It is clear that unconscious attitudes influence us. I should like to suggest that attitudes of this kind have influenced the way society perceives jobs, and the way some segments of society separate the professions from occupations.

Of the four occupations that are traditionally identified with women—nursing, teaching, librarianship, and social work—only social work is seen by some of the guardians of the professions as likely to achieve professional status.

It is interesting to note that the proportion of men to women in social work has changed significantly in recent years. In 1945, only 5 percent of the master's degrees in social work were awarded to men, whereas in the past decade the percentage has increased to more than 40.

University teachers—predominantly male—are considered professionals. School teachers—predominantly female—are not. Yet there is certainly no abstract knowledge base in teaching. If we look at such indicators of the professions as an abstract knowledge base, the ideal of service and the ability of its practitioners to engage in abstract or theoretical thinking, we find strange contradictions. Nurses are excluded from the professions, but some sociologists who make these distinctions include engineers in the professions.

Is it possible that the low status and respect which has traditionally been afforded women has carried over into the occupations in which they are predominant?

Women, it has been assumed traditionally, are incapable of abstract thought. Since women can succeed as nurses, librarians and teachers, then there can be no significant base of knowledge for these occupations. They are all right for nice gentlewomen, but they are not to be considered the equivalent of what thoughtful professional men do.

Unconscious attitudes of this sort—some call them sexist—interfere with the way sociologists and others establish criteria for separating occupations from professions.

## D. Driving

You are assigned to cover a talk at the luncheon of the Freeport Rotary Club, at the Barton Hotel. The speaker is Johnson J. Burdette, vice president in charge of statistical analysis for the Travelers Home Assurance Co. of Chicago. His subject: "How to Cope with the Traffic Toll." Your deadline is an hour after the speech concludes. Here is the prepared text:

Thank you, Bob. It's good to be in Freeport, this wonderful town my grandparents traveled through on the way west. It's changed a lot since then, and haven't all of us? And not for the better, I suppose. In those days the pace of life was set to the speed of the human being. Now we've got to adjust to the speed of the machine. I wonder if we'll ever be able to do it. The human body and mind are fragile things indeed. I wonder if we were designed to cope with all we're subjected to. I know that even what we call a leisurely speed on the highway is enough to break every bone in a man's body if there's an accident.

This is what I want to talk to you about today: death on the highway. Not a pleasant subject, but a pressing one when you consider that more people have been killed on our highways—many more—than have been slain by the enemy in all our wars.

Highway fatalities are our number one cause of accidental death. Every year, about 40,000 men, women and children die in grinding traffic accidents.

We're making progress in cutting this toll. For years, we had 50,000 fatalities a year. In recent years, we are down to 40,000, still too many.

What is the answer? First, let me ask: Do we want an answer? For there is no one who can say that he has not been touched by a traffic death—of a relative or a good friend. Personally, one of my best friends died just a month ago when his car ran off the road late at night.

John left a widow and three children, and how they are going to manage I don't know. I suppose Sue will have to go to work. And I imagine Ted and Betsy will have to drop out of college, at least until they can earn enough money to pay for another year.

These are the human dimensions behind the cold statistics you see in the newspapers.

I ask you again, what is the answer?

There is no single solution. In fact, it is absurd to talk of trying to eliminate all traffic deaths. It cannot be done. There are certain factors we cannot control.

But there are some that we can. We know, for example, that seat belts cut down on fatalities in collisions. I'd like to suggest a few lesser-known areas where action is possible. First, let me tell you what I do *not* have in mind.

I don't believe in billboards exhorting drivers to slow down. If they are soberly presented, the driver never sees them. If they are garish enough to attract his attention, he sticks his neck out the window to read and the next thing he knows he's broken his neck on the turn he never saw.

I don't believe in slogans . . . slow down and live . . . don't mix drinking with driving . . . don't drive if you are tired.

The fact is that most deaths occur at normal driving speeds, in daylight when road conditions are fine. And whoever heard of stopping a drinking driver by asking him to turn down that last cocktail?

No, I propose what I think are realistic methods. First, a tightening of driver's licensing tests and, next, a toughening of law enforcement.

In many states, the drivers license examination is a farce. It is far from strict—takes only a few minutes, and the agency doing the testing usually suffers from fiscal malnutrition. Testers are insufficient in number to give detailed examinations. Eye testing equipment is not used or is so old as to be worthless. So the incompetent driver, the physically handicapped driver, gets a license. My point is:

**Don't let him get behind the wheel** in the first place. Driving is not a right—it's a privilege, one which the state can give and *can* take away. I say: Make the giving tougher.

**And make the taking away easier.**

We find that in at least half of all fatal accidents one or both drivers had been drinking. In a 15-year period, arrests for driving under the influence of alcohol and other intoxicants increased 223 percent, whereas the number of drivers increased 42 percent. The cost is $10 to $15 billion a year for drunk driving. This is a phenomenal set of figures. It does mean that drinking and driving don't mix. But you won't stop it by asking the drinker not to drive. We must have laws that define drunk driving at .08 alcohol content of the blood, not .10.

We have proof what lowering the state's legal blood alcohol content will accomplish. California went from .10 to .08 and decided to revoke licenses of those in excess of .08.

The very next year, there was a 15 percent drop in alcohol-related traffic deaths and a 9 percent drop in injuries. Of course, a driver with .08 blood alcohol content is still three times more at risk of a crash than a driver with no alcohol in his or her system. But .08 is a lot better than .10, when a driver is 12 times more likely to be involved in a fatal crash than a non-drinking driver.

But we are behind other countries. England has .08 for all areas, parts of Australia use .05, and Sweden has .02. Not enough states here have .08 as the limit.

We have had some success with strict enforcement. In 1988, Wyoming became the 50th state to raise the drinking age to 21, and this has cut down on drunk driving. In 29 states, there are tough laws for drunk drivers under the age of 21. In these states, the standard for charging a driver under 21 is not 0.1 or .08 but .02. That's the equivalent of one beer.

Young people still drink. But Jim Hedlund, the director of alcohol and state programs at the National Traffic Safety Administration says that they "seem to take measures not to drink and drive." The alcohol industry's Century Council says drunk driving among young adults ages 21 to 34 "is a tough nut to crack."

Well, let's crack down harder. In too many states, people are still driving after their third conviction for drunk driving.

Take the license away on the first offense. Not permanently, but for 30 or 60 days. Long enough for the drinking driver to be genuinely concerned. On the second offense, no license for a year. And the third . . . permanent revocation *and jail*.

And this can be done only by law officers who are really interested in doing the job, who are supported by the local organizations—clubs such as yours—and the newspaper and leading citizens.

**Too often a patrolman simply takes the keys away** from a drinking driver and puts him in a taxi. **That way the patrolman is signing someone's death warrant.** And it might be your child's.

The patrolman doesn't want to handle the driver this way. But he feels he has to. The community wants him to. Oh, he will arrest the fellow driving an old Chevy or a battered Ford. But in the small town or the medium-sized city he will take the well-dressed drunk home. Or maybe the prosecutor will charge him with reckless driving instead of drunk driving in order to obtain a quick conviction.

Now these are only two steps. Yet I am certain—as certain as statistical analyses can lead me to be—that they will cut our traffic deaths in half.

Your editor tells you to write almost a column.

## E. *Mediocrity*

Here are excerpts from the remarks of Ted Koppel, anchorman of ABC News' "Nightline," made last night at a meeting of the International Radio & Television Society, which gave him its "Broadcaster of the Year" award. Write 300 to 400 words.

Koppel has been with ABC News since 1967 and was named anchorman of "Nightline" in 1980. From 1971 to 1980, he was the network's chief diplomatic correspondent. He joined ABC News at the age of 23 after working for a New York station, WMCA, as a desk assistant and off-air reporter. He was born in England and came to the United States with his parents at the age of 13.

I don't know what's happened to our standards. I fear that we in the mass media are creating such a market for mediocrity that we've diminished the incentive for excellence. We celebrate notoriety as though it were an achievement. Fame has come to mean being recognized by more people who don't know anything about you. In politics, we have encouraged the displacement of thoughtfulness by the artful cliché. In business, individual responsibility has been diffused into corporate non-accountability. In foreign affairs, the tactics of our enemies are used to justify the suspension of our own values. In medicine, the need to be healed is modified by the capacity to pay; and the cost of the cure is a function of the healer's fear of being sued. Which brings us to the law—the very underpinning of our system.

The law is supple and endlessly rich in meaning. It is also being abused as rarely before.

What Isaac Newton discovered to be true in physics is also applicable to the affairs of men: Every action has an equal and opposite reaction. I fear that unless we restore a sense of genuine value to what we do in each of our chosen professions, we will find that even the unprecedented flexibility of the American system can and will reach a breaking point. The legal profession is becoming an abomination; as often encouraging litigation purely for profits as for justice. The crimes and quarrels of the rich are endlessly litigated—until exhaustion produces a loophole or a settlement. The quarrels of the poor are settled in violence, and those crimes, in turn, are plea-bargained in courthouse corridors during a coffee break.

Our criminal justice system is becoming a playground for the rich . . . and a burial ground for the poor. It is increasingly difficult to argue that we were worse off when the rich resolved their disputes by dueling. It is even difficult, when one considers the conditions in most of our prisons, to make the case that we have progressed much beyond the brutal, but expedited justice of flogging and a day or two in the stocks.

Which brings me to my own profession; indeed, my very own job . . . and that of several of my distinguished colleagues here. Overestimated . . . overexposed . . . and by reasonable comparison with any job outside sports and entertainment . . . overpaid. I am a television news anchor . . . role model for Miss America contestants . . . and tens of thousands of university students, in search of a degree without an education. How does one live up to the admiration of those who regard the absence of an opinion as objectivity, or (even more staggering to the imagination) as courage?

How does one grapple with a state of national confusion that celebrates questions over answers? How does one explain, or perhaps more relevantly, guard against the influence of an industry which is on the verge of becoming a hallucinogenic barrage of images, whose only grammar is pacing . . . whose principal theme is energy?

We are losing our ability to manage ideas; to contemplate, to think. We are in a constant race to be first with the obvious. We are becoming a native of electronic voyeurs, whose capacity for dialogue is a fading memory, occasionally jolted into reflective life by a one-liner: "New ideas." "Where's the beef?" "Today is the first day of the rest of your life." "Window of vulnerability." "Freeze now." "Born again." "Gag me with a spoon." "Can we talk?"

No . . . but we can relate. Six-year-olds want to be stewardesses. Eight-year-olds want to be pilots. Nineteen-year-olds want to be anchorpersons. Grown-ups want to be left alone; to interact in solitary communion with the rest of our electronic, global village.

Consider this paradox: Almost everything that is publicly said these days is recorded. Almost nothing of what is said is worth remembering. And what *do* we remember? Thoughts that were expressed hundreds or even thousands of years ago by philosophers, thinkers and prophets whose ideas and principles were so universal that they endured without videotape or film, without the illustrations of photographs or cartoons. In many instances, even without paper; and for thousands of years without the easy duplication of the printing press.

What is largely missing in American life today is a sense of context; of saying or doing anything that is intended or even expected to live beyond the moment. There is no culture in the world that is so obsessed as ours with immediacy. In our journalism, the trivial displaces the momentous because we tend to measure the importance of events by how recently they happened. We have become so obsessed with facts that we have lost all touch with truth. . . .

It's easy to be seduced into believing that what we're doing is just fine; after all we get money . . . fame . . . and, to a certain degree, even influence. But money, fame and influence without responsibility are the assets of a courtesan. We must accept responsibility for what we do . . . and we must think occasionally of the future . . . and our impact on the next generation; or we may discover that they too have grown up . . . just like us.

## F. Cecil

You are covering a talk given by John R. Hunt, the Cobalt bureau manager for the *North Bay* (Canada) *Nugget*. Hunt has been with the newspaper 40 years and writes a widely read column and broadcasts a commentary for the Canadiard Broadcasting Corp. Presume that the talk was given at a Freeport Kiwanis Club luncheon meeting at Clark's Cafe. Write 250 to 300 words.

My car was making a funny noise the other day, so I took it to one of those antiseptic palaces, where I described the symptoms to a nice young lady, who called in a distinguished-looking gentleman with a stethoscope around his neck and a certificate on the wall which announced that he was a doctor of motors.

My car was taken away while I sat in a luxurious waiting room, reading old magazines and wondering what the experts were doing. Eventually I was told that my car was ready. I was presented with the bill and wrote a check, then drove frantically to my bank, where I persuaded the manager to cover it, and by the time I got home the car was making the same funny noise again. So I went for a beer at the Legion, and bumped into Cecil, the retired mechanic.

Cecil is retired, most reluctantly, because he is just about 65 years old. He doesn't see too well, because he always insisted on using a cold chisel without any goggles and got a chunk of steel in one eye, and then he damaged the other eye because he insisted on using a welding torch, again, without any goggles.

But oh, how I wish Cecil, and all the other old mechanics I have known, were still in business today.

They didn't wear white coats; in fact, they were usually covered in grease from head to foot. They didn't use a stethoscope. Cecil could stick his thumb against the block, feel the vibrations and tell you if you needed new spark plugs, new points or a ring job.

Cecil was a man of very strong opinions and ran his own garage for years. In fact, he refused to work on my car for a long time because he was a dog lover, and when I was a member of the local council, I hired a dog catcher who picked up Cecil's dog. Cecil beat the dog catcher to a pulp and paid a heavy fine. But he also refused to work on my car, or any one else's car who supported dog catchers. In fact, I believe he refused to work on the town truck, with the result that our snow-removal program was paralyzed.

If you called Cecil out late at night, he took a pair of pliers and some baling wire and a hammer. If he couldn't get the car to start with minor adjustments, he would attack it with the hammer and beat it into submission.

If you visited Cecil in his garage, you didn't sit in a waiting room. If you were lucky, you found an old crate or an orange box, and generally you took some newspapers with you to spread or you would have to take your clothes to the cleaners. And, if Cecil liked you, he would direct you to the back of the shop, where you could usually find some potent antifreeze and a fairly clean tin cup.

But Cecil could take the motor out of a Chev and put it into a Ford, welding new mounts and making new connections. He could take some beat-up jalopy that a teen-ager had paid twenty bucks for, and make it sing like a bird. And, if Cecil told you that your car was finished, you didn't argue, you had it towed to the dump.

And, when you got a bill from Cecil, you shoved it in your hip pocket and told him that you'd settle up on pay day, or maybe later, and he would only chuckle, or let rip with a few cuss words, and then crawl back into his grease pit and flail away with his hammer.

There are still a few Cecils out there. Running one-man garages, charging moderate bills and doing a good job. If you know one, cherish him, treat him gently, even buy him a drink, because as cars grow more complicated, and motorists more helpless, the Cecils of the automotive world are a precious and rare breed. But, I'd take him, covered in grease, smelling of booze and swearing like a trooper, in preference to all the white-coated doctors of motors that I know.

## G. Smokers

Dr. David A. Kessler, the Commissioner of Food and Drugs, is speaking at 11 a.m. on the Mallory College campus. You are told his subject is tobacco addiction. Kessler has been in the news lately with his campaign against tobacco companies for what he says is their "seduction of teen-agers." He has urged Congress to adopt stricter control over the sales of tobacco products, but the new Republican majority in Congress has shelved most of his recommendations. This talk is part of his campaign to take the issue to the public.

During Kessler's talk, he shows some slides which are reproduced here. Your editor tells you to write as much as you wish.

Here are some excerpts from his talk:

It is easy to think of smoking as an adult problem. It is adults who die from tobacco-related diseases. We see adults light up in a restaurant or bar. We see a colleague step outside for a cigarette break.

But this is a dangerously short-sighted view.

It is as if we entered the theater in the third act—after the plot has been set in motion, after the stage has been set. For while the epidemic of disease and death from smoking is played out in adulthood, it begins in childhood. If there is one fact that I need to stress today, it is that a person who hasn't started smoking by age 19 is unlikely to ever become a smoker. Nicotine addiction begins when most tobacco users are teen-agers, so let's call this what it really is: a pediatric disease.

Each and every day another three thousand teen-agers become smokers. Young people are the tobacco industry's primary source of new customers in this country, replacing adults who have either quit or died. An internal document of a Canadian tobacco company, an affiliate of a tobacco company in the United States, states the case starkly:

> If the last ten years have taught us anything, it is that the [tobacco] industry is dominated by the companies who respond most effectively to the needs of the younger smokers.

If we could affect the smoking habits of just one generation, we could radically reduce the incidence of smoking-related death and disease, and a second unaddicted generation could see nicotine addiction go the way of smallpox and polio.

The tobacco industry has argued that the decision to smoke and continue to smoke is a free choice made by an adult. But ask a smoker when he or she began to smoke. Chances are you will hear the tale of a child.

It's the age-old story: Kids sneaking away to experiment with tobacco, trying to smoke without coughing, without getting dizzy, and staring at themselves in a mirror just to see how smooth and sophisticated they can look. . . .

Between one-third and one-half of adolescents who try smoking even a few cigarettes soon become regular smokers.

What is perhaps most striking is that young people who start smoking soon regret it. Seven out of 10 who smoke report that they regret ever having started. But like adults, they have enormous difficulty quitting. Certainly some succeed, but three out of four young smokers have tried to quit at least once and failed.

Consider the experience of one 16-year-old girl, recently quoted in a national magazine. She started to smoke when she was 8 because her older brother smoked. Today, she says, "Now, I'm stuck. I can't quit. . . . It's so incredibly bad to nic-fit, it's not even funny. When your body craves the nicotine, it's just: 'I need a cigarette.' "

In her own terms she has summarized the scientific findings of the 1988 Surgeon General's report. That report concluded, "Cigarettes and other forms of tobacco are addicting" and "Nicotine is the drug in tobacco that causes addiction."

Let there be no doubt that nicotine is an addictive substance. Many studies have documented the presence of the key addiction criteria relied on by major medical organizations. These criteria include highly controlled or compulsive use, even despite a desire or repeated attempts to quit; psychoactive effects on the brain; and drug-motivated behavior caused by the "reinforcing" effects of the psychoactive substance. Quitting episodes followed by relapse and withdrawal symptoms that can motivate further use are some additional criteria of an addictive substance.

Are young people simply unaware of the dangers associated with smoking and nicotine addiction? No, not really. They just do not believe that these dangers apply to them.

For healthy young people, death and illness are just distant rumors. And until they experience the grip of nicotine addiction for themselves, they vastly underestimate its power over them. They are young, they are fearless, and they are confident that they will be able to quit smoking when they want to, and certainly well before any adverse health consequences occur.

They are also wrong. We see that documented in papers acquired from one company in a Canadian court case. A study prepared for the company called "Project 16" describes how the typical youthful experimenter becomes an addicted smoker within a few years:

> However intriguing smoking was at 11, 12, or 13, by the age of 16 or 17 many regretted their use of cigarettes for health reasons and because they feel unable to stop smoking when they want to. . . . Over half claim they want to quit. However, they cannot quit any easier than adults can.

Vern Herschberger, *Waco Tribune-Herald*.

Unfortunately, youth smoking gives no sign of abating. While the prevalence of smoking among adults has steadily declined since 1964, the prevalence of smoking by young people stalled for more than a decade and recently has begun to rise. Between 1992 and 1994, the prevalence of smoking by high school seniors increased from 17.2 percent to 22 percent. Smoking among college freshmen rose from 9 percent in 1985 to 12.5 percent in 1994.

And young people's addiction to nicotine is not limited to smoking. Children's use of smokeless tobacco, such as snuff and chewing tobacco, is also extensive. Today, of the seven million people in this country who use smokeless tobacco, as many as one in four is under the age of 19.

This epidemic of youth addiction to nicotine has enormous public health consequences. A casual decision at a young age to use tobacco products can lead to addiction, serious disease, and premature death as an adult. More than 400,000 smokers die each year from smoking-related illnesses.

Smoking kills more people each year in the United States than AIDS, car accidents, alcohol, homicides, illegal drugs, suicides and fires combined. And the real tragedy is that these deaths from smoking are preventable.

A year ago the FDA raised the question of whether the Agency has a role in preventing this problem. The FDA has responsibility for the drugs, devices, biologics and food used in this country. Over the last year, we have been looking at whether nicotine-containing tobacco products are drugs subject to the requirements of the Federal Food, Drug and Cosmetic Act. Our study continues. But we already know this: Nicotine is an addictive substance, and the marketplace for tobacco products is sustained by this addiction. And what is striking is that it is young people who are becoming addicted.

Statements from internal documents by industry researchers and executives show that they understood that nicotine is addictive and how important it is to their product. Listen to these statements made decades ago:

"We are, then, in the business of selling nicotine, an addictive drug."

"Think of the cigarette pack as a storage container for a day's supply of nicotine. Think of the cigarette as a dispenser for a dose unit of nicotine. Think of a puff of smoke as the vehicle for nicotine."

And consider what a research group reported to one tobacco company about starter smokers who assume they will not become addicted:

"But addicted they do indeed become."

More recently, a former chief executive officer of a major American tobacco company, told *The Wall Street Journal*, "Of course it's addictive. That's why you smoke. . . . " And a former smokeless tobacco industry chemist was recently quoted as saying, "There used to be a saying at [the company] that 'There's a hook in every can' . . . [and] that hook is nicotine."

Nevertheless, the industry publicly insists that smoking is a choice freely made by adults. An advertisement by one of the major tobacco companies that appeared in newspapers across the country last year bore a headline that read, "Where Exactly Is the Land of the Free?" It suggests that the government is interested in banning cigarettes—although no one in government has advocated such a position. With some 40 million smokers addicted to nicotine, a ban would not be feasible.

We cannot adequately address this pediatric disease our country faces without recognizing the important influences on a young person's decision to smoke. One such influence is industry advertising and promotion. It is important to understand the effects of these practices on young people.

In the last two decades, the amount of money the cigarette industry has spent to advertise and promote its products has dramatically risen. Despite a long-standing ban on broadcast advertising, in 1992 alone the industry spent more than $5.2 billion. This makes it the second most heavily advertised commodity in the United States, second only to automobiles.

Tobacco advertising appears in print media, on billboards, at point of sale, by direct mail, on an array of consumer items such as hats, t-shirts, jackets, and lighters and at concerts and sporting events. The sheer magnitude of advertising creates the impression among young people that smoking is much more ubiquitous and socially acceptable than it is. In studies, young smokers consistently overestimate the percentage of people who smoke.

In addition, tobacco industry advertising themes and images resonate with young people. Advertising experts describe the cigarette package as a "badge" product that adolescents show to create a desired self image and to communicate that image to others. As a retired leading advertising executive has stated, "When the teenagers loose [sic] the visual link between the advertising and the point of sale . . . they will loose [sic] much of the incentive to rebel against authority and try smoking."

In recent years, the tobacco industry has been spending more money on marketing and promotion and less on traditional advertising. For example, it distributes catalogues of items that can be obtained with proof of purchase coupons attached to cigarette packs—such as Camel Cash and Marlboro Mile. These coupons are exchanged for nontobacco consumer items imprinted with product logos.

These items have proven to be a big hit with children and adolescents. Half of all adolescent smokers and one-quarter of adolescent nonsmokers own at least one promotional item from a tobacco company, according to a 1992 Gallup survey.

Sponsorship of athletic, musical, sporting and other events is another important way that the industry promotes its product. This links tobacco products with the glamorous and appealing worlds of sports and entertainment. And the logos of their brands are viewed during televised events, despite the federally mandated broadcast advertising ban.

Make no mistake: All of this advertising and promotion is chillingly effective. The three most heavily advertised brands of cigarettes are Marlboro, Camel and Newport. A recent study by the Centers for Disease Control and Prevention found that 86 percent of underage smokers who purchase their own cigarettes purchased one of those three heavily advertised brands.

The advertisements apparently have far less impact on adults. By far, the most popular brand choices for adults are the private label, price value, and plain package brands, which rely on little or no imagery on their packaging or advertising.

Let me describe two campaigns to illustrate the effects that advertising and marketing practices can have on young people. One campaign gave new life to a cigarette brand with an aging customer base. The other revitalized the dying smokeless tobacco market.

In the early 1980s, Camel cigarettes were smoked primarily by men over 50, and commanded about 3 to 4 percent of the overall market. So the company began to make plans to reposition Camel.

The new advertising for Camel was designed to take advantage of Camel's 75th birthday. The campaign featured the cartoon character "Joe Camel" as its anthropomorphic spokescamel who gave dating advice called "smooth moves" and who eventually was joined by a whole gang of hip camels at the watering hole.

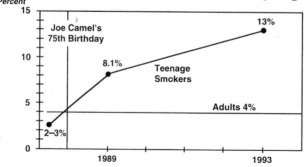

Centers for Disease Control and Prevention.

The campaign was variously described as irreverent, humorous and sophomoric. But Joe Camel gave the company what it wanted: a new vehicle to reposition the Camel brand with more youth appeal.

During the same time period, the company devised what it called a Young Adult Smokers program—which went by the acronym YAS. The program was designed to appeal to the 18 to 24 age group, and more narrowly to the 18- to 20-year-old audience. The program also had a tracking system to monitor sales in these groups.

Let me give you several facts about that program.

First, on January 10, 1990, a division manager in Sarasota, Florida, issued a memorandum describing a method to increase the exposure and access to the Young Adult Market for the Joe Camel campaign. The memorandum asked sales representatives to identify stores within their areas that "are heavily frequented by young adult shoppers. These stores can be in close proximity to colleges [and] high schools. . . ." The purpose of the memorandum was to make sure that those stores were always stocked with items that appeal to younger people—such as hats and t-shirts—carrying the Camel name and imagery.

A *Wall Street Journal* article revealed the contents of this letter and it also contained the company's response that the memo was a mistake. The company said the mistake had been corrected and explained that the manager had violated company policy by targeting high school students. However, on April 5, 1990, another division manager, this time in Oklahoma, sent a memo to all areas sales representatives and chain service representatives in parts of Oklahoma. The memo refers to what it calls "Retail Young Adult Smoker Retailer Account[s]" and goes on to say:

> The criteria for you to utilize in identifying these accounts are as follows: (1) . . . calls located across from, adjacent to [or] in the general vicinity of the High Schools. . . .

Second, an additional element of the Camel campaign was known as FUBYAS—an acronym for First Usual Brand Young Adult Smokers. The company's own research in the 1980s revealed a noteworthy behavior among smokers: The brand that they use when they first become regular smokers is the brand that smokers stay with for years. There is a great deal of brand loyalty among smokers.

Third, the next slide shows the effect of the YAS or young adult smoker campaign. Prior to the campaign, about 2 to 3 percent of smokers under the age of 18 named Camel as their brand. By 1989, a year into the campaign, Camel's share of underage smokers had risen to 8.1 percent and within a few years it had grown to at least 13 percent. During this same period, Camel's share of the adult market barely moved from its 4 percent market share.

The campaign succeeded in resurrecting the moribund Camel brand. But it also managed to create an icon recognizable to even the youngest children. Two studies, one by an independent researcher and one company funded, found that children as young as 3 to 6 easily recognize Joe Camel and know that he is associated with cigarettes. The company's researcher found that children were as familiar with Joe Camel as they were with Ronald McDonald. This fact is significant because children this young get most of their product information from television advertising. But cigarettes have not been advertised on television since 1970.

The campaign was clearly very effective with the target group—the YAS smokers. But it was also effective with the younger, under 18 smokers.

The second example of industry promotion concerns the largest smokeless tobacco company in America. It was also trying to revive the declining market for its product. By 1970, these products were used predominantly by men over 50. Young males had the lowest usage.

The company set about to redesign its products and refocus its advertising and promotion to target younger people, especially younger men. Its high-nicotine delivery products were apparently not well tolerated by new users. But as part of the redesign, it developed low-nicotine delivery snuff products in easy to use teabag-like pouches. Company documents indicate that these products were developed to create "starter" brands that would attract new users who could not tolerate the higher-nicotine delivery products.

A cherry-flavored product was also developed. In fact, one former company sales representative was quoted in the *Wall Street Journal* as saying that the cherry product "is for somebody who likes the taste of candy, if you know what I'm saying."

The documents also show that the company set out to produce a range of products with low, medium and high nicotine deliveries. One document shows that the company expected its customers to "graduate" upward through the range of nicotine deliveries. This chart, prepared by its marketing department shows the hierarchy of products, with arrows going from Skoal Bandits (the teabags), through Happy Days and Skoal Long Cuts and ultimately to Copenhagen—the company's highest nicotine delivery product.

The idea behind the advertising and marketing strategy was captured in a statement a few years earlier, in 1968, by a company vice president:

> We must sell the use of tobacco in the mouth and appeal to young people . . . we hope to start a fad.

The Camel and smokeless campaigns demonstrate how marketing and promotion targeted at younger tobacco users can also reach children and adolescents. And those young people who choose to smoke have easy access to the products. Tobacco products are among the most widely available consumer products in America, available in virtually every gas station, convenience store, drugstore and grocery store. And though every state in the country prohibits the sale of cigarettes to those who are underage, study after study demonstrates that these laws are widely ignored. Teen-agers can purchase tobacco products with little effort—and they know it. A 1990 survey by the National Cancer Institute found that eight out of 10 ninth graders said it would be easy for them to buy their own cigarettes. By some estimates, at least as many as 255 million packs are sold illegally to minors each year.

Younger smokers are more likely to buy their cigarettes from vending machines, where they can make their purchases quickly, often unnoticed by adults. The vending machine industry's own study found that 13-year-olds are 11 times more likely to buy cigarettes from vending machines than 17-year-olds. The 1994 Surgeon General's Report examined nine studies on vending machine sales and found that underage persons were able to buy cigarettes 82 to 100 percent of the time.

But the easy access does not stop with vending machines. Self-service displays allow buyers to help themselves to a pack of cigarettes or a can of smokeless with minimal contact with a sales clerk. This makes it easier for an underage person to buy tobacco products.

I've told you today that 90 percent of those who smoke began to do so as children and teen-agers. I've told you that most of them become addicted and that seven out of 10 wish they could quit. I've told you that the tobacco industry spends more than $5 billion a year to advertise and promote an addictive product and it uses cartoon characters, t-shirts and other gimmicks that appeal to children. I've told you that one company went so far as to develop a young adult smoker's program which, intentionally or not, increased cigarette sales to children.

Some may choose to ignore these facts. Some will continue to insist that the issue is an adult's freedom of choice. Nicotine addiction begins as a pediatric disease. Yet our society as a whole has done little to discourage this addiction in our youth. We must all recognize this fact and we must do more to discourage this addiction in our youth.

A comprehensive and meaningful approach to preventing future generations of young people from becoming addicted to nicotine in tobacco is needed. Any such approach should: First, restrict or ban the many avenues of easy access to tobacco products available to children and teen-agers in vending machines. Second, get the message to our young people that nicotine is addictive, and that tobacco products pose serious health hazards—and not just for someone else. Third, reduce the powerful imagery in tobacco advertising and promotion that encourages young people to begin using tobacco products.

These types of actions have been advocated by many public health experts and organizations, including most recently the Institute of Medicine which issued a report on smoking and children. And a recent public opinion poll sponsored by the Robert Wood Johnson Foundation showed widespread public support for measures to reduce smoking by young people.

When it comes to health, we Americans are an impatient people. We venerate the deliberate, cautious scientific method but we yearn for instant cures. We grow restless waiting years or even months for answers, yet today I am telling you to look to the next generation.

Certainly some of the 40 million addicted adult smokers in this country will succeed in quitting. Every addictive substance has some who are able to break its grip, and we should do all we can to support those who want to quit. But let us not fool ourselves. To succeed, we must fix our gaze beyond today's adults.

Of course we all want freedom for our children. But not the freedom to make irreversible decisions in childhood that result in devastating health consequences for the future. Addiction is freedom denied. We owe it to our children to help them enter adulthood free from addiction. Our children are entitled to a lifetime of choices, not a lifelong addiction.

# Meetings

## *Exercises II*

### A. Council

Write a story based on the following notes from a local city council meeting last night. Use all the facts here. The council decided:

1. To build a viaduct across railroad tracks at Lincoln Street, scene of three automobile-train accidents in the last seven months. To cost $300,000.

2. To dismiss George Q. Banks, welfare director. Successor not appointed. Banks criticized last month for "irregularities in finances of department," that the city manager found in an audit.

3. To add new inspector in department of sanitation. Appointed David Lowe. He has been assistant bacteriologist at Fairlawn Hospital.

4. To hold referendum at next election (May). Citizens to vote on $1,000,000 bond issue for replacement of sewers throughout downtown area. Present system in use since 1884. Leakage into ground water supply; system inadequate for load.

Sewer construction is the first part of the 10-year City Core Regeneration Plan. Traffic rerouting next; then the downtown mall.

## B. Boards

During the past week, stringers from nearby towns have been calling in with stories about meetings of their boards of education. You have written briefly about some of these meetings. Your editor now wants you to round up all of these for use in a Sunday story. Here is the material:

Selkirk: Board adopted $625,000 budget. Will hire three additional teachers, one speech therapist. Salaries up 2 percent. Turned down $175,000 request for bond issue to expand library. Property tax increased from $17 to $18/$100 in assessed valuation.

Wrigley: Board adopted budget almost same as last year, $890,000. No salary increases, no new teachers. The property tax kept at $24/$100.

Dease Lake: Board turned down request for $1 million bond issue. Bonds to be used for physical expansion of Dease Lake Junior High. Vote 5-0 after four-hour meeting at which members of Dease Lake Improvement Association asked for bond issue, but individuals said classes not overcrowded. Adopted $1,260,000 budget. Flat teacher-pay raise of $100. Tax rate continued at $28/$100.

Keno Hill: Acrimonious debate at board meeting over request by Keno Teachers Association to add 12 teachers and to increase salaries across the board by 12 percent. Association said, "Schools overcrowded," "teachers' average salary of $15,000 disgraceful." Board voted 3-2 against request. Teachers say won't sign contracts to teach next year. Board adopted $2,350,000 budget. Minor increases in most categories; 3 percent teacher salary increase. Keno Hill Real Estate Association told board property taxes now "prohibitive." Mill levy of $26/$100 retained.

Rockford: Ralph Robards, chairman of the Rockford Board of Education, said the board voted to "hold the line" in expenditures for the next school year. Robards said the board voted four to one to approve a school budget of $2,220,000.

This is an increase of $275,000 over last year. Robards said a 6 percent salary increase was voted for teachers; four new elementary school teachers will be hired; and major repairs made in the Rockford High School gymnasium.

"We managed to hold the line on our taxes, retaining the rate of $29/$100 because we anticipate new construction will enlarge the tax base," he said.

In other actions, the board turned down a request from the Rockford Committee of Concerned Citizens for $75,000 to be put into the budget for a pilot program to bus sixth-grade students from low-income areas to the recently constructed Albert Parker elementary school on Duane Street. It hired Dr. Selwyn C. Mann as principal of the Parker School. Dr. Mann is a native of Albuquerque, New Mexico, and recently was granted Ph.D. at the University of Minnesota.

## C. Legacy

The Black Student Group at St. Mary's College sponsored a discussion tonight, "The Legacy of Malcolm X." The speakers were Vincent Bivins, professor of political science at the college and faculty adviser to the BSG, and Judith Cramer, a member of the Freeport Human Rights Commission.

About 50 students attended the discussion on the campus. Half were black, half white. N. Francis Simms, college president, attended and said after the discussion, "This is the kind of opening up we must engage in so that we can understand each other. Discussion, debate, questions and answers do much more than confrontation."

Here are excerpts from Cramer's talk:

The legacy of Malcolm X derives from his appeal based on a strong belief in black pride and black identity, and his penetrating critique of racial inequality in this country.

In contrast to Martin Luther King, Malcolm X was the voice of the angry, dispossessed people of the northern ghettoes.

That's a section of society that's growing rapidly right now. As long as their problems exist, Malcolm X will continue to be relevant.

He was an inspirational figure who made a lot of us look in the mirror, so to speak, and be proud of who we were as black people and people of African descent.

A lot of what Malcolm dreamed is coming to pass, in some small ways.

We have to remember that Malcolm did not live to carry out the enormous changes he was in the process of making. He was murdered after he broke with Elijah Muhammad and the Nation of Islam. In 1964, after a dozen years of talking of the evil of the "white devil," he was moving to what Michael Eric Dyson, professor of African-American studies at Brown University, describes as "a broader philosophy of human community. We may conclude with certainty that Malcolm X had rejected the whites-are-devils pronouncements that helped to focus his earlier life and brought him to the attention and vilification of a nation."

But, as Professor Dyson says, "He simply did not live long enough to fulfill his promise. We are brought up short when trying to deal definitively with the universal humanitarianism of his latter days."

Here are excerpts from Bivins' talk:

> It's a multifaceted struggle—it wasn't Malcolm X, it wasn't Martin Luther King. Human struggles are much more complicated than any particular person.
>
> Malcolm functioned as a spokesman for a movement. He was an outspoken critic of America's racial situation.
>
> But we may be paying too much attention to one or two heroes while ignoring many others who were just as important.
>
> Clearly, Malcolm was an important figure. But I don't think he was the only person on the block. Emphasizing these one or two figures gives us a skewed view of history.
>
> We have to understand that Malcolm never registered anyone to vote. He never led a march against segregation. He never broke down any racial barriers himself.
>
> Given time, this could have changed. In the last year of Malcolm's life, he dropped the racist rhetoric of the Nation of Islam, thus earning him the enmity of people like Louis X, who is now Louis Farrakhan, head of the Nation of Islam. And in 1966, Martin Luther King began to move toward emphasizing black pride and the need for black economic health. We might have had a convergence of these two great figures.
>
> Studies of Malcolm must continue to be made. We have to foresake the uncritical endorsements and attacks and examine the man and his work.

Write 300 to 400 words about the discussion for tomorrow morning's newspaper, or write a long piece for tonight's local radio news.

## *Assignment*

### *Clubs*

Many civic organizations—Rotary, Kiwanis, Lions—have regular luncheon meetings at which invited guests give short talks. Sometimes these talks are newsworthy. Club officials often welcome student guests. A class may ask permission to attend for practice in speech coverage.

A number of other organizations usually hold regular meetings at which there are lectures or talks. The Audubon Society, the American Association of University Women, the League of Women Voters, the Sierra Club and many other national groups have local chapters. At times, the guests are men and women of some prominence.

Attend one of these meetings and write a story of 300 to 350 words.

# News Conferences

## *Exercises III*

### *A. Reject*

An organization known as the Concerned Parents Association two weeks ago presented a petition to the local school board asking for the removal of several books from the public schools. The association, which includes members of the three major religious groups and various racial and ethnic groups, has in past years confined its activities to submitting material, much of it used to encourage brotherhood studies in the schools. The books it asks to be removed are, according to the list of the group, *Manchild in the Promised Land,* by Claude Brown; *Laughing Boy,* by Oliver LaFarge; *The Fixer,* by Bernard Malamud; *The Adventures of Huckleberry Finn,* by Mark Twain; *Portnoy's Complaint,* by Philip Roth; and *Down These Mean Streets,* by Piri Thomas.

Five of the seven members of the city school board today issued the following statement at a news conference. The five are Albert Swimmer, Helen Epstein, Charles Thorne, Jean Silver and Salvatore Vincent. The other two are Edwin Minteer and John T. Voboril. Thorne, the president of the board, reads this statement:

> We intend to vote against the request when the board discusses the petition by the Concerned Parents Association next Monday. We have been holding meetings with teachers, parents and students, individually, as we promised two weeks ago when the matter was presented to the board.
>
> Several members of the association have been speaking to us, and although we believe we have heard ample evidence for the association's point of view, we certainly do not intend to prohibit them from speaking at Monday's meeting. It is possible that new arguments will be presented at that time.
>
> However, we have heard the supporters, read the books, spoken to many of those involved. The argument of the association and its supporters is best summed up by the statement of Mrs. Richard Farrington, who asks, "Why do they have to tell it the way it is? Some of these books print downright filth. As for Jim, in Huck Finn, he is portrayed as simple, superstitious, childlike, no role model for young blacks."

We agree that some of these books are realistic. Claude Brown's book does use street language, and it goes into detail about heroin use. *Huck Finn* is a subversive book; it does subvert the values of a society Twain disliked.

We respect the intention of these concerned citizens. But some arguments are as silly as the parents in a California school who asked that *The Red Badge of Courage* be removed from schools because they thought it was about a Russian war decoration.

We are also concerned that should we act as we are requested we would violate the law. The courts have said that a school board violates First Amendment guarantees if it removes books already on the library shelves. One federal court said:

> Here, we are concerned with the right of students to receive information which their teachers desire them to have. . . .
>
> A library is like a storehouse of knowledge. When created for a public school, it is an important privilege created by the state for the benefit of the students in the school. That privilege is not subject to being withdrawn by succeeding school boards whose members might desire to winnow the library for books the content of which occasioned their displeasure or disapproval.

In answer to a question, Swimmer, who is black, says:

> These books do denigrate certain groups. But that is only their superficial message. Each of them is written with a passionate regard for the dignity of mankind.
>
> But what happens when books are censored? Well, the immediate reaction here is that the popularity of these books has increased, school officials tell us. But for precisely the wrong reasons. In the long run, censorship is disastrous, for once censorship begins, it will not stop.

Epstein is asked if the charge that *The Fixer* has anti-Semitic stereotypes has some validity. She answers:

> I leafed through the book the other day after a few years, and I can see how someone would object, just as I would understand reactions to "The Merchant of Venice" and *Oliver Twist*.
>
> Clearly, Shylock and Fagin are anti-Semitic stereotypes. There is some debate about Shylock, who at times is a sympathetic character. But there is none about Fagin. Yet what good is served by censoring the books? Perhaps it is true that youngsters who cannot understand that these books reflect certain periods and feeling should not be asked to read them.
>
> I'd agree that small children have no business reading *Manchild,* but I read *Huckleberry Finn* to my 12-year-old daughter and she thought Jim was a wonderful human being.

She is asked about *Portnoy's Complaint:* Would you want your daughter to read it?

> Well, I wouldn't want her to have Portnoy for a boyfriend when she grows up. At her age—she's 12—she should not be exposed to that kind of book. But I see nothing wrong with having it on the shelves of the high school library and using it in the class for seniors.

Write a column of copy.

## B. Minors

The mayor's office distributes the following press release and says he will discuss it tomorrow at his 11 a.m. news conference. Write a precede.

THE CITY OF FREEPORT                                OFFICE OF THE MAYOR

    For Immediate Release

<u>Statement by Mayor Sam Parnass</u>
<u>on the Sale of Tobacco to Minors</u>

I am asking the chief of police and our city inspectors to step up their surveillance of the vendors of tobacco products. It has come to my attention that increasing numbers of teen-agers are smoking, despite the health risks, and I have had reports that some merchants are selling to underage buyers.

Tobacco takes the greatest toll on health of any substance that we are able to control. It is well established that at least a thousand deaths a day can be traced to tobacco. Recently, we have learned that there is even a toll on the unborn and the newly born. Researchers at the University of Massachusetts and at Brigham and Women's Hospital in Boston found that smoking mothers have 115,000 miscarriages a year and that 5,600 of their babies die each year. Also, they give birth to 53,000 low-weight infants and 22,000 who require intensive care at birth.

The financial toll is estimated at $43.8 billion a year in federal costs through Medicare, Medicaid and other federal entitlements.

The time to attack this problem is when potential smokers are young. We must do everything we can to prevent teen-agers from succumbing to tobacco addiction. The city will do its part through stepped-up law enforcement. I intend to ask the city council for more stringent punishments for offenders. I want their retail licenses suspended for the first offense and revoked for the second.

# Panel Discussions and Symposia

## *Exercises IV*

### *Teaching*

The school of education at St. Mary's University has held a symposium on "Teaching: What's Ahead?" The speakers are Sidney H. Ganch, York University, a visiting professor of English literature; Frederick L. Lynn, associate professor of English at the host school and moderator of the symposium; Herbert Gilkeyson, superintendent of the local school system. The symposium was held at 3 p.m. in the school's auditorium. Write about 250 words for tomorrow's paper from the following remarks:

**Gilkeyson:** The emphasis will be, I believe, on grade school education where the basic study habits are inculcated and educational values formed. We have overemphasized higher education, and the result has been a deficiency of resources allocated to the elementary schools. . . .

We all know the problems that students in college have cannot be remedied without massively expensive remedial aid. We must put that money into the lower grades.

At the same time, there must be rededication to teaching by the teacher. A sense of professionalism will have to reinvigorate teaching or nothing positive will result. . . .

The teacher who used to take papers home to read now wants to have preparation periods in the school to read them. Taxpayers won't pay for this, and so homework is not given with the frequency of past years. Consequently, students spend less time learning. . . .

I am confident the teacher is the key to a new spirit of learning in the future. . . .

**Lynn:** I would agree that teachers must re-examine themselves, but so must everyone else. Teachers are no different from doctors and ditchdiggers. They reflect the society at large, and it is society we must look to that establishes values that we all accede to.

**Ganch:** Students must be taught how to reason, how to learn. John Dewey recommended strong teaching, not the chaos we see in the curricula today with its permissive teachers. Samuel Johnson blessed the teachers who applied the birch rod to him. Teachers must put demands on students. . . .

## *Campus Project*

### *Altruism*

The former president of Harvard, Derek Bok, made these remarks in a commencement address:

During most of the 20th century, first artists and intellectuals, then broader segments of the society, challenged every convention, every prohibition, every regulation that cramped the human spirit or blocked its appetites and ambitions. Today, a reaction has set in, born of a recognition that the public needs common standards to hold a diverse society together, to prevent ecological disaster, to maintain confidence in government, to conserve scarce resources, to escape disease, to avoid the inhumane applications of technology. . . .

As people everywhere worry about our ethical standards, universities are bound to come under scrutiny. Almost every public servant, business executive, attorney, physician—indeed virtually all leaders in every walk of life—enter our colleges and professional schools and remain there for several formative years. . . .

In these circumstances, universities . . . need to think hard about what they can do in the face of what many perceive as a widespread decline in ethical standards.

Such evidence as we have about the values of college students only heightens these concerns. Several studies have found that undergraduates are growing less altruistic and more preoccupied with self-serving goals. In polls of entering freshmen over the past 15 to 20 years, the values that have risen most are the desire to be "very well off financially," to gain personal recognition and to have "administrative responsibility for the work of others." The goal that has plummeted furthest is the desire to find a "meaningful philosophy of life," while other values that have fallen include the desire to keep up-to-date in political affairs, to participate in community action programs and to help clean up the environment. Further studies suggest that the number of college students who admit to having cheated in class has risen appreciably over the past 30 years.

. . . what *can* universities do and what *should* they do to help students to achieve higher ethical standards?

What has your university done or is it planning anything to answer Bok's question? Check professional schools and departments to find the answer. Interview faculty members as well as the heads of departments about what has been done and how effective the action has been. Interview students to see whether they consider the action (lectures, reading, required courses) effective.

## Community Projects

### A. Mail

People are always complaining about how long it takes letters to arrive, and the postal service says it is constantly at work speeding up the process. Check the delivery time yourself.

Select friends and relatives at several different locations and send a letter with a self-addressed stamped envelope inside. Ask the recipient to note just when the letter was postmarked and received. A form could be used. At your end, note the date the incoming letter was postmarked and the date you received it.

Mail your letters on the same day as everyone else in your class.

### B. DWI

Statistics show that drunk drivers are repeaters. In New Mexico, for example, almost half the 14,000 drivers charged in a single year with drunk driving had at least one prior conviction on the charge. Traffic Bureau records show that nearly 3,500 had three or more convictions.

Make a study of figures for your city and for your state. How many of those convicted for driving while under the influence of alcohol had a prior arrest, more than one arrest? Are there any moves to tighten up the penalties for this offense?

## Home Assignment

### Oops

Newspapers and magazines are increasingly printing material with bad grammar, misspellings, wrong usage, incorrect punctuation. These are not typographical errors, mistakes in production; they are the handiwork of the newswriters. Look at these:

"As long as they respect my corner and I respect **their's,** there's enough to go around."—*The New York Times*.

Newark, N.J. (AP)—Americans are the worst spellers in the English-speaking world, according to the results of an international spelling bee. . . . Gallup's spelling test . . . follows a **simmlar** multination survey. . . .

That is just one reason to cheer the publishing of this **fulsome** biography. . . . —Book review in *Nieman Reports*. (**Fulsome:** gross; disgusting by excess.)

Spanish words seem to give *New York Times* reporters trouble, although the city has more than a million Spanish-speaking residents:

"I'll eat at home," he said, turning his back on the **cucinas** and Chinese restaurants. . . . (Not **cucinas,** *cocinas.*)

In a piece about the advertising business in Mexico, an account executive said he had to cope with the "**morbito,**" a colloquialism for *bribe*. (It's *mordida,* from the verb *morder,* to bite.)

For the next week, be on the lookout for errors of this sort in newspapers and other publications that you read. Do any publications have a preponderance of errors? Why?

## Class Discussion

### A. Indefensible

Every journalist who is not too stupid or too full of himself to notice what is going on knows that what he does is morally indefensible. He is a kind of confidence man, preying on people's vanity, ignorance, or loneliness, gaining their trust and betraying them without remorse.

This is the beginning of Janet Malcolm's book *The Journalist and the Murderer,* a description and commentary on how journalist Joe McGinniss ingratiated himself with triple-murderer Jeffrey MacDonald and then in the book *Fatal Vision* refused to accept MacDonald's version that an intruder was the killer.

Malcolm describes the relationship between journalists and their sources and subjects as one of exploitation, "seduction and betrayal," a "Devil's pact."

What do you think of Malcolm's assessment of journalistic morality?

## *DB/CAR*

### A. Chart

Obtain data from the state health department on causes of death in your state's counties over the past 10 years.

1. Make a graph of the changes in the death rates over the 10-year period.
2. Shade a county map of the state to indicate the rates.

You can select among the following causes: cardiovascular diseases, cancer, AIDS, respiratory ailments, cirrhosis of the liver, suicide, homicide, drug-related death, accidents, maternal and infant deaths.

## *Fix It: To the Point*

Here are some leads to the exercises in this chapter. Do they summarize what the speaker said; do they get to the point of the speech or talk?

1. *In-Depth*

Eugene Roberts, editor of *The Philadelphia Inquirer,* spoke about investigative reporting last night at the University of Southern California School of Journalism.

2. *Professions*

A library school dean last night asked his listeners whether the low status and respect traditionally given women has carried over into the occupations in which they are predominant.

3. *Driving*

An insurance company executive today described ways to cope with the nation's heavy highway traffic death toll.

4. *Mediocrity*

Ted Koppel, anchorman of ABC News' "Nightline," addressed the International Radio & Television Society last night. The Society gave Koppel its "Broadcaster of the Year" award.

5. *Legacy*

Malcolm X had discarded his racist rhetoric and was on the verge of a new approach to racism in this country, two speakers agreed last night.

## You Decide: Restrictions

1. A campus group has invited a controversial speaker to the campus. The speaker requests that the audience be limited to (consider each separately):
   (a) Faculty members.
   (b) Black men.
   (c) Women.

You are the editor of the campus newspaper, the *Spectator*. What do you do?

2. You are the sports editor of your campus newspaper and you have assigned a woman sportswriter to cover a football game between your team and a nearby institution on its field. Your reporter calls you and says she has been denied admission to the locker room by that institution's athletic department which has a "men only" rule. What do you do?

# 17 Hunches, Feelings and Stereotypes

Joel Sartore, *The Wichita Eagle-Beacon*.
**Journalists screen their emotions.**

### Introduction

Hunches and intuition can lead reporters to good stories. They do not, however, come out of the blue. They are the result of the reporters' accumulation of a large and varied background knowledge and an understanding of the behavior of people. The ill-prepared reporter does not have hunches. Feelings and emotions can distort observations and influence writing. But they also can lead reporters to uncover abuses and illegalities. Reporters monitor their feelings and opinions, and they make sure to avoid stereotypes in their reporting and writing. The reporter with fixed pictures in mind of people and groups produces distorted reporting.

## Exercises

### A. Burger

You check into the office one morning and find the nightside reporter has left some notes for you about what seems to be a routine police report. As the police reporter, it is your job to handle the story. You go to headquarters and look at the report.

The report by Patrolman Fred Galzo (all quotes are from his report) states that while two officers were chatting in the parking lot of the Burger King at 4700 Airport Road, a 1987 white Dodge pulled in at "a fast rate of speed." Galzo asked the operator for license and registration and, his report continues, "checked vehicle and found it unsafe and informed Officer (Paul)

Burns to inform headquarters that a tow truck was wanted for an impoundment of motor vehicle." Galzo then issued two summonses to the operator, George Post, 18, of 25 Domino Road. Vehicle was registered to the passenger, Thomas Polk, 18, of 10 Topeka St.

"After said vehicle was taken, the above two in question were standing in the lot and informed me that they are not going to leave and began to get loud and abusive." At this time, two other officers arrived and Galzo told them he needed help. "Who the fuck do you think you are taking our car?" one of the youths said.

"Both men were using indecent language with the indecent word (fuck) in their conversation. I informed both that they were under arrest, and the officers assisted me in arresting the accused. At this time, both men refused to get in the patrol car and became violent while we attempted to place same in the rear seat of the police vehicle.

"After the necessary amount of force was used and the arrest was completed they were transported to headquarters and booked." The two continued to make "comments about the police and our headquarters, and Post went on to say that they should burn this shit down and that he could build better shit than this and was taking out our cards from the rack and making comments about same. I asked this person several times to keep quiet and to stand at the other end of the room.

"Not replying to my request which I made several times I got up from my chair and extended my left hand outward to escort him to far side of room. He was stepping backward and tripped over Officer Gerber's chair and fell to the ground. At this time he got up and stated that his arm was broken and to send him to the doctor's. The lieutenant called the ambulance, which transported him to Community Hospital.

"Both men were charged with using loud and abusive language and failing to obey an officer's orders."

On the notes the night-side reporter left is the notation, "Released $25 bail each pending hearing tomorrow night. Post said he had fractured left wrist."

You have 15 minutes to deadline. What do you do?

## B. Politico

You cover the statehouse in a state with a large Spanish-speaking population. The primary elections are coming up and the incumbent attorney general, Ralph Martinez, a Democrat, has indicated he plans to run for governor. You hear that this annoys the leadership of the Democratic Party because Martinez—a popular, crusading official—might win the party nomination. In the general election, the Democratic Party leaders believe, the Republicans would have a decided advantage if they presented a non-Spanish-speaking candidate.

You have been around state politics long enough to know that there is some logic to this thinking. Some people do vote along ethnic lines, and your study of county returns has proved to you that, although the state has had a Democratic governor for the past 12 years, there might be some trouble for a Democratic candidate with a Spanish surname.

You check with your sources and contacts to get the lay of the land. There is no question that the party leadership is worried by Martinez. He could lose the gubernatorial race—thus eliminating thousands of patronage jobs, inside information on contracts and the various spoils of office—and, even if he were to win, his reputation as an independent is not liked by the party regulars. Some of his assistants in the attorney general's office are known to be Republicans.

One of your sources, Charles DuParte, a former reporter who is secretary to the governor, says the Democratic leadership has been meeting to discuss the situation. The last meeting was at the home of the state party chairman, Walter Kegel. The governor, John Mabee, who is retiring from politics at the expiration of his term, sat in the meeting but said nothing. He is taking a hands-off position. "It's too incendiary," DuParte says, "for him to get involved. He wants to go out smiling, and this Spanish thing has got everybody tense."

No, you cannot quote him on any of this. You know he is truthful, and you ask him whether you can use the information without his name. He says he doesn't care so long as you keep the governor out of the scene. It's yours exclusively, he says.

At this point, you can write an interpretative story if you wish to. Make it about 250 words.

You continue to report. A county chairman of the Democratic Party, Alberto Gonzales, is in the state capital and you run into him. He says he was chatting with Don Sanchez, a state corporation commissioner, and Sanchez "was making sounds like a candidate." A candidate for what? Gonzales motions you over to a side corridor. "For governor," he whispers.

You know that Sanchez won his last race by a whisker and has had a bland career in his job as a commissioner. As a candidate for governor, he makes no sense. You tell Gonzales this, and he smiles knowingly. With a bit of condescension in his voice, he says, "Well, I thought you knew politics. Strange things happen, don't they? Especially when the right people get together."

What right people? Has Sanchez been meeting with anyone? Did he see Kegel lately? You shoot the questions at Gonzales, but all he does is smile. You decide to see Sanchez.

After the usual chitchat, you ask him what he thinks of Martinez as a candidate for governor. "Oh," says Sanchez, "I didn't know he's running." So that's to be his game, you think, and you take a risk:

"I heard that's what you and Walter talked about at that meeting the other night."

Sanchez is an old hand at politics, and you watch him carefully. He won't fall out of his chair, perhaps not even blink if you hit home. He does start, and he begins to finger some papers on his desk. You've hit home. You press on.

"I heard that the fellows think you would make a good candidate." Appeal to his vanity. "They say that Martinez is not really popular up north, where you have always done well."

Sanchez melts a bit. "Yes, they liked my campaigning up there," he says. "But I'm not sure I'll run. I said that. I told them I couldn't be sure. I have two more years in this job, you know, and there are many things I want to finish up."

You know that the best thing to do now is to keep him talking, and you tell him you think that one area he could look into is the interstate trucking situation involving independent truckers, a subject he has spoken about. He warms to that. You let him talk, and then you mention that such a record would look good in a gubernatorial campaign—a candidate who has tried to bring down fees for truckers so that food and other material they bring in won't cost so much.

"Yes, I'd have something to say, all right," he says.

Of course, you tell him, he would be head-and-head with Martinez should the attorney general run, and you know what that would mean. (You are not really sure what he will take that to mean. It's an open-ended probe that he could interpret as meaning a tough campaign up north for both of them since Martinez is popular there, too. Or it could mean his candidacy would clear the way for a non-Spanish-speaking candidate to win because the Spanish-speaking electorate would split its vote.)

"What would it mean?" he asks you suspiciously.

"What everyone is saying," you answer. "That you would be a stalking horse."

"Nobody's saying that," he says testily. "Tell me who says I'm out to kill off Martinez and I'll call him a liar. Just print that, you hear. Print that when I make my decision, I'll be a candidate. I'll run and run hard and all those who make those accusations will be outside when I'm up there in the governor's office." He points to the floor above him, the governor's suite.

"Are you a candidate?" you persist.

"I'll make up my mind next week. I'm seriously thinking of it. You can say that."

You call Kegel from your office in the statehouse and try to bluff him. It doesn't work. Finally, you ask, "Are you going to tell me that Sanchez is a liar, that he is trying to commit you to something that's all a dream? That's going to look good, Walter."

He replies, "I will say that I will neither confirm nor deny that Mr. Sanchez met with the party central committee the other day. You know we cannot support a candidate. That's illegal as hell. He may have been in there to chat. He's a loyal Democrat and he has good ideas about party matters and state government. Don's one of our best state servants."

You have heard enough. You call the city editor and tell him you are ready to write an interpretative piece about the possibility of a stalking horse in the Democratic gubernatorial primary election. He tells you to give it 400 words.

### C. Racial-Religious

The Black Students' Organization at Mallory College has invited Khalid Abdul Muhammad, Minister of Information of the Nation of Islam, to speak on the campus, and you attend the speech. Muhammad had visited Mallory two years before and had aroused the anger of several groups, especially Jewish students.

At that time, he had described Mallory as "Jewniversity," and in his talk he had described New York City as "the city of Jew York."

The material you receive from the Black Students' Organization states that Muhammad has been a "professor of Pan-African studies at the State Universities of Los Angeles and Long Beach." He was invited, the BSO states, to discuss

*The Columbia Spectator.*

**Khalid Abdul Muhammad—"crackers" and "devils."**

Malcolm X, who had at one time been a major figure in the Nation of Islam. Muhammad is the associate director of the Urban Crisis Center in Atlanta.

Prior to his appearance, Gerald Stern, head of the Mallory Jewish Student Union, said, "It is unbelievable that this man is coming back to the campus."

In defense of the invitation Stanley Morson, head of the Black Students' Organization, said, "He is simply here because he represents the viewpoint of some members of the organization."

There were 250 people in the audience, almost all students. There were no empty seats. During his talk there were frequent cheers, many boos and shouts of anger.

During his appearance, Muhammad frequently addressed the white students in bitter, mocking tones. He referred to white people as "blue-eyed devils" and said Jews had been involved in the African slave trade.

Here are some excerpts from the talk:

> Whites and Jews have oppressed my people through the centuries. The wealthiest Jewish families had domestic slaves as a rule.
>
> From the cracking of the whip and the cat-of-nine tails on our backs, you've earned it (his reference to white people as "crackers" and "devils"). And I will always call you a cracker and a devil, and I will never let you off the hook.
>
> It's the white man who gave us all of these ills. You've got fire on one end of a cigarette and a fool on the other end of a cigarette. He makes the liquor, the beer, the whiskey, the wine and all of the ills.
>
> You have charged my leader, the Honorable Louis Farrakhan, with calling Judaism a gutter religion. I am here tonight to tell you in your face that you are a goddamned liar.
>
> He never called Judaism a gutter religion, and if he called Judaism a gutter religion I would be strong enough to stand right in your face and tell you that this is my belief also.
>
> Malcolm X understood the oppression of our people and spoke out against our continued oppression. His message is as true today as it was then.
>
> Malcolm X is a sign and a symbol of the holocaust of the black people, the pain and suffering, the misuse, the abuse and the oppression of black people.
>
> The Jews don't want to hear the truth about their oppression of black people. They spend their time complaining, instead of admitting their sins.

Write 300 words for tomorrow's newspaper.

## D. Ethnic Scores

The College Board has released some figures for last year about averages on the Scholastic Aptitude Test by ethnic group. Along with the data are these general observations by the Board:

> The tests were taken by college-bound students. More than a million students took the tests. Slightly more than half (53 percent) of those who took the test are female. Across ethnic groups, more females than males took the SAT. The proportion of females to males with Black and Hispanic ethnicity is higher than for other test takers as a whole. Asian American test takers are most evenly divided between male and female test takers.
>
> Whites constitute the largest test-taking group, although the percentage has declined from 86 percent in 1974 to 69 percent last year. Asian American test takers increased by almost five times the number who took the test in 1974.

Presume that these figures have just been released:

| Ethnic Group | Last Year | Change from 1976 | Change from Previous Year |
|---|---|---|---|
| **SAT Verbal** | | | |
| American Indian | 396 | +8 | −4 |
| Asian American | 416 | +2 | +1 |
| Black | 352 | +20 | −1 |
| Mexican American | 372 | +1 | −2 |
| Puerto Rican | 367 | +3 | 0 |
| Other Hispanic | 383 | NA | −1 |
| White | 443 | −8 | −1 |
| Other | 425 | +15 | +3 |
| All Students | 423 | −8 | −1 |
| All Men | 425 | −8 | −3 |
| All Women | 421 | −9 | +1 |

| Ethnic Group | Last Year | Change from 1976 | Change from Previous Year |
|---|---|---|---|
| **SAT Math** | | | |
| American Indian | 441 | +21 | −6 |
| Asian American | 535 | +17 | 0 |
| Black | 388 | +34 | 0 |
| Mexican American | 427 | +17 | −1 |
| Puerto Rican | 411 | +10 | +2 |
| Other Hispanic | 435 | NA | +2 |
| White | 495 | +2 | +1 |
| Other | 480 | +22 | +3 |
| All Students | 479 | +7 | +1 |
| All Men | 501 | +4 | −1 |
| All Women | 460 | +14 | +3 |

Write a story for the following:

1. A general circulation daily newspaper.
2. A weekly newspaper with a black readership.
3. A weekly newspaper with a Native American readership.
4. A Spanish language television station's newscast.
5. A California-based monthly magazine with a mainly Asian American readership.

## E. Top Twenty

Every five years your newspaper publishes a list of the 20 cities in the United States with the highest Crime Index Rates. The rate is based on the number of felony crimes reported to local police per 100,000 residents and is the accepted measurement of a city's criminal activity.

Your editor tells you, "Look through the list for last year and compare it with the list we published five years ago. Don't just run off a batch of figures. See whether you can find some patterns in the lists."

| | Last Year | | Five Years Ago |
|---|---|---|---|
| Albany, Ga. | 8,703.3 | Albany, Ga. | 9,083.7 |
| Atlantic City | 8,498.4 | Albuquerque | 8,948.8 |
| Baton Rouge | 9,856.1 | Atlantic City | 10,242.3 |
| Corpus Christi | 8,384.9 | Dallas | 10,039.3 |
| Fayetteville, N.C. | 8,277.5 | El Paso | 8,937.3 |
| Fort Lauderdale, Fla. | 8,904.1 | Fayetteville, N.C. | 9,047.4 |
| Fresno, Calif. | 8,099.6 | Fort Worth | 10,143.4 |
| Gainesville, Fla. | 10,131.2 | Fresno, Calif. | 9,099.6 |
| Jackson, Tenn. | 8,381.0 | Gainesville, Fla. | 9,458.8 |
| Jacksonville, Fla. | 8,598.0 | Jacksonville, Fla. | 9,197.5 |
| Lakeland-Winter Haven, Fla. | 8,820.9 | Lakeland-Winter Haven, Fla. | 9,715.8 |
| Little Rock | 8,884.8 | Laredo, Tex. | 8,966.7 |
| Miami | 13,500.4 | Little Rock | 9,352.2 |
| Myrtle Beach, S.C. | 8,838.6 | Miami | 12,786.1 |
| New Orleans | 8,511.7 | New Orleans | 8,839.5 |
| San Antonio | 8,528.3 | Odessa, Tex. | 12,054.7 |
| Stockton, Calif. | 8,528.3 | San Antonio | 10,453.0 |
| Tallahassee, Fla. | 10,756.3 | Tallahassee, Fla. | 11,353.3 |
| Tucson | 9,219.9 | Washington, D.C. | 10,768.1 |
| Washington, D.C. | 11,676.1 | Wilmington, N.C. | 9,771.9 |
| **All-Cities Average** | **6045.1** | **All Cities Average** | **5,897.8** |

## Assignments

### A. Documents

1. Examine wills filed for probate with the county clerk or in probate court within the last week or month for a newsworthy filing.

2. Tax-exempt organizations must file a Form 990 with the Internal Revenue Service. Organizations also are required to show the form to those requesting a copy. Obtain one from any local charity and write a story.

3. Some cities, most states and the federal government require public officials to file public disclosure forms that list their assets. Locate a form for a city, state or federal elected official and write a story based on the filing.

4. Check the real estate holdings of a local official by examining deeds, mortgages, loans, real estate transfers.

### B. Pattern

Examine the latest edition of the FBI's Uniform Crime Report. Make a list of the 10 states with the highest crime rates for violent crimes—murder, non-negligent manslaughter, rape, robbery, aggravated assault—or for one of these crimes. Make a list of the 10 states with the lowest crime rates. Can you see any patterns? Write a story based on your conclusions.

### C. Gifts

Each year, alumni donate billions of dollars to their alma maters. At one time, the giving was unrestricted; the donors allowed their schools to use the money as the schools saw fit. But unrestricted giving has declined. "There are more gifts with strings attached," says Peter Buchanan, president of the Council for Advancement and Support, an organization serving university administrators in the areas of alumni relations, communications and fund raising.

Some schools are unhappy with such gifts; others find input from donors positive. But there are limits. Most schools will not allow donors to dictate the professors they hire or the students they must accept. Lee Bass donated $20 million to Yale with the provision he would have a say in the appointment of professors. The gift was refused.

What is the situation in your campus? How many gifts are unrestricted, how many restricted? What is the nature of some of the restrictions?

## Campus Projects

### A. Ratings

Schools and departments of colleges and universities are accredited by various agencies. Accreditation reports often cite areas for improvement and occasionally deny accreditation.

Also, independent organizations and individuals rank professional schools, and several publications rank entire colleges and universities.

Dig out these accreditation reports, ratings and assessments for your college or university and its various schools and departments. A computer search will be helpful. Cite positive and negative comments and interview students, deans and department heads, faculty members and others for comments.

### B. Remedial

About 30 percent of all college students take at least one remedial course. The costs are high, and in an era of budget cutting, some universities want out of the remedial business. They would have remedial teaching done by the community colleges, which is how Florida handles remedial instruction. Virginia, Arkansas and Texas have considered this change.

California's 20 campuses have seen a rise in remedial students. In 1989, 23 percent of entering freshmen needed help in mathematics, 36 percent in English. By 1993–94, 42 percent needed remedial instruction in mathematics, 43 percent in English.

What are the percentages on your campus at present and in the past, and what are the reasons for the increase or decrease? Have there been any moves to change the way remedial instruction is offered in tax-supported institutions? What percentage of remedial students pass their courses and are admitted to the regular program? What percentage graduate?

## Community Projects

### A. Purchase

How much does it cost your city to buy school supplies, such as paper, cleaning fluids, pencils; police department supplies and equipment, such as patrol cars; street department materials, such as highway paint and signs?

Compare these costs with those in a city of comparable size in your state. Were there bids for your city's purchases, or were they negotiated? What is the state law on purchases that require competitive bidding?

### B. Kids

More than half a million abused and neglected children are under state supervision. This is twice as many as 10 years ago. The child welfare system, say experts, is in chaos: Children drift from place to place as the courts and state agencies mishandle their cases.

These drifting children often become homeless, unemployed, drug-using adults.

What's the situation in your community and state? Ask authorities on campus and in the community for their opinions. Interview those in the courts and law enforcement agencies for their experiences.

## Home Assignment

### Tips

What would you do to develop stories from the following information?

1. The mayor is reported to have decided to run for governor but will not say anything himself.
2. A union is thinking of organizing the university work force: groundskeepers, librarians, secretaries, cleaning personnel.
3. An unexpected increase in strep throat has struck the city.
4. A national organization is quietly buying up property outside the city limits for construction of a large industrial park.
5. You hear through the police grapevine that soon a new police chief may be appointed and the current chief fired.

## Class Discussion

### A. Seeing

> We need intellectual vigilance now more than barricade journalism, and particularly the gift of seeing, and seeing in time, trends that may affect the life of the world.
> —James Reston

The kind of vigilant journalism Reston calls for is described by some journalists as "anticipatory journalism." It depends upon the journalist's sense of the world around him or her and upon the journalist's ability to pattern events.

In your reading, see whether you can find examples of articles in newspapers or magazines that anticipate developments or trends.

### B. Passive

What do you think of the prediction of Frank Deford, a sportswriter and television and radio commentator?

> I think we're almost reaching a point where we were centuries ago: A certain small percentage of the population reads, and nobody else does. It used to be just a question of literacy and illiteracy, but now we're moving toward what is essentially going to be a two-tiered population—one that reads, and one that simply watches television.
>
> I'm not a believer in "visual literacy." I find it awfully hard to believe that the written word can be replaced by the ability to play Nintendo well. You can perhaps be entertained more, but I think your intellect can only be advanced so far by visual images. At a certain point it just breaks down—it's just not sophisticated.
>
> Aldous Huxley in *Brave New World* was right. Orwell thought we were all going to be watched, oppressed from outside, but it is the other way around: We'll be doing the watching. We'll be our own oppressors. Eisenhower warned us of the military-industrial complex, but we needn't worry about that anymore. It is the entertainment-amusement complex that threatens us—benignly.

## DB/CAR

### Costs

How much does it cost to run your state and the state's cities, and how do these costs compare with those in other states? Some of the key figures are:

**Payrolls:** How many people are on the state and cities payrolls and at what total cost? What is the government employment rate per 10,000 residents?
**Schools:** How much does it cost to finance the public elementary and secondary schools, total and per pupil?
**Welfare:** What is the cost of administering and financing Aid to Families with Dependent Children?
**Medicaid:** How much is the total Medicaid bill and how much is it per capita?
**Police:** What do the state and the cities spend on police services? What is the per capita figure?

Rank your state in terms of these and any other expenses you consider important. What is the explanation of your state's standing? Interview authorities.

## Skill Drill: Auditing Your Emotions

Reporters, like everyone else, have feelings that influence the way they see the world. Sometimes these emotional responses obstruct observation. You might audit your feelings by checking the boxes that follow and then matching your responses with those of other students.

|  | Positive | Neutral | Negative |
|---|---|---|---|
| Arabs | ☐ | ☐ | ☐ |
| Bill of Rights | ☐ | ☐ | ☐ |
| Bird Watchers | ☐ | ☐ | ☐ |
| Black Muslims | ☐ | ☐ | ☐ |
| Capitalism | ☐ | ☐ | ☐ |
| Catholics | ☐ | ☐ | ☐ |
| Communism | ☐ | ☐ | ☐ |
| Democrats | ☐ | ☐ | ☐ |
| Gays and Lesbians | ☐ | ☐ | ☐ |
| Housewives | ☐ | ☐ | ☐ |
| Jews | ☐ | ☐ | ☐ |
| Ku Klux Klan | ☐ | ☐ | ☐ |
| Liberals | ☐ | ☐ | ☐ |
| The Mafia | ☐ | ☐ | ☐ |
| Nation of Islam | ☐ | ☐ | ☐ |
| New Yorkers | ☐ | ☐ | ☐ |
| Radicals | ☐ | ☐ | ☐ |
| Rap singers | ☐ | ☐ | ☐ |
| Republicans | ☐ | ☐ | ☐ |
| The Rotary Club | ☐ | ☐ | ☐ |
| Scandinavians | ☐ | ☐ | ☐ |
| Sierra Club | ☐ | ☐ | ☐ |
| Socialism | ☐ | ☐ | ☐ |
| Southerners | ☐ | ☐ | ☐ |
| Texans | ☐ | ☐ | ☐ |
| Unitarians | ☐ | ☐ | ☐ |
| The United Nations | ☐ | ☐ | ☐ |
| Veterans | ☐ | ☐ | ☐ |
| Wall Street | ☐ | ☐ | ☐ |
| Zionism | ☐ | ☐ | ☐ |

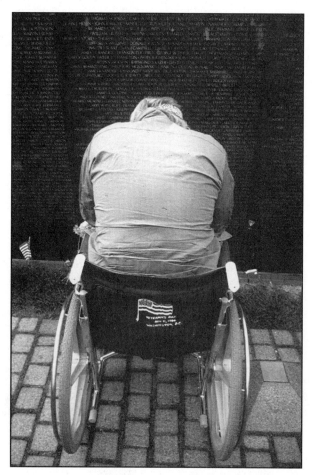

Dave Kline, *Lancaster* (Ohio) *Eagle-Gazette.*

## *What's Wrong?: Hopped Up*

A reporter need not accept as true, or valid, information from sources. Are there any clues in this old wire service story that indicate some of the information is suspect? If so, rewrite to eliminate the suspicious material.

SAIGON—North Vietnamese troops reported "hopped up" on marijuana attacked a U.S. reconnaissance patrol Thursday night in the central highlands and got to within hand grenade range before U.S. jets hit them with fiery napalm and they retreated.

None of the Americans, members of the 4th Infantry Division, were killed or wounded.

"These guys are hopped up on pot," radioed SP/4 Joseph F. Dean Jr., Orlando, Fla. "They're crazy, real crazy. You can smell the pot up here."

"We have bad guys all around this hill," he told a command post. "You can do anything you want, just don't shoot us."

A jet air strike sent napalm into the North Vietnamese ranks. Then helicopters, taking advantage of a break in heavy monsoon rain clouds, sighted in on the napalm fires and picked up the patrol.

Crewmen of the chopper said they spotted the bodies of Communist troups in the area and that all of the Americans were rescued.

HG739PED

## *You Decide: Claims*

A young woman told authorities that her two small boys had been kidnapped by a carjacker on an isolated country road. Sobbing and badly shaken, she described the carjacker as a black man wearing a cap. The woman, 23 years old and white, said the event occurred late in the evening.

Police artists drew a sketch of the suspect based on the woman's description, and it was used in newspapers and on television stations across the nation.

Your newspaper recently ran a long story about a woman who claimed that her daughter had been kidnapped while the child was waiting in her baby carriage as the mother stopped to buy a soft drink. The woman's claim turned out to be a hoax and she was arrested and charged with murder shortly after the child's body was discovered in a dumpster.

What do you do about this new kidnapping story?

# PART FIVE

From Accidents to Education

# 18 Accidents and Disasters

Ricardo Ferro, *St. Petersburg Times.*

**A basic assignment—the accident.**

### Introduction

Motor vehicle accidents are among the most common stories a reporter covers. Accuracy is essential, which means double-checking official reports of the names and addresses of those involved, avoiding giving the cause of the accident unless it is part of the official record. Eyewitness accounts of accidents and disasters animate the story, as do the accounts of those involved—investigating officers and victims. The essential aspect of these stories is accurate information about those injured or killed. Property losses and effects on the community are important parts of this story.

## Accidents

### Exercises I

#### A. Pedestrian

From the police reports: James Reynolds, 48, sign painter, 35 Palisades Ave. Struck by automobile at Georgia Avenue and Topeka Street, 4 p.m., Fairlawn Hospital. Critical injuries, including skull fracture. Car driven by Robert F. Magione, 872 Ogden St. Says pedestrian stepped into intersection suddenly. No charges. Investigation by Officer Sigmund Gerter.

A call to the hospital indicates that Reynolds is in intensive care. Write three paragraphs for the morning newspaper.

#### B. Three Dead

State highway patrol responds to your check with the following information: collision on Route 16, where it intersects with State Highway 65, 18 miles north of town. Three dead, all in the car coming out of Route 16: Stanley Shaeffer, 68, of 45 Madison St.; Mildred Shaeffer, 65; their granddaughter, Anne Shaeffer, 17, of Chicago, who was visiting her grandparents while en route to Boston University where she was to be a freshman student. The second car was driven by Louis Kruger, of Hutchinson, Kansas. Kruger was taken to Fairlawn Hospital for treatment of leg fractures and internal injuries. Time: 11 last night.

Investigating officers, Albert Doris and Ben Sandler, said the Shaeffer car was turning into 65 and had apparently not stopped for the stop sign. Possibility Shaeffer had a stroke. Write four paragraphs for the afternoon newspaper.

*C. Truck*

Report from Clovia police with a fatal: Irwin Soto, 22, of Clovia, was killed instantly at noon on access road four miles west of Clovia. Police say he apparently had a flat and had stopped to change tires, propping up his pickup with a bumper jack. Somehow he got under the truck, it slipped, and he was crushed. Severe chest injuries, says Dr. Wayne L. Stapleton of Fairlawn Hospital.

He is survived by parents, Jack and Eileen Soto, of Clovia; his widow, Alice; and an infant daughter, Adeilada. Funeral services pending. Body at Heavenly Rest Chapel. He was a local boy who played in all the high school sports and was a star sprinter. He spent two years at the University of Tennessee on a track scholarship but came home to run his father's dairy farm two years ago.

*D. Speed*

A patrolwoman you know tells you that there was a strange accident early this morning on Massachusetts Avenue. Several cars were struck by a teen-age driver, she says. The records and a conversation with the investigating officers, Sam Ratcliffe and Brut Kazazian, disclose the following: At 2 a.m., a car driven by George R. Dugan, 17, of 89 Georgia Ave., struck six cars on Massachusetts Avenue, southbound lane. No injuries, although Dugan's vehicle was demolished. The six cars were parked along the street when Dugan drove by.

"He just tore through town, probably at 70 or 80 and lost control, near as we can figure," Kazazian says:

Dugan doesn't remember a thing. Not that he's hurt. We took him to Fairlawn and all he has is a headache and a black eye. But he has got a lot to worry about: driving without a license, speeding, reckless driving citations. He told us he had never driven before two days ago when his brother started to teach him to drive. He said he took the car belonging to his brother Ralph and decided to go on a "solo" trip to prove he could do it.

He says he was at a party with some girls and other guys and they made fun of him because he was 17 and couldn't drive, so he took off and got the car to show them up. No alcohol or drugs present.

The way he went through there his car was like a Ping-Pong ball, banging this way and that. He also smashed a lamppost. It's lucky no one was on the street at the time.

*E. Flagg*

Police reports: Arnold Flagg, 52, waiter, drunk driving citation. Arrested State Highway 166 three miles east of town, going east. Driving erratically. Address: 571 Broadway. Time: 5 p.m. State Patrolman Pat Gallagher made arrest after call from motorist on highway. Also charged with speeding. Registered .20 on blood alcohol test.

Your newspaper carries short pieces on all drunk driving arrests. Write this for the newspaper.

## Assignments

*A. Reports*

Obtain from the police department copies of several newsworthy vehicular accident reports, and write stories based on the information presented. Explain your reasons for using the reports you selected.

*B. Dangers*

Examine the annual report of the traffic department of the state highway department. Usually, records are kept as to the location, day of week and time of day of fatal accidents on the state's highways. There also is usually a listing by cause. See whether you can find any patterns in these fatal accidents. To do this, set up hypotheses and check them:

Are weekends more dangerous than weekdays?
Are the evening hours more dangerous than daylight hours? (Do not ignore differences in traffic volume.)
Are some parts of the state, some roads or highways more dangerous than others?
Is speed, alcohol, snow, rain or some other factor a major cause of fatals?
Have the authorities developed a test for drivers they suspect of driving under the influence of drugs?

# Disasters

## Exercises II

### A. Gas Leak

A railroad tank car carrying chlorine gas has been cracked by a collision with another train on a siding four miles east of town, and the gas is seeping out of the tank. The sheriff's office, which is responsible for the area outside the city limits, has ordered an evacuation of the area in which there are 15 residences with a total population of 70 persons.

The first word came at 7:20 a.m. from the Union Pacific office, the sheriff says. One trainman, Albert Funster, 25, of Redding, Calif., was overcome by fumes. He is in Fairlawn Hospital, where his condition is reported as not serious.

You have an early edition, and you put this in a story. You check the railroad, and an official estimates it will take no more than a few hours to clear the track.

"We will put the families in a few motels, even if it is for a few hours," says the spokesman, Francis Praxton, of the local rail office.

As you prepare your story for the final edition, the police reporter calls you and says a family of four has just been taken to Fairlawn Hospital in serious condition from chlorine inhalation. You call the hospital and learn their names: Dayid Lewin, 35; Alice Lewin, 34; their son, Freddie, 7; and their daughter, Barbara, 3. They are listed by authorities as being in critical condition. They apparently live near the tracks. A hospital official says, "We understand there are several houses along there and that they are making a house-to-house search. I think the gas was seeping in all night."

You call back the railroad spokesman and he verifies that they believe the accident occurred during some siding activity last night. You tell him about the family in the hospital. He has no comment.

You call the sheriff's office again and ask about the search. He confirms it. All available officers have been sent to the area, and a contingent of state troopers—about a dozen—was sent out. The Red Cross emergency unit and some fire equipment are there.

As you are again ready to write, the police reporter calls and says a body, unidentified, has been removed from a house on U.S. 58 and taken to the North Funeral Home. It is a middle-aged woman. "We think there are more coming," he says.

You have no more time and must write.

### B. Rain

You work for the UPI bureau in Houston and are told to send out a story about a rainstorm that has struck the city. You are told to write about 200 words. The information:

1. Rain began to fall at 1 p.m. Continued for seven hours. Total fall, more than 7 1/2 inches, which some people say is total rainfall for the year in some parts of Texas.
2. Hardest hit area southeast of Houston where Texas Medical Center is located.
3. Creeks and bayous flooded out of banks and streets were flooded and motorists stranded. Still too early to tell if there are any casualties, but no word of any so far.
4. To baseball fans, this was a disaster. For first time in the history of Astrodome, built in 1965, the Houston Astros baseball team had to call off the game. Not because of wet grounds; dome covers field. But only a couple of hundred hardy fans reached the park.
5. "We couldn't have gone on anyway," says a dome official. "Half the players weren't here before the game either. The bat boy would have had to bat cleanup if we'd played."

## Assignment

### Preparations

Make a survey of disaster organizations in your community. Name them, give their functions and equipment and look into their history. When were they last used? Any changes in equipment, approach in recent years?

Citizens are expected to take certain precautions for an emergency, and once it strikes they are expected to know what actions to take. Include these in your story.

## Campus Project

*Auditing the Campus*

Using the chart in Chapter 17, *Auditing Your Emotions,* survey students, faculty members, administrators, support staff. Are there significant differences among these groups?
You can make subgroups as well: sex, age, race, etc.

## Community Projects

*A. Feedback (1)*

The Gannett newspapers use extensive polling and conduct focus groups to find out what readers want in their newspapers. Some of the findings include "more positive news, more human interest stories. Readers complain about too much negative news and news that's 'immoral,' " a Gannett columnist wrote. They complained about the coverage of "gays and AIDS."

A Gannett guidebook for its 93 newspapers suggests covering "shopping trends and sales, new products and restaurants" and reducing the coverage "that is institutionally driven," such as the coverage of city hall and the local planning commission. Some of the areas recommended for coverage are health, fitness and local entertainment.

Do a study of your own among residents. What do people want from their local newspaper?

*B. Environment*

Two out of five Americans live in areas where the air is unhealthful, reports the Environmental Protection Agency. Also, 40 percent of the nation's rivers and lakes are unfit for drinking, swimming or fishing.

"We should celebrate progress," says Fred Krupp, the executive director of the Environmental Defense Fund. "We have made a lot of progress in this country—even if it's also true that we've got a long way to go."

Among the problems is controlling the runoff of fertilizers, silt and pesticides from farms and cities. The runoff affects aquatic life. One of the consequences is that 362 species of fish have been extinguished or endangered. Some experts say that the fate of the American landscape and waters and the creatures who live there is the major domestic, environmental problem the country is not coping with.

The National Biological Service reports that natural ecosystems amounting to at least half the area of the 48 contiguous states have declined to the endangerment point.

More than 5 percent of the native plant species are lost or in peril in Delaware, Maine, Vermont, Rhode Island, New York, Pennsylvania, New Jersey and Maryland. Three to 5 percent are endangered in Ohio, Indiana, Iowa, Missouri and Kansas.

From the late 1980s to the 1990s, most states improved the quality of their air. New Mexico, Virginia, New Jersey and New Hampshire had a decrease in air pollution of more than 50 percent. But the percentage change in emissions of hazardous air pollutants increased in five states: Nevada, Alaska, Montana, North and South Dakota.

Freshwater fish species are imperiled in the streams of every state. Those with 10 or more imperiled species are Oregon, California, Nevada, Utah, Arizona, New Mexico, Texas, Oklahoma, Missouri, Arkansas, Louisiana, Mississippi, Alabama, Georgia, Florida, Tennessee, Kentucky, North Carolina, Virginia and New York. Heading the list, according to the National Biological Service, are California, 42; Alabama, 30; Texas, 23; Arizona, 22; Virginia and North Carolina, 21; and New Mexico and Georgia, 20.

Make an environmental study of your state. Where does it rank in cleansing its air and water and in protecting wildlife and plant species?

## Home Assignment

*Readable*

Clip from a newspaper stories that demonstrate these principles of good writing:

- Show, don't tell.
- Place quotations that reflect the thrust of the event high in the story.
- Personalize the event through human interest anecdotes high in the story.

## Class Discussion

### Feedback (2)

Discuss your findings in the Community Project in this chapter. Do the suggestions of local people include the watchdog function of the press, the obligation of newspapers to ferret out significant information, whether readers enjoy reading about it or not?

Does the study show that what Gannett recommends in the area of writing—shorter, snappier stories—leads to an informed community? That is, do people want their newspaper primarily to entertain them? Or do they recognize that the newspaper has a dual function that includes explaining complex matters so that they, the public, can make informed decisions on important matters?

## DB/CAR

### Stolen

Here is a list of the cities with car theft rates that exceed the national average of 721.4 per 100,000 inhabitants:

| City | Rate | City | Rate |
|---|---|---|---|
| Atlanta | 895.7 | Milwaukee | 855.8 |
| Baltimore | 799.6 | Modesto, Calif. | 822 |
| Baton Rouge | 931.3 | Newark | 1,302.6 |
| Beaumont-Port Arthur, Tex. | 754.5 | New Orleans | 1,194.1 |
| Boston | 861.8 | New York City | 1,368.8 |
| Bridgeport | 1,191.1 | Oakland | 891.3 |
| Brockton, Mass. | 1,054.3 | Orange County, Calif. | 848.1 |
| Dallas | 877.4 | Philadelphia | 758 |
| Detroit | 1,041.9 | Phoenix | 1,045.6 |
| El Paso | 902.9 | Portland, Ore. | 833.5 |
| Flint, Mich. | 763.6 | Riverside | 1,088.1 |
| Fort Meyers, Fla. | 766 | Sacramento | 1,240.5 |
| Fort Worth | 734.1 | San Diego | 1,263.4 |
| Fresno, Calif. | 2,045.3 | San Francisco | 949.6 |
| Gary, Ind. | 1,002.5 | Springfield, Mass. | 1,059.7 |
| Houston | 1,125.8 | Stockton, Calif. | 1,112.8 |
| Jackson, Miss. | 1,086.2 | Tallahassee | 1,119.6 |
| Jacksonville, Fla. | 1,009.4 | Tampa | 808.7 |
| Jersey City, N.J. | 1,258.2 | Toledo | 821.2 |
| Lakeland, Fla. | 926.5 | Trenton, N.J. | 1,154.9 |
| Las Vegas | 922.8 | Tucson | 912.6 |
| Lawrence, Mass. | 1,195.2 | Tulsa | 732.6 |
| Los Angeles | 1,378.2 | Washington, D.C. | 1,394.8 |
| Memphis | 1,424.1 | Waterbury, Conn. | 878.3 |
| Miami | 2,113.6 | | |

Write these stories:

1. Rank the list. Then write a story about the top five or 10 cities on the list.
2. Localize the list, using your city or one near you.
3. See whether you can find any patterns in the list.

For all these stories, obtain background about the subject by calling up material about car thefts on your database. Also, interview local authorities on the subject.

*Test V: Case*

Choose the correct answer.

1. He is the person _____ asked to leave. **(a) who (b) whom**
2. The one student _____ the principal chooses is fortunate. **(a) who (b) whom (c) that.**
3. The hamburgers were distributed among **(a) we (b) us** students.
4. You like chocolate cake more than **(a) I (b) me**.
5. He discussed the problem with _____ would listen to him. **(a) whoever (b) whomever**
6. I get tired of _____ being late. **(a) you (b) your (c) you're**
7. He doesn't believe that _____ story. **(a) witness' (b) witness's**
8. The _____ team lost the last six games. **(a) mens' (b) men's**
9. The _____ office is locked. **(a) boss's (b) boss'**
10. _____ book is this? **(a) Whose (b) Who's**

# 19 Obituaries

Cloe Poisson, *The Hartford Courant.*
**At a slain police officer's burial.**

### Introduction

The obituary section is one of the most frequently and thoroughly read parts of the newspaper. The obituary usually focuses on the accomplishments or achievements of the deceased and then describes the cause, time and place of death. Survivors and the funeral and burial plans are also included. Sometimes, as in the case of AIDS, survivors request that the cause of death be omitted. Increasingly, journalists are ignoring these requests so that the full impact of the disease toll is recognized. Accuracy is essential: The obituary is the one story above all others that is preserved by family and friends.

## *Exercises*

### A. Perkins

You receive this paid advertisement from classified:

PERKINS—William F., of 1105 Madison St., on March 14, beloved husband of Josephine Parker Perkins. Service at Heavenly Rest Chapel, 10 a.m., Wednesday. Visiting hours 7 to 9 p.m., Tuesday. In lieu of flowers, contributions to Community Hospital Medical Center will be appreciated.

You telephone Mrs. Perkins and are given the following information:

Perkins was with O'Connor & Perkins, successor to Rich & O'Connor, which he joined in 1956. He was president of the state bar association in 1980 and had been active in the National Foundation for Infantile Paralysis, which no longer has that name because of the success of the Salk vaccine. He was chairman of the foundation's local chapter for several years. He was born in Altoona, Pa.

He graduated from a college in Pennsylvania that is now Penn State, where he was a cross-country runner. He went to Harvard, where he was active in the law review and coached a soccer team made up of law students.

He died after a heart attack. He was 73.

Write four paragraphs.

### B. Tsouprake

The following comes up from classified:

TSOUPRAKE—Demetrios Athanasias, 560 Tudor St., on March 21, beloved husband of Juliana (Lappas); adored father of Natalie Arruzel, of Florence, Italy, and Christine Alice Costa, of New York City; grandfather of four; dear brother of Constantine, Stephen, George, Ann, and the late Chloe. Funeral service, Wednesday, March 26, 11 a.m., at the Greek Orthodox Cathedral of the Holy Trinity.

You obtain the following information. Write five paragraphs.

Age: 75.
Died last night in Community General, lung cancer.
Born: Athens, Greece.
Education: LL.D., Athens University.
          A.M., School of Political Science, Paris.
          LL.B., Stanford University.
Honors: Robert Kent Award of the Patent, Trademark and Copyright Research Institute of Oxford University, 1968. U.S. delegate to the Lisbon Conference to revise the international treaty on patents, 1958.
Author: *Protection of Industrial Property.*
        *Protection of Literary and Artistic Property.*

### C. Swimmer

You are a new reporter on the Freeport newspaper and are on general assignment, and this morning you are handling obits. The Prewitt Mortuary has dropped off a notice of the death of Albert F. Swimmer, and as you look it over, one of the older hands remarks that Swimmer was an interesting character.

You get his file out of the library and glance through it before going up to the city editor to ask him how much he wants on Swimmer.

He tells you that Swimmer was a "controversial character" and that his obituary is worth at least five takes.

"Don't write one of these deadly death notices," he tells you. "Give me a good story. I want to use some art with it."

**Prewitt Mortuary**
840 Stanford Avenue

| | |
|---|---|
| **Name:** | Albert F. Swimmer. |
| **Birth Date:** | Jan. 25, 1915, Birmingham, Alabama. |
| **Address:** | 1405 Sunset Drive. |
| **Cause of death:** | Cirrhosis of the liver. |
| **Where died:** | Fairlawn Hospital. |
| **Time:** | 5:45 a.m. |
| **Organizations:** | Legion Post No. 156, VFW Post 22, Optimist Club, NAACP, Urban League, Phi Beta Kappa. |
| **Church:** | Freeport First Baptist. |
| **Survivors:** | Wife, Ada Ruth Johnson Swimmer, second wife; son, Sam; daughter, Linda, by his first wife, Mrs. Martha Lupton, deceased; sister, Mrs. Dodge Henry, Birmingham; three nieces and six nephews. |

\* \* \* \* \*

Morgue clip, June 29, 1933

Arthur Monde and Albert F. Swimmer shared scholastic honors last night at the Freeport High School graduation. Monde, the son of Mr. and Mrs. Philip C. Monde, of 1145 High St., was the valedictorian and Swimmer was the salutatorian. Swimmer is the son of Mr. and Mrs. Temple Swimmer, of 303 Manley St.

Morgue clip, July 16, 1933

BERKELEY, Calif.—The University of California announced today it has granted the Thomas E. Roselle scholarship to Albert F. Swimmer, of Freeport. The scholarship was established by Mr. Roselle, a graduate of the University who practiced law in Freeport for 42 years prior to his death in 1920. It is awarded to a Negro high school graduate who intends to pursue pre-law courses.

* * * * *

Morgue clip, Aug. 3, 1933

Word was received here today of the arrest in Alamagordo, New Mexico, of Albert F. Swimmer of this city on a charge of disturbing the peace.

Swimmer, 18, apparently was on his way to California to enroll in the University of California. His parents said he left here 10 days ago for the coast with limited funds. He had received a scholarship to the University of California.

* * * * *

Morgue clip, Aug. 6, 1933

Albert F. Swimmer, son of Mr. and Mrs. Temple Swimmer of this city, was sentenced to 10 days in county jail in Alamagordo, New Mex., for disturbing the peace.

His parents said he was on the way to the University of California where he was to have enrolled next week. Mr. Swimmer said his son told him there was an altercation in a local restaurant. Swimmer had pleaded not guilty.

* * * * *

Morgue clip, Dec. 13, 1936

BERKELEY, Calif.—(API)—A talented California fullback and a tough line combined to upset highly favored Stanford 7-0 today.

The game's only score came on a 101-yard runback of the kickoff opening the second half. Al Swimmer, big fullback for the University of California, scampered the length of the field.

But the lead was in peril all during the remainder of the second half. The California line had to hold off repeated thrusts of the Stanford team which managed to get down to the California 20 with ease but could never penetrate beyond the 17-yard line.

Stanford was a two touchdown favorite.

Albert Swimmer is the son of Mr. and Mrs. Temple Swimmer, 303 Manley St., and is attending the University of California on a scholarship. He was a well-known football player at Freeport High and graduated second in his class with an A-average.

The senior Swimmer is employed by Houk's Barber Shop. Mrs. Swimmer is a teacher in the G.W. Carver Grade School. They will visit their son this Christmas as the result of a gift to the Swimmers by the Freeport Junior Chamber of Commerce.

* * * * *

Morgue clip, June 6, 1937

The University of California student newspaper yesterday reported the marriage of Albert Swimmer, a graduate of Freeport High School who is attending the California institution, to Miss Martha Stratton.

The newspaper reported Miss Stratton and Mr. Swimmer eloped. She is the daughter of Robert Stratton, a former governor of the State of Washington. The couple was married in Arizona. California has a law against interracial marriages.

Swimmer is the son of Mr. and Mrs. Temple Swimmer, of 303 Manley St. Swimmer will graduate next week. During his last three years at the University he was the starting fullback. He was the second leading ground gainer in the school's history and averaged 4.5 yards a carry.

His father said his son has been offered a contract by the Chicago Bears but may attend law school instead.

The elder Swimmer said his son, who was initiated into Phi Beta Kappa, an honorary scholastic fraternity, has a fellowship from a national organization to the law school at the University of Iowa.

* * * * *

Morgue clip, March 13, 1940

Albert F. Swimmer, of 140 California Ave., and F.T. Macdonald, of 32 Brighton Ave., were among the 235 persons who passed the state bar examination.

* * * * *

Morgue clip, Sept. 15, 1941

Albert F. Swimmer was the main speaker at the Freeport Kiwanis Club at noon today. He spoke on "An Untapped Human Resource, the Negro Worker."

Swimmer said that "discrimination and racial bigotry" keep Negroes in low-paying jobs. He said federal figures reveal that Negroes have an average income of about half the average white worker's.

Swimmer recently passed the state bar examination and is in practice with State Sen. Robert Wright.

* * * * *

Morgue clip, Nov. 7, 1941

Mr. and Mrs. Albert Swimmer, of 140 California Ave., today announced the birth of their first child, Linda. Mrs. Swimmer is the former Martha Stratton. Mr. Swimmer, a local attorney, enlisted in the U.S. Navy last month and is a recruit at the Bainbridge Naval Training Station in Maryland.

* * * * *

Morgue clip, April 16, 1943

HONOLULU—Steward Second Class Albert Swimmer of Freeport has been awarded the Navy Cross for heroism while on duty aboard the U.S.S. Covington, the Navy News Service reported this week.

Swimmer was the only man on an anti-aircraft detail who survived an enemy airplane attack. Despite serious leg wounds, Swimmer directed a makeshift crew which destroyed one attacking aircraft and damaged another. His commanding officer, Commander Frank C. Barnes, said Swimmer stayed at his post for six hours while the Covington was under attack.

Swimmer is in a base hospital at Pearl Harbor.

Swimmer is the husband of Mrs. Martha Swimmer, of 140 California Ave., and was on his third tour of duty with the Covington.

U.S. Navy.

* * * * *

Morgue clip, April 18, 1946

Albert F. Swimmer became the first Negro to serve on the city council in Freeport's history. He led the successful Veterans Group in a sweep of the five council seats.

Swimmer defeated Morgan B. Simms 2,345 to 2,088 in a bitterly contested campaign in the Second District. Swimmer had accused Simms, the incumbent, of "complete inability to react to the times." At one time he referred to Simms as "our Stone Age councilman."

The Second District is a residential area, long considered Freeport's finest. Swimmer was the target of some resentment when he moved into the district last year. But a bi-racial citizens group was formed and the opposition died down.

The other successful candidates . . .

* * * * *

Morgue clip, May 19, 1950

The author of several unsuccessful bills to eliminate discrimination in public places in the city, Councilman Albert F. Swimmer said in an interview today his faith remains strong in the "essential goodness" of Freeport residents.

Swimmer, the only Negro ever to serve on the council, said that with summer weather near he hopes to have the council adopt an ordinance that would prohibit local swimming pools from keeping Negroes from using their facilities.

"When I was a child I used to stand outside the gates on hot August days and watch kids from my school splashing in the pool," he said. "I don't want any more youngsters to suffer as I did, and I think my fellow councilmen will . . . "

* * * * *

Morgue clip, Oct. 3, 1952

Albert Swimmer, long active in the Democratic Party, announced his support of Dwight D. Eisenhower, at a luncheon of the Freeport Democrats for Eisenhower today.

Swimmer said he based his decision on "the inability of the Democratic Party to cope with the paramount issue of our times, civil rights."

Swimmer has been elected to the city council four times as an independent but has been closely connected with Democratic party affairs. Last year, he was unsuccessful in an attempt to push through the council an ordinance prohibiting discrimination in hotels, restaurants and other establishments offering their services to the public. At the time, he said his proposal was defeated because "local Democrats who had promised assistance refused to take a stand when the going got rough."

At the luncheon, Chairman Robert F. Rockford, said . . .

\* \* \* \* \*

Morgue clip, Aug. 3, 1954

A car driven by City Councilman Albert F. Swimmer of 69 Harvey St. struck a telephone pole and overturned last night on U.S. 43 north of Freeport.

Swimmer suffered head injuries and was reported in good condition in the Fairlawn Hospital. A passenger, Ruth Humphrey, of 42 Broad St., was treated for cuts and released.

Freeport police cited Swimmer for reckless driving.

\* \* \* \* \*

Morgue clip, Oct. 26, 1954

Magistrate Ann Rogers today dismissed reckless driving charges against City Councilman Albert F. Swimmer, 69 Harvey St., on motion of District Attorney Thomas Chambers.

\* \* \* \* \*

Morgue clip, May 15, 1955

City Councilman Albert F. Swimmer today was appointed to the city board of education by Mayor Sam Weale. He is the first Negro to serve on the board. . . .

\* \* \* \* \*

Morgue clip, Sept. 7, 1956

A family squabble that began with a glass of spilled milk ended with pistol shots and the hospitalization with chest wounds of City Councilman Albert F. Swimmer, 69 Harvey St.

Police said Swimmer was found unconscious in the kitchen, his sobbing wife at his side. Police said Mrs. Swimmer told them that her husband had come home late last night and had asked her to get out of bed and prepare his dinner.

When she handed him a glass of milk, it slipped from his hand. He became angry and beat her, police said Mrs. Swimmer told them. Swimmer then took a pistol from his pocket and waved it at her. When she struggled with him the gun went off and a bullet struck him in the chest.

Police said Swimmer had been drinking heavily at a meeting at the George Washington Carver Club before he left for home.

\* \* \* \* \*

Morgue clip, Nov. 10, 1957

District Court today granted an uncontested divorce to Mrs. Albert Swimmer, 69 Harvey St.

Mrs. Swimmer had accused her husband of "habitual drinking, mental cruelty and behavior that embarrassed the family."

\* \* \* \* \*

Morgue clip, April 15, 1958

The George Washington Carver Club today presented its annual Good Citizen award to Albert Swimmer, 1405 Sunset Drive.

Swimmer was honored for his "constant work in behalf of better understanding between the races."

Dr. Frederick Y. Herbert, who made the award, said that Swimmer had been chosen because he represented the "new generation which is striving for equality of opportunity for Negroes so that they can move out of their poverty into the sunlight and share in the wealth of this country."

Swimmer is serving his seventh consecutive term in the City Council.

\* \* \* \* \*

Morgue clip, March 1, 1960

This is a campaign biography of Swimmer, a candidate for re-election to the City Council for his eighth term on the Fusion ticket:

Swimmer, 45, is an active attorney in Freeport. He is a member of the Veterans of Foreign Wars, American Legion and many civic clubs. In the service of his country he lost his right leg. He won a Navy Cross in World War II. He is the father of Linda, 18, a freshman at the state university, and Sam, 14. A star football player on the high school team, he was graduated from the University of California, where he also played football, and the School of Law at the University of Iowa.

\* \* \* \* \*

Morgue clip, April 17, 1960

The Fusion party retained its control of city hall by easily winning four of the five district races.

Its only defeat came in the Second District where Martin Gabel trounced Albert Swimmer, 7,503 to 4,654. The campaign in the district was described as the most bitter in the memory of local politicians.

Gabel had accused Swimmer of being "incapable of sober judgment." In turn, Swimmer had charged Gabel with "turning his back on the real problems of Freeport."

Swimmer, a veteran of local politics, had served seven consecutive terms on the city council. In his last term he had often constituted a minority of one in council votes. He had urged higher taxes and city-financed projects to stop what he described as the "growing decay of the city core."

In his campaign, he accused Gabel of "representing the lily whites of suburbia whose interests are barbecue pits, golf and bridge."

In the other district races . . .

\* \* \* \* \*

Morgue clip, Dec. 15, 1965

The George Washington Carver Club today announced it will send four Freeport youngsters to Disneyland in California.

Albert F. Swimmer, the Club president, said the children, ages 8–12, were picked by teachers in the public schools. Their entire expenses will be borne by the Club.

"Most of these children have never been out of Freeport in their lives," he said. . . .

\* \* \* \* \*

Morgue clip, July 5, 1969

Albert F. Swimmer, a local attorney, told members of the American Legion Post 156 last night that the "patriotism that is confined to flag saluting but not to patriotic acts is anti-American."

His remarks were made at the annual July 4 ceremonies at the Legion Hall. Swimmer, a decorated World War II hero, defined patriotic acts as . . .

\* \* \* \* \*

Morgue clip, Sept. 21, 1971

Gov. William Buckley announced today he will appoint Albert F. Swimmer to the State Board of Education.

Buckley said the board needs "new perspectives, new ways of looking at some of our persistent problems."

Swimmer would be the first black to serve on the board . . .

\* \* \* \* \*

Morgue clip, Nov. 25, 1975

A local attorney paid a return visit to the Freeport Kiwanis Club today after an absence of 35 years, and his speech touched off a harsh debate.

Albert Swimmer, former city councilman, political activist and decorated war hero, bluntly told the club members the day is not far off when "a huge social, economic and political revolution will take place.

"I'm talking about a revolution that will be caused by the unemployed, the poor and the oppressed who are now without a voice but won't be long finding one."

Swimmer recalled he had spoken in 1941 to the club about the failure of U.S. industry to use blacks.

"I reread that speech the other day and I found that the same things I said then could be said now. The only difference is that there are more than only black people involved, there is an entire group of abused, underused and forgotten people who will not stand for much more."

In the question period, Swimmer was asked to set a date for "the revolution." He replied:

"That kind of idiotic question indicates the attitude you men have toward this problem. Either you cannot or you will not take this matter seriously.

"Well, gentlemen, it's your turn now. But it won't be for very long."

\* \* \* \* \*

Morgue clip, May 3, 1976

Albert F. Swimmer, a local attorney and long a maverick within the Democratic party locally, today urged his fellow party members to support Jimmy Carter for the Democratic presidential nomination.

"He's a winner," Swimmer said in telegrams sent to members of the Democratic State Central Committee, of which he is a member. "We must get aboard the victory train now or be left behind when our needs must be considered," he wired. . . .

\* \* \* \* \*

Morgue clip, Nov. 1, 1978

Albert F. Swimmer, a local attorney and former city councilman, said he will fly to New Jersey tomorrow to spend the last days of the campaign working for Bill Bradley, a former basketball player who is the Democratic candidate for United States Senator.

Swimmer said he intends to campaign "among the people Bradley can help most, the minority groups." He said he met Bradley several years ago on a business trip to New York City when Bradley was playing for the New York Knicks.

\* \* \* \* \*

Morgue clip, Dec. 12, 1983

Albert F. Swimmer, a local attorney, said today he will open headquarters here for the presidential campaign of Walter F. Mondale, the vice president under President Jimmy Carter.

Asked why he had decided to support Mondale, Swimmer replied, "The country has seen enough of Ronald Reagan and his utter disregard for the poor and the afflicted. We need a man of understanding and compassion back in the White House."

He added that he hoped that "my old friend, Bill Bradley of New Jersey, will be Mondale's running mate." Bradley was elected to the U.S. Senate on the Democratic ticket in 1978. Swimmer went to New Jersey to campaign for Bradley.

\* \* \* \* \*

Morgue clip, Jan. 14, 1987

Albert F. Swimmer, former city council member and long a Democratic Party local leader, said he is considering running for the city council.

He said local government "needs someone who will try to stop the almighty dollar from being the dominant voice in city hall." He said he referred specifically to the "steady pressure on the elderly and the working people that is forcing them out of their homes."

Swimmer was a member of the city council for . . .

\* \* \* \* \*

Morgue clip, Feb. 18, 1987

Albert F. Swimmer today took himself out of the race for city council.

Swimmer, 72, said that he saw little chance that "Freeport would support a person who sees race and class as destructive." In an interview, Swimmer, the city's first black councilman, said his election in 1946 "was a sign of hope, an indication the people wanted to solve these persistent problems.

"But now, some 40 years later, those hopes are gone. I am leaving the race more in sadness than in anger. . . . "

\* \* \* \* \*

Morgue clip, Feb. 9, 1988

Local Democratic leaders appear to favor the presidential candidacy of Michael S. Dukakis over his leading opponents.

An informal poll of political opinion shows that Dukakis has at least half of the city's party leadership behind him with several others indicating their support will soon be announced.

Among the 20 Democratic leaders interviewed, Dukakis had 10 definite supporters, four probables and two swinging his way. Sen. Albert Gore had three behind him and Jesse Jackson trailed with one, Albert F. Swimmer.

Swimmer was the most outspoken of those interviewed.

"Of course, I'm the only one in the party establishment who will come out and say Jackson is the only candidate fit for the presidency," Swimmer said. "Everyone in the establishment is scared silly that a black man at the top of the ticket will wreck the party.

"Also, they know that Jackson is not going to play ball with them because he is tuned in to those who have never had power before. . . . "

Note in file from Bob Phelps, reporter. 3/18/88

Swimmer tells me he is under a lot of pressure to stay with Jesse Jackson but figures Jackson "will never get the nomination." "Why chase a rainbow?" he said. Keep in touch with him.

\* \* \* \* \*

Morgue clip, Nov. 24, 1989

Martha Lupton, 69 Harvey St., died last night at her home after a long illness. She was 72 years old and had been hospitalized for cancer of the liver until a week ago when she returned home.

Mrs. Lupton was the former wife of Arthur F. Swimmer, and two years after their divorce in 1957 she married Arthur Lupton, a retired executive with the B.C. Krebs Manufacturing Co. . . .

\* \* \* \* \*

Morgue clip, Jan. 25, 1990

Freeport politicians and citizens turned out last night to pay tribute to Albert F. Swimmer on the 75th birthday of the civic leader and civil rights pioneer.

Mayor Sam Parnass described Swimmer as a "local treasure of national stature." More than 250 people dined on chicken kiev at the $150 a plate dinner at the Regis Hotel ballroom. Proceeds were donated to local child care centers at Swimmer's request.

Swimmer, still vigorous and outspoken, warned his listeners: "We still have enormous work to do in eradicating that seemingly permanent stain on the American character, racism. The question before us is whether it is indelible. I grow less optimistic with the years. . . . "

\* \* \* \* \*

Morgue clip, Oct. 5, 1992

Democratic presidential candidate Bill Clinton will campaign in Freeport Oct. 25 after he completes a California tour.

Albert F. Swimmer, head of the local Clinton headquarters, said Clinton had agreed to make the unscheduled stop in response to a personal plea Swimmer made.

"I told him that Freeport is a model of great achievements in racial harmony and in the enormous work that remains to be done," Swimmer said, "and that it is a symbol of what Clinton can do with his message of healing. . . . "

\* \* \* \* \*

Morgue clip, Jan. 25, 1993

Albert F. Swimmer, former city councilman and major local Democratic leader, today said President Bill Clinton has promised to return to Freeport later this year.

Swimmer, Clinton's guest at the inauguration in Washington, said Clinton was grateful for the large vote he received locally and in the state. . . .

\* \* \* \* \*

Morgue clip, May 10, 1995

Long-time Democratic Party leader Albert F. Swimmer said yesterday his party "might have to foresake President Clinton for renomination."

In a luncheon talk at the Kiwanis Club, Swimmer said the party "needs a stronger voice to oppose the heartless, greed-driven opposition." But Swimmer left the door open for Clinton: "If the president returns to the populism that marked his run for the presidency in 1992, and that he reaffirmed in his visit to Freeport the following year, then we will have a fighter for the principles the Democratic Party has always stood for."

In search of anecdotes and some background material you call the president of the George Washington Carver Club, Matthew Bennington Rogers, who tells you:

Al used to have a wonderful sense of humor, but in the last few years he was more and more worried. You fellows didn't cover a talk he gave here three months ago, but none of us who heard it will forget a few of the things he said. Wait a minute, I think I jotted it down and put it in a drawer. Yes, here it is: He told us that he was in despair that blacks were the victims of racism that infects the entire society.

Incidentally, not many people know this—and your people refused to carry it when we sent in an announcement two years ago—but Al set up a $1,000 college scholarship award to the best black student in town. Said it was a repayment of a sort for his scholarship. He told me it was his move toward "compensatory payments" that he hoped would catch on. Guess it didn't. We're cooperating with the First Baptist Church tomorrow at 11 a.m. services. He will be buried in our cemetery, Carver Cemetery, at 2 p.m. that afternoon. By the way, in your story last month about the Black Parents Association wanting the schools to ban several books, you remember that Al voted against the association. He got a lot of criticism from blacks for that. He was a man of principle.

You call Gabel, Swimmer's 1960 election opponent, who says:

> Al Swimmer was an unprincipled character, I'm sorry to say. I don't like to speak ill of the dead, but he drank too much, was intemperate and had regard only for himself. You notice how well he lived? Check the cost of his place—he paid $60,000 when a dollar was worth something. You notice the Cadillac he drove around? Did you know that he was earning twice as much as most lawyers in town with that colored practice? He bled in public for blacks, but in private he bled them. Sure, it's sad he had to go like he did. But he knew what he was doing and could have stopped any time. Say, don't quote me on any of this. Just say that Freeport has lost a sincere and beloved public servant.

## *Assignments*

### *A. Advance*

Your editor tells you she wants you to prepare background material for the files on the following persons, to be used at the time of their deaths. Write the story so that only the lead and one or more paragraphs need be placed at the top of your copy. Funeral and burial arrangements can be put at the end. You should try to interview your subjects.

**President:** The president of the local college or university.
**Mayor:** The mayor of the city in which you live.
**Governor:** The governor of the state.
**Professor:** The senior member of the English Department (or any prominent members of the faculty).
**Chief:** The chief of police.
**Operator:** The switchboard operator at a large local business, law firm or educational institution.
**Senior:** The senior member of a local law firm.
**Publisher:** The publisher of the daily newspaper in the city.
**Chef:** The head cook at the leading restaurant in town.
**Head:** The head of the city board of education.
**Merchant:** A prominent local businessman or businesswoman.
**Prelate:** The highest ranking prelate of the Roman Catholic Church in the city.
**Rabbi:** The head of a local synagogue.
**Doctor:** The medical chief of a local hospital.
**Athlete:** A well-known former athlete living in town.

Look for human interest as well as the vital statistics of birth, birthplace, education, work history and relatives.

### *B. Classmate*

Interview a classmate for background material for an obituary. Use any cause of death. Then write a 250-word obituary.

## *Campus Projects*

### *A. Requirements*

Educational observers are concerned over the decline in the abilities of college graduates to handle mathematics, and they worry that the colleges and universities are not emphasizing scientific studies.

Make an assessment of the requirements in these areas for students on your campus. Are there required courses in chemistry, biology and physics, or are they the so-called "soft" science courses—"astronomy for poets," for example? How much mathematics is required, and are these courses college level?

Does your school give entering freshmen tests to determine their competence in the sciences and mathematics? If so, what has the administration learned and what has been done about the findings?

Interview faculty members to determine whether they believe the physical sciences and mathematics have a role in the education of liberal arts majors.

How have the curriculum and the requirements for graduation changed in the last 25 years?

### B. Smokers

In 1955, 28.4 percent of women smoked; today, 22.8 percent do. In 1955, 56.9 percent of adult males smoked. Now, 28.4 percent do.

*The New York Times* comments, "The figures for adult females are less heartening. . . . The death toll among females is horrendous. More American women die each year from lung cancer than from breast cancer."

Survey men and women on campus and see what their smoking habits are. Obtain background data. Reportedly more than 400,000 Americans die annually from diseases related to smoking.

## Community Project

### NAEP: Math

The mathematics examination of the National Assessment of Educational Progress reveals what Albert Shanker, president of the American Federation of Teachers, describes as "disastrous" results. Although two of three students in grade school do work at course level, their mathematical proficiency declines as they move through high school.

At the senior high school level, about half the students manage to do seventh-grade mathematics. At the top achievement level, which indicates that a student knows some algebra and is prepared to do college mathematics, only 5 percent (one in 20) of high school students show proficiency on the NAEP test.

What has happened, is happening and is being done about this situation? Are school officials in local schools aware through their own findings of low mathematics levels? Obtain some local scores. How much mathematics is required in high school for graduation? Is this a change from 10, 20 years ago?

The government report *A Nation at Risk* said graduating high school seniors averaged 2.3 years of mathematics and 2.0 years of science. It recommended a minimum of three years for each subject. Japanese students are required to take six mathematics courses and five science courses.

## Home Assignments

### A. Suicide

The textbook describes the imitative effect of newspaper stories about teen-age suicides. *The New England Journal of Medicine* reports that studies by scientists at the University of California at San Diego and at Columbia University found that teen-age suicides increase after television news stories and made-for-television movies about teen-age suicides are broadcast. Does this mean editors and news directors should treat such stories with special care?

Locate some suicide stories through a database search or other references and see how they were handled. Were the stories handled in ways you approve of?

### B. AIDS

You have just received tables with last year's rates for people with AIDS. Your editor asks you to list the 10 states and the major cities with the largest number, with emphasis on localizing the situation if possible.

Rates are based on the number of cases per 100,000 population, and thus the listings are comparable.

Select a state or city in which you live or attend school or one that is nearby and presume this is the community in which you are working. Compare with three years ago. Blend background with the data.

Toby Gardner.
**Remembering the victims.**

## AIDS Cases Rates by State

| | Last Year | | | Three Years Ago | |
|---|---|---|---|---|---|
| Rank | State | Rate | Rank | State | Rate |
| 1 | New York | 82.2 | 1 | New York | 60.9 |
| 2 | New Jersey | 63.2 | 2 | Florida | 56.2 |
| 3 | Florida | 61.8 | 3 | California | 41.7 |
| 4 | Maryland | 54.4 | 4 | Delaware | 38.3 |
| 5 | California | 38.6 | 5 | New Jersey | 37.4 |
| 6 | Delaware | 38.4 | 6 | Georgia | 33.6 |
| 7 | Georgia | 31.8 | 7 | Missouri | 32.9 |
| 8 | South Carolina | 31.6 | 8 | Nevada | 32.4 |
| 9 | Louisiana | 28.7 | 9 | Texas | 31.0 |
| 10 | Connecticut | 27.8 | 10 | Maryland | 30.8 |
| | **National State Average** | **30.0** | | **National State Average** | **26.9** |

## AIDS Cases Rates by Metropolitan Area

| | Last Year | | | Three Years Ago | |
|---|---|---|---|---|---|
| Rank | Metro Area | Rate | Rank | Metro Area | Rate |
| 1 | San Francisco | 158.0 | 1 | San Francisco | 209.0 |
| 2 | New York | 153.4 | 2 | Jacksonville, Fla. | 89.8 |
| 3 | Miami | 153.3 | 3 | Miami | 84.6 |
| 4 | Jersey City, N.J. | 152.1 | 4 | West Palm Beach, Fla. | 80.6 |
| 5 | Ft. Lauderdale, Fla. | 106.1 | 5 | New York City | 74.5 |
| 6 | Newark, N.J. | 98.0 | 6 | Ft. Lauderdale, Fla. | 68.7 |
| 7 | Baltimore | 76.8 | 7 | Orlando, Fla. | 63.8 |
| 8 | West Palm Beach, Fla. | 75.3 | 8 | Houston | 56.8 |
| 9 | New Orleans | 53.2 | 9 | Dallas | 56.2 |
| 10 | Washington, D.C. | 53.1 | 10 | Austin | 51.2 |
| | **National Metro Area Average** | **41.4** | | **National Metro Area Average** | **37.4** |

Source: Centers for Disease Control and Prevention, 1993.

## Class Discussion

### Disclosure

I do not think newspapers should require reporters to show stories to sources. That would risk lawsuits on those few occasions when it is not possible to reach a source. What I suggest instead are a few limited, casual experiments, and I know a good place to start. There is one kind of news story—the obituary—where errors can cause real emotional pain. The only time most people ever have direct contact with a journalist is when they are interviewed for an obituary on their father or mother in the local paper. A mistake, even a small one, feels like someone scratched the coffin with a rusty nail.

Why shouldn't editors encourage obit writers to show such stories to relatives before publication? No one is going to leak the story to the competition. No one is going to try to take political advantage. Time is rarely an issue. It would be the simplest thing to fax a draft to a son or daughter to check for factual errors. If that worked, who knows what might happen next?

As reporters we are accustomed to exposing automakers who slap together cars and depend on recalls to make everything right. We have excoriated prosecutors who locked up innocents and then, discovering their error, set them free with a bare apology. Many of my colleagues think that front-page corrections are preferable to leaping into the unknown, but I don't. It's time we applied the principles of openness and accuracy we monitor in others to the practices we engage in ourselves.

—Jay Mathews, *Newsweek*

What do you think of this proposal for obituaries, for other kinds of stories?

## DB/CAR

### A. Deaths

You have received a government report that gives the leading causes of death and the annual death toll as:

> **Cardiovascular diseases:** 980,000
> **Malignancies:** 465,000
> **Accidents:** 95,000
> **Pulmonary diseases:** 75,000
> **Pneumonia:** 70,000

But if we count the number of years of life lost from these causes of death—for those who die before reaching the age of 65—the four biggest killers in order are:

> Accidents
> Cancer
> Heart disease
> Suicide and homicide

Obtain data for your state or city in the above categories. Take both the national figures and the local figures and write a 350- to 500-word article.

### B. Creationism

School boards around the country are being called on to introduce "creation science" into the science curriculum. *Creationism* has been defined as the belief that human beings are descended from Adam and Eve in the Garden of Eden and is sometimes offered as an alternative theory to the theory of Darwinian evolution. The proposals have led to acrimonious school board meetings and civic battles. In Plano, Tex., for example, the school board rescinded its move to adopt a creationist textbook, *Of Pandas and People: The Central Question of Biological Origins,* after a raucous board meeting.

Despite a Supreme Court ruling in 1987 (Edwards vs. Aguillard), groups described as the Religious Right are pushing creationism as an alternative theory to evolution. In the high court ruling, Justice William Brennan wrote that public schools can teach "a variety of scientific theories about the origins of humankind" if they are nonreligious in nature. Opponents of evolution see this as a loophole in the decision, and *Of Pandas and People* has been selected as a means of moving through the loophole. Its backers say it proposes an "intelligent design" underlying the creation of the world but avoids discussing the "designer."

Rob Boston, assistant editor of *Church & State,* describes the book as "a slick repackaging of creationist ideas under a different name." His magazine is published by Americans United for Separation of Church and State.

The book has been urged for adoption by biology classes in communities in Florida, Ohio, Alabama, Idaho, New Hampshire, Pennsylvania and New Mexico.

Jon Buell, the head of the Foundation for Thought and Ethics, which published *Of Pandas and People,* says that 15 school districts have purchased the book, which is in its second printing. Creationism or "creation science," is also known as "abrupt appearance theory," or "intelligent design theory."

Do a database search on the book, its publisher and its proponents and opponents. Write a 400-word story.

Has there been any local push for including creationism in the school curriculum or adding this book to the library or reading lists?

### Fix It: Obits

Correct the errors or suggest changes in the following material taken from obituaries:

1. Alfred (Alf) Felter, 42, died today after a long illness. Felter, an accountant, lived at 45 Ervin Ave. and was a founder of the Gay Men's Liberation Movement, a local group that sought to modify . . . (You find out he died of AIDS.)

2. The family asked that in lieu of flowers donations be sent to the American Cancer Society.

3. Police said that the youth carefully planned his death. Yesterday, he purchased 15 feet of garden hose from Barton's Department Store. He also bought a roll of duct tape. While his parents were asleep . . .

4. He was one of the few men decorated with the Congressional Medal of Honor for service in the Korean War. Fewer than 100 servicemen received the award in that war.

5. He was active in local organizations supporting the U.N. and fostering international understanding. He said that the greatest event he had witnessed as a young man in the Army was the drafting of the charter of the United Nations some 50 years ago in California.

## *What's Wrong?: Prizewinner*

The Pied Piper Award usually goes to a specific tobacco advertising campaign. But with this issue we are giving a special award to Sports Illustrated, a popular magazine among teenagers. S.I. is one of the most aggressive of all publications in it's eagerness to promote tobacco addiction for a profit. As documented in an article on page 16, SI has been one of the tobacco industry's most valuable allies in recruiting youthful replacement smokers through their willingness to associate tobacco addiction with athletic excellence.
—*Tobacco Free Youth Reporter*

## *You Decide: Anti-Gay*

A group seeks to initiate an anti-gay state law. It asks your newspaper to run a 16-page paid advertising supplement that includes articles under headlines such as "Homosexual Agenda Exposed," "Consequences of Sodomy: Ruin of a Nation," "What Schools Teach Children About Gay Sex" and "Medical Consequences of What Homosexuals Do."

The initiative would bar marital or spousal status for gays and lesbians and would affect school instruction in homosexuality. Would you accept the advertisement?

# 20 The Police Beat

### Introduction

Stories of crime, detection and arrest are avidly read. Most of these stories are culled from the reports and records kept by the police department which the reporter checks on his or her rounds. Names and addresses are always double-checked for accuracy. Given time, the reporter will follow up some of these reports with interviews of the victims and, when possible, of the investigating and arresting officers. These interviews provide the human interest details lacking in the reports. Police reporters also write general stories, such as the effectiveness of the police department in crime prevention and in solving crime.

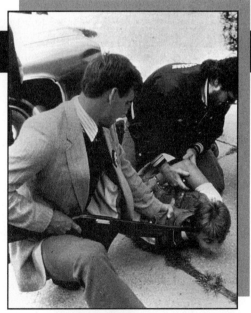

Michael Rafferty, *Asbury Park Press.*
**Young murder suspect captured.**

## Exercises

### A. Drugs

Your editor hands you this story and tells you he wants a more dramatic lead, even if you have to neglect the today angle. Rewrite the story.

> A local youth is scheduled to be arraigned in district court here today on charges of possession of a narcotic and resisting arrest.
> Police said that the youth, Mark Reib, 17, 338 Topeka St., was arrested yesterday after a downtown footrace between Reib and two sheriff's officers.
> Police said Reib tried to obtain narcotics from the Stuben Drug Store on Massachusetts Avenue by giving false information over the phone.
> The caller claimed to be a physician and said the prescription would be picked up shortly. The store clerk became suspicious and notified local police, who were waiting for the pickup to be made.
> The chase occurred after Reib left the drugstore, police said.
> Reib was freed on $5,000 bail, pending arraignment.

### B. Arrested

The police announce the arrest of Carl Morton on a charge of murder. He was sought for six days in the slaying of Mildred Miller, 47, a pianist who lived at an inexpensive hotel, The Plaza, where Morton also had a room. The police announced at the time of her slaying that she had been raped and strangled. The slayer also had set her bed afire and taken a television set and radio.

Det. Sgt. Richard Raskover said that Morton, an unemployed truck driver, had been sought because Mrs. Miller's radio was found in his room. His girlfriend, who was not identified by the police, said Morton had left the night of the slaying after depositing the radio in their room and telling her he had just sold a television set and was going out to buy some food.

When she asked Morton where he had obtained the radio and television set, Raskover said, he told her not to tell anyone about them.

Morton was picked up at a downtown hotel this morning. Police would not disclose how they learned of his whereabouts. But it is a well-known police procedure to question hotel clerks about new guests.

Raskover says that Morton will be questioned about several other deaths in The Plaza. Four women died there within the past six months under strange circumstances. All were past 60.

He did not resist arrest. No bail is set on capital charges.

You ask if Morton has a record and Raskover suggests you obtain that information elsewhere. Through a contact, you learn Morton is 37 years old, was arrested in 1978 on a robbery charge and sentenced to 2 1/2 to 5 years in the state penitentiary. Three years later, he was sentenced to 90 days on a misdemeanor, loitering, after his arrest for possession of dangerous drugs, a felony. In 1983, he again benefitted from plea bargaining, being sentenced to 90 days for attempted theft following his arrest for robbery in the second degree and criminal possession of stolen property, both felonies. In 1988, he was sentenced to two years for burglary.

Write a 300-word story.

### C. Cookies

Your editor likes short features—she calls them "brights"—from the police beat, and the following information from a crime report sounds like a good "bright":

> The day-care center of the Freeport School District holds its classes in the basement of the United Methodist Church, 850 Brighton Ave. During the evening, a basement window on the north side of the building was broken and the basement entered. Margaret Reeder, the director of the center, said all that appeared taken was a carton containing four boxes of chocolate cookies. She says the cookies were so stale the children wouldn't eat them and the center was planning to return them.

### D. Crime Reports

Total crimes, Precinct No. 2.

|  | Last Year | Previous Year |
| --- | --- | --- |
| Total crimes reported | 1,844 | 1,753 |
| Auto thefts | 262 | 202 |
| Theft from motor vehicles | 556 | 468 |
| Burglaries | 673 | 610 |

|  | Last Year | Previous Year |
|---|---|---|
| Purse snatching | 55 | 55 |
| Robbery | 265 | 378 |
| Murder | 6 | 6 |
| Rape and attempted rape | 16 | 18 |
| Possession of dangerous drugs | 11 | 16 |

The city police department released citywide totals on crimes reported for last year which your newspaper ran yesterday. You go to Precinct No. 2, in which St. Mary's University is located, in order to write a piece on crime in that area since it was the subject of intensive police action after a record number of crimes, 3,299, were reported in the precinct three years ago. The year following the transfer of additional officers to the precinct, the number of crimes dropped to 1,753. Last year, the number inched upward.

Police Captain Stanley Solomon tells you that the situation in the precinct is "steady," that the figures "reflect a citywide trend over the past two years of more property thefts in middle and upper income areas. We have always been a prime area for auto thefts. These foreign cars are attractive for some reason. Also, people around here tend to be absent-minded, and there are always the newcomers who think they're back home where they never locked their car doors. Anyone with a stereo or a camera in full view inside a car is asking for trouble."

Precinct No. 2 covers eastern Freeport. In the immediate area around the university, described as Police Post No. 3, total crimes reported went from 148 two years ago to 220 last year, the largest increase in the precinct. Most of the crimes involved thefts from motor vehicles (81) and burglaries (103). Write 300 words for the local newspaper. Then write the first four paragraphs of a story for the campus newspaper.

## E. Bite

In making routine checks of major hospitals, you are told at 2 p.m. that a police officer has been admitted with a severe dog bite. The admitting clerk at Community Hospital identifies the officer as William Trevor, age 39. His condition is good. His injury is a dog bite to the right wrist. He was brought to the hospital by ambulance at 1:15 a.m. (today) after being picked up at his home. That is all the information she can give you.

Next you reach the public relations office at the hospital and ask for additional information. In response to questions, and after checking with others at the hospital, Beverly Collins, the director of public information, tells you that Officer Trevor has been treated with antibiotics to ward off infection from inch-deep bites to the bottom and top of his wrist. The bites reached the bone. He has been given a sedative and is resting quietly. He is expected to be released from the hospital tomorrow. He is not to take shots to prevent rabies, because the city's standard dog-bite form, which was completed by ambulance attendant K.L. Ross, indicates that the dog has been seized by an animal control officer and is being held for observation in the city dog pound. You are told that the officer is asleep and cannot be disturbed by a telephone call.

You go to the police records room, where you learn there is a written report of the incident. It was prepared by Patrolmen B.J. Kirby and A.M. Dunning. It is headed "Attempt Burglary." It says that at approximately 12:45 a.m. (today), an attempt was made to burglarize Apartment 205, the home of William Trevor. The body of the report reads as follows:

> Victim states that he was in the bedroom when he heard the balcony door open. Door is sliding type and was unlocked. Victim got out of bed, turned on light situated on bedside table and obtained service revolver, .38 Police Special, from holster in chair. On entering living room victim spotted white male, age approx. 30, in room. Victim stated, "Hold it right there," and suspect turned and ran out of sliding door. Victim aimed revolver to fire, but as he was about to fire victim's dog became excited and bit victim. Victim taken to Community Hospital with dog bites to right wrist.

The report describes the suspect as wearing a Mickey Mouse T-shirt and blue jeans but no shoes.

You check with the personnel department of the police department and are told there is no William Trevor on the local police force. You recheck the offense report and note that Trevor's business address is listed as "Clovia P.D." You call the police department in Clovia and reach the police chief, Irving Scillicide. He confirms that William Trevor is a member of his police force. He is assigned to the K-9, or dog unit. You ask Scillicide if he knows what happened. He tells you, "It's my understanding Bill surprised a burglar in his apartment and struggled with him, and Rusty bit Bill instead of the burglar. It's a damn shame when a police dog bites the wrong person."

Write 150 words.

*F. Dangerous*

The textbook lists the 10 cities with the highest murder and violent crime rates among metropolitan areas in the country. See Chapter 20.

1. Write a 750-word roundup for a Sunday feature.
2. Presume that you work in one of the top five cities in the list of violent crimes. Write a 500-word feature.

*G. Bingo*

Here is an arrest report from the Sacramento police department. Presume the incident occurred last night. Write 250 words.

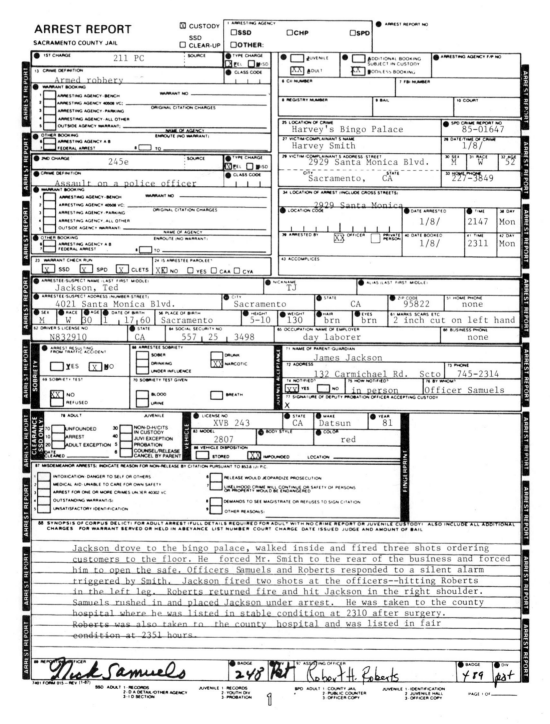

*H. Chen Arrest*

Police reported the arrest of Dong Lu Chen, 51, 1658 Broadway, a janitor with the B.C. Krebs Co. He was arrested last night in connection with the death of his wife, Gian Wan Chen, 40, last night.

A police spokesman said the woman suffered a number of blows to the head from a hammer. Her death followed a domestic quarrel, police said.

His wife and two children, a son, 16, and a daughter, 14, have been living in Freeport since 1986 when they and Chen came to this country from China. He was unable to find work then and moved to Maryland. But six months ago he moved back to Freeport.

## Assignments

*A. Age*

Obtain latest local arrest figures for the following categories and write a story based on a comparison of data for preceding periods: murder, rape, assault, robbery, burglary, auto theft, drunk driving. Check the ages of those arrested.

*B. Arrest Report*

Go to the local police station or a nearby precinct and ask to see some of the arrest reports turned in over the last 12 hours. Select one you consider newsworthy and do a story based on it. Include the suspect's criminal record if it is available and it is legal to use it.

*C. Crimes*

Take any one- or two-hour period or more over the past 24 hours, and do a total of crimes reported by category. For this story, you will have to obtain the dispatcher's record or the records of the police officer who takes all incoming calls on crimes. Some of these calls may not be serious, but record them anyway. This will be a narrow peek at a period in a day of the life of a police department.

*D. Police*

Interview a police officer who walks a beat or is assigned to a patrol car. Try to accompany the officer on his or her rounds or ask for a description of a typical day. Include the strong opinions the officer may have of the people he or she deals with, and ask what the officer thinks of the court system.

*E. Investigation*

Interview a police officer who was instrumental in solving a recent crime. How was the case broken?

*F. Prevention*

David Schreiber, *The San Bernadino Sun.*
**Fighting drug dealing takes increasing police work.**

Unique methods have been adopted in some cities to prevent crime. One of the most common is the computerized study of high-crime areas and periods and the assignment of officers to these areas in town during the specified times. What methods are being used in your city?

*G. Complaints*

Is there a bureau or department in the city that handles complaints against the police? Do a story on the kinds of complaints registered and the way they are handled. Have any officers been suspended or fired as a result?

The Police Beat

## Campus Projects

### A. Crime Count

Studies of crime indicate that many more crimes are committed than reported. Make a survey of students and determine how many have been victims of a crime within the past year on campus. Did they report the crime to campus or local police?

Failure to report is especially high among victims of sex crimes. You might want to make a separate category for this crime and investigate the situation in depth.

### B. Policy

Campus newspapers have gone to court to open campus police records, and the courts have agreed that the public has access to these records. Disciplinary records, however, are closed to the press as the courts have ruled that they fall under the protection students have from the so-called Buckley Amendment.

What is the situation on your campus? Are reporters allowed to examine campus police records? If so, does the campus newspaper and/or local newspaper examine these records on a regular basis?

### C. Campus Crime

Make a study of crime on the campus for last year and compare it with the preceding year, noting any significant changes. Compare your campus crime totals with the campuses with the highest crime totals for a recent year as follows:

**Total Violent Crime**

| | |
|---|---|
| University of Medicine and Dentistry, Newark | 85 |
| University of California at Berkeley | 54 |
| Arizona State University | 47 |
| University of Maryland, College Park | 46 |
| North Carolina State University, Raleigh | 42 |

**Forcible Rape**

| | |
|---|---|
| University of Alaska, Fairbanks | 8 |
| Florida State University, Tallahassee | 6 |
| Indiana University, Bloomington | 6 |
| Boston College | 6 |
| Jackson State University, Mississippi | 6 |
| Mary Washington College, Virginia | 6 |
| Washington State University | 6 |

**Motor Vehicle Theft**

| | |
|---|---|
| San Diego State University | 135 |
| University of Florida | 131 |
| University of California, Los Angeles | 112 |
| California State University, Long Beach | 100 |
| San Francisco State University | 96 |

**Total Property Crime**

| | |
|---|---|
| University of Michigan | 1,845 |
| Ohio State University | 1,699 |
| University of California, Davis | 1,602 |
| University of California, Berkeley | 1,540 |
| Michigan State University | 1,467 |

Source: *Crime in the United States, Uniform Crime Reports,* 1993.

## Community Projects

### A. Car Theft

More than 1.5 million vehicles are stolen annually. Their value is estimated at $7.5 billion. The recovery rate for stolen vehicles is around 60 percent nationally and much lower in metropolitan areas. The national motor vehicle theft rate is 605 per 100,000 people, broken down as 721 in metropolitan areas, 224 in cities outside these areas and 110 in rural counties. An average of one of every 125 registered vehicles is stolen each year.

California has the highest state rate of motor vehicle thefts. Washington, D.C., has the highest city rate with New York and Los Angeles close behind.

Talk to police officers, garage mechanics and others about the local car theft rate and car insurance rates. Find out the best way to protect cars against theft: alarms, steering wheel immobilizers, the Lojack, ignition cutoff systems?

### B. Efficiency

One measure of police efficiency is the comparison of arrests to citizen complaints. Take the numbers of each in the categories of burglary and robbery. In large urban areas, the ratio is about one arrest for every five reported burglaries and robberies.

You might extend this to all categories of crime, and if the community has precincts, you can make a precinct-by-precinct analysis.

A further analysis can be made to see whether police are assigned to precincts on the basis of the incidence of crime. Make a tabulation of the number of officers assigned to each precinct and the police strength per 1,000 residents of the precinct. Compare the assignments to your crime-incidence figures. You might check these figures against the economic, racial and ethnic nature of the precincts.

### C. Firearms

The FBI reported that 56.7 percent of murder victims died from handgun violence in 1993. The Coalition to Stop Gun Violence states, "America is bleeding to death from gun violence and there's only one reason why it's been allowed to continue: the NRA."

The National Rifle Association counters: Guns do not kill. People do. Moreover, defenders of the right to keep firearms say that the Constitution protects gun ownership.

The National School Safety Center says 135,000 children carry handguns to school every day and another 270,000 have carried a gun to school at least once. Many inner-city schools have installed metal detectors to keep guns out.

Gun-control legislation in Congress usually is stalled, frequently by legislators who receive large contributions from the NRA. Have members of your congressional delegation received NRA money? How have they voted on gun-control legislation?

How do people in your community feel about more stringent gun-control legislation?

## Home Assignment

### Holes

Stories that do not include the information that readers and listeners expect to be given are said to contain holes. Clip from a local newspaper a story that you think does not include one or more facts necessary to a complete understanding of the event. (Here is an example of a hole in a brief: "A burglar broke into the home of Mr. and Mrs. Hector Berlin, 311 Cross Lane, last night and took a silver tea service while the couple slept." The hole: What was the value of the set?)

## Class Discussion

### Banner

Oswald Garrison Villard, 1872–1949, was the editor-owner of *The Nation,* an outstanding liberal political weekly, until 1932. In a commentary on journalism, he wrote:

> It must ask last of all what were the returns of the counting room but must first inquire what ideals a given journal upheld, what moral aims it pursued, what national and international policies it championed, what was the spirit of fair play and justice which activated it, and above all on whose side and under whose banner it fought.

Ask these questions of a newspaper or magazine that you read, and give the answers. Are you happy with your answers? Why?

## DB/CAR

### A. Handguns

Here is an alphabetized list by state of the percentages of murders involving handguns in 48 of the 50 states. Use the computer to rank them from highest to lowest percentage. Then make a database search for material about the actions that state governments and the federal government have taken regarding control of handgun sales. What is the situation in your state?

| State | Percent | State | Percent |
|---|---|---|---|
| Alabama | 49.47 | Montana** | NA |
| Alaska | 37.04 | Nebraska | 25.00 |
| Arizona | 50.91 | Nevada | 61.24 |
| Arkansas | 51.23 | New Hampshire | 25.00 |
| California | 63.73 | New Jersey | 43.54 |
| Colorado | 53.88 | New Mexico | 41.05 |
| Connecticut | 56.80 | New York | 66.42 |
| Delaware | 50.00 | North Carolina | 47.73 |
| Florida | 39.74 | North Dakota | 27.27 |
| Georgia | 58.00 | Ohio | 62.60 |
| Hawaii | 27.91 | Oklahoma | 48.16 |
| Idaho | 45.16 | Oregon | 39.86 |
| Illinois** | NA | Pennsylvania | 60.45 |
| Indiana | 63.03 | Rhode Island | 41.03 |
| Iowa | 22.22 | South Carolina | 56.80 |
| Kansas** | NA | South Dakota | 44.44 |
| Kentucky | 48.73 | Tennessee | 60.22 |
| Louisiana | 72.12 | Texas | 51.68 |
| Maine | 57.14 | Utah | 29.31 |
| Maryland | 67.56 | Vermont | 41.67 |
| Massachusetts | 28.57 | Virginia | 60.30 |
| Michigan | 41.11 | Washington | 48.11 |
| Minnesota | 38.93 | West Virginia | 42.40 |
| Mississippi | 64.68 | Wisconsin | 39.64 |
| Missouri | 59.34 | Wyoming | 37.50 |

**No data.

### B. Driver Check

A school bus driver was recently arrested for speeding and your editor asks you to run a check of computer tapes to see whether any of the school bus drivers in your state has had a conviction for a serious driving offense, has ever had his or her driver's license revoked or has ever been convicted of a sex offense.

## Skill Drill: Police Vocabulary

Beginning reporters on most news staffs are expected to handle stories originating in or involving the police department. Accidents, reports of crimes, arrests, searches, investigations, administrative activities, corruption and other newsworthy activities require reporters to deal with the police and with material from the police. There is simply too much news for the police reporter to handle alone. This list includes terms every reporter should know and a handful with which only the police reporter might be familiar. Define:

1. ADW
2. APB
3. Arrest warrant
4. Bail
5. Booking
6. Burglary
7. Citation
8. Crime report

9. Decoy
10. Detention
11. Entrapment
12. Felony
13. Grand larceny
14. Homicide bureau
15. Interrogation
16. Miranda card
17. Misdemeanor
18. On the pad
19. Pigeon drop
20. Robbery

## Fix It: Tighten, Adjust

Edit or rewrite these sentences to rid them of unnecessary words and phrases or to make them read better.

1. BEIJING (AP)—American evangelist Billy Graham today praised Chinese leaders, saying that they are working to broaden freedom of religion in their country.

2. The nation's largest organization of doctors called for shifting the main point of attack from trying to catch drug traffickers to working to reduce demand for their illegal products by expanding treatment of abusers.

3. NICOSIA (AP)—Hundreds of Iranian mourners shouted "Revenge, revenge" as they buried 44 sailors killed in the widespread battles in the Persian Gulf with the U.S. Navy this week.

4. MIAMI (AP)—A museum official, under fire for including in a recent auction works by artists considered sympathetic to the Cuban government, accused his detractors of using the type of totalitarian tactics they say they oppose.

5. TOKYO (AP)—Asserting it has opened its markets to U.S.-made computer chips, Japan today repeated earlier requests that the United States remove trade restrictions imposed by President Ronald Reagan.

# 21 The Courts

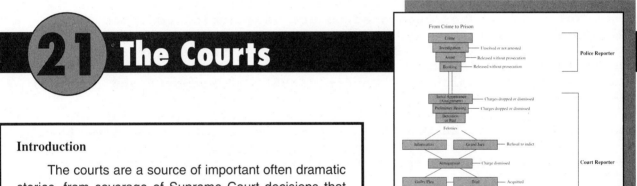

### Introduction

The courts are a source of important often dramatic stories, from coverage of Supreme Court decisions that affect every aspect of our lives to decisions by local courts that determine which criminal defendants will be sent to prison and which will be placed on probation. The two basic systems are the federal and state courts, and within these systems civil and criminal cases are heard. In civil cases, actions are initiated by an individual, usually suing another for damages. In criminal law, the government takes action for violation of the criminal statutes. Most of these cases, civil and criminal, are settled to avoid trial.

## Exercises

### A. Dogs

Presume that you are a courthouse reporter for a newspaper in Perth Amboy, N.J., and you come across this suit in the state Superior Court. You call your city editor and describe the case to him. He suggests you give it 150 to 200 words and says, "Keep it light."

```
Wilentz, Goldman & Spitzer,
Attorneys for Plaintiffs,          SUPERIOR COURT OF NEW JERSEY
252 Madison Avenue,                LAW DIVISION, MONMOUTH COUNTY
Perth Amboy, New Jersey            Docket No.
Telephone (201) 826-0700

STANLEY S. BEY, individually and   :
STANLEY S. BEY, guardian ad litem
for Wendy Bey and Jeffrey Bey,     :

              Plaintiffs,          :
                                        Civil Action
     vs.                           :
                                        COMPLAINT
JOHN L. MONTGOMERY, JR. and        :
MARION
MONTGOMERY,
                                   :
              Defendants.
                                   :
```

Plaintiff, Stanley S. Bey, is the father of Wendy Bey, age 7, and Jeffrey Bey, age 6, and has no interest contrary to that of the said Wendy Bey and Jeffrey Bey in this action.

Stanley S. Bey has consented to act as guardian ad litem for Wendy Bey and Jeffrey Bey, infants.

Plaintiffs, Stanley S. Bey, individually and Stanley S. Bey, guardian ad litem of Wendy Bey and Jeffrey Bey, residing at 6 Woods End Road, in the Borough of Rumson, County of Monmouth and State of New Jersey, complaining of the defendants, say:

1. Plaintiffs, Wendy and Jeffrey Bey at all times relevant, were the owners of an Old English Sheep Dog bitch named "Samantha."

2. Said Samantha was of pleasant temperament possessing excellent physical qualities and had been exhibited at various dog shows.

3. The relative scarcity of the breed, the purity of the blood lines of Samantha and her condition and temperament resulted in said canine having deep sentimental ties to her owners and other members of their household, having great value both for her qualities as well as the value of her prospective litters.

4. At all relevant times, defendants were the owners of a Golden Retriever named "Barney."

5. The aforesaid Barney had a propensity for running loose and causing mischief and damage, particularly the attacking and sexual violation of female canines in the neighborhood, all of which was known to the defendants.

6. Defendants, negligently and in wanton disregard of the rights of plaintiffs in the enjoyment of their pet and the sanctity of their household, continued to permit Barney free and unsupervised license to roam.

7. On June 15, Samantha was upon the premises of her owners in a specially constructed dog run, which run was to house, contain and protect Samantha.

>      8. On said date, the defendant's dog Barney, unleashed, unsupervised and unattended, entered Samantha's run and attacked, sexually violated and mauled Samantha.
>      9. The result of said attack caused physical damage, alteration of temperament and impregnation.
>      10. The wounds and injury suffered by Samantha have effectively removed her from competition at dog shows.
>      11. The pregnancy required an abortion and caused the omission of Samantha's next blood litter.
>      12. In addition to the foregoing, plaintiff, Stanley S. Bey, was required to expend monies for medical treatment of Samantha directly resulting from the attack.
>      WHEREFORE, plaintiffs demand judgment in such amount as the court may find due, together with interest and costs of suit.
>
>                                        WILENTZ, GOLDMAN & SPITZER
>                                        Attorneys for Plaintiffs
>
>                                     By:
>                                        Allen Ravin
>                                        Member of the Firm.

## B. Life

In Chapter 25, **Exercise A. Slay,** a man is arrested in connection with the death of a young woman. A year later, he goes to trial, and after a two-week trial in which the defendant asserted he was not at the scene of the crime, a jury convicted Hosie Gene Jones after three hours of deliberations. Today, a month after he was found guilty, he was sentenced to life in prison without parole by District Court Judge Samuel A. McMillan. In his comments, Judge McMillan said:

> This was a deliberate murder for gain, and although the gain was slight, a few dollars, this man was willing to kill for it. He took the life of a young woman with most of her life ahead of her. He is the lowest order of human we can imagine.
>
> It is clear from crimes of this sort that the state legislature must reinstitute the death penalty for murder committed while engaging in a felony, such as was the case here.

Present law allows the death penalty only for killing a police officer or other law enforcement agent. Write a story about the sentencing.

## C. Conviction

In Chapter 12 of the textbook, the arrest of Calvin Jackson in connection with a series of murders is described. It is now some 18 months later and Jackson has been on trial for nine murders. The case went to the jury today, and after four hours and 11 minutes of deliberations, a guilty verdict was returned.

Jackson was convicted of killing nine women. He faces life in prison with a mandatory minimum of 25 to 30 years. Sentencing will be two weeks from today. District Court Judge Aloysius J. Melia, who presided over the six-week trial, will do the sentencing next month.

Jackson's defense was insanity. But a three-hour tape-recorded confession he made to the police, which was played to the jury, was full of details of the various crimes, and jurors said, after the trial, this convinced them he was sane at the time of the slayings. Write a story about the verdict.

## D. Chen Indict

Dong Lu Chen, 51, of 1658 Broadway, who was arrested 10 days ago in connection with the death of his wife, Gian Wan Chen, was indicted today by a grand jury. (See Chapter 20, **J. Chen.**)

He was charged with second-degree murder. He has been held without bail and was returned to jail pending felony arraignment on the charge.

*E. Chen Sentence*

District Court Judge Marvin Hurley held a nonjury trial for Dong Lu Chen, 51, who was charged with second-degree murder in the death of his wife, Gian Wan Chen, 40.

Chen spent 18 months in jail pending trial, which began five days ago.

Judge Hurley reached a decision yesterday of second-degree manslaughter. Two hours later, he sentenced Chen to probation of five years.

During the trial, testimony showed that while Chen was in Maryland and his wife and children were in Freeport, his wife took a lover. The children testified that their mother taunted Chen about her affair.

After an argument that the children overheard, Chen knocked his wife down on the bed and hit the slight, 99-pound woman at least eight times with a hammer.

A second-degree manslaughter conviction carries a penalty of five to 15 years. But Hurley said that he imposed probation because of the "cultural aspects" of the case. Hurley cited "the effect of his wife's behavior on someone who is essentially born in China, raised in China and took all his Chinese customs with him to the United States."

One of Chen's witnesses was Nicholas Trowbridge, chairman of the psychology department at Mallory College, who said that marriage in China is sacred and that a husband could be expected to become enraged on learning of his wife's infidelity. The defense attorney, said, "The basis of this defense is not that it's acceptable to kill your wife as a result of her infidelity. The basis is the special high place the family holds in the Chinese community. This act of adultery would bring great shame and humiliation his entire life."

He said that because of Chen's mental state there could be no intent, and intent is essential to second-degree murder or first-degree manslaughter.

You have not covered this trial and so you will have to recapitulate much of the testimony. Your editor tells you to obtain a statement on the judge's sentence from the district attorney, Paul Robinson, who states, "Anyone who comes to this country must be prepared to live by and obey our laws. Anything less than the maximum sentence suggests that women's lives, minority women's lives are not valued."

He added, "There should be one standard of justice, not one that depends on the cultural background of a defendant."

*F. Chen React*

The day after Chen was sentenced, Mayor Sam Parnass issued the following statement for immediate release:

THE CITY OF FREEPORT                  OFFICE OF THE MAYOR

For Release: Immediate

STATEMENT

I am shocked and dismayed by District Court Judge Marvin Hurley's decision to impose a sentence of probation on a man who killed his wife with a hammer.

Judge Hurley's explanation of his nonjail sentence in the case of Dong Lu Chen was that the defendant's Chinese "cultural background made him susceptible to cracking under the circumstances" and that he was unlikely to kill again. Accordingly, the judge refused to impose a prison sentence.

This reasoning is both an affront to those of Chinese heritage and inconsistent with the philosophy that sentences for crimes should punish the offender, deter the individual from a repetition of such conduct and serve to deter others from engaging in similar conduct. Additionally, sentences for criminal conduct should communicate a message about societal values that the laws seek to promote, uphold and protect.

If Judge Hurley's reasoning were accepted, it would be used to argue mitigation for those who commit crimes against persons because of the offender's objection to the cultural, racial, sexual, religious or other characteristics of the victim. A judge in Texas recently applied this irrational philosophy when he accepted a killer's distaste for a homosexual lifestyle as an explanation for his murders and gave him a reduced sentence.

I reject stereotyping and bias based on cultural, ethnic, racial, sexual, religious or other such grounds and I urge everyone to reject it. While cultural, ethnic and other diversity are important ingredients of a heterogeneous society, diversity should not be used to excuse or justify conduct that is contrary to accepted societal norms.

### G. Chen Judge

Two days after you wrote about the conviction of Dong Lu Chen (*E. Chen Sentence*) the judge who sentenced him speaks out in defense of his sentence. Here are excerpts from his statement to you in an interview. Write 300 words.

> If a judge made a ruling on a cultural background it would be wrong. It wasn't that it was a defense, but it totally affected this man.
>
> He's not a loose cannon. That's the point. He never displayed psychopathic tendencies.
>
> This guy is not going to do it again, and he has suffered. There's no question he's going to suffer every day of his life.
>
> If you kill someone you should face some jail time. I don't find any violence acceptable . . . but in this case it wasn't that his cultural background excused him. It just made him more susceptible to cracking under the circumstances. I don't think this man would have killed her under any other circumstances.
>
> If he went to jail at some point he might come out a real time bomb. Under my mandate, he is under intense supervision.
>
> This is just a terrible tragedy all around. If you could just see this broken and dejected man and his poor family . . . this guy is not going to do this again and there's no question he's going to suffer every day for the rest of his life.

Hurley said Chen had been isolated in jail because he speaks a rare Chinese dialect and had been beaten by other inmates. He said the children asked that their father be given probation, not jail, and that Chen had suffered remorse.

Also, the National Organization for Women said it intends to file a complaint with the State Commission on Judicial Conduct.

## *Assignments*

### A. Rural

Rural prosecutors infrequently have the heavy case load of violent crime that burdens the urban prosecutor. Interview a rural prosecutor about his or her cases. Has there been any change in their nature? Also, what are the prosecutor's personal ambitions? Many rural prosecutors see the job as a stepping stone to higher political office. Most are paid little, and the job can be held in association with a private practice. Are these generalities true of your interviewee?

### B. Urban

Accompany an urban prosecutor through a day in court. Keep precise track of what he or she faces by singling out some cases and following them. This is best done at arraignment, where the bulk of plea bargaining occurs. What is the prosecutor's case load? What does he or she see as the solution to the case load?

### C. Legal Aid

In most large cities, the court appoints lawyers for defendants unable to hire defense attorneys. The task is usually filled by the local legal aid organization. Interview a legal aid lawyer and follow the lawyer through a day's work on specific cases. Try to have the lawyer explain how he or she balances the case load. What are the lawyer's ambitions? Go into his or her background.

### D. Bankrupt

If there is a federal courthouse in your area, it will have a bankruptcy court, which you can visit. Find out the total individual and total business bankruptcies for the last full year and the preceding year. Why the increase or decrease?

How are bankruptcies handled? Give specific examples of cases and the settlements reached. (See *Workbook*, Chapter 23, **Community Projects:** *Broke.*)

### E. Selection

Sit in on a jury selection at a trial. Try to determine the type of juror the prosecutor and the defense attorney want to seat. At a recess or adjournment, interview each and try to draw portraits of the prosecutor's and the district attorney's views of the perfect juror for this case.

*F. Arraign*

Visit arraignment court. In large cities, an arraignment is a confusing and inaudible proceeding. You will have to make arrangements with the court clerk and, if possible, with the presiding judge for permission to sit close to the bench. In some communities, judges are allowed to have guests sit with them on the bench. Try to follow the main course of action and, when possible, examine one or two typical cases in detail to buttress your major conclusions about the process.

*G. Indict*

Determine what process of indictment your state uses: grand jury action or the information. Then follow a case through this process—through indictment or the handing up of an information.

*H. Reduce*

Obtain data of the number of felony arrests, felony indictments, sentences on felony pleas and trials in your city. This will give your reader an idea of the extent of plea bargaining.

*I. Trial*

It is possible to cover the high point of a trial: introductory statements of attorneys, a key witness's testimony, summaries of the attorneys, jury verdict or sentencing. Through reading of the daily newspaper, you may be able to learn when such events will occur in an interesting trial. Verify with the court clerk to avoid a wasted trip. Put the day's activities in context.

*J. Youthful*

Do a background story on family court or juvenile court. How many cases are on the docket each month? How does this compare with previous years? What kinds of offenses are most frequent? Make a table that shows the frequency of certain offenses. If possible, attend a session to see how the court works.

*K. Indigents*

In most cities, 60 percent or more of those arrested are unable to hire attorneys. How does your community, state or bar association handle this problem? Invite a representative of the system to speak to the class about it. Then do some reporting to find out whether the system is satisfactory to defendants, local attorneys, the bar association, judges, law professors.

*L. Bail*

What is the bail policy of the local court where defendants are arraigned? Some criminal courts release defendants on their own recognizance if they have jobs or a family. Others set bail, depending on the severity of the crime. There have been charges that some courts have bail policies that discriminate against members of minority groups. Make a study of actual cases over the past week.

*M. Bondsman*

Interview a local bail bondsman. What does this person do? How much does he or she charge? What happens when a person skips bail? In the last 10 years, how has the business changed, and why?

*N. Crowding*

In a number of cities and states, the courts have ordered that prisoners be given decent conditions in which to serve their sentences. This has led to early releases, and some see it as the beginning of the decriminalization of some crimes. Check the local situation. Are such crimes as marijuana possession and shoplifting decriminalized?

## *Campus Project*

*Binges*

The *Journal* of the American Medical Association reports that a study of 17,592 students on 140 campuses shows that 44 percent reported binge drinking, which is defined as having five drinks in a row for men and four for women on at least one occasion in the two weeks before the survey. (Women's bodies generally have a higher fat content than men's and, as a result, it takes women longer to metabolize alcohol, resulting in women being more affected by lesser amounts.)

One-fifth of all students (19 percent) were found to be frequent binge drinkers, defined as those having at least three binges during the two-week period. Some other results:

- Binge drinkers were seven times as likely to have unprotected sex as nonbinge drinkers.
- They were 10 times as likely to drive after drinking.
- They were 11 times as likely to fall behind in their schoolwork.
- About one-third of the colleges surveyed had more than 50 percent of students as binge drinkers; one-third had fewer than 35 percent.
- Residential colleges and those in the Northeast and North Central states had a higher rate of binge drinking.
- Women's and black colleges had a lower rate than other colleges.
- Sober students at the big drinking schools were twice as likely as binge drinkers to be assaulted and to be the victims of sexual advances from students who had been drinking.
- Few students sought help for their drinking problems.

Do a similar study and reach conclusions about drinking on your campus. Has the school any program for informing students about drinking, any special treatment or counseling program for heavy drinkers? Find someone on campus to comment on this statement by Henry Wechsler, director of the Alcohol Studies Program at the Harvard School of Public Health:

Students on campuses where there's a lot of binge drinking are affected in a number of ways—including physical assault, sexual harassment, property damage and interrupted sleep or study time.

## Community Projects

### A. White Collar

Sentence inequities have been demonstrated by journalists in a number of cities: light treatment of white-collar crime committed by middle-class managerial types, heavy sentences for low-income and minority defendants accused of theft or larceny. Obtain court documents and interview lawyers, judges, probation workers, court clerks. Can you find any pattern in sentencing?

### B. Plea Bargain

Most cities encourage defendants to plead guilty in return for lesser charges. The arrangement is known as plea bargaining and affects 70 to 85 percent of all criminal cases in large cities. The arrangement is the result of the huge increase in criminal cases and the effect on the criminal justice system.

Without plea bargaining, say some legal experts, the system would be overwhelmed. But critics say it puts criminals back on the streets too soon. One district attorney decided to eliminate plea bargaining and in doing so voiced a belief held by police and many in the public. Plea bargaining, he said, "means that society has ceded control to those it has accused of violating its laws. And it means that our system is running us and not the other way around."

In reply, a criminal court judge said, "Plea negotiations are as vital to the system as breathing and eating and sleeping are for human survival. You have a limited number of tax dollars. You can't build a courthouse as big as the Triborough Bridge, manned by half the population of the Bronx to try the other half of the Bronx."

A civil rights lawyer said the elimination of plea bargaining has been considered by many cities and states but is in effect in few jurisdictions. Plea bargains, he continued, are "the aspect of the judicial system which most undermines confidence in it. People feel that their representative, the public prosecutor, has given in and the defendant has gotten a good deal."

Examine the situation in your city. What percentage of cases are plea bargained? Interview judges, police officers, lawyers and others for an article on how the system works locally and what its effects are.

### C. Execution

At any one time, there are about 2,700 convicts on death row in the nation's state penitentiaries. The record number of executions in a single year occurred in 1935 when 199 persons were executed. Watt Espy, a historian of capital punishment, estimates that the number of executions will reach 300 a year by the turn of the century.

Espy says that 200 to 300 men and women are added to death house cells each year. He believes that there is "a danger that you can have a quiet bloodbath which the people won't even notice as executions become more common and less newsworthy."

Thirty-six states and the federal government permit the death penalty, 22 of them and the federal government allowing death by lethal injection. Additional states are considering adding execution to their penal codes.

"Study after study shows retribution is behind the push for capital punishment," says Kica Matos, research director for the Capital Punishment Project of the NAACP's Legal Defense and Educational Fund.

Advocates contend that the death penalty acts as a deterrent to crime. The United States and South Africa are the only industrialized nations that have not abolished capital punishment.

Studies have demonstrated that a disproportionate number of black defendants have been sentenced to death, and some opponents of the death penalty contend that racism is a powerful factor underlying pro–death-penalty arguments. Espy, who has documented 18,482 executions in the United States since 1608, cited a headline written some 75 years ago to illustrate the powerful emotional elements in the argument:

Black Fiend Hanged<br>Jerked to Jesus

Make a survey in your city of how people feel about capital punishment and its use in your state. If there is such a law, is there any move to repeal it? If there is no such law, are there advocates of its adoption?

## Home Assignment

### Graffiti

On the opposite page is a court document. Write a 300-word story.

## Class Discussion

### A. Family Court

What are the pros and cons of opening family or juvenile court to the public, which includes the press? Some proposals call for open court but a prohibition on using the names of juvenile offenders. The courts have ruled that the press can use the names of juvenile offenders if reporters can obtain them, but most courts are closed and deal harshly with those who disclose names of juvenile offenders. Most newspapers will refuse to use the names but make exceptions in unusual cases or when a competitor has disclosed an identity.

You might invite to class a juvenile court judge, a social worker or an attorney who handles such cases.

### B. Harassment

You receive the following press release from the office of Mayor Sam Parnass:

> Mayor Sam Parnass and the Human Rights Commission Director, Stanley Downey, announced today the settlement of a sexual harassment case involving a young Freeport proofreader who worked for the Freeport Press Corporation.
>
> In the settlement, the corporation agreed to pay the complainant "Jane Doe" a total of $44,200.
>
> In a complaint filed in 1995, a woman in her teens charged that from her first day of employment at Freeport Press, three male employees—Anthony Blount, Donald Trump and Henry Morton—sexually harassed her. The harassment allegedly included obscene jokes and sexist remarks about her and other female employees. The complainant specifically charged that Blount, a typesetter and assistant supervisor, fondled her, touched her hair with his face and brushed against her.
>
> Mayor Parnass said, "There is no such thing as an 'okay' amount of sexual harassment or discrimination. It is incumbent on employers to keep their workplaces free of these egregious behaviors and to treat their employees' concerns about them seriously.
>
> "Unwarranted sexual advances, sexist statements and derogatory comments based on one's gender are simply unacceptable. If employers lack the resolve to prohibit these practices from the workplace or to respond vigorously when they appear, the city will step in, as we have in this instance, to make sure the proper protections are afforded to Freeport workers."
>
> Human Rights Commission Director Downey said, "Many women who find themselves subjected to sexist remarks and lewd behavior at work are unsure of what to do for fear of losing their jobs. This courageous woman took action and brought her case to the Commission on Human Rights. While I'm sure no amount of money would make up for this reprehensible and illegal sexual harassment, this settlement from this company sends a message to employers that they must not discriminate and that they are responsible for the behavior of their supervisors and employees."
>
> The complainant also alleged that her own efforts to address the situation through her supervisor led to public ridicule by the male management. A requested transfer to another shift and a formal complaint filed with the Special Project and Art Composition Room Manager were unsuccessful. Finally, in August 1992, after a conflict with her supervisor, the complainant became emotionally upset and went home sick. The next day she was terminated. (*Continued on Page 196.*)

**DISTRICT COURT OF FREEPORT**

The City of Freeport
    —Plaintiff
  —against—
Paul Godfrey and Claudine Godfrey
    —Defendants

Complaint: 416-CH

Plaintiff, by its attorney, Paul Robinson of the City of Freeport, respectfully alleges upon information and belief:

1. Plaintiff City of Freeport is a municipal corporation organized and existing under state laws.
2. Defendant Paul Godfrey resides at 870 Blue Ridge Rd., Freeport.
3. Defendant Claudine Godfrey is the mother of defendant Paul Godfrey, and resides at the same address.
4. The City owns a part of the city overpass at U.S. 81 and State Highway 166.
5. The City is responsible for maintaining the highways within its boundaries, including the overpass. In fulfillment of that responsibility, the City, acting through its Department of Transportation, removes graffiti from the retaining walls of the overpass.
6. On or about the night of July 6, defendant Paul Godfrey willfully, maliciously, and unlawfully damaged the walls of the overpass by spray-painting his nickname, or "tag," consisting of the name "REAL," on those walls.
7. By reason of the foregoing acts of trespass, plaintiff has sustained damages for the costs of materials, supplies, and labor expended by plaintiff to remove the graffiti from the overpass.

### First Cause of Action

8. The acts of defendant Paul Godfrey constitute a trespass, and Paul Godfrey is liable to the City for the damages to City property resulting from those actions.
9. Because the actions of defendant Paul Godfrey were unlawful, willful, and wanton, and were undertaken with the intention of damaging public property, Godfrey is liable for punitive damages in addition to whatever compensatory damages may be awarded.

### Second Cause of Action

10. The foregoing acts subject defendant Paul Godfrey to the penalties of State Highway Law § 320, which provides that "[w]hoever shall injure any highway or bridge maintained at the public expense . . . shall for every such offense forfeit treble damages."

### Third Cause of Action

11. Paul Godfrey is a minor over the age of ten and under the age of eighteen, and lives in the custody of his mother, defendant Claudine Godfrey.
12. Under State General Municipal Law § 78-a, defendant Claudine Godfrey is liable for up to $2,500 of the damages caused by defendant Paul Godfrey.

WHEREFORE the plaintiff demands judgment against the defendants as follows:

a) On the first cause of action, against Paul Godfrey, compensatory and punitive damages resulting from trespass, or, in the alternative, restitution;

b) On the second cause of action, against Paul Godfrey, treble damages for injuries to the highway;

c) On the third cause of action, against Claudine Godfrey, damages up to $2,500, or, in the alternative, restitution, for damages to City property;

Together with the costs and disbursements of this action and such further relief as is just and proper.

Dated: August 4

Paul Robinson
District Attorney,
The City of Freeport,
Attorney for the Plaintiff

(**Note**—Paul Godfrey is 16 years old.)

*Continued*—Freeport Press has agreed to adopt and distribute a sexual harassment policy to all employees and conspicuously place posters outlining the new procedures for handling sexual harassment complaints. The company agreed to conduct special sensitivity training programs for all its supervisors and employees. Additionally, the firm agreed that the supervisory personnel responsible for enforcing the policy would have to attend an initial training session and be reviewed regularly.

Joseph Finnegan was the prosecutor for the Commission's Law Enforcement Bureau, and Pamela Bell represented the complainant.

\* \* \* \* \*

You dig into this case, the first sexual harassment settlement in Freeport, and you learn that the "Jane Doe" is Sandra Begley, 17-year-old daughter of the city clerk.

1. Do you use her name in the story?
2. Do you use the names of the three employees who are named in the press release?
3. How much space or time would you give this story, and where in the newspaper or on a local news broadcast would you place this item?

## DB/CAR

### A. Rape

Considerable debate developed after *The Des Moines Register* ran a lengthy series about the experiences of a rape victim who identified herself. The newspaper editor said that newspaper silence about sex crimes should be lifted, but few newspapers have agreed to identify victims without their consent.

Make a check of the pros and cons in this discussion and summarize them in a feature or an interpretative column of no more than 700 words.

### B. SLAPP

Free speech in the United States has a price tag. Although the Constitution guarantees the right to speak out, Americans are being sued because they have voiced their opinions.

People who have opposed developers building housing atop a community's drinking supply have been sued by the developer. A California pediatrician who warned against drinking raw milk was sued for $110 million by a raw milk producer. The Sierra Club and some members who opposed a timber cutting proposal to a federal agency were sued for $11 million.

These cases are described with the acronym SLAPP, for Strategic Lawsuit Against Public Participation. The suits are designed to stifle public debate through intimidation, say legal experts. Often, the plaintiffs do not care whether the case goes to court, only that it silences critics. The National Science Foundation funded a study of these suits.

Make a database search for material about SLAPP and write a 350-word story based on the material and interviews.

## Skill Drill: Court Terms

Define or explain the following terms:

1. Appellant
2. Arraignment
3. Bail bondsman
4. Character witness
5. Felony
6. Cross-examination
7. Directed verdict
8. Dismissal for cause (of a juror)
9. Dissenting opinion
10. Indeterminate sentence
11. Indictment
12. Mistrial
13. Peremptory challenge (of a juror)

14. Plaintiff
15. Plea bargaining
16. Preliminary injunction
17. Probation
18. Rebuttal
19. True bill
20. Waiver of immunity

## Test VI: Usage

Choose the correct answer.

1. We don't know what **(a) affect (b) effect** the strike will have on production.
2. Yesterday he **(a) lay (b) laid** down for a nap.
3. This medicine has **(a) proved (b) proven** successful in curing hypertension.
4. This shirt has one of **(a) it's (b) its** buttons missing.
5. Salem is Oregon's **(a) capital (b) capitol.**
6. Today America has **(a) fewer (b) less** farmers than it did 25 years ago.
7. The killer will be **(a) hung (b) hanged** tomorrow at sunrise.
8. In a crowd Mary is quite **(a) reluctant (b) reticent,** but in a small group she is outspoken.
9. I **(a) imply (b) infer** from your comments that you consider me guilty.
10. The enrollment dropped **(a) due to (b) because of** rising tuition.
11. **(a) Can (b) May** I be excused to go to dinner?
12. The salad is **(a) comprised of (b) composed of** tomatoes, lettuce and celery.
13. We **(a) convinced (b) persuaded** the coach to use a different offense.
14. The senators bitterly differed **(a) from (b) with** each other during the debate.
15. **(a) Hopefully, (b) I hope** the package will arrive today.

# 22 Sports

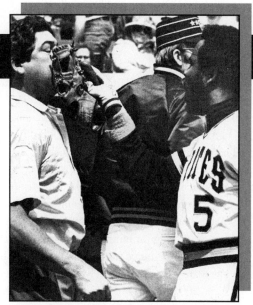

Robert J. Pavuchak, *The Pittsburgh Press.*

**"He's safe? In your face."**

### Introduction

The largest single department on most newspapers is the sports department, a reflection of reader interest in spectator sports. The growth of big-time sports—collegiate as well as professional—has created an audience in almost every city for intense coverage of basketball, football and baseball. Even hockey has expanded to areas that have never seen an ice-covered pond. Sports coverage is best when it is objective, when the reporter is not a home-team rooter. As television coverage expands, newspaper accounts increasingly emphasize the game's turning points, strategy and after-the-game comments over a running account of scoring.

## Exercises

### A. Runner

Here are some notes from an interview with Arthur Baron, a biology major, who is a member of the Mallory College cross-country team that returned two days ago from finishing fourth at the NCAA Division III meet at Franklin Park in Boston. Baron finished 11th—considered a good finish—and this is the second time he has been in the top 25 in the annual meet. The newspaper has run a story on the meet. You are to do an interview. Here are your notes:

> Baron is 5'11", weighs 150, has brown hair, wears glasses.
> Runs 20 miles a day—twice what most run—seven days a week in summer, lifts weights and swims as part of his training. In winter, runs at least 10 miles a day unless snowbound. Yesterday, the day after returning from Boston, he did seven miles of road work at a minus 20 degree temperature.
> Baron says his coach, Steve Helmer, tries to develop internal motivation among the runners:
>
>> It's unlike high school where everything has a rigid schedule. Steve is more oriented to the athlete than the program. You're given credit for being able to think.
>> At other schools, win-oriented coaches burn out their athletes. At some schools, the runners put in twice as much road work, but there is a point of diminishing returns.
>> We have no athletic scholarships here, and there is no physical education major. None of us who ran in Boston came here to be athletes. We're here for the academic program. The coach knows that the Big Ten and other big conferences attract athletes. But running, the coach says, 'is for intrinsic reasons, not money.'
>
> Asked about the success of the team despite the small size of the school and its lack of scholarships, Baron says the team uses a tactic called "pack running." Instead of each running his race, the four stay together until the last mile. The effect on other teams is demoralizing, particularly when the four run in front, as they try to do.
> "I could possibly run faster times away from the pack on my own, but there is a mental strain to running in front all alone. Also, the feeling of running with your team can cause you to beat a better runner.
> Baron is thinking of studying medicine. The other three are going into science-related fields, physics, chemistry and biology.
> A call to Helmer turns up the following information:
>
>> Cross-country runners are highly disciplined and demand top performance of themselves. If there is a problem, it is that they do train to excess. They are very demanding.
>> Cross-country runners in this country tend to come from the middle and upper classes and are good students, whereas the sprinters often are from less affluent homes. The situation in Egypt, where I spent a year, is reversed. There the military officers are the sprinters; the laboring class provides the long distance runners.

Write 400 to 450 words.

### B. Trade

Willie Suarez, an outfielder with the local professional baseball team, the Red Sox, has been complaining about playing in the northern climate and has asked to be traded. He has played three seasons in Philadelphia and one season in windswept Candlestick Park in San Francisco. He is 28 and from Puerto Rico.

"Last season, my first season here, I felt the weather bad," he said in an interview last week. However, he batted .310 and drove in 101 runs. This year, after 50 games, almost one-third of the season, he has 20 runs batted in and is hitting .274.

This afternoon, you have a call from the Sox front office. The management decided to trade Suarez to the Braves in Atlanta. They received in return Dave Martin, a utility infielder batting .246, and a reserve outfielder, George White, batting .265.

You say you don't think the team received very much.

"Well, you might say we weren't getting very much from Willie either, and since he wouldn't play in cool areas, there wasn't much bidding for him. He's got great potential, but he'll kill his career with this kind of attitude."

Your ball club source says he can't be quoted by name but you can use the fact that it came from a person "close to the club."

The team is in fourth place, 12 games out of first.

Write 200 to 250 words, preferably with a delayed lead and a feature touch.

## C. Reds-Braves

Here are the lineups and an inning-by-inning account of a baseball game between the Reds and the Braves. The Braves lead the Reds by two games for the division leadership before the game. Lemon is a left-hander, Katz a right-hander. Katz, 7-4, has lost two games to the Braves this year. Lemon, 11-3, has never faced the Reds. It is midseason. There is no need to identify the teams any further or to place them in any league. (You could place them in the Western Division of the National League in a game between the Cincinnati Reds and the Atlanta Braves.)

First, devise the box score. Next, write a 400-word story for the morning newspaper. This is an evening game played in the Reds' hometown, your town.

### Lineups

| Braves | Reds |
|---|---|
| Bumiller, Ernie cf | Eddings, Bobby ss |
| Vorobil, Maury ss | Manoff, Stan lf |
| Weiner, Tommy rf | Douge, Harry 3b |
| Wallis, Mike lf | Cruz, Al 1b |
| Hand, Denny 3b | Marwell, Chuck c |
| Sherman, Gene 1b | Gougeon, John cf |
| Day, Karl c | Kelso, Jack 2b |
| Weir, Rick 2b | Barrett, Eddie rf |
| Lemon, Carl p | Katz, Art p |

### Play by Play

**1st inning**

*Braves:* Bumiller walks on five pitches. Vorobil hits a 3-1 count to center-field wall; Gougeon makes putout. Weiner hits first pitch to center field for single. Bumiller goes to third. Wallis hits into double play, Eddings-Kelso-Cruz.

*Reds:* Eddings grounds out, Lemon to Sherman. Manoff looks at third strike. Douge flies out to Wallis.

**2nd inning**

*Braves:* Hand takes first when Kelso bobbles grounder. Sherman strikes out. Day singles to center, Hand going to third. Weir pops to Cruz. Lemon swings at and misses three pitches.

*Reds:* Cruz grounds out, Weir to Sherman. Marwell flies out to Weiner. Gougeon grounds out, Hand-Sherman.

**3rd inning**

*Braves:* Bumiller flies to Manoff. Vorobil singles to center. On one-one count to Weiner, Vorobil out trying to steal second. Weiner pops to Cruz.

*Reds:* Kelso fouls out to Day. Barrett hits 3-0 pitch to center-field wall for double. Katz grounds out, Sherman unassisted, Barrett taking third. Eddings flies to Weiner.

**4th inning**

*Braves:* Wallis grounds to deep short and is safe on close play. Reds Manager Bordewich argues to no avail. Hand bunts Wallis to second, Douge throwing Hand out at first. Sherman grounds out, Kelso to Cruz. Wallis goes, taking third. Day strikes out on four pitches.

*Reds:* Manoff hits first pitch into left-field stands for a home run, his 15th of the season, his 76th RBI. Douge grounds out, Vorobil to Sherman. Cruz pops to Hand. Marwell flies out to Wallis.

**5th inning**

*Braves:* Weir singles on ground over second. Lemon sacrifice bunts Weir to second, Cruz to Kelso covering first. Bumiller tops pitch that dribbles toward third, and everyone is safe, Weir on third, Bumiller on first. Vorobil hits first pitch to deep center, Gougeon making catch. Throw to plate too late to catch Weir. Weiner grounds out, Eddings to Cruz.

*Reds:* Gougeon hit on ankle by pitch, takes first. Kelso, trying to bunt, pops to pitcher who doubles Gougeon off first. Barrett flies to Weiner.

**6th inning**

*Braves:* Wallis walks and steals second on 2-1 pitch to Hand, who then pops to Eddings. Sherman grounds out Kelso to Cruz. Day hits grounder past first, Barrett throwing Wallis out at plate on close call that Wallis protests vehemently. He is warned by plate umpire.

*Reds:* Katz grounds to Sherman unassisted. Eddings flies out to Hand in foul territory. Manoff grounds out Weir to Sherman.

**7th inning**

*Braves:* Weir grounds out Eddings to Cruz. Lemon strikes out. Bumiller singles to left. Vorobil forces Bumiller, Eddings to Kelso.

*Reds:* Douge walks on five pitches. Cruz singles to left, Douge going to second. Marwell hits into double play, Vorobil-Weir-Sherman, Douge taking third. Gougeon pops into center, the ball dropping in front of Bumiller, Douge scoring on the single. Kelso forces Gougeon, Weir stepping on second unassisted.

**8th inning**

*Braves:* Weiner flies to Barrett. Wallis doubles down first-base line. Hand grounds out Douge to Cruz, Wallis remaining on second. Count goes to 3-0 on Sherman, and Marwell goes out to talk to Katz. Calls trainer who examines Katz's hand. Blister is developing. But Katz says he is OK. (He has not pitched a complete game this year.) Sherman walks. Day grounds to third, Douge stepping on bag, forcing Wallis.

*Reds:* Barrett flies out to Bumiller. Katz looks at three strikes, never lifting bat off shoulder, apparently unwilling to put stress on pitching finger with blister. Eddings flies out to Weiner.

**9th inning**

*Braves:* Weir hits 3-2 pitch into center for a single. Ahearn pinch hits for Lemon; infield expects him to bunt. Ahearn swings at first pitch and it narrowly misses being fair past first. Infield drops back. Ahearn then bunts toward third and beats throw to first. Reds manager goes out for mound conference, leaves Katz in. Bumiller hits line drive to Kelso, who makes sideways leaping catch. Runners stay put. Vorobil hits into game-ending double play around the horn, Douge throwing to Kelso for the out at second and on to first.

The game took two hours and four minutes, and the attendance was 16,069 paid.

## D. Loser

You cover the local team, the Red Sox, and it has just lost 2-0 to the Twins in an afternoon game. The winning pitcher was Randy Jones, the loser Bob Pierce. The Sox got six hits, the Twins 10 off Pierce. The winning runs were scored in the fourth on a base on balls to Marty Balzer and successive doubles by Gene Mica and Tom Kemper.

You interview Ted Schmidt, the Sox leading hitter, after the game, who went nothing for four and struck out twice.

"I can't recall striking out twice in a game in my life in this league," he says. "But I did." He kicks his locker. "If I were a pitcher I'd be embarrassed to go to the mound with the kind of stuff Jones has. A nothing pitcher. Nothing."

You then talk to the Sox manager, Danny Appel, and you ask him about Jones. "A helluva pitcher. He's won 12 games and the season's one-third old. A lot of the guys say he's a nothing pitcher, but what you need to stay alive in this league is control and pinpoint pitching. The guys who have a lot of stuff but can't get it over the plate bomb out fast."

"Just between us, Schmidt had a bad day and was bitching. Heck, I'd give anyone on my team for Jones. The guy's worth a sure pennant to any contending team."

Jones is now 12-2 and Pierce is 6-5. The leading team in the league, the Athletics, lost a game in the standings to the Twins by losing 5-3 to the Rangers and the Twins now trail the Athletics by two games.

Write a game story with a feature lead for a morning newspaper.

## E. Racism

Here are excerpts from an interview with Linda Greene, professor of law at the University of Wisconsin and a specialist in sports-related civil rights issues:

> Baseball is not the only sport, or institution, to adhere to the unstated rule that African-Americans should not exercise power over whites. But with so few management positions in baseball being held by members of minority groups, it is even more obvious here that African-Americans crash into the glass ceiling when what's at stake is authority and power in relation to their white counterparts. . . .

Bob Thayer, *The Journal-Bulletin.*

**High slide . . . relay to first . . . double play.**

This controversy is not about racism that is personal, but rather racism that is institutional. The owners must acknowledge that they inherited an institution with a long history of racially discriminatory behavior that will not be eradicated by business as usual. The business as usual *is* racism. New business practices must be instituted.

There are concrete ways to do this. Why not agree to a time frame within which the sport must achieve a significant number—to be defined—of African-American coaches and managers? Why not agree to approve ownership bids on a basis of a history of demonstrated commitment to equal opportunity? . . .

. . . racism is currently reflected in the failure to meaningfully incorporate African-Americans in coaching, management and front-office positions. . . .

Write 300 words.

## F. Probation

Here is a news release distributed by the National Collegiate Athletic Association. Although the violations occurred in the 1990–91 and 1991–92 academic years, the NCAA has just completed its investigation. Write a 400-word story for a San Francisco newspaper.

FOR IMMEDIATE RELEASE  
Tuesday, February 15

CONTACT:  
Kathryn M. Reith  
Director of Public Information

*SAN FRANCISCO STATE RECEIVES THREE-YEAR PROBATION*  
*FOR ELIGIBILITY VIOLATIONS*

OVERLAND PARK, KANSAS—The NCAA Committee on Infractions has placed the athletics program at San Francisco State University on probation for three years for violations of NCAA legislation concerning the eligibility of student-athletes. San Francisco State allowed the participation of 27 student-athletes in eight sports who had not met satisfactory academic-progress requirements.

The violations took place during the 1990–91 and 1991–92 academic years. The men's sports involved were baseball, football, soccer, swimming, track and field and wrestling. The women's sports involved were basketball and track and field.

The case was handled under the summary disposition procedures, which the institution and the NCAA enforcement staff can agree to follow in major infractions cases. This process may be used if the member institution, involved individuals and NCAA enforcement staff agree on the facts and that those facts constitute violations of NCAA legislation. The institution proposes suggested penalties, which the Committee on Infractions can accept, reject or change.

The committee adopted the following sanctions as proposed by San Francisco State:

- Prohibiting postseason competition for one year in all sports in which ineligible student-athletes participated.
- Vacating team records in all sports in which ineligible student-athletes competed during the 1991–92 academic year.
- Forfeiting two football games.
- Recertifying current athletics policies and practices.
- Reprimand and censure of the university's athletics program.
- Letter of admonition to the director of athletics.

The committee imposed two penalties in addition to those suggested by San Francisco State. Those penalties were an extension of the university's proposed two-year probation to three years and a requirement for the continued development and implementation of the institution's comprehensive educational program for athletics.

The committee found NCAA rules violations including:

- San Francisco State counted credit hours in remedial, tutorial or noncredit courses taken during an academic year other than the students' first year of college.
- San Francisco State counted repeated courses above the allowable number.
- San Francisco State mistakenly used more than the permitted 70 transferable credit hours.
- San Francisco State used credit hours that cannot be applied to the students' designated degree program.
- A lack of institutional control also was found.

The committee's findings normally would subject the institution to minimum penalties prescribed by the NCAA membership for major violations. These penalties include a two-year probationary period, elimination of expense-paid recruiting visits for one year, elimination of off-campus recruiting for one year, possible termination of the employment of all staff members who condoned the violations and the loss of postseason competition and television opportunities for one year.

The NCAA membership has, though, given the committee the authority to impose lesser penalties if it determines that the case is unique. The committee concluded that this case was unique because:

- the institution conducted a complete and thorough investigation of possible violations;
- the institution cooperated in the processing of the case, and
- the institution initiated numerous corrective actions.

The corrective actions that San Francisco State took were:

- Implementing a new advising format.
- Instituting new procedures for monitoring the academic progress of student-athletes.
- Improving the education component of orientation for student-athletes.
- Eliminating physical education activity classes from satisfactory-progress calculations.

San Francisco State University admitted the violation of NCAA rules under the summary disposition procedures, accepted the penalties proposed by the Committee on Infractions and waived its opportunity to appeal. The members of the Committee on Infractions who heard this case are Richard J. Dunn, associate dean of the College of Arts and Sciences at the University of Washington; Jack Friedenthal, dean of the school of law at George Washington University; Roy F. Kramer, commissioner of the Southeastern Conference; James L. Richmond, retired judge and attorney; Yvonne (Bonnie) L. Slatton, chair of the department of sports studies at the University of Iowa; and committee chair David Swank, professor of law at the University of Oklahoma.

A copy of the complete report from the Committee on Infractions is attached.
KMR:jmq

## G. Players

Here are the rankings of the colleges and universities that have sent players to the National Football League. Write a 450-word sports page column.

| College | NFL Players | College | Players |
| --- | --- | --- | --- |
| Southern California | 38 | Oregon | 8 |
| Notre Dame | 34 | Wisconsin | 8 |
| Miami | 30 | Hawaii | 7 |
| UCLA | 29 | Minnesota | 7 |
| Tennessee | 27 | Nevada-Reno | 7 |
| Ohio State | 24 | Virginia Tech | 7 |
| Washington | 24 | South Carolina | 7 |
| Florida State | 23 | Tennessee State | 7 |
| Penn State | 23 | Tulane | 7 |
| Colorado | 22 | Florida A&M | 6 |
| Texas A&M | 22 | Jackson State | 6 |
| Auburn | 21 | Memphis State | 6 |
| Florida | 21 | Rutgers | 6 |
| Michigan | 21 | Temple | 6 |
| Pittsburgh | 20 | Texas A & M-Kingsville | 6 |
| Alabama | 18 | Alcorn State | 5 |
| Georgia | 17 | East Carolina | 5 |
| North Carolina | 17 | Kansas | 5 |
| Clemson | 16 | Middle Tennessee | 5 |
| Louisiana State | 16 | Mississippi State | 5 |
| Nebraska | 16 | Missouri | 5 |
| Michigan State | 15 | Nevada-Las Vegas | 5 |
| Stanford | 15 | Oklahoma State | 5 |
| Syracuse | 15 | Southern Mississippi | 5 |
| California | 14 | Southern | 5 |
| Illinois | 13 | Western Carolina | 5 |
| North Carolina State | 13 | Wake Forest | 5 |
| Texas | 13 | Texas Tech | 5 |
| Virginia | 13 | Toledo | 5 |
| Arizona | 12 | Alabama State | 4 |
| Arizona State | 12 | Appalachian State | 4 |
| Baylor | 12 | Mississippi Valley | 4 |
| Iowa | 12 | Eastern Kentucky | 4 |
| Louisville | 12 | Idaho | 4 |
| Mississippi | 12 | Iowa State | 4 |
| Boston College | 11 | New Mexico | 4 |
| Georgia Tech | 11 | N.W. Louisiana | 4 |
| Houston | 11 | Pittsburg, Kan. | 4 |
| Indiana | 11 | San Jose State | 4 |
| Kentucky | 11 | South Carolina State | 4 |
| Purdue | 11 | Southern Methodist | 4 |
| Maryland | 10 | Texas A&I | 4 |
| Oklahoma | 10 | Western Illinois | 4 |
| Washington State | 10 | Texas-El Paso | 4 |
| West Virginia | 10 | Arkansas State | 3 |
| Fresno State | 9 | Ball State | 3 |
| Grambling | 9 | Carson-Newman | 3 |
| Louisiana Tech | 9 | Cincinnati | 3 |
| San Diego State | 9 | Duke | 3 |
| Arkansas | 8 | Eastern Washington | 3 |
| Brigham Young | 8 | James Madison | 3 |
| N.E. Louisiana | 8 | Kansas State | 3 |
| Northwestern | 8 | Kent State | 3 |
| Ohio Wesleyan | 8 | Northern Arizona | 3 |

| College | Players | College | Players |
|---|---|---|---|
| Northern Iowa | 3 | Chadron, Neb. | 1 |
| Northern Michigan | 3 | Citadel | 1 |
| Oregon State | 3 | Clark Atlanta | 1 |
| Rice | 3 | Connecticut | 1 |
| S.W. Louisiana | 3 | Dartmouth | 1 |
| Tulsa | 3 | Delaware | 1 |
| Utah State | 3 | Delaware State | 1 |
| Vanderbilt | 3 | Delta State | 1 |
| Western Michigan | 3 | East Texas State | 1 |
| Winston Salem | 3 | Eastern New Mexico | 1 |
| Albany State, Ga. | 2 | Emporia State | 1 |
| Cal State-Fullerton | 2 | Evangel | 1 |
| Cal State-Long Beach | 2 | Ferris State | 1 |
| Cal State-Sacramento | 2 | Ferrum, Va. | 1 |
| Central Arkansas | 2 | Ft. Hays State | 1 |
| Central Florida | 2 | Gardner-Webb | 1 |
| Central State, Ohio | 2 | Georgia Southern | 1 |
| Cheyney, Penn. | 2 | Graceland | 1 |
| Colgate | 2 | Grand Valley State | 1 |
| Colorado State | 2 | Holy Cross | 1 |
| Eastern Illinois | 2 | Idaho State | 1 |
| Ft. Valley State | 2 | Jacksonville State | 1 |
| Hampton | 2 | Kutztown, Penn. | 1 |
| Howard | 2 | La Crosse, Wis. | 1 |
| Illinois State | 2 | Lenoir-Rhyne | 1 |
| Indiana State | 2 | Livingstone | 1 |
| Liberty | 2 | Marshall | 1 |
| Maine | 2 | McNeese State | 1 |
| Montana | 2 | Mesa, Colo. | 1 |
| Montana State | 2 | Millikin | 1 |
| New Hampshire | 2 | Milton, Wis. | 1 |
| New Mexico State | 2 | Mississippi College | 1 |
| North Dakota State | 2 | Montclair State | 1 |
| Oregon Tech | 2 | North Carolina Central | 1 |
| Pacific | 2 | N.E. Missouri | 1 |
| Pennsylvania | 2 | N.E. Oklahoma | 1 |
| Stephen F. Austin | 2 | Navy | 1 |
| Sam Houston State | 2 | Nebraska Wesleyan | 1 |
| Towson State | 2 | New Haven | 1 |
| Valdosta State | 2 | Nicholls State | 1 |
| West Chester, Penn. | 2 | North Alabama | 1 |
| William & Mary | 2 | North Texas | 1 |
| Air Force | 1 | Northeastern | 1 |
| Akron | 1 | Northern Illinois | 1 |
| Alabama A&M | 1 | Ohio Northern | 1 |
| Angelo State | 1 | Portland State | 1 |
| Augustana, S.D. | 1 | Princeton | 1 |
| Bloomsburg, Penn. | 1 | S.W. Texas State | 1 |
| Boise State | 1 | Santa Clara | 1 |
| Boston University | 1 | Savannah State | 1 |
| Bowling Green | 1 | Sioux Falls, S.D. | 1 |
| Bucknell | 1 | Sonoma State | 1 |
| Cameron, Okla. | 1 | South Dakota State | 1 |
| Central Oklahoma | 1 | Southern Illinois | 1 |

| College | Players | College | Players |
|---|---|---|---|
| Texas Southern | 1 | Wayne State, Neb. | 1 |
| Texas-Arlington | 1 | Weber State | 1 |
| Utah | 1 | Wesleyan | 1 |
| Virginia State | 1 | West Texas State | 1 |
| Virginia Union | 1 | Wichita State | 1 |
| Wabash | 1 | Wyoming | 1 |

## Assignments

### A. Links

Go to the local golf course and chat with players and the people running the golf shop. Who are the best golfers in town, the man, the woman and the youngster? Try to interview one of them for a profile. Is the person a Sunday golfer or a regular player? How did the golfer start to play? How much of a handicap do competitors have to be given?

### B. Bowler

Make the rounds of the local bowling lanes and find a league in which there are some good bowlers. Then go out one night when one of the good teams is bowling. Do a story on the players, personalizing the match if possible.

### C. Minor

Many high school and college sports do not have the spectator appeal of basketball and football, but the participants enjoy them and there are vociferous and steady fans. Do a profile of one of these sports by interviewing the coach, players and fans: tennis, crew, swimming, cross country, field events (track), wrestling, fencing, soccer, golf, field hockey, rugby, lacrosse, squash, ice hockey.

### D. Ambition

Interview one of the prominent players on the local college or university team about his or her ambitions; continued amateur play or professional status; the driving force behind his or her desire to play; the help of coaches; the relationship of athletics and studies.

### E. Spectator

Are most students spectators, or do they work out regularly? Are students exercising sufficiently for good health? Have they embarked on exercises and sports that will engage them for their active lives, or are they playing sports that they will have to drop after they graduate?

## Campus Project

### Coverage

Cover a game or a meet on campus. Give yourself 90 minutes to write the story after the game. If no game is available, cover one on television.

## Community Project

### Fitness

Is the community aware of the need to provide facilities for residents who want to stay fit? Some communities have paths for walkers and bicyclists. Some have jogging areas, and some have set aside an area with equipment for aerobic exercises. Make a check of what is available and its use. Interview local doctors about what they consider the fitness level of local residents.

## Home Assignment

### Graduates

College athletic departments are now required to disclose the graduation rates of student athletes. This follows what many consider a shameful period of recruiting students with little or no ability to do college work, exploitating them and then dumping them.

Colleges and universities maintained the eligibility of illiterate athletes with fake grades and nonacademic courses. Some were kept around long enough to play two or three years. The most victimized, critics said, were black athletes. At Memphis State University, for example, over a 12-year period, only four of 38 varsity basketball players graduated, none of them black.

Round up the data on graduation rates of athletes of the schools in your college's or university's conference, including your school. Make a list by sport. If you can, make a graph to illustrate your findings and accompany your story.

## Class Discussion

### A. Reds and Howard

Three of the most influential sports journalists of the last 50 years were Red Barber, Red Smith and Howard Cosell. Barber was an announcer for baseball teams around the country, and Smith was a sports writer for New York City newspapers. Cosell was a broadcaster best known for "Monday Night Football." Examine the files through a database search or through reference works for background on the three and prepare a summary of their attributes that modern sports writers might want to emulate.

They were noted for their fairness and integrity. Barber left his job as announcer for Dodger games when the team moved from Brooklyn to Los Angeles and the team owner urged Barber to lend vocal support to the team in his announcing. Later, when he was broadcasting Yankee games, he reported that the last place team had drawn a total of 413 fans. The owners fired him for this embarrassing truth.

Smith always warned young sports writers never to root for the teams they covered, and he was a firm believer in keeping superlatives out of his copy. Cosell "entered sports broadcasting in the mid-1950s, when the predominant style was unabashed adulation," *The New York Times* said in its obituary of Cosell. "Mr. Cosell offered a brassy counterpoint that was first ridiculed, then copied until it became a dominant note of sports broadcasting."

### B. Millionaires

Who are the highest-paid athletes in major sports? Compare their salaries today with the highest salaries a decade ago. Baseball and basketball salaries in excess of $1 million are common now. How many million-dollar players were there 10 years ago? Write 300 to 350 words.

## Skill Drill: Sports Vocabulary

Briefly define, describe, identify the following:

### A. Baseball

1. MVP
2. Pinch runner
3. Sacrifice fly
4. Save
5. Scratch hit
6. Texas leaguer

### B. Basketball

1. Dunk shot
2. Give and go
3. NIT
4. Top of the key
5. Trailer
6. Zone defense

### C. Football

1. Flanker
2. Flare out
3. Blitz
4. Sack
5. Tight end
6. Run and shoot

### D. Golf

1. Eagle
2. PGA
3. Par-four hole
4. Slice

### E. Hockey

1. Face off
2. High sticking
3. Icing
4. Red line
5. Sudden death

### F. Soccer

1. Direct kick
2. Indirect kick
3. Goal kick
4. Yellow card
5. Trap

### G. Tennis

1. Ace
2. Double fault
3. Mixed doubles
4. Passing shot

### H. Thoroughbred Horse Racing

1. Claimer
2. Fractions
3. Maiden race
4. Stretch runner
5. Turf race

## You Decide: No English

Your sports reporter has just returned from interviewing a local high school football player who is being sought by dozens of football powerhouses. During the interview, the reporter asked the young man what the recruiters had offered him as inducement to play for their schools.

In passing, the player said that the recruiter from the local university had told him about the fine academic program at the school. The player had said that he wasn't too sharp in English Comp. "Oh, don't worry," he said the recruiter informed him. "You won't have to take English Comp."

Everyone at the local university is required to take English Composition in the freshman year, the reporter points out in his story.

You know that if the story is published, the football coach will blacklist the newspaper. He is a no-holds-barred type. What do you do with the story?

# 23 Business Reporting

New York Stock Exchange, Inc.
**Trading on the NY Stock Exchange.**

### Introduction

Business stories have become popular reading. Most people have a bank account, and many have a mortgage and debts to a bank and credit card company, own stocks and bonds, take part in a pension fund and either run or work for a business. All of these topics are the subject of business reporting, which, because of this diverse audience, is now written in everyday language. Business reporters know how to translate the complexities of finances and economics into their consequences for the livelihood of working people. Because of the private nature of most business, reporters cultivate insiders for information for their stories.

## Exercises

### A. Stocks

You are to do a feature story on a club that buys stocks. The members, 10 women who have been investing together for seven years, include four homemakers, two teachers, the manager of a local drugstore, a hairdresser and two secretaries. The club has invested about $100,000 to date, and its stocks have a market value of $162,000. All dividends have been put back into stock purchases. The women say their plan is to sell all the stock and divide the revenue in three years. Each member puts up $1,500 a year.

"This was a 10-year plan," says Mrs. Arlene Robbins, who acts as secretary of the group. "We've lost on some stocks and done well on others. We meet monthly at one of the member's homes and make a decision on buying and selling. The next meeting is Thursday at my place." You go to 65 Bismark St. to attend the meeting.

Seven of the women are there. One is ill and two are working late. The discussion is about whether to sell 1,000 shares of Goodyear and whether to buy 100 shares of Motorola, 100 shares of News Corp. preferred, 1,000 of J.C. Penney, and 100 of Texas Instruments.

The club makes its own decisions on buying and selling. Five of the women were assigned to study the stocks considered for purchase and the two others were asked to examine the merits of selling Goodyear and to report next month.

"We are doing well this year," says Mrs. Robbins. "But I am not so sure that we shouldn't consider looking at bonds as well as stocks. Let's think about that."

Mildred Bannister, 15 Hawthorne Drive, says that had the group gone into the bond market several years ago it would have done well. "The bonds were paying high interest rates to attract capital in a high-interest market situation," she said.

Alice Thomas, 56 Western Ave., cautions the women doing the checking on buying and selling to watch the yield- and price-to-earnings ratio and to report on them.

You tell the city editor what you have and he suggests that you do some checking yourself so that you can give the current closing prices of the stocks they discussed. He adds, "Make sure you explain all the terms they used. Let's make this an educational feature."

He tells you to write 350 to 500 words.

## B. Tourism

The Chamber of Commerce secretary, Fred Graham, tells you that the hotel occupancy rate is down. Last month, he says, 64 percent of all hotel rooms in the metropolitan area were occupied, compared with 67 percent a year ago and 82 percent three years ago, the best tourist year in the past decade.

Last month 50,300 rooms were filled. That's up slightly from last year's 49,100 but, because of the increase in the number of units available as the result of new construction, the percentage is down.

"Clearly, the people who are in the hotel business are not discouraged," Graham says. "A new hotel is going up downtown and another is in the planning stage."

You ask why present occupancy is so far down from the 82 percent. "First place, tourists aren't coming in the numbers they used to," he answers. "Also, the economy was better. Firms were out looking for business, and salesmen were on the go. Also, the area attracted a number of large conventions and annual meetings. Now, companies are not sending out the waves of salespeople they used to, and conventions are being held closer to the home office, or there are regional meetings." He adds, "We are optimistic. I predict that next year our occupancy rate will be in the 70s. You watch for it."

Write 150 words.

## C. Reorganized

Atlas Equipment Associates of Freeport filed under Chapter 11 of the federal bankruptcy laws a year ago. Today, it released a statement saying its board has given approval to a reorganization plan. Creditors have tentatively accepted the plan.

Under the plan, the company will be recapitalized with 45 percent of new stock going to National Corporation, which lent the company $1.5 million 10 months ago. The company has applied for a favorable tax ruling, and the plan depends on such a ruling. Other stock will be distributed: 5 percent to existing common shareholders, 7.5 percent to existing preferred stockholders, and 42.5 percent to the creditors. Atlas manufactures road-building equipment.

Write 125 words.

## D. Layoff

The Exton Electric Co., a local commercial cabinet manufacturing concern, says it is laying off 150 workers the first of next month. "Poor conditions in the housing market necessitate our cutting back," said Alexander Sanchez, president. "With housing starts in this area down 15 percent from last year, which was a bad year to begin with, we have fewer purchasers for our products." Exton had previously laid off 750 employees this year. Its total work force is 3,000. "I cannot say that this is the end of the layoffs," Sanchez said. "If the market picks up, we'll hire. Otherwise, we will be forced to continue to lay off workers."

Write 125 words.

## E. Annual

The Baldwin Protection Systems Co., a local industry that manufactures burglar alarms for vehicles, homes and industry, announced its earnings for last year:

|  | Last Year | Previous Year |
|---|---|---|
| Revenue | $4,073,421.00 | $3,467,656.00 |
| Net income | 282,382.00 | 137,935.00 |
| Share earns | .83 | .34 |
| Shares outstanding | 340,422 | 400,070 |

Company president Felix Parrington—who founded the company 10 years ago after tinkering with alarms in his garage with a borrowed set of tools—said that the increase in income was the result of "a new sales force that is expanding our contacts with retail outlets." Baldwin products are sold over a four-state area. Parrington, who lives at 76 Roth Road, said he plans to have his alarm system sold nationally "within three years."

You check with local brokers and find that the stock is traded in the over-the-counter market and that the price per share has been around $10. The company has been conservative in its policies and has put most of its earnings back into the business. Last year, it paid a 20-cent dividend. The previous year, it was 10 cents. The broker said that the "increase in crime has been good for Baldwin. Parrington has some excellent patents, and the company clearly is a growth operation."

Write 200 words.

*F. Digital*

The Digital Equipment Corporation issued its earnings report for the first fiscal quarter of the year. You know that there has been increased competition in the computer industry, which could explain the decline in Digital's earnings. You ask for some comments from business analysts and they say they think Digital did better than they had expected. "We were expecting a per-share income of 90 cents to $1 a share," said Paul Olsen, office equipment analyst at Burns & Allen Investment, Inc. Digital is the world's leading manufacturer of networked computer systems, those that can communicate with each other and share workloads and common databases. Write 150 words.

|  | This Year | Last Year |
|---|---|---|
| Revenue | $1,623,927,000 | 1,515,263,000 |
| Net income | 72,325,000 | 144,216,000 |
| Share earns | 1.20 | 2.45 |
| Shares outstanding | 63,927,102 | 59,164,197 |

*G. Car Costs*

Each year, the American Automobile Association estimates the cost of owning and operating a new car. For last year, the AAA reports, the cost was $6,255 for a six-cylinder, four-door sedan driven 15,000 miles. Here are last year's costs compared with the previous year:

|  | Last Year | Previous Year |
|---|---|---|
| Gas and oil | 6.0¢/mile | 6.3¢/mile |
| Maintenance | 2.6¢/mile | 2.4¢/mile |
| Tires | 1.4¢/mile | .9¢/mile |
| Insurance | $716 | $720 |
| License, taxes, registration | $211 | $172 |
| Depreciation | $3,099 | $2,549 |
| Finance charges | $729 | $622 |

Write 250 words for the business section.

## Assignments

*A. Imports*

Interview dealers in domestic automobiles to see how imports have affected their business over the past year compared with the competition in previous years. Support the interview with data from automobile registrations by manufacturer, making annual comparisons for the last few years.

*B. Pulse*

Take the pulse and blood pressure of a variety of local businesses. Make a list of the points of measurement (gross revenues, net revenues, etc.) and use these as the vital signs of health or illness. Ascertain what elements have caused each business to be robust or ailing (location, competition, changes in taste, etc.).

*C. Inventory*

Make an inventory of government agencies—city, county, regional and federal—that are concerned with local business activities. Make a thumbnail sketch of the activities and powers of these agencies.

*D. Authorities*

Compile a list of the names of sources who can provide background for business news stories. For each authority, give the individual's credentials: position, background, area of competence.

*E. Labor*

How strong is organized labor in the community? Would you classify your community as pro-labor or anti-labor? First, devise ways of making this determination. One technique would be to see whether local industries have been organized by the major unions, whether industries have closed or open shops. The comments of labor leaders and local officials would be useful as well.

*F. Market*

Interview securities dealers to see how many people in your city invest in the stock market occasionally and how many buy and sell on a frequent basis. Try to interview individuals in each category. Why do they invest in stocks? How well have they done lately? What are some of their successful investments; some losers? If there is a local investment club, do a story on how it has fared.

*G. Index*

Three yardsticks of the economy are issued monthly by the government: consumer price index, wholesale price index and the index of leading economic indicators. Go to the reference library to obtain material for a story that traces the fluctuations in these indices over the past year. Do you discern some kind of trend or pattern? Can you link it to any major economic or political events?

*H. Nonprofit*

Do a profile of a nonprofit organization in the community. Examine the forms that it is required to file with the government and interview some of the organization's officials.

*I. Open-Closed*

Locate an open shop and a closed shop among the businesses in the city and compare them in terms of:

1. Reasons for status.
2. Salaries.
3. Worker satisfaction with the plan.
4. Owner's view of the situation.

*J. Survey*

Find out the going loan interest rates for home mortgages, automobiles, home improvement and for personal and business purchases. Compare these to the prime rate. Locate someone who has decided to take out a loan or not to borrow because of the rate, and personalize the piece.

*K. Sharing*

If there is a profit-sharing business or cooperative in town, do a historical profile of it. Find out who founded the business and why. How has the business fared? What do workers and management think of the arrangement?

*L. Rent*

Do a housing rental survey of the community. If you prefer to limit it to student rentals, fine. Find out about availability of rental units, going rental charges, quality of housing.

*M. New Business*

Interview the owner of a newly opened business. In your story, balance the financial aspect of the investment with the human interest detail that will personalize it. How much was borrowed? At what interest rate? How much of the person's savings were involved? What are the anticipated earnings? What does the owner's family think of the new business? Has the owner had any experience in the field? Does the business have any novel approaches? Remember, this is not a publicity puff but a careful examination of the facets of a new business.

*N. Promotion*

Locate a company official who recently has been promoted and write a profile, blending the person's business life with his or her personal background.

*O. Execs*

How many women are in executive positions in the city's major industries and businesses? Women constitute what percentage of the total number of executive positions? How recently have they been hired or promoted? What do they think of the status of women in business?

*P. Construction*

Obtain information on building permits over the last quarter, half year or year and compare it with previous periods. Interview people connected with the building trades. What is the overall situation?

*Q. Prime*

Localize the latest prime rate. Talk to bankers, officials of savings and loan associations, builders, automobile dealers and others to ascertain the local consequences. Put this latest figure in the context of the past several months and look for a trend.

*R. Shares*

Find a local company that has issued stock that is actively traded. It may not be listed on the New York Stock Exchange or other exchanges in your newspaper, but local brokers may trade it in the over-the-counter market. Trace the history of the stock: its price fluctuations, earnings, dividends, major stockholders. Interview company officials to determine whether they plan any new offerings or are trying to buy back stock.

*S. Finance*

How do local people or companies raise money to start a business? Ask some local business leaders, bankers, securities dealers.

*T. Handouts*

Many newspapers carry public relations releases in their food, business, fashion, real estate and travel sections. Does yours?

*U. Broker*

Many people invest in mutual funds offered by large investment companies such as Prudential Securities and Twentieth Century Investors. These funds are sold by brokers, who receive a commission on the funds they sell. A study has shown that brokers will push hardest the funds that give them the highest commission, regardless of the performance of the fund. Investigate this situation by interviewing local brokers and consulting sources of background material such as *Consumer Reports* and others that offer information to consumers about best buys.

# Campus Project

## *Market Basket*

Do a market basket survey of groceries and supermarkets that students patronize. This list contains 39 items. You may want to add some. Reach general conclusions on the basis of your survey.

| **Item** | Store A | Store B | Store C |
|---|---|---|---|
| Wonder Bread, 22 oz. package | _____ | _____ | _____ |
| Kellogg's Corn Flakes, 12 oz. box | _____ | _____ | _____ |
| Carolina Long Grain Rice, 3 lbs. | _____ | _____ | _____ |
| Ronzoni Spaghetti, 1 lb., No. 8 strand | _____ | _____ | _____ |
| Gold Medal Flour, 5 lbs. (bleached) | _____ | _____ | _____ |
| Domino Sugar, 5 lb. package | _____ | _____ | _____ |
| Nabisco Chocolate Chip Cookies, 19 oz. bag | _____ | _____ | _____ |
| Minute Maid Frozen Orange Juice, 12 oz. can | _____ | _____ | _____ |
| Del Monte Canned Fruit Cocktail, 1 lb., 1 oz. | _____ | _____ | _____ |
| Birdseye Frozen Green Beans, 9 oz. | _____ | _____ | _____ |
| Green Giant Canned Green Peas, 1 lb., 1 oz. package | _____ | _____ | _____ |
| Campbell's Canned Vegetable Beef Stock Soup, $10\,^3/_4$ oz. | _____ | _____ | _____ |
| Mazola brand Corn Oil, cooking oil, 24 oz. | _____ | _____ | _____ |
| Del Monte Canned Corn, 1 lb., 1 oz. | _____ | _____ | _____ |
| London Broil, 1 lb. | _____ | _____ | _____ |
| Hamburger—ground round, 1 lb. | _____ | _____ | _____ |

| Item | Store A | Store B | Store C |
|---|---|---|---|
| Bacon—store brand, per lb. | _____ | _____ | _____ |
| Oscar Mayer Bacon, 8 oz. | _____ | _____ | _____ |
| Pork Chops, center cut, 1 lb. | _____ | _____ | _____ |
| Perdue Whole Roasting Chicken, 1 lb. | _____ | _____ | _____ |
| Frying chicken, cut up, no spec. brand, 1 lb. | _____ | _____ | _____ |
| Chicken of the Sea Tuna in oil, chunk, $6\frac{1}{2}$ oz. | _____ | _____ | _____ |
| Eggs, grade A large, 1 doz. | _____ | _____ | _____ |
| Fleischman's Stick Margarine, 1 lb. | _____ | _____ | _____ |
| Land O'Lakes Butter, stick, 1 lb. | _____ | _____ | _____ |
| Whole milk, homogenized, 1 qt., list brand | _____ | _____ | _____ |
| Skim milk, 1 qt., list brand | _____ | _____ | _____ |
| Maxwell House Coffee, 1 lb. can | _____ | _____ | _____ |
| Pepsi Cola, 6 pack, 12 oz. cans | _____ | _____ | _____ |
| Taster's Choice instant regular coffee, 8 oz. | _____ | _____ | _____ |
| Miller Beer, 6 pack, regular cans | _____ | _____ | _____ |
| Tetley Tea, 48-bag package | _____ | _____ | _____ |
| Red delicious apples, per lb. | _____ | _____ | _____ |
| McIntosh apples, per lb. | _____ | _____ | _____ |

| Item | Store A | Store B | Store C |
|---|---|---|---|
| Bananas, medium size, 1 lb. | _____ | _____ | _____ |
| Carrots, packaged, medium bunch | _____ | _____ | _____ |
| Iceberg lettuce, per head | _____ | _____ | _____ |
| Yellow onions, per lb. | _____ | _____ | _____ |
| Potatoes, per lb. (Idaho, Maine, Long Island specified) | _____ | _____ | _____ |

## Community Project

### Broke

Visit the federal bankruptcy court and make a list of five filings. Examine the filings collected by other students. Can you see any patterns in the master list?

Some of the bankruptcies could lead to feature stories. Interview those involved in one of the bankruptcies. Here is some background:

When bankruptcy is declared under a provision of the federal bankruptcy act, three possible types of bankruptcy are involved, each designated by a different chapter number in the federal bankruptcy act—7, 11 or 13. A bankruptcy can be voluntary or involuntary. An involuntary proceeding is filed by creditors who seek to prevent the company from disbursing its assets before it pays its bills. Voluntary proceedings are filed by the company.

**Chapter 7:** This is the traditional form of bankruptcy. The assets of the company are liquidated and the proceeds are paid to creditors. When a company files under Chapter 7, it is proper to say that the firm has declared bankruptcy or has gone bankrupt.

**Chapter 11:** The purpose of a firm filing under this chapter is to reorganize its business under the federal bankruptcy laws. Since the company continues in business, it is not correct to state that it has gone bankrupt.

The firm seeks a federal order that relieves it from lawsuits by creditors while it develops a plan to set its finances in shape. The court must approve the reorganization plan of the firm, and a majority of the creditors has to approve the final plan. The firm may pay off all or part of its debts under this plan.

When a firm files under Chapter 11, the reporter must be careful not to describe it as bankrupt. Here are some leads recommended by Louis D. Boccardi, editor of the AP, for Chapter 11 proceedings:

- XYZ Corp. filed for protection under the nation's bankruptcy laws today.
- XYZ Corp. filed for reorganization in the federal bankruptcy court today.
- Creditors filed a bankruptcy petition against XYZ Corp. today, forcing it into reorganization proceedings.

The first two leads refer to voluntary proceedings in which the company filed the action. The third lead refers to an involuntary proceeding in which the individuals and companies to which the XYZ Corp. owes money have taken the action.

Should the reorganization plan fail, the company may be forced into bankruptcy and its assets liquidated. This is done under Chapter 11, but at this time the firm can be labeled bankrupt because it is being or has been liquidated.

**Chapter 13:** This proceeding involves individuals only, and it must be voluntary. When a person files under Chapter 13, he or she is protected by the court against creditors while working out a plan to repay the debts, which may be paid partially or in full.

It is not correct to describe someone filing under Chapter 13 as bankrupt. Here are two leads Boccardi suggests:

- Hugh Mulligan filed for protection from his creditors under the bankruptcy laws today, seeking court protection while he works out a repayment plan for $500,000 in debt.
- Hugh Mulligan filed a bankruptcy petition today, seeking court protection from his creditors while he works out a repayment plan to settle his debts.

## Home Assignment

### High-Low

Check the performance so far this year of newspaper stocks. You can find them listed weekly in *Editor & Publisher*. Select a particular stock and consult the listings in today's newspaper for its current price and the year's high and low, dividend, yield and any other information the stock tables list.

Then make a study of the company's historical performance by examining evaluations of its earnings and other indexes of performance in a stock-rating publication such as *Value Line*.

Generally, newspaper stock prices were depressed in the early 1990s because of a falloff in advertising income and then made a comeback by the mid-1990s. How did that affect earnings and dividends for your stock?

Write a 350-word piece on your stock.

## Class Discussion

### A. Puff

A store has an anniversary sale. A car dealership has been sold. A clothing store adds a new line of merchandise. Where is the line between free advertising and legitimate news? Draw some guidelines and apply them to the following summaries of press releases from local sources:

1. Jack A. Serge, manager of the Kmart Eastview store, today announced the opening of an expanded apparel section.
2. The Metropolitan Transit Authority today contracted to buy 25 specially designed buses from General Motors at a cost of $5 million.
3. The XYZ Repair Shop has opened in a new shopping center outside town and is having a lottery to give away a laptop computer tomorrow.
4. Wayne Miller, an employee of the Amidon Photo Exchange, is retiring after 35 years with the store.
5. Stacy Backman is being honored by the Allstate Insurance office in town for 25 years' service. She will be given a diamond pin at a dinner Friday night.
6. Robert Salmi, cashier at the First National Bank, has been promoted to assistant vice president in charge of credit.

### B. Jargon

Look through the business pages of a few issues of the local newspaper; listen to the business news on radio and television. Collect words and phrases that you consider the jargon of business journalism. Take them to class for discussion. (Jargon is the technical language of a field.)

## Skill Drill: Business and Labor Terms

Define these terms:

1. Bear
2. Board of directors
3. Bond
4. Chairman(-woman) of the board
5. Closed shop
6. Common stock
7. Insolvent
8. Liquidation
9. Municipal bond
10. Open shop

11. Prime rate
12. Public/private company
13. Proxy
14. Receiver
15. Stock split

## Fix It: Match 'Em

Look at the Consolidated Balance Sheet for the appropriate values for last year and match the definitions from the alphabetized list on the next page.

| Item | Value | Definition |
|---|---|---|
| 1. Accounts receivable | $_____ | _____ |
| 2. Inventories | $_____ | _____ |
| 3. Fixed assets | $_____ | _____ |
| 4. Depreciation | $_____ | _____ |
| 5. Accounts payable | $_____ | _____ |
| 6. Notes payable | $_____ | _____ |
| 7. Accrued expenses payable | $_____ | _____ |
| 8. Debentures | $_____ | _____ |
| 9. Preferred stock | $_____ | _____ |
| 10. Common stock | $_____ | _____ |
| 11. Accumulated retained earnings | $_____ | _____ |
| 12. Net working capital | $_____ | _____ |

### Consolidated Balance Sheet (in thousands of dollars)

| Assets | Last Year | Previous Year | Liabilities | Last Year | Previous Year |
|---|---|---|---|---|---|
| Current assets | | | Current liabilities | | |
|   Cash | $ 20,000 | $ 1,000 |   Accounts payable | $ 72,000 | $ 69,000 |
|   Marketable securities—cost market value: 1995, $42,000; 1994, $34,000 | 40,000 | 32,000 |   Notes payable | 51,000 | 61,000 |
| | | |   Accrued expenses payable | 30,000 | 36,000 |
| | | |   Federal income taxes payable | 17,000 | 15,000 |
|   Accounts receivable—less allowance for doubtful accounts: 1995, $2,375; 1994, $3,000 | 156,000 | 145,000 | **Total current liabilities** | **$170,000** | **$181,000** |
| | | | Long-term liabilities | | |
| | | |   Deferred income taxes | $ 10,000 | $ 9,000 |
| | | |   Debentures 12.5%, due 2010 | 136,000 | 136,000 |
|   Inventories | 180,000 | 185,000 | **Total liabilities** | **$316,000** | **$326,000** |
|   Prepaid expenses | 4,000 | 3,000 | Stockholders' Equity | | |
| **Total current assets** | **$400,000** | **$380,000** |   Preferred stock $5.83 cumulative, $100 par value, authorized 60,000 shares, outstanding 60,000 shares | $ 6,000 | $ 6,000 |
| Fixed assets | | | | | |
|   Land | $ 30,000 | $ 30,000 | | | |
|   Buildings | 125,000 | 118,500 | | | |
|   Machinery | 215,000 | 186,100 |   Common stock $5.00 par value; authorized 20,000,000 shares; outstanding 1995, 15,000,000 shares; outstanding 1994, 14,500,000 shares | 75,000 | 72,500 |
|   Office equipment | 15,000 | 12,000 | | | |
| **Total property, plant and equipment (fixed assets)** | **$385,000** | **$346,600** | | | |
| Less accumulated depreciation | 125,000 | 97,000 |   Capital surplus | 16,000 | 7,500 |
| **Net fixed assets** | **$260,000** | **$249,600** |   Accumulated retained earnings | 249,000 | 219,600 |
| Intangibles (goodwill, patents) | 2,000 | 2,000 | **Total stockholders' equity** | **$346,000** | **$305,600** |
| **Total assets** | **$662,000** | **$631,600** | **Total liabilities and stockholders equity** | **$662,000** | **$631,600** |

## Definitions

a. Property, plant and equipment; not intended for sale.

b. Amount owed to employees in salaries and wages, interest on bank loans, interest to bondholders, pensions, insurance premiums, attorney fees.

c. Raw materials to be used in the product, partially finished goods in process of manufacture, finished goods ready for shipment to customers.

d. Amount not yet collected from customers to whom goods were shipped prior to payment.

e. Formal promissory note issued by the company; money received by the company as a loan from bondholders, who in turn are given a certificate called a *bond* as evidence of the loan.

f. Stock issued by the company to raise cash; no limit on dividends, which are set annually by the company.

g. Decline in useful value of a fixed asset due to wear and tear from usage and passage of time.

h. Earned surplus; the amount left after preferred and common stockholders have been paid in dividends.

i. Amount the company owes to its regular business creditors from whom it has bought goods or services on open account.

j. Money owed a bank or other lender; a written promissory note is given the lender by the company.

k. Stock or shares issued by the company that have some preference over other shares with respect to dividends and distribution of assets in case of liquidation. A specific amount or rate of return is set, which may be cumulative.

l. The difference between total current assets and total current liabilities.

The material here has been taken from "How to Read a Financial Report," by permission of Merrill Lynch, Pierce, Fenner & Smith Incorporated. © Copyright 1985 Merrill Lynch, Pierce, Fenner & Smith Incorporated.

## *What's Wrong?: Look Again*

Correct these leads and sentences from business stories.

1. The Albright Corp. today reported record income for last year with sales rising almost 50 percent, from $55 million to $82 million last year.

2. The Y-Mart furniture chain reported record sales last year, an increase of almost 100 percent over the previous year. Sales last year totaled $62,500,000, compared with $42,750,000 the year before.

3. A record number of bait-and-switch charges were made by customers to the state consumer agency last year. The agency head, Alfred Wilson, said in his annual report that 57 state businesses were charged with the illegal sales tactic. The report also cited "considerable improvement" in compliance with the state's new restaurant inspection law.

4. Although the Consumer Price Index has more than tripled over the past 30 years, Acuff said, prices on small consumer items have not gone up that much. "Kids aren't being hurt when they buy gum or chocolate bars," he said. "Prices haven't increased that much."

5. Allison Equipment Corp., a local manufacturer of machine tools, today reported revenues of $26.5 million, the highest in its 26-year history. Total income last year was 15 percent over the previous year, F.L. Briggs, the president, announced yesterday. However, because of higher costs and a tax ruling the company had futilely protested, net earnings were down from $1.50 a share two years ago to $1.38 a share last year.

# 24 Local Government and Education

Joel Strasser.

**City problem: poor children.**

### Introduction

Cities are the custodians of public health, welfare and education. They collect our trash, regulate our traffic, tell us where we may and may not park and build and maintain our streets, schools and bridges. Reporters regularly check our caretakers to see what they are doing and how well they are doing it. A central indicator of the city's priorities is the budget, which establishes the ways the city collects and spends taxes and fees. Budgets are made in an arena in which competing interests vie for favor. Journalists cover the entire process, not just the final stage of budget adoption.

## *Exercises*

### *A. Budget Talk*

Last night you attended a city council meeting at which the city manager, Harold Born, submitted an idea for financing long-range construction that would avoid the issuance of bonds. Born also submitted three sets of tables regarding his proposed budget:

1. The total budget proposed for next year and the current year's budget (Table 24.1).
2. A breakdown of the general operating fund, much of which is used for salaries of employees in the city's offices (Table 24.2).
3. Itemization of the ad valorem tax (property tax) requirements that are included in the proposed budget. The total $821,175, will have to be raised from the tax levied on owners of real estate in Freeport through a mill levy (Table 24.3).

You show the city editor your notes from the portion of the meeting that was concerned with the budget. Here are your notes:

Council members: Albert Fuentes, Bernard Garner, Fred E. Smith, Martin Davis and Marcia Gold.
*Fuentes:* "I think we owe thanks to Harold for the splendid job. I know he's spent considerable time working with department heads over the past few months, adjusting their needs to our realities."
*Garner:* "Right. This looks like a hold-tight budget, and I think we all like it. Except for one item, the one that says General Improvement in Lieu of Bonds."
*Born:* "Let me explain that. We need to put away money for what I project as a needed expansion of the sewage treatment plant and water lines. Also, we will have to lay out some new roads to the subdivision south sooner or later. I don't see anything immediate but I want to start building up a fund. That way we won't have to borrow and pay interest. Right now interest rates are way up and we are bonded close to our limit. Also, our debt service is high."
*Smith:* "But it adds to taxes, doesn't it?"
*Born:* "Yes, a few mills."
*Davis:* "So the taxpayer has to shoulder the burden."
*Born:* "Less, actually, than if you had to sell bonds."

*(Excerpts continued on page 221.)*

## Table 24.1

| Current Year Expenditures | Funds | Proposed Expenditures |
|---|---|---|
| $ 576,945.00 | General Operating Fund | $ 626,715.00 |
| 15,000.00 | Cemetery | 15,000.00 |
| 32,000.00 | Improvements | 24,207.00 |
| 500.00 | Band | 500.00 |
| 47,725.00 | Library | 53,210.00 |
| 15,000.00 | Hospital | 13,500.00 |
| 19,500.00 | Firefighters' Pension | 19,500.00 |
| 16,500.00 | Police Officers' Pension | 16,500.00 |
| 2,500.00 | Bindweed | 2,500.00 |
| 20,560.00 | Social Security | 21,750.00 |
| 415,083.00 | Debt Service | 497,648.00 |
| 0.00 | General Improvement (in Lieu of Bonds) | 95,396.00 |
| $1,161,313.00 | | $1,386,426.00 |

Current year mill levy: **$20.920**

Tangible assessed value of real property: **$31,798,794.** (Assessed valuation is 50% of market value. Average home has market value of **$90,000.**)

Funds raised from ad valorem taxes are supplemented by fees, licenses, fines, etc. and the total makes up the total expenditure.

Total indebtedness January: **$6,611,372.**

Current year property tax revenue: **$665,200.**

## Table 24.2

| | Current Year | Proposed |
|---|---|---|
| City Council | $ 3,815.00 | $ 1,660.00 |
| City Manager | 10,760.00 | 11,890.00 |
| Planning and Research | 7,335.00 | 15,160.00 |
| City Clerk | 10,375.00 | 10,170.00 |
| Elections | 10,150.00 | 2,595.00 |
| City Treas.-Purch. Agent | 4,135.00 | 3,685.00 |
| Building Inspector | 9,035.00 | 11,565.00 |
| Buildings and Grounds | 34,445.00 | 26,055.00 |
| Legal | 7,650.00 | 8,350.00 |
| Police Court | 3,675.00 | 3,875.00 |
| Engineering | 37,845.00 | 45,360.00 |
| General Overhead | 8,295.00 | 14,400.00 |
| Police Department | 122,400.00 | 125,665.00 |
| Animal Control | 3,600.00 | 3,600.00 |
| Parking Meter | 13,520.00 | 0.00 |
| Fire Department | 123,350.00 | 133,995.00 |
| Street Department | 107,250.00 | 103,350.00 |
| Forestry | 6,000.00 | 10,000.00 |
| Street Lights | 18,200.00 | 19,480.00 |
| Park Department | 23,510.00 | 39,700.00 |
| Airport Maintenance | 2,100.00 | 6,160.00 |
| Health Department | 9,500.00 | 10,000.00 |
| Contingency Appropriation | 0.00 | 20,000.00 |
| | $576,945.00 | $626,715.00 |

## Table 24.3

| Funds | Ad Valorem Tax Requirements |
|---|---|
| General Operating | $330,275.00 |
| Cemetery | 7,545.00 |
| General Improvement | 24,278.00 |
| Band | 448.00 |
| Library | 48,499.00 |
| Hospital | 11,730.00 |
| Firefighters' Pension | 6,747.00 |
| Police Officers' Pension | 4,778.00 |
| Bindweed | 2,079.00 |
| Social Security | 4,288.00 |
| Bond and Interest | 285,112.00 |
| General Improvement (In Lieu of Bonds) | 95,396.00 |
| Totals | $821,175.00 |

*Gold:* "Of course we all want to save money, but isn't there also a principle involved, of making the people who benefit from the services pay for them? I mean, why should present taxpayers pay for future benefits? Bonds are a much fairer way of assessing costs."

*Davis:* "I have a feeling that all of us are a bit gun-shy of that item, Harold."

*Smith:* "Yes, we can't add to taxes now. The home owner is absolutely strapped, with this and the school tax going up."

*Garner:* "Suppose we cut it out. How much do we save on the mill levy, Harold?"

*Born:* "I can figure that out in a few ..."

*Davis:* "Don't bother now. Bring it in in two weeks when I think we're just going to go through the motions of adopting your budget without that item. Agreed?"

(Various nods and grunts of approval of Davis' statement.)

After reading these excerpts, the city editor says it seems certain the council will adopt the budget at the next meeting, after striking out the item for General Improvement in Lieu of Bonds. He says that it appears to him that you can figure out the budget yourself since all the figures are available. You look at him, trying not to appear too perplexed. He senses your trouble and volunteers to take you step-by-step through the figures and to the story, which he says you should then be able to write by yourself.

First, he says, look at Table 24.1 and strike the item General Improvement in Lieu of Bonds. Then refigure the proposed expenditures. He suggests you do that on your own and return with the total proposed budget for next year.

You go to your seat and do the figuring. No problem, really:

$$\begin{array}{r} \$1,386,426 \\ -95,396 \\ \hline \$1,291,030 \end{array}$$

As you are about to return to the editor, something strikes you. If you subtracted the same $95,396 figure from the total on Table 24.3 you would get the total ad valorem tax requirement. You know that this is the amount of money to be raised from the property tax.

So, on your own, you do that:

$$\begin{array}{r} \$821,175 \\ -95,396 \\ \hline \$725,779 \end{array}$$

That is a key figure. It is going to be the basis of the mill levy, you know. But you cannot recall how the levy is figured. You ask the city editor to tell you.

He says that if you multiply the total assessed valuation by the mill levy, you will get the funds raised from the property tax, also known as the mill levy.

This, you see, makes the following equation:

$$\text{mill levy} \times \text{assessed valuation} = \text{total raised from the property tax}$$

You pick up the assessed valuation of the city's real estate from Table 24.1 and from Table 24.3 you take the total taxes needed from the property tax or mill levy:

$$\text{mill levy} \times \$31{,}798{,}794 = \$725{,}779$$

Or, to put it in easy form for figuring out:

$$\text{mill levy} = \frac{\$725{,}779}{\$31{,}798{,}794}$$

$$\text{mill levy} = \$.0228241$$

That is 2.282 cents on the dollar, and since your city uses a mill levy on $1,000 assessed valuation, the tax levy on property is $22.82/$1,000 in assessed valuation.

You show this to your editor and he congratulates you and suggests you check it with the city manager. Born verifies your figures and confirms your feeling that the budget will be adopted at the next meeting without his item, which would have added three mills, or $3/$1,000 in property tax, he tells you.

Write a story of 800 to 900 words, quoting from the commission meeting.

## B. School Board

The Pennsbury School Board met last night and adopted next year's budget by a vote of 5-1. The board had discussed the budget during the spring. This meeting took 10 minutes. Three board members were absent. You are to write 500 to 750 words from the following information:

The expenditures will total $21,743,000 as compared with $20,617,000 last year. The new budget will require a property tax of 108.5 mills, compared with 102.5 last year. When the school district first presented the budget to the board last spring, a 13.5 mill increase would have been necessary. Over the past several weeks, the board cut various items from the budget on its own and after public hearings.

Board member Francis Martin, the lone dissenter, said, "I'd like to save the taxpayer money. I'd like to see the athletic account back to where it was last year. I'd like to see more money taken out of the budget reserve to decrease the millage." He said the savings could be half a mill off the school tax.

Raymond Wiese, vice president of the board, opposed the suggestion. "I think if we did that we'd be cutting it pretty close. There are a number of factors that may hit us, like a wrong guess on heating and lighting costs. There's the unknown impact of children leaving nonpublic schools and the cost of transportation into New Jersey, especially if some of these schools start holding Saturday sessions."

Those voting to adopt the budget were Morris Feldman, president of the board; Wiese; William Gummere; George Littleton and Robert McKelvie.

Presume this is June 27, and next year's budget will take effect in the school year beginning in September. Tables 24.4–6 and Figures 24.1–2 are sheets from the budget you must consult for background for your story.

The average home in the Pennsbury School District is assessed at $30,000, but many people live in homes assessed at half that. Use both figures in your estimates of what the home owner will pay.

Of the total $21,743,000 budget, $15,140,421 will be raised through the property tax.

### Table 24.4
### Proposed Budget for Next Year
### Summary of Receipts

| | |
|---|---:|
| 1. Anticipated Balance (end of this year) | $ 540,000.00 |
| 2. Current Taxes | 15,571,421.00 |
| 3. Delinquent Taxes | 125,000.00 |
| 4. Other Local Sources | 378,000.00 |
| 5. State Sources | 5,128,579.00 |
| | $21,743,000.00 |

### Table 24.5
### Budget Comparisons Pennsbury School District

| | Actual Last Year | Actual Current Year | Anticipated Next Year |
|---|---:|---:|---:|
| Classrooms | 591 | 591 | 591 |
| Schools | 18 | 18 | 18 |
| Students | 13,292 | *13,025 | 12,880 |
| | | | |
| Classroom Teachers | 673 | 670 | 650 |
| Specialists | 32 | 30 | 30 |
| Administrators | 34 | 36 | 36 |
| Guidance | 28 | 28 | 28 |
| Curriculum Coordinators | 9 | 10 | 10 |
| Nurses | 20 | 20 | 20 |
| **Total Professional** | **796** | **794** | **774** |
| | | | |
| Secretaries, Clerks and Supervisors | 93½ | 89½ | 86 |
| Bus Drivers and Bus Maintenance | 71 | 73 | 72 |
| Custodians, Whse. and Etc. | 144½ | 144½ | 142 |
| Cafeteria | 141 | 141 | 139 |
| Maintenance | 28 | 30 | 29 |
| Paraprofessionals | | | |
|   Teacher Aides | 23 | 37 | 38 |
|   Transportation Aides | 10 | 10 | 9 |
|   Management Assistants | 4 | 4 | 4 |
| **Total Noninstructional** | **515** | **529** | **519** |
| | | | |
| **Total Employees** | **1,311** | **1,323** | **1,293** |
| | | | |
| Students/Classroom Teacher | 20.0 | 19.4 | 19.8 |
| Students/Noninstructional Employee | 26.2 | 24.6 | 24.8 |
| Students/Professional Employee | 16.9 | 16.4 | 16.7 |
| Students/Total Employee | 10.3 | 9.8 | 10.0 |

*Actual student enrollment as of March 1 this year

Local Government and Education

## Table 24.6
### Budget Comparisons Pennsbury School District

| | Budget<br>Current Year | Tentative Budget<br>Next Year |
|---|---|---|
| Total Budget | $20,617,000.00 | $21,743,000.00 |
| Number of Students | *13,025 | 12,880 |
| Decrease in Students | **−(2.01)% | −(1.11)% |
| Increase in Budget Over Last Year's Budget | 9.28% | 5.46% |
| Cost per Student | $1,582.88 | $1,688.11 |
| Number of Employees | 1,323 | 1,293 |
| Decrease or Increase in Employees | .91% | −(2.27)% |
| Total Salaries | $14,166,733.68 | $15,080,849.47 |
| Increase in Salaries | 8.36% | 6.45% |
| All Other Expenses | $6,450,266.32 | $6,662,150.53 |
| All Other Increases | 14.53% | 3.28% |
| Salaries Cost per Student | $1,087.66 | $1,170.87 |
| All Other Costs per Student | $495.22 | $517.24 |

*Actual student enrollment as of March 1 this year
**Decrease from June last year average daily membership as of March 1 this year

### New Positions—Next Year

| Account Number | Classification | Number |
|---|---|---|
| 0218 | Security Guard | 1 |
| 0513 | Mechanic | 1 |

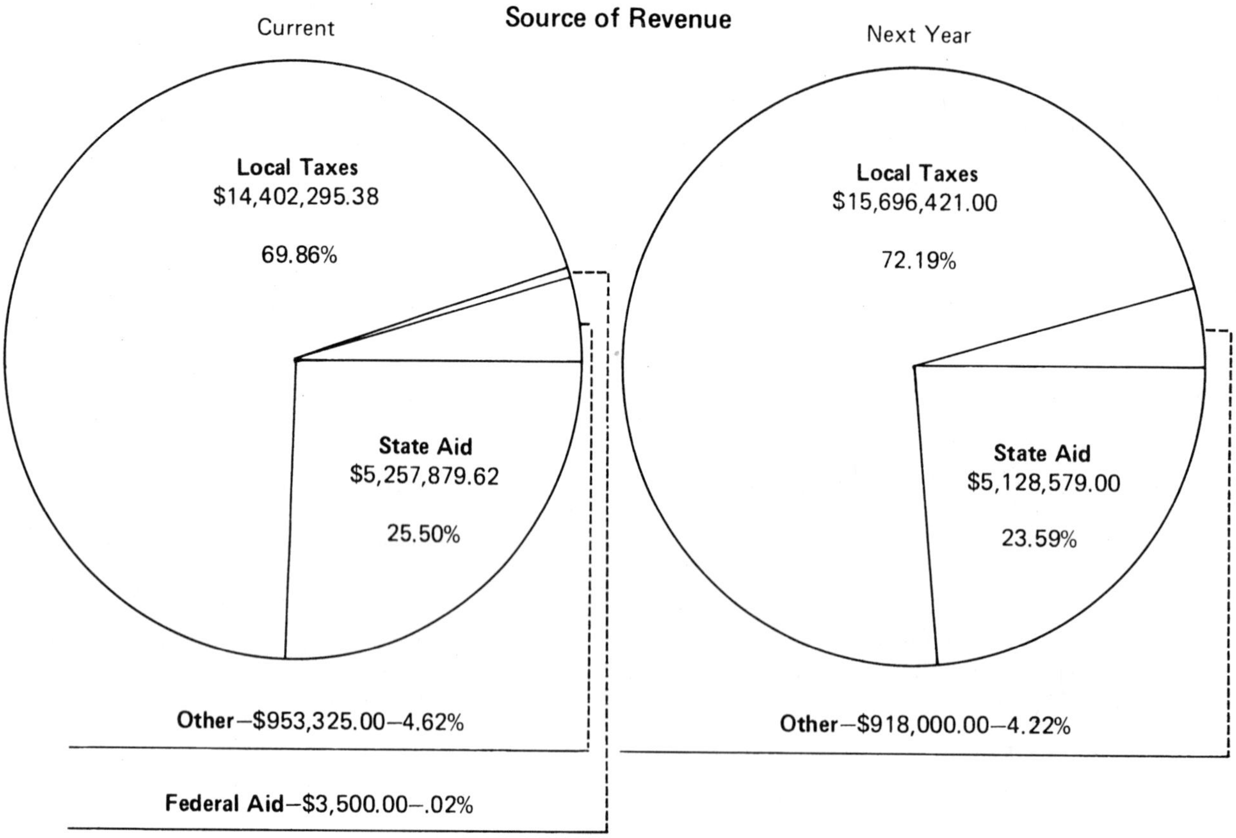

### Source of Revenue

**Current**
- Local Taxes $14,402,295.38 — 69.86%
- State Aid $5,257,879.62 — 25.50%
- Other—$953,325.00—4.62%
- Federal Aid—$3,500.00—.02%

**Next Year**
- Local Taxes $15,696,421.00 — 72.19%
- State Aid $5,128,579.00 — 23.59%
- Other—$918,000.00—4.22%

**Figure 24.1**

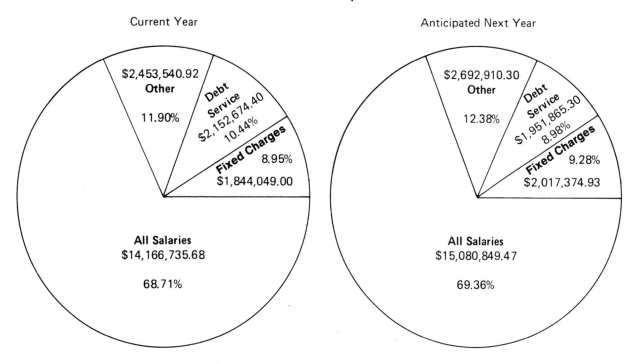

**Figure 24.2**

*C. Proposed*

It is now April of the year following the budget adopted in **B. School Board.** The district superintendent of the Pennsbury School District, Ernest H. Mueller, last night submitted the school budget to the Pennsbury School Board for the coming year.

The proposed budget totals $24,168,000. A total of $18,413,449 will be raised from the property tax toward the total budget. This will necessitate a property tax of 130 mills, or $130/$1,000 in assessed valuation. You have the current year's budget totals (See **Exercise B. School Board**) and you can compare the two.

From these comparisons and the pages taken from the proposed budget (Tables 24.7–9 and Figures 24.3–4), write a 500-word story.

Local Government and Education   **225**

**Pennsbury School District**  
**Fallsington, Pennsylvania**

April 12

MEMO

To: Pennsbury School Board
Fr: Ernest H. Mueller, District Superintendent

I hereby transmit to you the Pennsbury School District's tentative budget proposed for the next school year.

This document is the result of many hours of deliberation on the part of individual building staffs and central administration. Only through the cooperation and input of everyone concerned with the budget has it been possible to prioritize the district's needs and produce a budget that will provide those basic needs and still not overburden the tax-paying community.

We are fully aware of what burdens these fiscally difficult times place upon the taxpayers, yet they, too, must be aware that the same inflationary escalations that affect their family and business budgets also seriously affect a school budget. Holding the total tentative budget increase to only 11.15% has required maximum efforts in all departments to make the necessary revisions and deletions without downgrading the quality of education in Pennsbury.

Since State Aid provided 23.59% of the revenue for the current budget but will provide only 18.45% for next year's budget, anyone can realize that an 11.15% increase is modest indeed. An uncontrollable fact is that the amount of receipts required from local sources has increased a full 10% in two years.

This next year 4.8 mills of the 21.5 mills required for the budget increase are a direct result of the decrease in state aid. Of the remaining 16.7 mills, 14.4 mills are required for Debt Service, Fixed Expenses and All Salaries. Only 2.28 mills of the increase go for educational supplies, utilities and custodial and maintenance supplies. This is a surprisingly low increase when one examines the real inflationary costs that affect all consumers today.

Accompanying this year's budget is the board's adopted Goals and Objectives for next year, including the financial impact that it has on the proposed budget; therefore, it is possible for the board and the community to observe that any increases, no matter how slight, are a direct result of educational commitments on the part of the board, administration, staff and community.

Since the administration and the staff, through many meetings and deliberations, have been able to effect a $418,638 (almost three full mills) reduction in the budget as it was originally drawn up, there remains little opportunity for further reductions. My staff and I, however, will stand ready to exert maximum effort to comply with the board's wishes. What we ask is that we be permitted to continue offering the kind and quality of education that the Pennsbury community needs and desires.

**Table 24.7**
**Proposed Budget Next Year**
**Summary of Receipts**

| | |
|---|---:|
| 1. Anticipated Balance July 1 | $    356,000.00 |
| 2. Current Taxes | 18,785,449.00 |
| 3. Delinquent Taxes | 200,000.00 |
| 4. Other Local Sources | 367,000.00 |
| 5. State Sources | 4,459,551.00 |
| | $24,168,000.00 |

## Table 24.8
## Budget Comparisons Pennsbury School District

|  | Actual Last Year | Actual This Year | Tentative Next Year |
|---|---|---|---|
| Classrooms | 591 | 591 | 591 |
| Schools | 18 | 18 | 18 |
| Students | 13,025 | *12,777 | 12,500 |
| | | | |
| Classroom Teachers | 670 | 655 | 656 |
| Specialists | 30 | 30 | 31 |
| Administrators | 36 | 36 | 35 |
| Guidance | 28 | 28 | 28 |
| Curriculum Coordinators | 10 | 10 | 9 |
| Nurses | 20 | 20 | 20 |
| **Total Professional** | **794** | **779** | **779** |
| | | | |
| Secretaries, Clerks and Supervisors | 89½ | 86 | 88 |
| Bus Drivers and Bus Maintenance | 73 | 72 | 72 |
| Custodians, Whse. and Etc. | 144½ | 142 | 143 |
| Cafeteria | 141 | 140 | 140 |
| Maintenance | 30 | 29 | 32 |
| Paraprofessionals | | | |
|   Teacher Aides | 37 | 38 | 39 |
|   Transportation Aides | 10 | 9 | 9 |
|   Management Asst's. | 4 | 4 | 4 |
| **Total Noninstructional** | **529** | **520** | **527** |
| | | | |
| **Total Employees** | **1,323** | **1,299** | **1,306** |
| Students/Classroom Teacher | 19.4 | 19.5 | 19.1 |
| Students/Noninstructional Employee | 24.4 | 24.5 | 23.7 |
| Students/Professional Employee | 16.4 | 16.4 | 16.0 |
| Students/Total Employee | 9.8 | 9.8 | 9.6 |

*Actual student enrollment as of March 1 this year

## Table 24.9
### Budget Comparisons Pennsbury School District

| | Budget Current Year | Tentative Budget Next Year |
|---|---|---|
| Total Budget | $21,743,000.00 | $24,168,000.00 |
| Number of Students | *12,777 | 12,500 |
| Decrease in Students | **–(1.41)% | –(2.17)% |
| Increase in Budget Over Last Year's Budget | 5.46% | 11.15% |
| Cost per Student | $1,701.73 | $1,933.44 |
| Number of Employees | 1,299 | 1,306 |
| Decrease or Increase in Employees | –(1.81)% | .54% |
| Total Salaries | $15,080,849.47 | $16,053,305.16 |
| Increase in Salaries | 6.45% | 6.45% |
| All Other Expenses | $6,662,150.53 | $8,114,694.84 |
| All Other Increases | 3.28% | 21.80% |
| Salaries Cost per Student | $1,180.31 | $1,284.26 |
| All Other Costs per Student | $521.42 | $649.18 |

*Actual student enrollment as of March 1 this year
**Decrease from June last year to March 1 this year

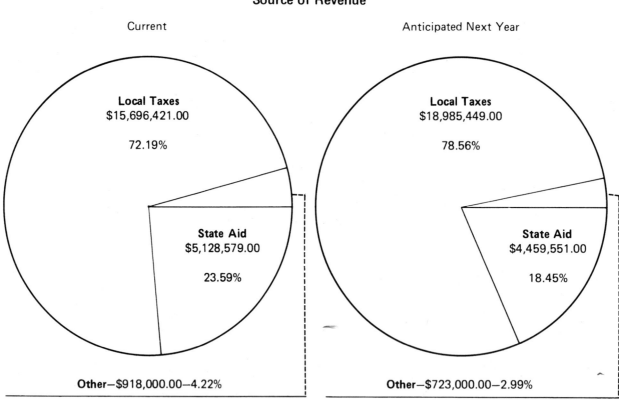

Figure 24.3

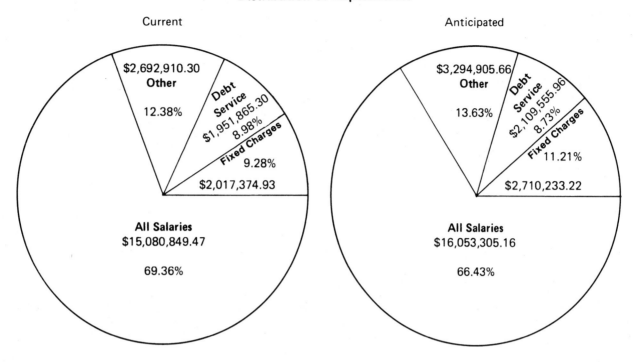

**Figure 24.4**

## Assignments

### A. Constituencies

There are five major sources of news on local government finances. These organizations and groups have varied interests in how much the city spends and where the expenditures are directed, and they are concerned about how revenues are gathered. The groups are:

1. **Government:** the various departments, agencies, bureaus, their directors and employees.
2. **Money-providing constituencies:** the chamber of commerce, local real estate groups, property-owners associations, taxpayer and merchant groups, banks.
3. **Service-demanding groups:** organized groups seeking such city services as welfare, health care, police and fire protection.
4. **Organized bureaucracies:** public employees, municipal unions, retirement fund manager.
5. **Independent groups:** League of Women Voters, various municipal information organizations.

List the people you would seek out for information about their groups' reactions to the present budget. Interview these sources about the current or the coming budget.

## B. Bonds

Cities, counties, school districts and special assessment districts finance major construction by selling bonds. Examine the bonding situation of one of these governmental units and discover:

1. The plans, if any, for new construction; the anticipated interest rate; the value of the bonds.
2. The interest rate on the last bond issue sold.
3. The rating of the unit's borrowing health by one of the rating services (Moody's Investors Service Inc., Standard & Poor's Corp. and Fitch Investors Service Inc.)
4. Taxpayer reaction to issuance of bonds in the past.

## C. Schools

At what level in the budget-making process is the local school district? Write a story on what has been accomplished and what remains to be done. Keep an eye on actual or anticipated major changes from the current budget.

## D. Record Keeping

Go to the office of the city clerk (or the county clerk, if appropriate) and ask for the previous month's (or quarter's or year's) records for the following: marriage licenses, births, divorces, deaths, building permits, trust deeds, real estate transfers. Write a story comparing them with a comparable period one year earlier and five years earlier.

## E. Business

Business conditions directly affect the city's finances. Look into a new business. One way to check on new businesses in the community is through the telephone company, which often makes available new business telephone listings. Interview the owner of a new business about plans, number of people to be hired, reason the business opened, the services to be offered, the owner's background. What are the owner's reactions to the local tax structure?

## F. Data

Some journalists have done stories that show a correlation between income and employment and such factors as crime, delinquency, truancy and poor health. Where income and employment are low, deviant behavior is above average for the city, these stories indicate.

If your city has clearly identifiable income areas and you can isolate data for other factors in these areas, you can do similar stories. If the data clearly indicate relationships, you should check your findings with local officials and with authorities on the subjects on the campus and elsewhere. These sources may assist you in interpreting your findings.

Some of the basic data you will need follow. The Census Bureau has material on population density, housing quality and the racial and ethnic composition of the areas under study.

1. **Unemployment:** Unemployment by age group, race, ethnic background.
2. **Health:** Fetal deaths, infant mortality, early infancy diseases, tuberculosis, drug-related deaths, suicide.
3. **Crime:** Rates and totals for homicide, rape, assault, robbery.
4. **Education:** Absences, truancies, percentage of students graduating from high school, percentage going to college.

## G. Process

Here is a story that appeared in a local newspaper. Write a similar story for your community, or select a stage in the current budget and emphasize that in your story.

**City Budget to Start**

The first of many steps in compiling data for next year's city budget will start next week, City Manager Eric Turner said today. But the process of financing next year's city operations will not be finished until late in the summer.

"Next week, we will give budget request forms to all our city department heads," Turner said. "They then will have until about June 15 to compile all the programs they wish included in their operations, along with a 'narrative' telling why the programs are justified."

### Past Budgets Studied

The department heads must look at last year's budget, the current budget, amounts spent during the first four months of this year and numerous other figures in order to arrive at next year's needs.

"We also have to re-evaluate the remainder of the current year's budget, in light of expenditures during the first four months," Turner pointed out. He explained that some departments may have had an expense in one phase of their operations that was greater than anticipated. But since the budget is fixed, other operations must be curtailed, or costs cut elsewhere, so that the year's total expenses will remain within the allowable total.

"On about June 15, I'll begin meeting with the department heads to work out the various details of the budget and to put all the requests into one balanced program," Turner said. "We won't take any phase of the budget to the city commission for approval until all proposals are laid out in detail."

### Figures Translated

From July 1–15, Turner must translate the budget "figures" into "words," he said. He will compile a "narrative," or word explanation, of each number and need of the overall budget. This narrative will accompany budget requests submitted to the commission."

"I hope to get the narrative finished and to the commission by July 16. But this really is rushing things," he added. The complete budget is about 100 pages long. The commissioners then will have until approximately the end of July to study the proposals.

Moving on into the next phase of the operation, the city commission will meet in a lengthy session and go through all the proposals an item at a time. From this they will arrive at a final budget figure for each operation.

Following a public hearing, at which various items can be lowered but not raised, the commissioners will pass an ordinance levying the taxes to finance next year's city operations.

### Budget Figures

Last year, the commission budgeted $2,621,315, of which $1,441,723 was to be raised from property taxes. These taxes, based on the assessed valuation of property, were based on a 19.89 mill levy, or $19.89 for each $1,000 property valuation. The total assessed valuation was $72,500,000.

Turner said that for the last several months, the various department heads have been listing ideas of how to increase their particular budget or to introduce new department programs at a minimum increase in expenditures.

"If they have a new program they feel is justified, they are asked to translate the money needs into a narrative. Additional equipment often can lessen one particular department cost and eventually reduce the overall department expenditures," Turner said.

He pointed out how one new machine may release manpower to be used elsewhere, where it actually is needed more. This makes it possible for a department to avoid hiring more manpower and the new machine "pays for itself within a short time because of this."

## *H. Records*

Make a list of the following over the past 24 hours: fire calls, crime reports, arrests, hospital admissions and discharges, motor vehicle accident reports, births, deaths, marriage licenses issued, business licenses issued, property sales and transfers.

1. Indicate where and from whom such information is available.
2. Include enough information to help an editor decide which items are newsworthy. Indicate why items are worth stories.
3. Select one of the newsworthy items from each category and write a story.

## *I. Assessments*

Interview the county assessor and obtain a breakdown of assessed valuation of real and personal property for the current year. Any overall changes from the past year? Any changes in assessments of major property? Ask for the property tax rate; has that changed? Has there been an unusual number of complaints about assessments or has it been a quiet year? Obtain figures on the amount of tax-exempt property and list them if you think they might be interesting.

*J. Licensing*

State licensing boards decide who can practice medicine, cut hair, build and sell houses, bury the dead. Every state has such boards, some as many as 40, some as few as 10. Their purpose is to establish and enforce standards of professional competence and ethics, but many are criticized as self-serving. Write 300 to 400 words on one state licensing board. Cover the following areas:

1. How are the members appointed? Who recommends, clears, makes the appointments? How powerful is the influence in the appointment process of the trade or professional group that is being regulated?
2. What are some of the board's most recent actions?
3. Has the board been accused of practicing restrictive and exclusionary practices to cater to special interest groups?
4. How does one become licensed by the board to practice? Does it give tests, interviews? How many applicants were there for licenses and how many licenses were granted?

*K. Recipiency*

Using a map of the city divided into districts, chart the changes in the number of people receiving welfare assistance. Gather data for the last year for which figures are available and for five and 10 years previous. Are there any factors you would want to correlate with welfare assistance?

*L. Vigilant*

I think we should be walking through the jungle listening for odd noises and reporting exactly what we see and hear—and be wary and vigilant.
—Mary McGrory (on the job of the reporter covering public affairs)

Select an office, department, bureau or agency of local government and obtain answers from officials and townspeople to these questions and others you may devise:

1. What is the function of the office? What is its budget allocation, number of employees, current major projects?
2. Is the function necessary to meet public demands and needs?
3. Is the office functioning at optimum level in the opinion of its head or director, the second-in-command, some of the career employees and the newer employees?

Write a story of about 600 words based on your findings.

*M. Education*

Here are some assignments on education subjects:

**Majors:** Survey a group of high school seniors or incoming college freshmen to see what subjects they intend to major in. One of the fastest-growing majors is business, going from about 10 percent of incoming freshmen in the 1970s to 24 percent in the 1990s. Language majors dropped to 1 percent, history to 1.8 percent. Compare these national figures with your findings.

**Textbooks:** Bias, prejudice and discrimination have been found in high school textbooks. Make a check of textbooks in various fields: U.S. history—how Native Americans are treated, whether attention is paid to black and Hispanic contributions, adequate treatment of women; biology—adequate treatment of evolution, inclusion of women scientists, adequate discussion of venereal diseases; world history—adequate treatment of Holocaust and Judaism, suffrage, imperialism and the slave trade, Latin America, Africa and Asia.

**Movement:** Are job and educational opportunities luring high school and college graduates to other states? Survey these groups.

**Accountability:** How well are schoolchildren taught, and how well do they perform? Can you and your colleagues make a list of criteria to be used as the basis for reporting the effectiveness of the educational system?

Ken Eklins, *The Anniston* (Ala.) *Star.*

**The student is the school's measure.**

One measure is how well students do on national tests such as the Scholastic Aptitude Test. For grade school children, there are standardized tests. Another measure could be the percentage of freshman students who graduate from high school or the percentage of graduating seniors who go on to college.

**Homework:** Another way of looking at educational effectiveness is to examine what is being done in the classroom. How much homework is assigned daily? Give some examples of the homework assigned in English, history and arithmetic classes. What are students assigned to read in junior and senior high school English classes? How many compositions, essays, reports are they asked to write?

Do students think they have enough, too much, too little homework? What do their parents think?

**Curriculum:** Interview teachers about their suggestions for basic changes in the curriculum. How do their opinions differ from those held by principals and the schools' superintendent?

**Math:** A fourth of the students in the country could not multiply 671 by 402 and get the correct answer, 269,742. Of all 13-year-olds, a third could not do the multiplication. Fewer than half of all the teen-agers tested could figure out the area of a square given the length of one side. Find out the mathematical profile of students in local high schools. Look at the SAT scores for mathematics over the last few years and compare them to SAT figures for 10 and 15 years ago. Interview mathematics teachers and high school students.

**Bright:** Examine the college yearbook of 10 years ago and read news stories about graduation. Select three to five of the students considered the brightest. Where are they now? Interview them, friends, associates.

### N. Comparison

Here are data that an education reporter gathered for an article comparing two adjacent cities in terms of the quality of education. List the questions you would ask at each school for a story.

|  | Spencer | Ruston |
| --- | --- | --- |
| Per-capita income | $15,094 | $25,051 |
| Residents 25 or over with 4 years or more of college | 12.5% | 45.7% |
| Graduates attending college | 50% | 78% |
| Average SAT score | 871 | 1,021 |
| Percentage taking test | 48% | 80% |
| Percentage of teachers with master's degrees | 21.6% | 84% |
| Per-pupil spending | $3,848 | $5,691 |
| Median teacher's salary | $22,160 | $36,820 |
| Enrollment | 993 | 2,362 |
| Student/teacher ratio | 13.8:1 | 11:1 |

### O. Zoning

Attend a meeting of the planning and zoning body and cover a single request that seems to you to be worth following up with interviews. Use this as an example of the problems the community faces in planning.

### P. Land Use

Develop a feature story on the land use design for the city and surrounding areas. What are the latest developments? Anything unforeseen when the plan was made? Any people opposing its development?

### Q. Developers

Interview real estate developers and others to obtain some sense of where they think the next major moves of residential and commercial development will occur.

### R. Shoppers

What has happened to the neighborhood grocery store, drugstore, shoe store? Have shoppers deserted them for the supermarket outside town? Are these now mostly chain stores? Interview shoppers, store owners.

### S. Housing

In 1975, the standard-size home under construction for a middle-income family was 1,500 square feet. What is it today in your community and why? Interview builders and real estate agents.

### T. Inspection

Does the city or the state enforce health laws for restaurants, food producers, markets? Accompany an inspector as he or she makes the rounds. Look for particular items and match local enforcement against agreed-upon general standards. For example, the federal health standards for soft ice cream are 50,000 bacteria/gram and 10 coliform bacteria/gram.

### U. Continents

A sociologist wrote, "The city is filled with dark continents that remain impenetrable to the inhabitants of other spaces." Another sociologist described some of these areas as "dreadful enclosures." In these areas, the crime rate is high, rates for diseases and deaths such as pneumonia and infant mortality exceed the average, unemployment is above average, welfare recipiency is high and educational attainment is low. Look through census data and check city and state records for such areas or districts in your city. Then interview residents of one of these areas: To what do they attribute their area's conditions; have they hope for improvement; would they want their children to remain; have they any ideas for changing the situation?

*V. City-Suburb*

One of the assumptions in politics is that big cities vote Democratic in national elections and suburbs and small towns vote Republican. How true is this in your state?

*W. Garbage*

How much trash and garbage does your city toss out each day, and what does it do with the material? If it uses a dump or landfill, how long will it last? If there are plans for a change in garbage and solid waste disposal, what new methods are being considered: recycling, separation, incineration for energy?

*X. Compare*

Here is the beginning of a news story in a Springfield newspaper:

> Springfield now spends close to $700,000 a year for parks and recreation, a per capita expenditure of $3.37.
> Nearby Mt. Pleasant, with about the same population, spends $1,600,000 a year for the same purposes, an expenditure of $7.27 per resident.
> Mt. Pleasant has five times as many municipal swimming pools as Springfield and is scheduled to open four more this spring. Mt. Pleasant has more than 21,000 acres of park land, nearly 20 times the acreage in Springfield, half of which is undeveloped.
> Springfield last year opened its first municipal golf course; Mt. Pleasant has two and is building two more.

Make a similar comparison for your community and others in the state. In addition to parks and recreation, you can use education, social services, health, streets, police and fire.

*Y. Vouchers*

A number of state legislatures have adopted or are considering school voucher plans that allow students to enroll in parochial and other private schools and pay for tuition with tax-funded vouchers. In Ohio, the plan permits funding for vouchers for 2,000 students in Cleveland. The governors of Texas and Pennsylvania called for voucher legislation. In Arizona, North Dakota and Indiana, legislatures killed voucher proposals.

What has your state legislature done with voucher proposals? Who is behind them, who against?

## Campus Project

### Right-Left

On a speaking tour of colleges, Nadine Strossen, the president of the American Civil Liberties Union, said she was shocked to find so few liberal political groups on campuses. Whereas the conservative Federalist Society had a large network of campus chapters, she said she found only one unit of the ACLU in the northeast and few liberal political groups elsewhere.

Are there political groups on your campus? Describe their orientation, purpose, membership, funding. Attend a meeting and report the discussion.

## Community Project

### Status

The budget is an ongoing matter and many factors affect it: business conditions, state politics, demands of various groups, resistance of tax-paying organizations. Here are several questions that can be used as the basis of interviews with those involved in city or county finances. You may want to select one or a group of questions for interviews with the appropriate people. Some questions could be asked of different groups which would then be the basis of a roundup. For example, city officials could be asked their view of 1; health and welfare groups could be asked about 1a, and the local chamber of commerce and taxpayer organizations about 1a and 1b:

1. Is the government managing to balance the needs of those demanding services and the needs of those who provide the taxes to keep government in operation?
    a. Are services adequate or inadequate because of tax cuts and subsequent declines in numbers of municipal workers and in facilities and equipment?
    b. Are taxes onerous, threatening to increase? Are business conditions being affected by the tax structure?
2. What changes will have to be made as the result of experiences with the current budget?
3. Will any new programs require budget changes?
4. Is any decline in revenues anticipated?
5. Are per-capita costs in any particular area showing a steep increase or decline? Explain.
6. Is assessed valuation increasing as anticipated?
7. Are any long-range population or economic changes seen that will affect taxes or business conditions?
8. Are there any attempts under way, or is there any thinking about, regional cooperation to share the costs of services, such as solid-waste disposal, air-pollution abatement and recreation?
9. Are there any new kinds of taxes, such as nuisance taxes? Are new sources of revenue foreseen?
10. What specific pressures is the unit going to be subjected to during budget making this year?
11. Have any studies been made of employee productivity? If so, what do they show? If not, why not?
12. Is there any attempt to shift local burdens to the state or federal governments? What costs could be taken over by these larger units?
13. Have there been any significant shifts in the major source of revenue? How does the local experience compare with the national trend toward declining property tax revenues and increasing state and federal grants-in-aid?
14. What tax anticipation notes have been issued recently? What was the rate of interest on an annual basis? Have these notes been sold to the banks on a competitive basis?
15. Are there any special demands from either the money-providing constituencies or the service-demanding groups?
16. Has there been any significant shift in the so-called high-cost population, which usually demands or needs considerably more in local services than it can pay for in taxes?
17. Has there been any shift toward borrowing as a means of raising money because of the resistance to any increase in taxes?
18. How has the city fared in its relations with the state and federal government in receiving grants-in-aid? Is there any chance of greater assistance in the future?

## *Home Assignment*

### *Cities (2)*

How livable is your city? There are many measures that can supply the answer. *Money* magazine each year ranks the livability of 300 of the largest U.S. metropolitan areas. The federal government and various state and city agencies collect data that can be used as indicators. Make a list of the factors that you would use to measure the livability of your city.

## *Class Discussion*

### *Cities (3)*

After you have listed the categories to be used in judging the livability of your city (see **Home Assignment** in this chapter), make a determination of how livable your city is. How do you think it ranks with other cities in the state, in the region? Give supporting data.

## *DB/CAR*

### *A. Income*

Your newspaper has received Census Bureau data on family incomes and the percentages of Americans in poverty. Here are the figures:

|  | Year | White | Black | Native American | Asian | Hispanic |
|---|---|---|---|---|---|---|
| **Median Household Income** | 1980 | $29,632 | $18,340 | $20,541 | $33,463 | $22,629 |
|  | 1990 | $31,435 | $19,758 | $20,025 | $36,784 | $24,156 |
| **Percentage Below Poverty Line** | 1980 | 9.4% | 29.9% | 27.5% | 13.1% | 23.5% |
|  | 1990 | 9.8% | 29.5% | 30.9% | 14.1% | 25.3% |
| **Children Below Poverty Line** | 1980 | 11% | 37.8% | 32.5% | 14.9% | 29.1% |
|  | 1990 | 12.3% | 38.8% | 37.6% | 16.6% | 31% |

Use a database to bring these figures up-to-date.

Write the first three paragraphs of a news story for:

1. A medium-size daily newspaper in an affluent suburb.
2. A metropolitan daily newspaper with a large Hispanic and black population.
3. A weekly newspaper that is directed at Asian residents of the state.
4. A newspaper adjacent to a large Native American reservation.

## B. Judges

Federal appointments to judgeships are made in a political atmosphere. Here are the percentages of female and minority appointments made by four presidents:

**Carter:** 38%
**Reagan:** 14%
**Bush:** 28%
**Clinton:** 60%

Find out who was appointed to the federal courts in your area during these presidencies and check the appointees' backgrounds. What factors do you find influenced these appointments?

## C. Amendment

Republicans in Congress have declared that a school prayer constitutional amendment is a major priority. The proponents consist of a wide spectrum of religious and political groups. Some want a proposal that would be directed primarily at student religious expression in public schools, while others want a measure that would include granting religious groups access to public funding. Opponents say most of the measures would repeal church-state separation.

Obtain information for an update on the situation. Where is the proposal in Congress now? What are the positions of local leaders and the members of your state's congressional delegation? Have any prominent local citizens or religious and civic groups taken a position?

Place this information against background that includes Supreme Court rulings in 1962 and 1963 that barred school-sponsored prayer and other religious devotions. Check the comments and activities of the American Civil Liberties Union, the American Center for Law and Justice, the Christian Coalition, the Christian Legal Society, the Liberty Counsel, the National Association of Evangelicals, Concerned Women for America, the Family Research Council, the Christian Action Network, Americans United for Separation of Church and State, the Southern Baptist Christian Life Commission, the Rutherford Institute.

## Skill Drill: Property Assessments

Fill in the answers:

1. A family whose home is valued at $200,000 on the market lives in a community where real estate is valued at 45 percent of market value. The house is assessed at $ _____ .
2. Last year, the owner of the home paid a school property tax of $95 per $1,000 of assessed value. Her school property tax for the year was $ _____ .
3. The home owner decided to figure out exactly how much she was paying in property taxes and she jotted down the following figures (in $/$1,000 in assessed valuation) she had obtained from a lawyer friend:

**School:** 95
**City:** 28
**Special Assessment Districts:** 12

By adding these up and applying them to her assessed valuation, she found she was paying a total of $ _____ in property taxes.

4. She decided that with her three children grown she could use a smaller house in the $100,000 price range. Since she will retire soon, she needs to save money also. If she bought a $100,000 home, her new total property tax would be $ _____ . (Assume she continues to live in the same special assessment districts.)

5. That would be a tax savings of $ _____ a year.

## *Fix It: Basic Budget*

Paul Danison, of the *Times-Advocate* in Escondido, Calif., says of hiring new reporters, "I want someone who has enough up top to be able to walk into a budget session that's real basic and be able to make the calculations himself or herself."

Make the following calculations:

1. The proposed budget is $185,650,000, compared with the current year's budget of $175,450,000. This is a _____ percent increase.

2. The average home is valued at $150,000. With a property tax of $22.50 per thousand dollars valuation, the annual tax on the average home would be $ _____ .

3. The school budget proposes enough revenue to increase the number of teachers to 264. With 5,270 students in the city school system, this would be a _____ student/teacher ratio.

4. Pensions and union-contract wages for city employees amount to $662,000 of the $1,390,000 current budget, which means that _____ percent of the expenditures is untouchable.

5. The councilman would cut band ($15,683), library acquisitions ($10,652), playground equipment ($6,965) and audio-visual materials ($5,846) from the proposed budget, a total of $ _____ , or _____ percent of the proposed increase in the school budget of $122,480.

## *Test VII: Troublesome*

On a language test given to reporters, these questions proved difficult for more than half of those taking it.

1. Of **(a) harrass, (b) Fahrenheit** and **(c) tomatoes,** which is spelled incorrectly or are **(d) all spelled correctly** or **(e) all spelled incorrectly?**

2. Curtis__ and Hilda's house is for sale. **(a)** ' **(b)** 's **(c)** s' **(d) no punctuation needed.**

3. History is one of the subjects that **(a) interest (b) interests** her.

4. He discussed the problem with **(a) whoever (b) whomever** would listen to him.

5. This medicine has **(a) proved (b) proven** successful in curing hypertension.

# PART SIX
## Laws, Taste and Taboos, Codes and Ethics

# 25 Reporters and the Law

### Introduction

Journalists have First Amendment protection, which grants them freedom to publish. But they must work within the limits of the laws of libel and privacy. Most violations of the libel law are accidental, the result of mistakes in names and addresses and the misreading of police and court documents. Accuracy, which results in a truthful account, is the best protection. Privilege permits journalists to report the activities of official groups without fear of libel. Intrusions into the private lives of nonpublic figures can lead to privacy suits. Eavesdropping and trespassing for a story are prohibited.

**Police records are privileged.**

## Exercises

### A. Slay

You are the police reporter for a local newspaper and have been told that the police have arrested a murder suspect, Hosie Gene Jones, 55, 1347 Oklahoma Ave., a handyman and ex-convict who is known to be a drug addict. You obtain the background of the slaying, and along the way manage to obtain the criminal record (rap sheet) of the suspect.

Your editor tells you he wants about 400 words and if you can put the man's record in the story, to do so. He says he has recently heard that it may not be legal in the state to use anything but convictions, and he asks you to check. It is supposed to be prejudicial to the suspect, he says.

Write the story, but be sure to determine whether you can use parts of the suspect's record.

Here is the background provided by police:

Jones is accused of stabbing to death a 24-year-old advertising copywriter. The young woman, Dorothy F. Roberts, was in the habit of returning to her apartment at 242 Madison St. to take lunch with a friend. She worked for Trimbel's Department Store.

Yesterday when Miss Roberts entered the hallway of her four-story building, she was accosted by Jones, who demanded her purse. She resisted.

He is charged with stabbing her in the chest and back with a knife and stealing her purse containing $7.

When he was captured several blocks away, police found a sales slip addressed to Miss Roberts rolled between the $7 and tucked into Jones' pocket. He quietly surrendered.

Jones' criminal record runs to three sheets. He has had two aliases, Sonny Boy and Tom Stacey. The record contains 22 arrests beginning in 1960 with a conviction for burglary. He was sent to jail or prison 15 times. Here are the crimes for which he was convicted and the disposition of the cases:

| Date | Charge | Disposition |
|------|--------|-------------|
| 1/4/63 | Rape | Convicted, felony court, 3/5/63, 10 mos. |
| 4/10/64 | Burglary | Convicted pet. larc., 6/8/64, 90 days. |
| 12/1/65 | Petit larceny | Convicted pet. larc., 12/12/65, 60 days. |
| 1/28/68 | Grand larceny | Convicted pet. larc., 2/7/68, 90 days. |
| 4/11/69 | Burglary, unlawful entry | Convicted, 4/30/69, 1 yr. on 1st chg., 4 mos. on 2nd chg., concurrent. |
| 4/26/70 | Possession of hypo. needle | Convicted, 4/28/70, 90 days. |
| 3/9/71 | Burglary | Convicted gr. larc., 4/27/71, 2 yrs. |
| 7/6/73 | Petit larceny | Convicted, 7/19/73, 6 mos. |
| 8/17/74 | Possession heroin | Convicted, 10/27/74, 1 yr. |
| 10/22/78 | Burglary | Convicted, 11/21/78, 6 mos. |
| 9/11/81 | Burglary | Convicted, 9/16/81, 6 mos. |
| 1/7/83 | Burglary | Sent to drug center, rlsd. as cured after 6 mos. |
| 5/12/85 | Possession of hypo. needle | Convicted, 5/26/85, 90 days. |
| 6/12/89 | Burglary | Convicted, 6/29/89, 8 mos. |
| 1/19/91 | Possession of crack | Convicted, 2/3/91, 11 mos. |
| 2/7/94 | Burglary | Convicted, 9/10/94, 13 mos. |

## B. Endorse

The Sunday editor of your magazine section hands you the story that follows and tells you that she would like you to follow it up for a feature piece for her section. The story is from a newspaper in your state.

"I have a feeling that the college president has acted illegally," the editor tells you. She says she has read that students on tax-supported campuses such as Jefferson have the same constitutional protection as professional reporters.

"Dig up some of this material. If you know of any relevant cases or incidents, use them. What's the situation on campuses in the state? Give me a roundup of about 500 words."

Your survey of local colleges and the state university turns up the following notes:

The state university daily newspaper has an adviser, K.C. Franks, who says he does not examine copy before publication unless a student asks him to read it. "My job is to advise. That's all I can do, according to the clear rulings of the court." Franks is an assistant professor at the department of journalism, which uses the student newspaper for course work in reporting and editing. Two community colleges in the area have weekly student newspapers. The adviser of Selkirk Community College, Beatrice Kellogg, says she understands that it is her job to "get anything out that does not represent the college at its best." Asked how she squares this with federal court rulings, she replied, "This is the way it's always been done here." She teaches English at Selkirk. At the other school, Madison College, Ralph Barnes, the adviser, said he has "been at it 10 years and I pretty much let them print what they want. When they get a little stupid and want to use four-letter words and put the president of the school in jail for molesting freshmen, I tell them to grow up. It works. Persuasion, not censorship."

The adviser to the Mallory College *Spectator* says he does not read stories or editorials before publication. "It is clearly unconstitutional to censor a newspaper on the campus of a tax-supported institution," said Robert Figuera, the adviser. "Although Mallory receives most of its support from private sources, I prefer to abide by the courts' interpretation of the First Amendment."

Make a list of the sources you would consult, and then write the story. Here is the story your editor gives you:

A March 19 edition of the *Harbinger,* the Jefferson College student newspaper that contained endorsements of two candidates for the college board of trustees, was seized last month on orders of the college president, Ray Henry. The 1,000-copy edition then was reprinted, but without the endorsing editorial.

Henry defended the action, saying it was not an effort at censorship, but the result of a college policy against involvement in partisan politics. The college is in Hillsboro.

The endorsements were of two candidates, James A. Peek of DeSoto and Sandra Taliaferro of Arnold, who sought seats on the Junior College District Board in this week's election, and appeared in an editorial in the March 19 edition of the *Harbinger.*

When Henry learned of the editorial, he had copies of the paper picked up from the campus, and ordered reprinting without the editorial.

An article in which all six candidates for the two contested seats answered a set of questions was left undisturbed.

"Under no circumstances was this censorship," Henry said yesterday. "I have turned my back on articles of questionable taste and on some that were critical of the college administration.

"But this was entirely different. The policy against any phase of college activity becoming involved in partisan politics was restated last July and it was widely distributed at that time. The board of trustees set that policy for good reason."

The endorsements were written by the co-editors of the paper, Peggy Eades and Alice Humble.

"After our interview with President Henry," Humble said yesterday, "we understand about the policy. We don't totally agree with the policy and we hope to change it, but we understand it."

An issue of the four-page paper to be distributed on campus Monday contains an interview with Henry by the two editors in which he explains the reasons for his action.

Humble said that the six student reporters on the paper had agreed with the editors' position in making the endorsement. They had felt that the board of trustees would benefit from stronger representation from the northern area of the district and from having a woman and a student as members, Humble said. Taliaferro would have satisfied the first two qualifications and Peek the third.

Humble said some students thought the college was right and others really didn't have an opinion. "It's no big thing," she said.

"The administration feels the paper represents the college and we felt it represented the students' views," she said. The paper is distributed free with costs paid by the college.

David Braum, faculty adviser for the paper, said he had been aware of the college's nonpartisan policy. Asked why he had approved the publication of the editorial, he said, "It became a matter of interpretation." He said the staff and the paper had been given wide latitude on coverage and comment on other issues.

In the board election Tuesday, Peek and Taliaferro finished at the bottom in the field of six. Two incumbents, Charles B. Long, who is Jefferson County circuit clerk, and Donald Fitzgerand, Mayor of Hillsboro, were re-elected.

## Assignments

### A. Freedom

In a number of decisions since 1966, the federal courts have given college journalists at tax-supported institutions First Amendment freedoms. The courts have done so with a clear objective in mind: to encourage the press to a full, free and critical examination of society. The situation for high school journalists is less clear since the Supreme Court decided *Hazelwood v. Kuhlmeier* in favor of the high school administration having the right to determine content.

Go to the reference section of a law library and look for the volume assigned to you from the list that follows. Take notes on the judge's ruling and write a story as though the decision were made today. You may want to refer to prior decisions cited in the ruling. Do not use subsequent decisions.

Remember that your readers are not legal experts. You also may want to provide background from your own knowledge. The citations are read as follows:

> *Antonelli v. Hammond* means *Antonelli*, the plaintiff, is suing *Hammond*, the defendant.
>
> *F. Supp.* is the *Federal Supplement*, a series of volumes that carry federal district court decisions.
>
> **308 F. Supp. 1329 (1970)** refers to Volume *308*, page *1329* where the Antonelli case will be found. The decision was made in *1970*.

**College Cases**

*Antonelli v. Hammond*, 308 F. Supp. 1329 (1970)
*Bazaar v. Fortune*, 476 F. 2d 570 (1973)
*Brooks v. Auburn University*, 412 F. 2d 1171 (1969)
*Channing Club v. Board of Regents of Texas Tech University*, 317 F. Supp. 688 (1970)
*Dickey v. Alabama State Board of Education*, 273 F. Supp. 613 (1967)
*Joyner v. Whiting*, 341 F. Supp. 1244 (1972)
*Kania v. Fordham*, 702 F. 2d 475 (1983)
*Koppell v. Levine*, 317 F. Supp. 456 (1972)
*Korn v. Elkins*, 317 F. Supp. 138 (1970)
*Leuth v. St. Clair County Community College*, 732 F. Supp. 1410 (1990)
*Papish v. Board of Curators of University of Missouri*, 93 S. Ct. 1197 (1973)
*Schiff v. Williams*, 519 F. 2d 257 (1975)
*Stanley v. Magrath*, 719 F. 2d 279 (1983)
*State Board v. Olson*, 687 P. 2d (Colo. 1984)
*Trujillo v. Love*, 322 F. Supp. 1266 (1971)
*The UMW Post v. Board of Regents*, 774 F. Supp. 456 (1991)

## High School Cases

*Burch v. Barker,* 861 F. 2d 1149 (1988)
*Bystrom v. Fridley High School,* 822 F. 2d 747 (1987)
*Bystrom v. Fridley High School,* 855 F. 2d 855 (1988)
*Eisner v. Stamford Board of Education,* 440 F. 2d 803 (1971)
*Fraser v. Bethel School District,* 403 F. 2d 1356 (1985); *Bethel v. Fraser,* 106 S. Ct. 3159 (1986)
*Fujishima v. Board of Education,* 460 F. 2d 1355 (1972)
*Gambino v. Fairfax County School Board,* 429 F. Supp. 731 (1977)
*Kuhlmeier v. Hazelwood School District,* 596 F. Supp. 14501 (1985); *Hazelwood v. Kuhlmeier,* 108 S. Ct. 562 (1988)
*Planned Parenthood of Southern Nevada v. Clark County School District,* 941 F. 2d 817 (1991)
*Reineke v. Cobb County School District,* 484 F. Supp. 1252 (1980)
*Romano v. Harrington,* 725 F. Supp. 687 (1989)
*Schwartz v. Schuker,* 298 F. Supp. 238 (1969)
*Shanley v. Northeast Independent School District,* 462 F. 2d 960 (1972)
*Tinker v. Des Moines Independent School District,* 393 U.S. 503 (1969)
*Vail v. Board of Education of Portsmouth School District,* 354 F. Supp. 592 (1973)

## B. Sunshine

Just what campus meetings are open to the public and press under the state's sunshine law or other freedom-of-access laws or regulations: of the regents and trustees; of the faculty; of the academic senate? What records are open: budget; faculty, staff and administrative salaries; student grades and assessments; campus police actions?

## C. Citations

1. Find the citations in the Supreme Court for the following cases.
2. Select one and write a story as though the decision were made today.

### Access
*Branzburg v. Hayes*
*Gannett v. DePasquale*
*Houchins v. KQED*
*The Miami Herald Publishing Co. v. Tornillo*
*Nebraska Press Association v. Stuart*
*Press-Enterprise v. Supreme Court of California*
*Students Press Law Center v. Alexander*

### Libel
*Firestone v. Time*
*Gertz v. Robert Welch, Inc.*
*Herbert v. Lando*
*Hutchinson v. Proxmire*
*The New York Times v. Sullivan*
*Rosenbloom v. Metromedia*
*Wolston v. Reader's Digest*

### Privacy
*Time, Inc. v. Hill*

### Search
*Zurcher v. Stanford Daily*

## Campus Project

### Schedule

Where does your time go? How much of the day do you and your friends devote to study, sleep, bull sessions and the rest? Make a study of members of a class—say freshmen or seniors—and find out.

First, make a time log for seven days of the week. Down one side place the various activities students engage in, such as adviser-advisee consultations, reading, television viewing, attendance at sports events and social events such as dances and travel.

Then distribute the logs to a random sample of one class. You could use two classes and compare how freshmen and seniors, for example, use their time. Follow up with interviews.

One such study found that freshmen spend an average of 41 hours a week on all academic activities: classes, labs, study. They averaged two hours a day with their books, slept eight hours—going to bed after 1 a.m. most of the time—and felt television was a time waster.

## Community Project

### Channel One

If the schools in your community are wired into Channel One, the Whittle communications firm's daily television program that combines so-called educational material with commercials, make a study of a week's programs. With the assistance of educational experts, students, teachers and administrators, assess the contribution Channel One is making to the education of those who view it.

Here is how Helen Thompson of *Texas Monthly* described her experience with the channel, which is wired to 1,000 Texas schools:

> For schools on a tight budget . . . the offer was a once-in-a-lifetime chance to obtain unaffordable equipment . . . "It has worked real well for us," [a principal] says. "We couldn't have gotten this technology any other way." . . . the content isn't exactly conveying "world culture," as Whittle promised. . . . Here's the report from the classroom. The program begins with spunky graphics. . . . Today the subject is the Grammy Awards . . . (there's a two-minute news segment) . . . Flash! . . . we're back to the Grammy-goers . . . [including] the backup singers on the Diet Pepsi commercial [Pepsi is a sponsor of Channel One] . . . Ads for Clearasil and Bite-size Doritos are sandwiched between the Grammys and another series, *On the Money,* which tells the thirteen-through-eighteen-year-old viewers how to get a loan when the "$17,000 dream car you want is more than you can afford." Back to the Grammys again before the Kellogg's Corn Pops and Burger King ads. . . . Rummaging through recorded programs at home, I find one about . . . the Academy Awards which promises "the lowdown on the Oscar showdown," which should be interesting since six of the seven films are R-rated and Channel One viewers are actually too young to see them. Even so, the program features clips from each movie. . . . In Texas, says a parent, where "half our school population can't even afford a dollar for lunch, Channel One is a constant reminder of the need for a new car or new clothes." . . . some of the members of the State Board of Education have never even seen a Channel One program.

California, Massachusetts, North Carolina, New York and Washington have banned the channel, and several teacher and parent organizations oppose its use in schools.

Many have complained about the two minutes of commercials on the program. They say that allowing commercials to intrude on a captive audience results in a de facto endorsement of the advertised products. Also, as was charged in the debate over Channel One in New York's schools, with the set in the classroom, educators lose control over the curriculum. In reply, defenders of Channel One say that high school students are sophisticated enough to resist the influence of commercials for jeans, tennis shoes, snack foods, candy, acne creams and cosmetics.

K. Tim Wulfemeyer and Barbara Mueller of the journalism faculty at San Diego State University analyzed the commercials aired on Channel One "to determine the techniques, messages, values, themes and appeals used to persuade students to buy products or change their behavior." (See "Channel One and Commercials in Classrooms: Advertising Content Aimed at Students," *Journalism Quarterly,* Fall 1992.)

They found 86 percent of the commercials were for products, 14 percent were public service announcements. The breakdown: jeans, 14 percent; candy, 10 percent; shampoo, 9 percent; makeup, gum and razor blades, 8 percent each; breath mints and acne cream, 6 percent; deodorant, 5 percent; athletic shoes and corn chips, 4 percent; catsup and movies, 4 percent; and cough drops, 2 percent.

The most common public service announcements were about the dangers of drug abuse. None of the commercials was developed specifically for Channel One.

"Three major themes dominated the commercials on Channel One," the researchers found: " 'Be popular/have friends' (48%) was the most frequent, followed by 'be attractive' (46%) and 'have fun/have pleasure' (38%)." Other common themes were " 'Be cool' and 'be fit/healthy' (23% each) and 'self-actualization' (18%)."

Among the other findings: "Most of the dominant and secondary characters were young and white . . . (which) should be cause for some concern. . . ."

With a potential audience of seven million students, Channel One could have far-reaching effects on young people, the authors say, and they urged more research of the program's news and feature stories.

## Home Assignment

### Disparity

Women faculty members have contended that they are discriminated against in salary and promotion. They say that women receive less pay than do men of the same rank, and they point out that they are represented disproportionately in the ranks of instructor and full professor—that many women are in the lower ranks, few in the higher ranks.

You can obtain the national averages from the American Association of University Professors, which makes annual studies in these areas and publishes them in its magazine *Academe*.

Compare the national data with the situation on your campus.

Write 450 words.

## Class Discussion

### A. Con Artist

You are covering the federal district court and drop in to talk to Herbert N. Kaplan, an assistant U.S. attorney. He tells you about a case involving John DeLuria, 68, last known address in New York City:

DeLuria was born in Portugal and has a criminal record going back to 1944, when he was arrested for shoplifting in Philadelphia. He got off on that one and from most of the other charges, which included larceny, vagrancy, taking money under false pretenses, concealing leased property, fraud by wire, conspiracy. His latest caper was to convince businessmen to invest in a portfolio of stock that supposedly included blue-chip securities. Some men went in for as much as $200,000. The stock was offered through a New York firm known as Kimberly Beers Ltd., which DeLuria and his associates claimed was affiliated with DeBeers Consolidated Mines Ltd., of Kimberly, South Africa, the big diamond concern.

At least 40 victims were involved, and $750,000 in losses have been accounted for, but more losses are suspected. DeLuria was granted U.S. citizenship in 1959 despite government efforts to deport him. His record shows he served a two-year sentence in Lewisburg, Pa., beginning in 1970 for fraud.

DeLuria has had some interesting accomplices, one of whom served a brief prison term for participating in a $20 million religious fraud in the early 1970s. This was the Baptist Foundation of America caper.

DeLuria is an old hand at taking money from people, a typical white-collar criminal with a smooth line who steals from those who have a little larceny in their hearts themselves. We know how he operates. He claims to have inside contacts, especially with a couple of local politicians, including the congressman from this district. Maybe he does. When he got citizenship in 1959, the congressman in office then wrote letters for DeLuria to the immigration people. You want to know how he operates, talk to Benjamin Fields, owner of the North Funeral Home, who invested and lost $185,000. We're looking into Fields' income taxes, for that matter.

What would you do with this information under each of the following circumstances?

1. DeLuria was arrested last night on charges of securities violations in connection with the Kimberly Beers Ltd. stock sales.
2. DeLuria has been found guilty of securities violations in connection with Kimberly and is awaiting sentence.
3. DeLuria has been sentenced to 10 years in prison by Federal Judge Charles E. Stuart.
4. A warrant has been issued for DeLuria's arrest for securities violations.

# 26 Taste—Defining the Appropriate

Tim Lorette, *Foster's Daily Democrat.*
**Pictures draw the most complaints.**

### Introduction

What constitutes acceptable language and subject matter for the journalist cannot be precisely defined. What was taboo yesterday has become commonplace today. Definitions of acceptability vary with the nature of the medium, the audience and the status of the individuals involved. Magazines aimed at particular audiences feel free to explore the limits of acceptable taste, whereas small-town newspapers are more susceptible to pressures from organized groups. Television is regulated by the Federal Communications Commission, which sets standards.

## Exercises

### A. Questionable

Your instructor will make available to you material from events that included frank language and explicit detail on sexual matters. You are to write news stories for:

1. A newspaper of 15,000 circulation in a Kansas agricultural community.
2. A radio station in Chicago.
3. A metropolitan daily newspaper.

### B. Demographics

You receive a release from the mayor's office that includes data based on studies made by various city agencies. Your editor has examined the material and tells you to do a story that "makes some logical sense out of these figures." He says the mayor's statement should be helpful.

The statement says in part:

> The figures on income and unemployment indicate trouble spots for our community. Clearly, we have to do something about these factors because the consequences can be chilling for community life.
> In our country, problems of race and class are serious. We can see that they have come to Freeport.

You call around and learn that one of the "consequences" has been a record crime increase in districts 4 and 5, with felonies last year rising 18 percent in district 4 and 22 percent in district 5.

You check with the mayor's office and are told by an aide, "Mayor Sam Parnass says that increased crime in districts 4 and 5 is one of the consequences he was referring to."

You have no time to check further. (A map of the city districts is on Page 248. A demographic profile of Freeport is on Page 249.)

Write a 350- to 500-word story based on the data and the mayor's statement.

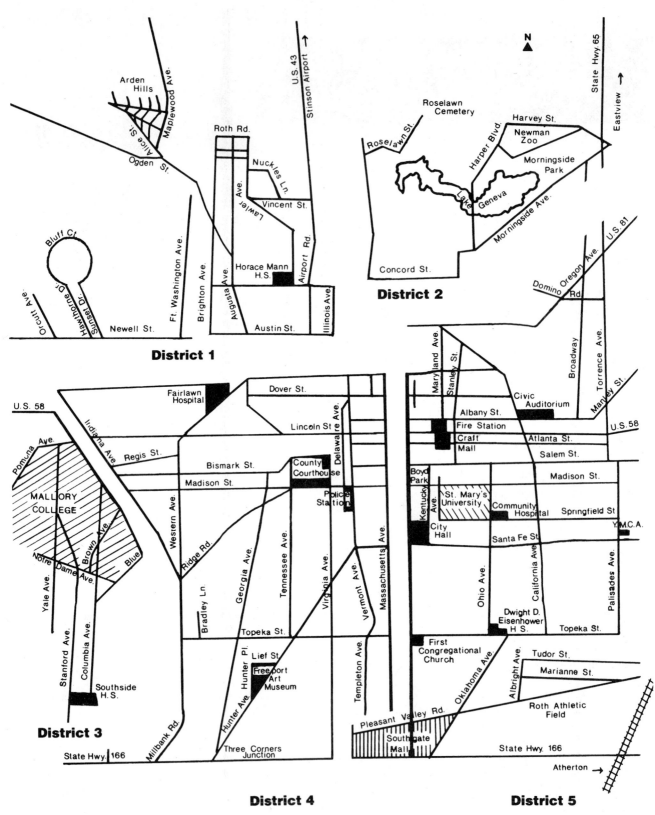

**Freeport Health Districts**

## Freeport

| District | Percent of Total Families with Female Householders, No Husband Present | Percent with 12 Years or More of Schooling | Mean Household Income | Percent of Total Population in the District that is Minority | Percent of Total Labor Force Unemployed |
|---|---|---|---|---|---|
| 1 | 14.7 | 53.3 | $36,842 | 18.5 | 6.3 |
| 2 | 10.8 | 88.8 | $59,113 | 12.4 | 4.1 |
| 3 | 11.5 | 64.5 | $47,406 | 21.7 | 4.9 |
| 4 | 31.6 | 43.6 | $16,327 | 37.6 | 13.4 |
| 5 | 41.2 | 41.4 | $11,669 | 56.3 | 17.8 |
| City | 19.4 | 53.5 | $24,895 | 26.6 | 8.4 |

| District | No. of Reported Felonies | Homicide Rate | Robbery Rate | Burglary Rate | Rape Rate |
|---|---|---|---|---|---|
| 1 | 1,922 | 16.8 | 117.1 | 1,566.9 | 6.9 |
| 2 | 2,612 | 3.0 | 142.6 | 1,485.3 | 20.8 |
| 3 | 2,533 | 20.2 | 224.8 | 1,333.8 | 16.7 |
| 4 | 2,956 | 38.3 | 244.9 | 1,876.2 | 133.5 |
| 5 | 3,297 | 45.7 | 276.9 | 2,002.8 | 78.3 |
| City | 13,320 | 20.9 | 258.6 | 1,592.3 | 38.7 |

*C. Racial-Religious Folo*

The appearance of Khalid Abdul Muhammad on the Mallory College campus last week (see *C. Racial Religious,* Chapter 17) caused a massive reaction. Your editor tells you that he wants a Sunday piece rounding up opinions expressed at several subsequent campus meetings and the reactions of Mallory administrators and faculty members. He wants 500 to 750 words.

Here is the material you have gathered:

Ruth Pitts Renaldi, president of Mallory College:
Mallory is a place where ideas are exchanged, examined, debated and judged. Some ideas are misguided, but we count on the bright light of reason to expose and shrivel them. The answer to hate is more speech, not enforced silence. I note with pride that this point has been widely understood in the Mallory community.

I have also said that, "We must work to ensure that all our dealings with each other are marked by decency and characterized by civility. We must do what we can to engender mutual respect, understanding, even empathy." Every campus organization has the right to invite speakers of its choice, but having the right, or freedom, or power to do something is the beginning of ethical inquiry, not the end of it. "I have the rights to do what I am doing" is very different from "I am doing what is right." Many Americans miss that distinction.

A hateful speaker has come and gone and I hope we can heal the wounds caused by his visit, though they are deep and painful. It is time for those who exercised their right to invite him to ask themselves whether they did the right thing. Can they in their hearts feel good about having been so indifferent to the feelings of their colleagues as to invite back to Mallory a man who had openly insulted Jews on his last visit?

This is a good time for all of us to think about what we owe one another. This is a good time to remember that there can be no community without mutual respect, understanding, even empathy.

Stanley Morson, head of the Black Students' Organization:
"I just hope people really heard what he had to say. His message was inspiring."

Gerald Stern, head of the Jewish Student Union:
"The speech blew apart anything I'd ever experienced in terms of anti-Semitism, racism and the proliferation of hatred. It was disgusting to the point of nausea. I sat there shaking in my seat. It was like a police state."

A member of BSO who spoke at a forum sponsored by the college: "I am outraged by the level of religious intolerance at this school. The Nation of Islam is a religion, whether you like it or not. People are interested in Malcolm X. The Nation of Islam is the group closest to him."

A dialogue between a white student and a black student at the forum. They would not give their names:
Black student: "We were curious to hear what he had to say. We want an opportunity to hear leaders of our community speak."
White student: "Suppose a group here invited the Ku Klux Klan to send a speaker because it wanted to hear what the Klan has to say for itself?"

Black student: "There is racism here on the campus, and this attack is part of it."

White student: "After this incident, I no longer care about your aims, no matter how laudable they may seem. Your means are despicable."

The student newspaper, the *Spectator,* carried a long editorial on the talk that included the following:

The Black Students' Organization has sponsored anti-Semitic speakers on this campus over the past three years. We are tired of these offensive actions.

The BSO understood full well the nature of the talk their invited speaker was likely to give. It also knows that the Nation of Islam is notoriously anti-Semitic.

If the BSO cannot explain its action we must conclude that the organization is itself anti-Semitic.

The BSO can invite anyone it wishes, but that invitation does not establish the validity of the content of the speech. Nor does an invitation to a speaker promoting hatred constitute responsible behavior by the organization.

A letter to the editor by a student, Charles Stalworth, stated, "The claim that the Nation of Islam can speak for Malcolm X is spurious. Malcolm broke with the Nation in his maturity, when he dropped his racist oratory. He understood how he was spreading hatred and he was killed because he broke with the hate peddlers."

The BSO held a discussion to go over the concerns raised by its invitation to Muhammad. "We need to recognize the prejudice we have against other groups before we can move towards tolerance," said Hilton Barrows, the BSO vice president. Several BSO members said they felt no need to apologize for their invitation. Florence Halter, a BSO member, said, "You cannot tell the BSO what kind of statement to issue because perhaps the BSO doesn't feel that way."

Stern, who attended the meeting, said that he had felt threatened by Muhammad's bodyguards several times during the speech.

"Good," said a BSO member. "Jewish students should feel uncomfortable so you can understand the hostility black students face here daily. Mallory black men are hassled by security and generally not recognized as members of this community. It is a fallacy to say that BSO is destroying a sense of community, because for us there is no community to destroy."

Stern replied, "I don't believe that blacks are anti-Semitic. But surely the campus organization could have issued a statement that it does not agree with the bigotry expressed by its speaker here on two occasions."

"The silence is frightening. That silence means approval," Josh Friedman, a member of the audience said.

Fred Long, a BSO member, replied: "Dr. Muhammad's message provided pride and love in one's race and religion."

A black member of the audience, unidentified, said, "If the source of pride in one's race and religion is based on hatred of other groups and people rather than the beauty of your own, then one degrades his own culture, race or religion."

At a meeting called by the Student Government Association, Professor Dalton Dennis of the psychology department said, "Racial tensions on the campus are the worst I have seen in 30 years." The SGA voted to draft a letter to the faculty to hold seminars and teach-ins on race relations on campus. The SGA also decided to hold a "town meeting to discuss the implications of the Muhammad appearance."

The dean of students, William Sharman, stated in a letter to the *Spectator,* "The BSO has acted irresponsibly by inviting a known anti-Semite and hate-monger to this campus to air his message of religious intolerance." The BSO responded by accusing Sharman of racism. A petition in support of Sharman's letter was signed by 800 Mallory College students.

William Parrington, professor of political science, said in an interview, "The position of the BSO is clearly indefensible. It cannot deny that the anti-Semitic sentiments of its speaker were well known. It knew full well what it was doing when it invited him. It is strange that college students should be so committed to a philosophy of religious hatred. Polls show that intolerance declines as the level of education increases.

"In one recent poll, 37 percent of the blacks interviewed were classified in a category described as the 'most anti-Semitic.' But the percentage declined dramatically for college students. Seventeen percent of whites, by the way, were in the most anti-Semitic group."

You ask Parrington to hazard a guess as to the reason the speaker was invited.

"There are two obvious reasons. First, the organization has an agenda determined by a few leaders, and the membership feels it must go along in the name of group solidarity. I have had students, members of the BSO, come up to me and say they are ashamed of what the organization is doing but that they cannot speak out for fear of causing dissension. The second is that these few leaders who espouse anti-Semitism realize they are untouchable since on a liberal campus no one wants to be seen to be critical of blacks, whatever wild cause they endorse."

Parrington, who is black, is the author of many articles and books on the experiences of African Americans in the United States.

Franklin Besoyan, a member of the sociology department, said the situation at Mallory follows a well-established pattern on campuses throughout the country. A speaker is invited by a group that knows the speaker will attack Jews. He referred to the appearance at the University of Washington of Abdul Alim Musa, who was invited by the Black Students Commission, the Associated Students of the University of Washington and the International Muslim Student Association. In his talk, Musa charged that America is "controlled by an influential Jewish community, determined to keep minorities repressed and powerless," and that "Jews control American domestic policy," and that "they are the enemy of humanity." He predicted a second holocaust, this one in the United States, where "Jews will be slaughtered in a popular uprising."

In a day-long silent protest in the middle of the campus, the BSO attacked Sharman. BSO president Stanley Morson said, "We have been silenced by the media. The president and the dean's office have condemned us. Certain students are threatening us physically and financially. This kind of intimidation cannot go on on a free and democratic campus."

## *Assignment*

### *Chitchat*

Handle this assignment with the technique of unobtrusive observation. (See the textbook for a definition and examples.) Visit a high school cafeteria or a luncheonette where students eat or visit a student hangout. Report verbatim what students are talking about, what subjects occupy them. Write the story precisely as you heard it. Discuss in class whether you can use some of the language and subject matter for the local newspaper or radio station.

## *Campus Project*

### *Voters*

Political scientists and pollsters have drawn two conclusions about young men and women eligible to vote: Those under 30 are mostly Republican, and most of those under 21 do not bother to vote.

Of those under 30, 27 percent say they are Democrats, 34 percent Republicans, 39 percent independents. This compares with figures for those in their 60s: 46 percent Democrats, 30 percent Republicans, 24 percent independents.

One explanation for this difference is the Impressionable Years Hypothesis, which states that when people become old enough to vote they are influenced by the party then in power. "These first loyalties are powerful throughout life," says Everett C. Ladd, executive director of the Roper Center, which studies political polls and trends. Older voters came of age politically during the New Deal and Harry S. Truman's presidency, whereas younger voters established voter eligibility during Republican administrations.

As for under-21 voters, their participation in elections worries people. In some parts of the country, fewer than a third eligible to vote cast ballots in the last presidential election.

Test these assumptions and findings by conducting a poll of students on your campus. Poll a sufficiently large number so that you also can make subgroups: men and women; age brackets; percentage voting of those who consider themselves Democrats, Republicans, independents. You might ask about their parents' political affiliations to see whether students shifted loyalties.

Pool your data and write a story on the findings.

## *Community Project*

### *Sex Education (1)*

Teen-age pregnancies are at all-time highs in some cities, and the incidence of AIDS and sexually transmitted diseases is increasing among young men and women. Two-thirds of sexually active adolescents have had two or more sexual partners, up from 39 percent 20 years before.

Of sexually active women under 20, a third have had four or more sexual partners, and 5 percent reported 10 or more partners.

The Alan Guttmacher Institute reports that there is a steady trend "toward multiple sexual partners." Its study said this "means we need to be facing the reality of the risks of sexually transmitted diseases. We need to be concerned not only about preventing unintended pregnancy, but about guarding against sexually transmitted diseases such as H.I.V. and chlamydia and gonorrhea, which can cause infertility."

Dr. Jacqueline Darroch Forrest, author of the study, said younger women are growing up in "an era of relaxed sexual mores," and this increases their vulnerability.

What is the status of sex education and education on AIDS and other sexually transmitted diseases in your junior and senior high schools? Is there counseling on birth control, distribution of condoms? Classes in sex education?

Interview students, teachers, parents. What do they think schools should do in this area?

## Home Assignment

### Policy

The editor of the local newspaper (50,000 circulation in a county seat in Illinois) has asked you to draw up for her a policy statement on taste that she will consider for adoption by her staff. Write about 500 words as a "position paper" and include some general suggestions and your reasons for them. Cite actual cases and the comments and experiences of reporters and editors.

## Class Discussion

### A. Guidelines

Where do you draw the line?

When Col. Oliver North testified before Congress that Rep. Ron Dellums of California should not be on the House Intelligence Committee because he opposed the Vietnam War, Rep. Pete Stark, another Democrat from California, said to North, "Frankly, Colonel, you are full of shit."

The actress Regina Taylor recalled that in the early 1970s she was among the first group of blacks to integrate a junior high school in Oklahoma. The first day in class she was seated next to a white girl who told the teacher, "I do not want to sit next to this nigger."

In the lyrics of a rap song by 2 Live Crew, the group recites, "I'll break ya down and dick ya long/Bust your pussy then break your backbone."

Earl Butz, a member of President Ford's cabinet, said in the hearing of a reporter, " . . . coloreds only want three things: first, a tight pussy; second, loose shoes; and third, a warm place to shit. That's all."

Madonna at a Live Aid concert refused to take off her blazer. "I'm not taking shit off."

For a profile, Clint Eastwood told the interviewer he could not accept the notion of a wrathful god—"some great villain who would come down and beat the shit out of you if you sinned."

What would you do with this language and with any other words and situations you have come across in your reading and experience? Can you suggest guidelines?

### B. Johns (2)

You receive this press release from the mayor's office:

Scott Martin, *The Blade*.

**Neighborhoods demand the police crack down on cruising Johns.**

> Mayor Sam Parnass today announced that the Mayor's Office of Midtown Enforcement and the City Police Department last night closed three houses of prostitution on Torrence Avenue. Also last night, the Public Morals Division of the Police Department arrested 29 prostitutes and eight of their clients and confiscated three automobiles at 10 locations along Torrence Avenue.
>
> Mayor Parnass said, "Last month, after consultation with District Attorney Paul Robinson, I directed my Office of Midtown Enforcement to assist the Police in their efforts to address the growing prostitution problem. As a result, six illegal brothels were closed last week and three more were closed last night.
>
> "These achievements bode well for the success of interagency cooperation and I am confident that with city agencies working together with the support of the District Attorney's office, the quality of life will improve for our citizens."
>
> The three illegal businesses—located at 6310, 6522 and 6770 Torrence Ave.—were closed last night pursuant to the City's Nuisance Abatement Law, which provides for the immediate closure of establishments that have a history of prostitution

arrests during the previous year. Midtown Enforcement attorneys initiated the three lawsuits based on numerous prostitution arrests made by the Police Department's Public Morals Division. The closing orders were signed by District Judge Mary Farrell.

Also, we are confiscating cars belonging to men who cruise looking for prostitutes. We will not have our neighborhoods used for illicit purposes.

You check the arrest records and obtain the names of seven of those arrested. The officer in charge suggests that you check the ownership of the three confiscated automobiles, and you do so with the motor vehicle department. You learn one of the automobiles is registered in the name of Herbert Blitzer, dean of the school of journalism; the other two are registered to two of the seven arrested.

You ask who the eighth person was and the police tell you they are holding his name because he is a minor. Through sources, you learn he is Donald Blitzer, the 16-year-old son of the dean.

How would you handle the story?

1. Would you use the names of the prostitutes, some of whom have local addresses?
2. Would you use the names of the local men?
3. Would you use Donald Blitzer's name? (The law does not prohibit publication of the names of minors; it penalizes those who disclose them.)

## *DB/CAR*

### *Safe Sex*

Many studies indicate that the majority of college students are not practicing safe sex. Dr. Karen Kotloff, an associate professor of pediatrics at the University of Maryland School of Medicine, sampled 2,013 undergraduates and found:

- 48.5 percent of heterosexual partners used condoms when having intercourse.
- 36.8 percent of gay students always or almost always used condoms; 28.2 percent said they never used condoms.

Make a database survey to obtain material for a story on sexual practices and supplement it with interviews on your campus.

## *Fix It: Leave or Delete*

1. A story about a Michigan-Michigan State basketball game included this paragraph:

After talking with reporters, Frieder walked past Skiles and said with a grin. "I'm glad we've got only one more goddamn game with you."

Is the quotation OK?

2. An American Indian woman was quoted in a news story: "This is my native, ancient land. My great, great ancestors were living here when Columbus touched Manhattan Island, and we don't know how long before that." Do you use the quotation as is?

3. A woman driving to work sees an accident a few blocks from her home. The wreckage is of a sports car that looks familiar. She asks a police officer, and he confirms her fears: The dead man in the wreckage is her husband. A free-lance photographer records her anguish and the picture is published on page one, in color. Readers describe the newspaper as insensitive, irresponsible, exploitative and sensationalistic.

Would you have used the picture?

4. A story about a bar that caters to gay men begins:

A reedy man about 30 years old, wearing nothing but magenta leg warmers, closes his eyes and eases back against a wooden beam inside the Mine Shaft, a gay sex bar in Greenwich Village, while a paunchy, middle-aged man drops to his knees and performs oral sex.

Do you use this lead as is?

5. President Reagan is pressed hard to answer some questions at a news conference. He dodges them and when the conference is over, he is heard to mutter, "Sons of bitches," in obvious reference to the reporters. You have it on tape; do you broadcast the direct quote? You heard it; do you use it in your news story?

## Test VIII: Define

What do these words or terms mean?

1. Muckraker
2. Coup d'etat
3. Felony
4. Unicameral
5. DNA
6. Pork barrel
7. Lame duck
8. Dow-Jones average
9. Indictment
10. HIV-positive

## You Decide: Rapper

A member of the "gangsta rap" group the Geto Boys "ignited a furor," according to *Editor & Publisher,* with remarks he made at the annual convention of the National Association of Black Journalists. The rapper, Bushwick Bill, frequently referred to women as "bitches" and "hos," according to the account in *E&P*. When he was asked why he used these terms, he replied that the "only women he knows are 'bitches and hos,' " *E&P* reported. The article in the journalism publication continued:

> Audience grumbling turned to outrage, however, when *Asbury Park* (N.J.) *Press* recruiter Karyn Collins asked him what he called his mother.
> According to witnesses, Bushwick Bill replied that he called his mother a woman, adding, "I'm not fucking my mother. If I was fucking you, you'd be a bitch.
> More than 200 people, mostly women, stormed out of the session.

If you were the editor of *E&P* would you have allowed the offensive language to appear as it did? Why?
If you were the following, what would you have done with Bushwick Bill's language?:

- News director of a local radio station covering the convention.
- Editor of the city's daily newspaper.
- Author of an article or book about changing standards of taste in the media.

# 27 The Morality of Journalism

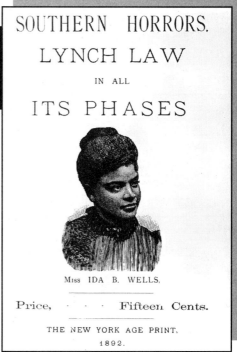

Making journalism out of injustice.

### Introduction

Journalism is a moral enterprise. Journalists recognize their obligation to check on power as the reason they are given First Amendment protection. They understand they are the conscience of the community, that they not only transcribe the community's formal activities but also actively seek out information that helps all of those in the community to lead happy, fruitful lives. Journalists subscribe to a code of ethics and a personal credo that make public service journalism's major obligation. Journalists are expected to be impartial in their reporting and free of conflicts of interest.

## *Exercises*

### A. Quit

You are covering Washington for your newspaper and a congressman from a district in which your newspaper circulates calls you in to announce he has managed to keep a post office building in your city. The Postal Service had intended to consolidate it with a post office in the nearby city of New Plains as an economy move. The service, he said, has cancelled its plan. The congressman, William Hartwell, has served six terms in the House. He is a Democrat. He has been a good source for years, a friend.

You chat with him about the criticism of Congress as a contentious, even capricious body, beset by political considerations, unable to act decisively. He agrees that there is merit in the criticism, and then goes on:

I am having second thoughts about staying in Congress. An office holder has to ask himself if he is serving the public interest to the best of his ability. It really has to be a passion. I have gradually become aware that my enthusiasm for public service has been waning under the weight of my frustrated hopes, others' unreasonable pressures and the job's persistent demands.

People want you to act for their interests, and often this is against the public interest. But how can you build a political base without catering to local demands? Yet it is the increasing narrowness, the declining public spirit that you see locally that you can't really cater to.

The years have eroded my tolerance, stamina and patience. I am tiring of the criticism and the demands of my constituents. I am not sure I can continue to live with Jefferson's dictum, "When a man assumes a public trust, he should consider himself public property."

It is difficult for a public servant to live in an atmosphere of suspicion and distrust. It may be that the ineffectiveness of Congress is the result of these pulls and tugs.

The other night, I was working past midnight when I spotted a letter from a constituent that complained I should not have voted for a pay raise, that I did not deserve one because I don't work hard enough. Here it was, 1:30 in the morning and I was starting to write to her. Then I thought, "Do I have to take this?"

People are cynical about politicians. They shoot you down first and then ask questions. Let's be realistic. Most of us are not in this for the money. We get some sort of ego satisfaction in serving; some like the opportunity of moving up to something higher. But the grind is too great. I've had 69 days of vacation since I've been in Congress, and my marriage broke up because I could not afford to have my wife and four children in Washington, and we were separated for long periods.

Maybe my time is running out anyway. I may be too liberal for my constituents. I've supported programs for the poor, and these are becoming less and less popular in my district. Also, I hate the prospect of having to raise so much money for the campaign. . . .

You are taking careful notes as he speaks, and he suddenly stops to ask, "You're not going to use that are you?" You say that you intend to, and he says he was not speaking for the record. You ask if he intends to run for re-election or is only thinking about running or not running, and he answers that he has definitely made up his mind to go home, to quit. All the more reason, you say, you want to use the story. He owes it to his constituents to tell them he is not going to seek re-election.

No, he answers. Not now. You remind him of your understanding with your sources: no retroactive off-the-record remarks. He says he understands that, but he hopes you will hold off a while.

1. What do you do?
2. Presume you will write a story and write 300 words.

### B. Death

You decide to follow up on the demographic material that you wrote about a few weeks ago. (See Chapter 26, *B. Demographics.*)

You visit the city health department and obtain data from last year on causes of death. The mayor had mentioned "poor health" as a consequence of the data he had released then.

You look at the figures, and it is evident that the mayor was on the right track. You show the data to your editor and he tells you he wants 500 words on the subject. (A map of health districts is on Page 257.)

"I want you to make clear correlations between these figures and social and economic factors," he tells you.

## Freeport

| District | Percent of Total Families with Female Householders, No Husband Present | Percent with 12 Years or More of Schooling | Mean Household Income | Percent of Total Population in the District who Belong to Minority Group | Percent of Total Labor Force Unemployed |
|---|---|---|---|---|---|
| 1 | 14.7 | 53.3 | $36,842 | 18.5 | 6.3 |
| 2 | 10.8 | 88.8 | $59,113 | 12.4 | 4.1 |
| 3 | 11.5 | 64.5 | $47,406 | 21.7 | 4.9 |
| 4 | 31.6 | 43.6 | $16,327 | 37.6 | 13.4 |
| 5 | 41.2 | 41.4 | $11,669 | 56.3 | 17.8 |
| City | 19.4 | 53.5 | $24,895 | 26.6 | 8.4 |

## Death Rates

| District | All Causes | Infant Mortality | Heart Disease | Cancer | Flu and Pneumonia | Cirrhosis of Liver | AIDS | Drug Dependence | Homicide | Accident | Suicide |
|---|---|---|---|---|---|---|---|---|---|---|---|
| 1 | 10.1 | 11.8 | 489.2 | 179.3 | 45.6 | 14.9 | 14.0 | 8.5 | 16.8 | 13.6 | 7.7 |
| 2 | 10.9 | 5.1 | 520.7 | 236.0 | 39.5 | 15.6 | 9.4 | 6.5 | 3.0 | 1.8 | 10.1 |
| 3 | 11.1 | 7.6 | 572.8 | 202.3 | 44.2 | 16.9 | 8.8 | 5.2 | 20.2 | 16.5 | 4.4 |
| 4 | 7.1 | 13.8 | 182.1 | 147.9 | 67.7 | 22.0 | 57.2 | 53.2 | 38.3 | 14.5 | 8.7 |
| 5 | 11.2 | 16.5 | 338.1 | 318.9 | 63.3 | 40.9 | 66.5 | 36.9 | 45.7 | 14.4 | 12.6 |
| City | 10.8 | 11.0 | 401.5 | 196.1 | 46.2 | 15.9 | 37.5 | 10.8 | 20.9 | 7.7 | 7.1 |

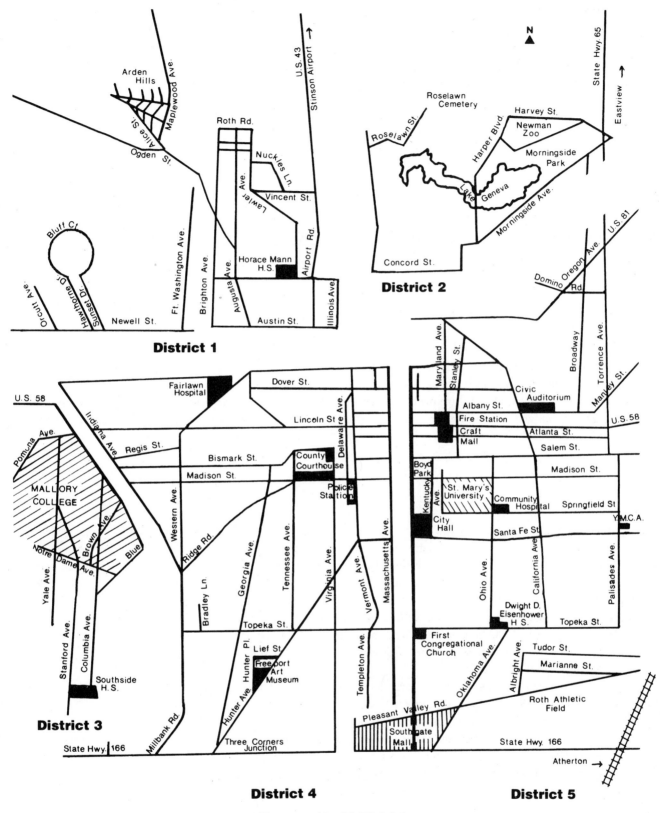

**Freeport Health Districts**

## Assignments

### A. Pose

Reporter teams have posed as couples needing loans and as the owners of malfunctioning automobiles. The textbook describes the differing views of the morality of using disguises in reporting. Interview a local editor about his or her views.

### B. Problems

Interview a reporter or editor of a local newspaper or broadcast station about an event or a story that posed ethical problems. What was the issue and how was it resolved? In class, discuss any generalities that can be drawn from the variety of experiences the interviews turn up.

### C. Appointment

Newcomers in many communities find it hard to obtain appointments within a reasonable time with pediatricians, ophthalmologists, gynecologists and other kinds of doctors. A Michigan newspaper reporter called all the doctors listed in the yellow pages and detailed the difficulties. Try this locally.

## Campus and Community Project

### Omission

Survey students on the campus and residents in the community: Are there activities, events, personalities, problems that the campus or community newspapers or broadcast stations are not covering?

Or is your criticism broader, that the media that local people read, listen to and watch are primarily bulletin boards, offering only overt events and matters of record, not digging into problems, not initiating or enterprising coverage?

## Campus Project

### Segregated

Campus ethnic groups have successfully sought separate housing and dining facilities on many campuses since the 1960s. In recent years, the concept has come under attack. Kenneth B. Clark, professor emeritus at the City College of New York and a major figure in the Supreme Court's desegregation of public schools, argues that black, Native American and Latino dormitories violate the 1964 Federal Civil Rights Act, which forbids federal financial support to institutions that permit racially segregated facilities.

Clark compares such segregation and its defense by some institutions such as Cornell University as akin to the "rationalizations that guardians of the Old South offered in defense of their racist traditions."

In commenting on the resistance of Cornell to desegregate, Clark and Michael Meyers, the executive director of the New York Civil Rights Coalition, wrote:

"In accommodating the mindlessness of race-based campus housing in Ithaca and accepting the alibis for separatism, Cornell and the Board of Regents are accessories to a functional repeal of the Supreme Court's *Brown v. Board of Education* pronouncement that separate education is inherently unequal."

What is the situation on your campus? Is there racially separate housing and are other facilities separated? Has there been a drive for such? Obtain the comments on this subject from a variety of perspectives: black, Native American and Latino students; university administrators; members of the faculty.

## Home Assignments

### A. Contribution

On the opposite page is a list of men and women who have made some kind of contribution to journalism. Select an individual and write a 300- to 350-word profile about his or her role in journalism:

| | |
|---|---|
| Paul Y. Anderson | Edward R. Murrow |
| Nellie Bly | Al Neuharth |
| O.K. Bovard | Drew Pearson |
| Edna Buchanan | Lillian Ross |
| Janet Cooke | Edward W. Scripps |
| Elmer Davis | Hazel Brannon Smith |
| Frederick Douglass | Lincoln Steffens |
| Bernard Kilgore | I.F. Stone |
| John Knight | Ida M. Tarbell |
| Walter Lippmann | Oswald Garrison Villard |
| Ralph McGill | Ida B. Wells |
| Rupert Murdoch | Walter Winchell |

## B. Heroes

> I guess I grew up in a different era, with people with moral courage around me who spoke out against injustice, who made such issues central in their lives. . . . I have learned that my students don't have living moral heroes.
> —Susannah Heschel, professor of religion, Case Western Reserve University

Have you a hero in journalism? Perhaps one of those listed in the preceding assignment would meet the criterion Heschel sets. Select a journalist who has "moral courage" and discuss his or her attributes and accomplishments.

## Class Discussion

### A. Agenda

George Orwell said a strong motive in his writing was to right wrongs. Some journalists agree. They say they have an agenda for their communities and that they practice an activist journalism.

On the other hand, some believe the press should not lead, not take an activist position.

"It is not the role of the press to fix the problems of society," said Katherine Graham, chairman of the board of *The Washington Post*. "We need to broaden our coverage, to show the problem and how it's being fought. We can't and shouldn't lead in that sense (as advocate). What we can do is to report it better. . . .

". . . newspapers are information bringers, not advocates. . . . when you get into being a leader in a campaign, you screw up your news. . . ."

Here is the view of Eugene Patterson, former editor of the *St. Petersburg Times*:

> The press is not anointed to set the public's agenda for it. However, it is situated, and in the best sense obligated, to be the listener and messenger that hears and conveys the people's own agenda to the public arena. . . .
> . . . reporters are beginning to turn where they should, back to the people, to hear their definitions of the real issues that touch their lives. By giving those concerns sharper voice in the politician's press conferences, the press is starting to interrupt the political vaudeville of past campaigns and ask the legitimate questions, those of the public. . . .

Yet many of the great achievements in journalism—see the work of the muckrakers—were those of journalistic advocates.

What is your position in this debate over the role of the journalist? Should the journalist have an agenda? Should he or she be active in digging out news relevant to items on the agenda? Is it advocacy when a reporter who finds a high rate of infant mortality in the community bases his or her journalism on lowering the rate?

### B. Dumb-Down

Newspaper advertising was down. Circulation was failing to keep up with population growth. Studies showed that the precise audience, the men and women ages 25–43, who are big buyers of the products newspapers advertise, were not reading newspapers.

In what amounted to a massive self-analysis, publishers, editors and reporters tried to find a formula that would bring back the newspaper reader. Here are excerpts from one response to some of the remedies. It is by David Nyhen, columnist for *The Boston Globe,* and was printed in the Winter 1991 issue of *Nieman Reports:*

Of all the problems crunching the newspaper business, the info-glut is heaviest. . . .

We were . . . brought up to believe that the more information we gave the citizenry, the more informed they'd be and the better citizens they'd become. Guess what? The more information we give them, the more confused and dispirited they become. . . .

Newspapers have been fighting off the TV monster for so long, we've turned our newspapers into black-and-white-and-color replications of television—in print.

Our editors now think in terms of television. You can't really blame them. They watched this gunk seven hours a day, like most everyone else, and their brains were turned to jellied eel. . . .

[We are] dulling [newspapers] down. Dumbing them down, "Safing" them down, by reducing friction with local advertisers, interest groups or loud-mouthed lobbies. . . . Newspaper proprietors, a notoriously timid bunch, weighed their various alternative strategies for the Nineties, and came to the near-unanimous conclusion: time to hunker down. Boat-rocking is definitely out. Pulling in your journalistic horns is definitely in. . . .

What do you think?

## DB/CAR

### A. Opposites

Among the issues that have divided individuals and groups are abortion, school prayer, welfare reform, gun control, protection of the environment, instruction in evolution.

On one side are conservative groups such as the Moral Majority, the Catholic League for Religious and Civil Rights, the Eagle Forum, Citizens for Excellence in Education, the Christian Broadcasting Network, Citizens for Decency Through Law.

On the other side are groups such as Americans United for Separation of Church and State, People for the American Way, The American Civil Liberties Union.

Select one issue and make a database search for the stand of these organizations. Localize your reporting by interviewing local members of these organizations.

### B. Scorecard (1)

Make a legislative scorecard for your state legislators. First, compile a list of the important issues before the legislature, and then find the votes of those from your community, area and the entire state. For guidance, you might turn to various groups such as the American Civil Liberties Union and League of Women Voters and special-interest groups to see what bills they considered important.

Among the key issues to face state legislatures in recent years were abortion, regulation of gun ownership, the death penalty, privacy, pornography, preventive detention, harsher penalties for crimes.

Write 450 words.

### C. Scorecard (2)

Conduct a database search to find out how the representatives from your area and the state's two senators have voted or expressed themselves on these controversial issues in Congress: Prayer in school, abortion, constitutional amendment to prohibit flag desecration, federal minimum wage, vouchers for private schools, aid to parochial schools.

Add any other issues you deem appropriate. If you can find nothing on an issue, write your representative or senator. Write a 450-word story on your findings.

## Skill Drill: Ethical

Discuss the journalistic ethics involved in the following situations:

1. Your editor has told you to get a story on a local men's club that is discussing the admission of women to membership. The meeting is closed, but an adjoining room is vacant and you can hear the discussion. Should you listen in?

2. You are a sports reporter covering participant sports, and the manager of a local bowling alley that is on your beat offers to buy you a drink on your rounds, buy you lunch. Do you accept?

3. You are a consumer reporter doing a check on local auto repair shops. Upon completion, you ask a local association of automobile dealers for a comment, and the executive director says that he will advise his members to pull their advertising if you print the story. What do you do?

4. An executive session is being held by the local Independent Party to select a candidate for mayor. You can hear the closed-door discussions across an air shaft; you can hear them better if you toss a small microphone on a long cable over the air shaft to a window sill and record the discussion. Do you listen in?

5. A good source has told you that he can obtain a document about candidates for the job of city manager, including their personal records. Do you ask him to slip you the material?

6. You cover city hall. A local wrestling promoter has asked the sports editor to recommend someone who can write weekly news releases on the wrestling matches in the two-state area the promoter covers, and the editor gives him your name. He offers you the job. Do you take it?

7. A source inside the police department who has given you considerable information not otherwise available was transferred from the vice squad to a low-level desk job for an infraction. He indicates that if you run a story about him you have lost him as a source. Do you write it?

8. You cover the state legislature and develop some personal friends among legislators and lobbyists. They have a friendly weekly poker game and invite you to join them as a regular. Do you?

9. You are going over data on homicides and other violent crimes for the past year, and you notice that race and ethnic origin are included in the homicide figures but not in the rape data. You ask for the data and the police chief says that the department keeps it but has not distributed it because it is "volatile." You obtain the material and understand what he means. Almost 80 percent of the rape arrests involve members of minority groups. As in the case of homicides, the bulk of the victims were of the same race or ethnic origin as the alleged perpetrators. The chief warns you about using the rape data. "Murder is one thing. People can accept it. But rape. . . ." Do you use all the figures?

10. You cover business and finance. A local banker suggests you buy stock in his parent bank because of an expansion program yet unannounced. Do you buy?

11. Your newspaper, you learn from a confidential source, hired a CIA agent in the 1970s and gave him cover as a reporter. What is your obligation?

12. The local chapter of a medical organization is willing to finance your way to the annual convention of the American Medical Association because of the splendid way you have handled medical news over the past year. Your newspaper would like you to go but cannot afford the $1,500 in costs, the editor says. He tells you to use your judgment about accepting the offer. Do you go?

13. A reporter is asked out for an evening—dinner and the theater—by a source. The evening is a social engagement; it is not related to any story the reporter is covering. The reporter is attracted to the source, an attractive, friendly person. Should the reporter accept?

14. A source close to a federal government contract tells you that he has been involved in an illegal scheme to inflate costs. He names two other company officials, who deny the allegations. Your source gives you some documents that allude to the scheme but do not prove it. It is his word against theirs, and you believe him on the basis of long acquaintance. You know that if you run the story he will be fired.

15. You learn that the newspaper plant (or broadcast station property) is vastly underassessed. You plan to include this in a story about evaluation of downtown property. The editor sends the story upstairs, and mention of the newspaper (or station) is edited out. What do you do?

16. The textbook (Chapter 27) describes the ethical dilemma facing Kevin Krajick after he interviewed Paul Geidel, who had been imprisoned for 68 years. Do you agree with what Krajick did? What do you think of his reasons for running the story about the elderly prisoner?

17. A reporter for a weekly student newspaper at Dartmouth College attended a meeting of the Gay Students Association at the college and secretly taped the session. She wrote an article that contained excerpts of people describing their sexual experiences and she named two gay leaders. The moderator had read an oath of confidentiality at the start of the meeting. What do you think of the reporter's use of a secret tape recorder? Do you consider this an invasion of the privacy of members of the group?

18. The textbook gives opposing views on whether the press should examine the sexual lives of presidential candidates. Do you think it is morally correct to investigate the sex lives of candidates? Was the technique *The Miami Herald* used—staking out Gary Hart's home—ethical? Was the coverage of a woman's allegations of a lengthy sexual liaison with Bill Clinton ethical?

19. Many travel writers are guests of the hotels, cruise lines, tourist attractions that they write about. A number of articles have appeared that question the ethics of accepting these favors. Is the practice in your area newspapers obviously to accept gifts for coverage?

20. A standard January 1 story is about the first baby born in the new year. In Peoria, Ill., two local television stations, WMBD and WEEK, led their listeners to believe that Brooke Rochelle Hamby was the first. She wasn't. Actually, 45 minutes before, a 14-year-old unmarried black girl who hadn't known she was pregnant gave birth in an ambulance. The stations had decided to ignore the birth.

**Taking the sun at Gambia beach resort.**

"We've got to have pictures, video," said a TV reporter in defense of the decision. The hospital said it did not have permission to give out the mother's name and that her family did not want the story done.

The director of the Peoria Planned Parenthood office said, "I don't think the public is ever served by withholding such information. We have, as many communities do, teens giving birth. We'd all like to see something done about the problem, but we can't act as if it doesn't happen."

What would you have done if you were the manager of one of the television stations?

21. For a few years, several sportswriters knew that Arthur Ashe had AIDS. The world-famous tennis player, who had devoted his time after his playing days to teaching inner-city youngsters the game, had asked that journalists respect his privacy. But *USA Today* revealed that he had the disease. The reporter said the story was known too widely to suppress.

22. When Woody Hayes was coaching the Ohio State University football team, a crucial game was nearing the end and his team was behind. An opposing player intercepted an Ohio State pass, and as the player who had made the interception passed Hayes, the enraged coach punched him. ABC-TV, which was televising the game, did not show a replay of the incident, and its announcers did not discuss Hayes' reaction. Should ABC have shown and discussed Hayes' violence?

23. A columnist for the *New York Post* quoted in his column an anti-Semitic epithet that a New York Yankee baseball player directed at him. Does a journalist use personal experiences in his or her work?

24. Newspapers, magazines and television are charged with overemphasizing athletes and celebrities, with the result that younger readers have aspirations that rarely match their abilities and society's needs. What do you think of the media coverage in your area?

25. Have you discussed in class or found in your reading sufficient information to reach some decisions on a set of personal guidelines in areas such as the coverage of the personal lives of public figures, the acceptance of favors, taking a second job, using poses and disguises?

## *You Decide: Case Studies*

The four cases described here are drawn from the experiences of editors at *The Commercial Appeal* in Memphis, which asked its readers to comment. What would you have done?

### *Case No. 1*

Local government has redeveloped a section of an otherwise blighted part of the city. Tax incentives have encouraged business investment. The project was created as a stimulus for economic growth in the surrounding neighborhood. At first the project takes off: Businesses move in, curious shoppers are drawn to the stores, city officials report a growing sense of optimism.

But after a year, negative signs appear. A couple of the businesses close up. Curiosity satisfied, shoppers from other parts of the city stop patronizing the stores.

A reporter is assigned to find out whether other businesses there also are on the ropes. He comes back with a story that two more stores are about to fail. But there are complications. Officials have asked him not to print the story for a week because they have contracts out with three new companies. If the negative news runs in the newspaper before the signed contracts are returned, they say, the deals may fall through and taxpayer funds may end up wasted.

As an editor would you:

- Hold the story for a week?
- Publish the story, but either tone down the negative aspects or run just a brief version on an inside page?
- Publish the original story right away in a prominent place?
- Publish the original plus the request of the officials?

*Case No. 2*

A young couple telephones to ask that the newspaper not run an announcement of their marriage. The newspaper's policy is clear: Publish all marriage reports listed as a public record in the Court Clerk's office. This request, however, has an unusual twist.

The newlyweds are medical students. After falling in love, they tried for a while to live apart. But since they intended to get married when they were graduated from medical school anyway, they decided to become husband and wife without telling their families. The quiet marriage, they reasoned, would spare them out-of-town celebrations at a time when they needed to concentrate on their studies, while it also would allow them to economize on severely strained budgets. They did not want to live together out of wedlock.

Now they have a problem they want you to solve: Their families, knowing of their engagement, have surprised them with plans for a big wedding to be held after their final exams for the year. If the news of their marriage is published, the plans will be ruined, the families disheartened.

Would you:

- Make an exception to policy for them?
- Refuse their request on the grounds that it would set a precedent for other couples and make it difficult for you to maintain a policy based on equal treatment?

*Case No. 3*

A police reporter notes on the police log that the bomb squad has responded to a bomb threat at an abortion clinic. Although the squad did not find a bomb, the reporter writes a story about the police response.

The newspaper's policy is not to report bomb threats because such stories tend to encourage other threats. The policy is based on the lengthy experience of newspapers throughout the country. Years ago, for instance, there was a rash of fire alarms at local schools. At first, the newspaper reported each one, even with pictures of students parading out the school doors. The alarms multiplied until publicity stopped.

A threat at an abortion clinic falls into a different category, however. Clinics elsewhere in the country have been bombed. Does that elevate a local threat into a legitimate news story?

In addition, there have been unconfirmed reports that a person who is wanted in connection with a clinic bombing in another city has been seen in your city.

Would you:

- Run the story as is?
- Kill the story on the grounds of established policy?
- Hold the story until you can check with a superior, even though that would make it a day older getting into the paper?
- Hold the story until the representatives of local anti-abortion groups can be asked for their reactions?

*Case No. 4*

A 17-year-old juvenile is arrested for stealing a magazine from a convenience store. The newspaper reports shoplifting arrests in its daily agate roundup of police and court activity. But it would not ordinarily include this incident because it has a policy against publishing arrests for thefts that involve less than $10.

A reporter notices, however, that the last name of the juvenile is the same as that of the local juvenile court judge. He checks it out, and finds that the juvenile is the judge's son.

This complicates the editor's decision because the judge has been on a campaign against shoplifting by juveniles. The newspaper, in fact, had recently run a news story about the campaign and had quoted the judge extensively.

Would you:

- Follow policy and not run a report of the theft?
- Run the report because of the prominence of the father?
- Run the report because of the special circumstances of the judge's campaign?
- Ask the judge whether he thinks the story should run?
- Call the judge and ask for his comments; then run the story?

## *You Decide: Sex Education (2)*

The head of a national health organization is to speak in your city tomorrow evening. He is on a speaking tour in which he is calling for less media attention to exotic and rare diseases and greater stress on the prevention of diseases that afflict large numbers of people.

In his talks, he has emphasized that teen-agers who receive classroom sex education are less likely to engage in early or high-risk sex, and he has described violence as a greater threat to health than infectious diseases. He has stated that those who purchase handguns have a 40 percent risk of harming themselves because so many go off accidentally or are used in anger.

In the last city in which he spoke, several organizations picketed the auditorium in which he spoke, and there were fights between these pickets and those supporting sex education in the schools and gun control.

The sponsors of the talk ask you to give minimal emphasis to the speaker's coming appearance. They hope that by limiting prior reports, you will keep opposition groups from mustering a large following to picket the talk. How do you respond to this request?

# Freeport City Map

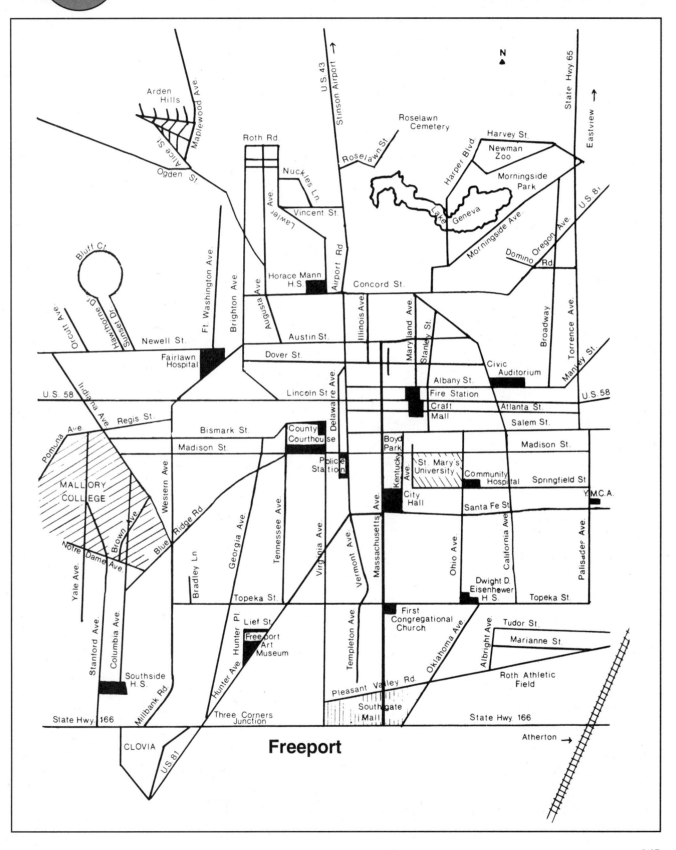

# Freeport Directory

Note: Unless designated otherwise—Av, Rd, Dr—addresses are for streets.

A-1 Shopping Center    77 Notre Dame Av
Abele Forrest L    Atherton
Abromovitch Sterling    2633 Springfield
Addison Rodney    424 Nuckles Ln
Adler Margot    728 Augusta
Alcohol Control Center    570 Western Av
Allen Hotel    212 Albany
Allstate Insurance Co    65 Atlanta
Aluko Sharon    2487 Oregon Av
American Cancer Society    10 Dover
Amidon Photo Exchange    70 Dover
Anders Sparky    18 Tudor
Appel Alan    1133 Madison
Applegate William    3 Hunter Pl
Arnold Alfred MD
   Ofc    10 Dover
   Res    1280 Lawler Av
Ashkinaze Thomas    61 California
Ashkinaze's Men's Styles    742 Springfield
Atlas Equipment Associates    97 Albany

B & D Butchers    742 Springfield
Backman Stacy    548 Atlanta
Baldwin Protection Systems Co    65 Lincoln
Banks George Q    928 Springfield
Bannister Mildred    15 Hawthorne Dr
Barber Billy Jo    56 Roth Rd
Barnes Jake    675 Stanford Av
Bartles Adele    431 Topeka
Barton Hotel    26 Vermont Av
Battle Richard    258 Topeka
Baylor Ulysses    3950 Broadway
Begley Vivian    1280 Madison
Bell Pamela E    606 Vincent
Belmont Motel    7989 Airport Rd
Bennett Elizabeth    88 Columbia Av
Berents Bernzar    76 Newell
Berlin John F    176 Tudor
Berry Lawrence    3468 Salem
Big Jo Lumber Yard    Clovia
Bishop Barney Advg
   Ofc    370 Massachusetts Av
   Res    12 Roth Rd
Bivins Vincent    479 Springfield
Blitzer Herbert    124 Georgia Av
Blount Anthony E    322 Oregon Av
Bob's Electrical Supply    Southgate Mall
Bokum Baths Inc    5200 Hunter Av
Born Harold    876 Palisades Av
Borns Claude    624 Dover
Borns Robert    438 Oklahoma Av
Bradford Hugh J    Atherton
Braverman C L    529 Palisades Av
Brezen Stanley    17 Tudor
Brown's Auto Supply    3355 Oregon Av

Brown Plumbing and Heating    Clovia
Burger King    4700 Airport Rd
Burgess-Stevens Architects    650 Massachusetts Av
Burns & Allen Investment Inc    370 Massachusetts Av
Burns Paul    Clovia

Cahan Daniel    515 Pleasant Valley Rd
Cahan Mildred    15 Lincoln
Camuto Philip    1338 Tennessee Av
Carruthers Helen    39 Lincoln
Carver Cemetery    2222 Salem
Catton Marianne    51 Vermont Av
Chaffee Frank    1440 Springfield
Chamberlain Thomas    88 Austin
Chang Jeff    316 Ogden
Chang & Sons Construction    9 Ft Washington Av
Chavez Daniel    479 Springfield
Chen Dong Lu    1658 Broadway
Civic Auditorium    3600 Albany
Clark's Cafe    3769 Oregon Av
Cohen Cory    479 Springfield
Collins Beverly    159 Orcutt Av
Community Hospital    200 Ohio Av
Cramer Judith    33 Springfield
Crane Ronald K    2063 Ohio Av
Croft Ronald C    865 Indiana Av
Crosson Cafe    127 Lincoln
Crosson Ralph    15 Blue Ridge Rd
Crossroads Grocery    8005 Hunter Ave

Daisy's Pet Shop    1270 California Av
Daly William H    402 Stanford Av
Dantzic Mervin    481 Springfield
David Ross    524 Springfield
Davis Martin    52 Lawler Av
Dean Jerry    479 Springfield
Deluxe Adult Videos and Books    4062 Airport Rd
Diamond Alvin    596 Austin
Digital Equipment Corp    18 Concord
Dimmesdale Arthur Rev
   Ofc    4700 Massachusetts Av
   Res    5587 Salem
Downey Anne    165 Vincent
Downey Stanley    165 Vincent
Dufur James    225 Ohio Av
Dugan Harold    89 Georgia Av
Dunning Arthur M    9868 Highway 166
Dwight D Eisenhower High School    216 Topeka

Earl Lloyd    1492 Brighton Av
Eighty-One Groceries    6730 Hunter Av
Eisenhower Dwight D High School    216 Topeka
Elman Richard    3732 Palisades Av
Elston Aaron    Arden Hills
Epstein Helen    864 Madison

Erlanger Donald       45 Domino Rd
Evans Charlotte DDS      66 Bluff Ct
Everingham Thomas      373 Vermont Av
Exton Electric Co      777 Atlanta

Fairlawn Hospital      570 Western Av
Falcione Marshall atty
   Ofc      370 Massachusetts Av
   Res      666 Western Av
Farrell Mary      86 Bradley Ln
Farrington Richard      332 Bismark
Feeney Raymond      167 Kentucky Av
Felson Charles      565 Concord
Feron Gerald      75 Hunter Pl
Fields Benjamin      1272 Broadway
Figuera Robert      97 Maryland Av
Finnegan Joseph      228 Vermont Av
First Baptist Church      1730 Atlanta
First Congregational Church      4700 Massachusetts Av
First National Bank      55 Massachusetts Av
Flagg Arnold      571 Broadway
Flynn Clark      9 Roth Rd
Forde Betty      896 Santa Fe
Fox Daniel      833 Santa Fe
Frank's Deli      740 Springfield
Fraser James      76 Albright Av
Freedman Martin      537 Dover
Freeport Auto Repair      1273 Santa Fe
Freeport Chamber of Commerce      22 Massachusetts Av
Freeport Dodge Inc      2121 Broadway
Freeport Golf Course      952 Airport Rd
Freeport Kiwanis Club      326 Albany
Freeport Motor Lodge      2485 Oregon Av
Freeport Press Corp      7620 Torrence Av
Freeport Rotary Club      6993 Lincoln
Fuentes Albert      720 Georgia Av
Fulton Robert Elementary School      1109 Santa Fe

Gabel Martin      1325 Morningside Av
Galzo Frederick      435 Albany
Gamm William atty
   Ofc      34 Massachusetts Av
   Res      583 Millbank Rd
Gap Clothiers The      1770 Broadway
Garner Bernard      72 Albright Av
George Packer Elementary School      66 Maryland Av
George Washington Carver Club      3030 Airport Rd
Gerber Phil      348 Millbank Rd
Gerter Sigmund      55 Templeton Av
Gilkeyson Herbert      1643 Newell
Glasser Sara F      555 Blue Ridge Rd
Godfrey Claudine      870 Blue Ridge Rd
Gold Marcia      831 Brighton Av
Golden Years Club      110 Newell
Gonzales George      1523 Ogden
Graham Fred
   Ofc      22 Massachusetts Av
   Res      71 Hunter Pl
Greek Orthodox Cathedral      1015 Indiana Av
Green David      104 Springfield
Green Richard MD
   Ofc      16 Dover
   Res      84 Maryland Av
Grimes E W Co      1560 Broadway
Grubbs Oscar      Smith Farms
Gruner Donald      280 Lawler Av
Gulf Drive-Up      4950 Oregon Av

Guth George T      626 Manley
Guzman Clifford      16 Brighton Av

Halpern William      479 Atlanta
Halpert Wesley Atty
   Ofc      370 Massachusetts Av
   Res      18 Marianne
Harris Arthur B      123 Western Av
Hastings Abner      576 Atlanta
Hay Peter      5 Nuckles Ln
Heavenly Rest Chapel      1485 Tennessee Av
Hecht's Fine Furniture      715 Vermont Av
Hedberg Milton      9843 California Av
Hedberg-Smith Stkbrkrs      690 Massachusetts Av
Heffner Albert      1842 Salem
Held Dennis      630 Orcutt Av
Helmer Steve      63 Lincoln
Helmer Steven      533 Yale Av
Hess James      867 Brighton Av
Hilliard's Body Shop      6584 Hunter Av
Himmelstein Dale L      42 Ft Washington Av
Ho Robert T F      763 Airport Rd
Hoch Arthur      474 Tudor
Holing John OD      53 Bluff Ct
Holy Trinity Church      300 Madison
Hosmer James      91 Tudor
Huff Martin      202 Blue Ridge Rd
Hulbert George W      69 Topeka
Hunscher David      1515 Salem
Hurley Marvin      1060 Columbia Av
Hurst Fanny MD      590 Brighton Av

IGA      135 Kentucky Av

Jack's Mobil Serve      6481 Hunter Av
Jacobs Anne      702 Bismark
Jacobson J      44 Austin
Jenkins Stephen C      89 Manley
Jones Hosie Gene      1347 Oklahoma Av
Jopper Frank      622 Broadway
Joseph Barney G      1625 Tennessee Av
Joseph Pharmacy      450 Stanley
Joshua Baptist Church      8724 Torrence Av
Joyce Coleman      44 Broadway

Kmart Eastview      4339 Oregon Av
Kaplan Herbert N      897 Madison
Katzen Arthur      12 Ft Washington Av
Kay's Diner      128 Atlanta
Kazazian Brut      515 Santa Fe
Keenan Kenneth      918 Blue Ridge Rd
Kempe Harry      7 Manley
Kilafar Dianne MD      324 Indiana Av
Kinney Fay      8280 Lincoln
Kirby B J      122 Oklahoma Av
Kliff Paul A      29 Tudor
Knudson Jerry Ph D      562 Bismark
Konner John      333 Austin
Kragler Bertha      2260 Bismark
Kramer John      164 Albright Av
Krane Ray      1215 Albany
Krebs B C Manufacturing Co      10 Concord
Kroeger B      88 Augusta Av

Lane Sarah      540 Regis
Leek's Cafe      15 Lincoln
Lemieux Jacques      225 Augusta Av

Lentz Robin     484 Springfield
Levine Leonard     264 Ogden
Levy Richard     54 Maplewood Av
Lewin David     8440 Lincoln
Logan Ann     2960 Salem
Longo Frank     465 Lief
Loran Anley     98 Western Av
Lowe David     19 Millbank Rd
Lucky 7 Grocery     1384 Santa Fe
Lynn Frederick L     18 Madison
Lyon P     77 Dover

Magione Robert F     872 Ogden
Mallory College     500 Indiana Av
Mann Horace High School     370 Concord
Marple Jane     6 Millbank Rd
Marvello Rosario     4143 Torrence Av
Mayfair Fabrics     740 Springfield
McCoy Frank     320 Manley
McMillan Samuel A     48 Orcutt Av
Melia Aloysius J     653 Madison
Metro Transit Authority     9643 Highway 166
Meyers Bernard A     3320 Madison
Miller Wayne     614 Albany
Minteer Edwin     8456 Lincoln
Mitchell & Co     889 Newell
Mohawk Brush Building     1620 Blue Ridge Rd
Mom's Maternity Fashion     91 Broadway
Morgan Robert     2255 California Av
Morton Henry     687 Pleasant Valley Rd

NCR Corporation     266 Atlanta
National Car Rental     6901 Airport Rd
National Kidney Foundation     729 Albany
Nelley Margaret     96 Albright Av
Nicholson Philip     18 Marianne
North Funeral Home     1620 Tennessee Av
Norton Ralph     6522 Torrence Av
No-Tell Motel     3969 Broadway

Olsen Paul     863 Morningside Av
Oregon Groceteria     5333 Oregon Av
O'Reilly Sandy     459 Brighton Av
Oshiro Mary     1360 California Av

Packer George Elementary School     66 Maryland Av
Palmer Thomas     568 Madison
Pardee Francis     1874 Ogden
Parker Bayard     1618 Brighton Av
Parnass Sam     716 Broadway
Parrington Felix     76 Roth Rd
Pearl Mildred     175 Virginia Av
Peat Marshall     84 Notre Dame Av
People's Bus Line Inc     1320 Torrence Av
Perkins William F     1105 Madison
Petrie Donald     386 Brighton Av
Phealan Ronald     526 Albany
Pietro Peter     824 Vincent
Plaza Hotel The     912 California Av
Podhoretz Hobart Bayward     82 Bluff Ct
Polk George     10 Topeka
Pop's Cleaners     249 Austin
Popvich Robert     81 Millbank Rd
Pork Parlor     405 Regis
Post Theodore     25 Domino Rd
Potts L P     52 Bradley Ln
Praxton Francis     1160 Broadway

Prewitt Mortuary     840 Stanford Av
Purdue Jack     726 California Av

Quick Stop Laundry     39 Millbank Rd
Quire Karl     38 Concord

Ramsgate Charles     265 Virginia Av
Raskover Richard     766 Augusta
Ratcliffe Sam     5 Hunter Pl
Reeder M     82 Hunter Pl
Regis Hotel     88 Dover
Reib Rachel     338 Topeka
Renaldi Ruth P     22 Columbia Av
Reynolds James     35 Palisades Av
Richards Donald L     94 Hawthorne Dr
Rieder's Trading Post     7935 Hunter Av
Robbins Edward     65 Bismark
Robert Matthew B     569 Blue Ridge Rd
Roberts Dorothy F     242 Madison
Robinson Paul     730 Georgia Av
Rogers M B     935 Millbank Rd
Roper Leon     6 Bradley Ln
Ross David     2920 Madison
Ross K L     323 Lief
Rothkrug Russell     37 Bluff Ct
Rubens Merle     648 Austin
Russ's Market     929 Indiana Av
Ryan Scott     1580 Oklahoma Av

St. Mary's University     290 Madison
Salmi Robert     1280 Blue Ridge Rd
Sanchez Alexander     86 Santa Fe
Sanchez Luis     54 Millbank Rd
Sandler Ross     355 Pleasant Valley Rd
Scarpino Joan     539 Columbia Av
Schneider Burton     269 Topeka
Schneider Stella     4 Hawthorne Dr
Schwartz Harry     768 Albany
Scillicide Irving     Clovia
Scott Building     2000 Torrence Av
Seaver Dorothy     1120 Brighton Av
Seaver Vincent     333 Millbank Rd
Serge Jack A     640 Columbia Av
Serpa Kelly     46 Topeka
Shaeffer Stanley     45 Madison
Shalom Moving & Storage     6432 Newell
Sharman William     522 Virginia Av
Sharon's Used Goods     65 Virginia Av
Shelly's Laundromat     402 Newell
Shelton O M     666 Stanley
Sherman Albert     266 Maplewood
Shilton Wendy     922 Airport Rd
Silver Isadore     88 Virginia Av
Silver Jean     88 Virginia Av
Simms N Francis     290 Madison
Simpson Motors Co     1880 Palisades Av
Sinclair Margaret     161 Albany
Skinner Vernon     9690 California Av
Slinkard Thomas     4 Bluff Ct
Smith Frances     132 Alice
Smith Fred E     66 Templeton Av
Smith Harvey     145 Nuckles Ln
Smith Walter     926 Columbia Av
Snead Daniel     481 Yale Av
Solomon Stanley     47 Palisades Av
Soto Irwin     Clovia
Soto Jack     Clovia

Southside High School    1370 Stanford Av
Stapleton Wayne L MD
  Ofc    10 Dover
  Res    2620 Morningside Av
Steinberg Alfred    145 Columbia Av
Stern Franklin W    9529 Millbank Rd
Stiga Stanley    909 Lawler Av
Stinson Airport    8900 Airport Rd
Stranger's Department Store    25 Massachusetts Av
Stroh Bruce    1215 Millbank Rd
Stuben Drug Store    472 Massachusetts Av
Sunoco Service    5431 Hunter Av
Sutherland Karl    368 Atlanta
Swimmer Albert F    1405 Sunset Dr

Taylor Alan    349 Santa Fe
Temple B'nai Shalom    1282 Airport Rd
Temple Emmanuel    457 Oregon Av
Terada Winifred    294 Broadway
Texaco Fuel Stop    4266 Oregon Av
Thames Arthur atty    416 Pleasant Valley Rd
Thomas Jules    56 Western Av
Thorne Charles    1855 Atlanta
Three Corners Cafe    4700 Hunter Av
Tobin Barry    112 Bismark
Trenzier William    460 Lincoln
Trevor William    Clovia
Trimbel Department Store    17 Vermont Av
Trowbridge Nicholas    90 Austin
Trump Donald    418 Palisades Av
Tsouprake Demetrios A    560 Tudor
Tucek Cyrus    1280 Bismark
Turner Eric    441 Georgia Av

United Methodist Church    850 Brighton Av

Venzon Jewelry    Southgate Mall
Vincent Salvatore    44 Concord
Voboril John T    1496 Blue Ridge Rd

Walker Damon    67 Roth Rd
Walnut J C and Co    850 Albany
Walnut James C    215 Manley
Walnut Theodore    1018 Millbank Rd
Walters Tess    843 Columbia Av
Ward Samuel    47 Harper Blvd
Wigglesworth James    349 Springfield
Williams Adam    1423 Harper Blvd
Williams Adam Rprs    3333 California Av
Williams Margaret    7 Bradley Ln
Williams Mildred C    1423 Harper Blvd
Williams Milton    496 Brighton Av
Wilson's Rest Stop    6631 Hunter Av
Wolfe T    6 Stanford Av
Woodcock Joseph C    784 Lincoln
Wright Beulah    26 Domino Rd
Wrightson Industries Inc    3640 Broadway
Wrightson James    4716 Airport Rd

X Francis T    677 Palisades Av
XYZ Typewriter Repair    345 Concord

York Alfred    15 Templeton Av
Young William    42 Broadway

Ziegler Alfred    444 Bismark
Zimmerman Martha    340 Lincoln

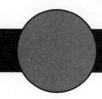

# Freeport Cross Directory

The **Cross Directory** is also known as the *reverse directory*.

**Airport Rd**
| | |
|---|---|
| 763 | Ho Robert T F |
| 922 | Shilton Wendy |
| 952 | Freeport Golf Course |
| 1282 | Temple B'nai Shalom |
| 3030 | George Washington Carver Club |
| 4062 | Deluxe Adult Videos and Books |
| 4700 | Burger King |
| 4716 | Wrightson James |
| 6901 | National Car Rental |
| 7989 | Belmont Motel |
| 8900 | Stinson Airport |

**Albany**
| | |
|---|---|
| 97 | Atlas Equipment Associates |
| 161 | Sinclair Margaret |
| 212 | Allen Hotel |
| 326 | Freeport Kiwanis Club |
| 435 | Galzo Frederick |
| 526 | Phealan Ronald |
| 614 | Miller Wayne |
| 729 | National Kidney Foundation |
| 768 | Schwartz Harry |
| 850 | Walnut J C and Co |
| 1215 | Krane Ray |
| 3600 | Civic Auditorium |

**Albright Av**
| | |
|---|---|
| 72 | Garner Bernard |
| 76 | Fraser James |
| 96 | Nelley Margaret |
| 164 | Kramer John |

**Alice**
| | |
|---|---|
| 132 | Smith Frances |

**Arden Hills**
| | |
|---|---|
|  | Elston Aaron |

**Atherton**
| | |
|---|---|
|  | Abele Forrest L |
|  | Bradford Hugh J |

**Atlanta**
| | |
|---|---|
| 65 | Allstate Insurance Co |
| 128 | Kay's Diner |
| 266 | NCR Corporation |
| 368 | Sutherland Karl |

| | |
|---|---|
| 479 | Halpern William |
| 548 | Backman Stacy |
| 777 | Exton Electric Co |
| 1730 | First Baptist Church |
| 1855 | Thorne Charles |

**Augusta Av**
| | |
|---|---|
| 88 | Kroeger B |
| 225 | Lemieux Jacques |
| 576 | Hastings Abner |
| 728 | Adler Margot |
| 766 | Raskover Richard |

**Austin**
| | |
|---|---|
| 44 | Jacobson J |
| 88 | Chamberlain Thomas |
| 90 | Trowbridge Nicholas |
| 249 | Pop's Cleaners |
| 333 | Konner John |
| 596 | Diamond Alvin |
| 648 | Rubens Merle |

**Bismark**
| | |
|---|---|
| 65 | Robbins Edward |
| 112 | Tobin Barry |
| 332 | Farrington Richard |
| 444 | Ziegler Alfred |
| 562 | Knudson Jerry Ph D |
| 702 | Jacobs Anne |
| 1280 | Tucek Cyrus |
| 2260 | Kragler Bertha |

**Blue Ridge Rd**
| | |
|---|---|
| 15 | Crosson Ralph |
| 202 | Huff Martin |
| 555 | Glasser Sara F |
| 569 | Robert Matthew B |
| 870 | Godfrey Claudine |
| 918 | Keenan Kenneth |
| 1280 | Salmi Robert |
| 1496 | Voboril John T |
| 1620 | Mohawk Brush Building |

**Bluff Ct**
| | |
|---|---|
| 4 | Slinkard Thomas |
| 37 | Rothkrug Russell |
| 53 | Holing John OD |
| 66 | Evans Charlotte DDS |
| 82 | Podhoretz Hobart Bayward |

**Bradley Ln**
| | |
|---|---|
| 6 | Roper Leon |
| 7 | Williams Margaret |
| 52 | Potts L P |
| 86 | Farrel Mary |

**Brighton Av**
| | |
|---|---|
| 16 | Guzman Clifford |
| 386 | Petrie Donald |
| 459 | O'Reilly Sandy |
| 496 | Williams Milton |
| 590 | Hurst Fanny MD |
| 831 | Gold Marcia |
| 850 | United Methodist Church |
| 867 | Hess James |
| 1120 | Seaver Dorothy |
| 1492 | Lloyd Earl |
| 1618 | Parker Bayard |

**Broadway**
| | |
|---|---|
| 42 | Young William |
| 44 | Joyce Coleman |
| 191 | Mom's Maternity Fashion |
| 294 | Terada Winifred |
| 571 | Flagg Arnold |
| 622 | Jopper Frank |
| 716 | Parnass Sam |
| 1160 | Praxton Francis |
| 1272 | Fields Benjamin |
| 1560 | E W Grimes Co |
| 1658 | Chen Dong Lu |
| 1770 | Gap Clothiers The |
| 2121 | Freeport Dodge Inc |
| 3640 | Wrightson Industries Inc |
| 3950 | Baylor Ulysses |
| 3969 | No-Tell Motel |

**California Av**
| | |
|---|---|
| 61 | Ashkinaze Thomas |
| 726 | Purdue Jack |
| 912 | Plaza Hotel The |
| 1270 | Daisy's Pet Shop |
| 1360 | Oshiro Mary |
| 2255 | Morgan Robert |
| 3333 | Williams Adam Rprs |
| 9690 | Skinner Vernon |
| 9843 | Hedberg Milton |

**Clovia**
- Big Jo Lumber Yard
- Brown Plumbing and Heating
- Burns Paul
- Scillicide Irving
- Soto Irwin
- Soto Jack
- Trevor William

**Columbia Av**
| | |
|---|---|
| 22 | Renaldi Ruth P |
| 88 | Bennett Elizabeth |
| 145 | Steinberg Alfred |
| 539 | Scarpino Joan |
| 640 | Serge Jack A |
| 843 | Walters Tess |
| 926 | Smith Walter |
| 1060 | Hurley Marvin |

**Concord**
| | |
|---|---|
| 10 | Krebs B C Manufacturing Co |
| 18 | Digital Equipment Corp |
| 38 | Quire Karl |
| 345 | XYZ Typewriter Repair |
| 370 | Mann Horace High School |
| 444 | Vincent Salvatore |
| 565 | Felson Charles |

**Domino Rd**
| | |
|---|---|
| 25 | Post Theodore |
| 26 | Wright Beulah |
| 45 | Erlanger Donald |

**Dover**
| | |
|---|---|
| 10 | American Cancer Society |
| 10 | Arnold Alfred MD Ofc |
| 10 | Stapleton Wayne L Ofc |
| 16 | Green Richard MD Ofc |
| 70 | Amidon Photo Exchange |
| 77 | Lyon P |
| 88 | Regis Hotel |
| 537 | Friedman Martin |
| 624 | Borns Claude |

**Ft Washington Av**
| | |
|---|---|
| 9 | Chang & Sons Construction |
| 12 | Katzen Arthur |
| 42 | Himmelstein Dale L |

**Georgia Av**
| | |
|---|---|
| 89 | Dugan Harold |
| 124 | Blitzer Herbert |
| 441 | Turner Eric |
| 720 | Fuentes Albert |
| 730 | Robinson Paul |

**Harper Blvd**
| | |
|---|---|
| 47 | Ward Samuel |
| 1423 | Williams Adam |
| 1423 | Williams Mildred C |

**Hawthorne Dr**
| | |
|---|---|
| 4 | Schneider Stella |
| 15 | Bannister Mildred |
| 94 | Richards Donald L |

**Highway 166**
| | |
|---|---|
| 9643 | Metro Transit Authority |
| 9868 | Dunning Arthur M |

**Hunter Pl**
| | |
|---|---|
| 3 | Applegate William |
| 5 | Ratcliffe Sam |
| 71 | Graham Fred Res |
| 75 | Feron Gerald |
| 82 | Reeder M |

**Hunter Av**
| | |
|---|---|
| 4700 | Three Corners Cafe |
| 5200 | Bokum Baths Inc |
| 5431 | Sunoco Service |
| 6481 | Jack's Mobil Serve |
| 6584 | Hilliard's Body Shop |
| 6631 | Wilson's Rest Stop |
| 6730 | Eighty-One Groceries |
| 7935 | Rieder's Trading Post |
| 8005 | Crossroads Grocery |

**Indiana Av**
| | |
|---|---|
| 324 | Kilafar Dianne MD |
| 500 | Mallory College |
| 865 | Croft Ronald C |
| 929 | Russ's Market |
| 1015 | Greek Orthodox Cathedral |

**Kentucky Av**
| | |
|---|---|
| 135 | IGA |
| 167 | Feeney Raymond |

**Lawler Av**
| | |
|---|---|
| 52 | Davis Martin |
| 909 | Stiga Stanley |
| 1280 | Arnold Alfred MD Res |
| 1280 | Gruner Donald |

**Lief**
| | |
|---|---|
| 323 | Ross K L |
| 465 | Longo Frank |

**Lincoln**
| | |
|---|---|
| 15 | Cahan Mildred |
| 15 | Leek's Cafe |
| 39 | Carruthers Helen |
| 63 | Helmer Steve |
| 65 | Baldwin Protection Systems Co |
| 127 | Crosson Cafe |
| 340 | Zimmerman Martha |
| 460 | Trenzier William |
| 784 | Woodcock Joseph C |

| | |
|---|---|
| 6993 | Freeport Rotary Club |
| 8280 | Kinney Fay |
| 8440 | Lewin David |
| 8456 | Minteer Edwin |

**Madison**
| | |
|---|---|
| 18 | Lynn Frederick L |
| 45 | Shaeffer Stanley |
| 242 | Roberts Dorothy |
| 290 | St. Mary's University |
| 290 | Simms N Francis |
| 300 | Holy Trinity Church |
| 568 | Palmer Thomas |
| 653 | Melia Aloysius J |
| 864 | Epstein Helen |
| 897 | Kaplan Herbert N |
| 1105 | Perkins William F |
| 1133 | Appel Alan |
| 1280 | Begley Vivian |
| 2920 | Ross David |
| 3320 | Meyers Bernard A |

**Manley**
| | |
|---|---|
| 7 | Kempe Harry |
| 89 | Jenkins Stephen C |
| 215 | Walnut James C |
| 320 | McCoy Frank |
| 626 | Guth George T |

**Maplewood Av**
| | |
|---|---|
| 54 | Levy Richard |
| 266 | Sherman Albert |

**Marianne**
| | |
|---|---|
| 18 | Halpert Wesley atty Res |
| 18 | Nicholson Philip |

**Maryland Av**
| | |
|---|---|
| 66 | George Packer Elementary School |
| 84 | Green Richard MD Res |
| 97 | Figuera Robert |

**Massachusetts Av**
| | |
|---|---|
| 22 | Freeport Chamber of Commerce |
| 22 | Graham Fred Ofc |
| 25 | Stranger's Department Store |
| 34 | Gamm William |
| 55 | First National Bank |
| 370 | Bishop Barney Advertising Ofc |
| 370 | Burns & Allen Investment Inc |
| 370 | Falcione Marshall atty Ofc |
| 370 | Halpert Wesley atty Ofc |
| 472 | Stuben Drug Store |
| 650 | Burgess-Stevens Architects |
| 690 | Hedberg-Smith Stkbrkrs |
| 4700 | Dimmesdale Arthur Rev Ofc |
| 4700 | First Congregational Church |

**Millbank Rd**
| | |
|---|---|
| 6 | Marple Jane |
| 19 | Lowe David |

| 39 | Quick Stop Laundry |
| 54 | Sanchez Luis |
| 81 | Popvich Robert |
| 333 | Seaver Vincent |
| 348 | Gerber Phil |
| 583 | Gamm William |
| 935 | Rogers M B |
| 1018 | Walnut Theodore |
| 1215 | Stroh Bruce |
| 9529 | Stern Franklin W |

**Morningside Av**
| 863 | Olsen Paul |
| 1325 | Gabel Martin |
| 2620 | Stapleton Wayne L Res |

**Newell**
| 76 | Berents Bernzar |
| 110 | Golden Years Club |
| 402 | Shelly's Laundromat |
| 889 | Mitchell & Co |
| 1643 | Gilkeyson Herbert |
| 6432 | Shalom Moving & Storage |

**Notre Dame Av**
| 77 | A-1 Shopping Center |
| 84 | Peat Marshall |

**Nuckles Ln**
| 5 | Hay Peter |
| 145 | Smith Harvey |
| 424 | Addison Rodney |

**Ogden**
| 264 | Levine Leonard |
| 316 | Chang Jeff |
| 872 | Magione Robert F |
| 1523 | Gonzales George |
| 1874 | Pardee Francis |

**Ohio**
| 200 | Community Hospital |
| 225 | Dufur James |
| 2063 | Crane Ronald K |

**Oklahoma Av**
| 122 | Kirby B J |
| 438 | Borns Robert |
| 1347 | Jones Hosie Gene |
| 1580 | Ryan Scott |

**Orcutt Av**
| 48 | McMillan Samuel A |
| 159 | Collins Beverly |
| 630 | Held Dennis |

**Oregon Av**
| 322 | Blount Anthony E |
| 457 | Temple Emmanuel |

| 2485 | Freeport Motor Lodge |
| 2487 | Aluko Sharon |
| 3355 | Brown's Auto Supply |
| 3769 | Clark's Cafe |
| 4266 | Texaco Fuel Stop |
| 4339 | Kmart Eastview |
| 4950 | Gulf Drive-Up |
| 5333 | Oregon Groceteria |

**Palisades Av**
| 35 | Reynolds James |
| 47 | Solomon Stanley |
| 418 | Trump Donald |
| 529 | Braverman C L |
| 876 | Born Harold |
| 1880 | Simpson Motor Co |
| 3732 | Elman Richard |
| 5677 | X Francis T |

**Pleasant Valley Rd**
| 355 | Sandler Ross |
| 416 | Thames Arthur atty |
| 515 | Cahan David |
| 687 | Morton Henry |

**Regis**
| 405 | Pork Parlor |
| 540 | Lane Sarah |

**Roth Rd**
| 9 | Flynn Clark |
| 12 | Bishop Barney Advertising Res |
| 56 | Barber Billy Jo |
| 67 | Walker Damon |
| 76 | Parrington Felix |

**Salem**
| 1515 | Hunscher David |
| 1842 | Heffner Albert |
| 2222 | Carver Cemetery |
| 2960 | Logan Ann |
| 3468 | Berry Lawrence |
| 5587 | Dimmesdale Arthur Reverend Res |

**Santa Fe**
| 86 | Sanchez Alexander |
| 349 | Taylor Alan |
| 515 | Kazazian Brut |
| 833 | Fox Daniel |
| 896 | Forde Betty |
| 1109 | Fulton Robert Elementary School |
| 1273 | Freeport Auto Repair |
| 1384 | Lucky 7 Grocery |

**Smith Farms**
| | Grubbs Oscar |

**Southgate Mall**
| | Bob's Electrical Supply |
| | Venzon Jewelry |

**Springfield**
| 33 | Cramer Judith |
| 104 | Green David |
| 349 | Wigglesworth James |
| 479 | Bivins Vincent |
| 479 | Chavez Daniel |
| 479 | Cohen Cory |
| 479 | Dean Jerry |
| 481 | Dantzic Mervin |
| 484 | Lentz Robin |
| 524 | David Ross |
| 740 | Frank's Deli |
| 740 | Mayfair Fabrics |
| 742 | Ashkinaze's Men's Styles |
| 742 | B & D Butchers |
| 928 | Banks George Q |
| 1440 | Chaffee Frank |
| 2633 | Abromovitch Sterling |

**Stanford Av**
| 6 | Wolfe T |
| 402 | Daly William H |
| 675 | Barnes Jake |
| 840 | Prewitt Mortuary |
| 1370 | Southside High School |

**Stanley**
| 450 | Joseph Pharmacy |
| 666 | Shelton O M |

**Sunset Dr**
| 1405 | Swimmer Albert F |

**Templeton Av**
| 15 | York Alfred |
| 55 | Gerter Sigmund |
| 66 | Smith Fred E |

**Tennessee Av**
| 1338 | Camuto Philip |
| 1485 | Heavenly Rest Chapel |
| 1620 | North Funeral Home |
| 1625 | Joseph Barney G |

**Topeka**
| 10 | Polk George |
| 46 | Serpa Kelly |
| 69 | Helbert George W |
| 216 | Dwight D Eisenhower High School |
| 258 | Battle Richard |
| 269 | Schneider Burton |
| 338 | Reib Rachel |
| 431 | Bartles Adele |

**Torrence Av**
| 1320 | People's Bus Line Inc |
| 2000 | Scott Building |
| 4143 | Marvello Rosario |
| 6522 | Norton Ralph |
| 7620 | Freeport Press Corp |
| 8724 | Joshua Baptist Church |

**Tudor**
| | |
|---|---|
| 17 | Brezen Stanley |
| 18 | Anders Sparky |
| 29 | Kliff Paul A |
| 91 | Hosmer James |
| 176 | Berlin John F |
| 474 | Hoch Arthur |
| 560 | Tsouprake Demetrios A |

**Vermont Av**
| | |
|---|---|
| 17 | Trimbel Department Store |
| 26 | Barton Hotel |
| 51 | Catton Marianne |
| 228 | Finnegan Joseph |
| 373 | Everingham Thomas |
| 715 | Hecht's Fine Furniture |

**Vincent**
| | |
|---|---|
| 165 | Downey Anne |
| 165 | Downey Stanley |
| 606 | Bell Pamela E |
| 824 | Pietro Peter |

**Virginia Av**
| | |
|---|---|
| 65 | Sharon's Used Goods |
| 88 | Silver Isadore |
| 88 | Silver Jean |
| 175 | Pearl Mildred |
| 265 | Ramsgate Charles |
| 522 | Sharman William |

**Western Av**
| | |
|---|---|
| 56 | Thomas Jules |
| 98 | Loran Anley |
| 123 | Harris Arthur B |
| 570 | Alcohol Control Center |
| 570 | Fairlawn Hospital |
| 666 | Falcione Marshall atty Res |

**Yale Av**
| | |
|---|---|
| 481 | Snead Daniel |
| 533 | Helmer Steven |

# Freeport Source List

**Freeport City Officials**
Airport manager — Marshall Peat
Budget director — Albert Heffner
Building inspector, chief — Barry Tobin
City clerk — Vivian Begley
City Council members — Albert Fuentes
Bernard Garner
Fred E. Smith
Martin Davis
Marcia Gold
City engineer — O.M. Shelton
City forester — John T. Voboril
City manager — Harold Born
City treasurer — Daniel Cahan
Computer and data communications services agency — Sterling Abromovitch
County manager — David Hunscher
Fire chief — Mervin Dantzic
Health Department director — Jane Jacobson
Health and Hospital Corp. director — Mildred Pearl
Housing Authority director — Charles Ramsgate
Human Rights Commission director — Stanley Downey
Human Rights Commission member — Judith Cramer
Land use board director — Matthew B. Robert
Latino affairs director — Marlene Figuera
Mayor — Sam Parnass
    Deputy Mayor — Stanley Brezen
Parks Department director — Thomas Chamberlain
Planning board chairman — Philip Nicholson
Planning board secretary — Betty Forde
Police chief — Lloyd Earl
Press Secretary to the Mayor — Leon Roper
Public Works Dept. director — Robin Lentz
    Deputy director — Ralph Norton
Sanitation commissioner — William Applegate
Social Services director — Cory Cohen
Voluntary Action Center director — Martha Zimmerman
Water Dept. superintendent — L.P. Potts
Welfare director — George Q. Banks
Zoning and Planning Board member — Harry Kempe
Zoo director — Cyrus Tucek
Zoo asst. director — Bayard Parker

**Freeport Court Officials**
Clerk of Court — Abner Hastings
Civil Court judge — John Kramer
City Court administrative officer — William Halpern
District attorney — Paul Robinson
    Chief asst. D.A. — Robert Morgan
    Asst. D.A. — Joseph C. Woodcock Jr.
District court administrative judge — Ross David
District judge — Mary Farrell
District judge — Marvin Hurley
District judge — Samuel A. McMillan
District judge — Aloysius J. Melia
District judge — Harvey Smith

**Freeport School Officials**
Board of education chairman — Rodney Addison
Board of education president — Charles Thorne
Board of education members — Albert Swimmer
Helen Epstein
Jean Silver
Salvatore Vincent
Edwin Minteer
John T. Voboril
Superintendent — Herbert Gilkeyson
English coordinator, high schools — F.W. Stern
Dwight D. Eisenhower H.S. principal — Bernard A. Meyers
Horace Mann H.S. principal — Richard Battle
Horace Mann asst. principal — Daniel Fox
Atherton school board chairman — Forrest L. Abele

**Mallory College**
Adviser, student paper — Robert Figuera
Arts & Science dean — Hobart Bayward Podhoretz
Basketball coach — George Gonzales
Committee on Academic Standing, member — Walter Smith
Dean of Students — William Sharman
    Associate dean — Claudine Godfrey
Education dept. chair. — Alfred Steinberg
English dept. chair. — Samuel Ward
Journalism dean — Herbert Blitzer
Library science dean — Donald L. Richards
Physics professor — Albert Sherman
President — Ruth Pitts Renaldi
Provost — Thomas Palmer
Psychology dept. chair. — Nicholas Trowbridge
Sociology dept. chair. — Margot Adler
Track coach — Steve Helmer
Trustee — Karl Quire

**St. Mary's College**
English assoc. prof. — Frederick L. Lynn
Financial aid director — C.L. Braverman
Political Science prof. — Vincent Bivins
President — N. Francis Simms
Provost — Stanley Stiga
Trustee — Dorothy M. Seaver

**Civic and Service Groups**
American Civil Liberties Union local chapter president — Sara F. Glasser
Elks (Benevolent and Protective Order of Elks or
    B.P.O.E.) secretary — Peter Hay
Freeport Chamber of Commerce
    President — Clifford Guzman
    Secretary — Fred Graham
    Public relations director — Thomas Everingham
Freeport Civic Society president — Lawrence Berry
Good Citizens League head — Alvin Diamond
Jewish Community Council director — Arthur Hoch
Kiwanis Club manager — John F. Berlin
League of Women Voters local chairwoman — Mildred Cahan

**Hospital Officials**
Community Hospital
    Director — Vincent Seaver
    Medical services director — Stanley Downey
    Medical staff director — Alfred Arnold
    Public information director — Beverly Collins
Fairlawn Hospital
    Alcohol control center head — Charles Felson
    Director — Milton Williams
    Medical resources director — Dianne Kilafar

**State Officials**

| | |
|---|---|
| Attorney General | Alfred Steinberg |
|     Deputy attorney general | Michael Canzian |
| State assemblyman | Peter Pietro |
| Commissioner of Aeronautics | William Sullivan |
| Comptroller | Thomas Wolfe |
| Public Utilities Commission chairman | Michael McKirdy |
|     Press officer | Jack Nagel |
| State senator | Joseph Margeretta |
| Governor | Janet Kocieniewski |
| Lieut. Governor | Harry Lee Waterfield |
| Ombudsman for state prisoners | Bruce Stroh |

**Federal Officials**

| | |
|---|---|
| U.S. Attorney | Stephen C. Jenkins |
|     Asst. U.S. Attorney | Herbert N. Kaplan |
| Congressman | William Trenzier |
| Senators | Janice Cooper |
| | James Dufur |

**Business Executives**

| | |
|---|---|
| Baldwin Protection Systems president | Felix Parrington |
| Exton Electric president | Alexander Sanchez |
| National Security Bank, Freeport branch, president | Elizabeth Bennett |
| People's Bus Line, Inc., owner | George W. Hulbert |

**Union Officials**

| | |
|---|---|
| City Trade Union Fed. director | Daniel Chavez |
| Hotel and Restaurant Workers union head, state | Bert Gentle |
| Nat'l Federation of Teachers, local head | Helen Carruthers |

# Index

## Exercises and Assignments

Accountant, 122
Acne, 113
Acquisition, 13
Admissions, 53
Advance, 175
Age, 183
Ambition, 205
Annual, 209
Applicants, 130
Appointees, 19
Appointment, 258
Appreciation, 19
Architecture, 72
Arraign, 192
Arrested, 180
Arrest Report, 183
Assessments, 231
Astrology, 78
Attribution, 17
Authorities, 210

Bail, 192
Balance and Fairness, 19
Bankrupt, 191
Barometers, 95
B Copy, 108
Behavior, 122
Belmont, 21
Bidding, 102
Bingo, 182
Bite, 181
Boards, 147
Bonds, 230
Bondsman, 192
Bowler, 205
Brevity, 19
Broker, 212
Budget Talk, 219
Burger, 153
Bus, 8
Business, 230

Calendar, 8
Camera, 72
Canines, 30
Car Costs, 210
Carols, 96
Cars, 121
Cars React, 123
Catholic, 82
Cecil, 141
Center, 29
Ceremonial, 89
Changes, 22
Charity, 12
Checks, 38
Chen Arrest, 183
Chen Indict, 189
Chen Judge, 191
Chen React, 190
Chen Sentence, 190
Children, 87
Chit-Chat, 251
Citations, 242
City-Suburb, 235
Class-Based, 130
Classmate, 175
Clubs, 148
Coach, 72
Commencement, 93

Commentary, 108
Compare, 235
Comparison, 234
Complaints, 183
Constituencies, 229
Construction, 212
Continents, 234
Conviction, 189
Cookies, 180
Copy Editing Marks, 2
Council, 146
Craftsman, 27
Crime Reports, 180
Crimes, 183
Criticism, 126
Crowding, 192
Cyanide, 87

Dangerous, 182
Dangers, 163
Daredevil, 9
Data, 230
Dates, 130
Death, 255
Degrees, 108
Delayed, 62
Demographics, 247
Deposits, 72
Developing the Story Idea, 6
Dickens, 61
Digital, 210
Dining, 80
Diseases, 81
District Attorney, 7
Diversity, 107
Divorce Rate, 123
Documents, 158
Dogs, 187
Donations, 122
Driving, 139
Drugs, 180
Dumped, 2

Edison, 85
Editing Your Copy, 1
Education, 232
Elephant, 9
Emergency, 30
Endorse, 240
Essays, 106
Ethnic Scores, 156
Execs, 212

Family, 103
Fans, 31
Fantasies, 130
Feet, 95
Fifty Common Errors, 68
Finance, 212
Fire, 7
Flagg, 163
Flies, 120
Foreign, 96
Freedom, 241

Galloway, 128
Garbage, 235
Gas Leak, 164
Genealogy, 80

Gifts, 158
Goals, 10
Golfers, 10
Government, 116
GP, 122
Grades, 73
Growth, 35
Gun, 52

Handouts, 212
Health Stats, 73
Heart, 87
Heir, 107
High Scorers, 40
Holiday, 80
Hoofer, 86
Hope, 88
Hot Line, 17
Housing, 234
Human Interest, 22

Ignorance, 113
Ignorance React, 117
Imports, 210
In-Depth, 134
Index, 211
Indict, 192
Indigents, 192
Infant, 37
Inflated, 22
Inflation, 72
Inspection, 234
Interpret, 95
Inventory, 210
Investigation, 183
Investment, 63
IRS, 79
Issue, 95

Jailed, 72
Journalism, 129

Kliff, 1

Labor, 211
Lakes, 86
Land Use, 234
Laundromat, 7
Law Students, 122
Lawyer, 122
Layoff, 209
Legacy, 147
Legal Aid, 191
Librarian, 72
Licensing, 232
Life, 189
Links, 205
Lobby, 51
Longo, 9
Loser, 200
Low Pay, 22
Lunch Box, 80

Market, 211
Mediocrity, 140
Med Students, 122
Meetings, 13

Memorial, 6
Merit, 6
Merit Folo, 13
Minor, 205
Minors, 149
Missing, 8
Mortality, 36
Museum, 80
Music, 122

Names, 31
New Business, 211
Newsstand, 100
New Voices, 62
No Baby, 79
Nonprofit, 211
No Phone, 39

Ombudsman, 7
Open-Closed, 211
Opening, 51
Opening React, 77
Outage, 9

Parade, 7
Parents, 89
Park, 52
Pattern, 158
Payroll, 95
Pedestrian, 162
Periodicals, 108
Perkins, 167
Pets, 79
Planning, 6
Players, 202
Poet, 27
Poetry, 18
Police, 183
Politico, 154
Portrait, 80
Pose, 258
Postal, 121
Preparations, 164
Prevention, 183
Prime, 212
Priorities, 34
Probation, 201
Problems, 258
Process, 230
Professions, 138
Projection, 36
Promotion, 212
Proposed, 225
Prospects, 121
Provost, 101
Pulse, 210

Questionable, 247
Quicksand, 52
Quit, 255

Racial-Religious, 155
Racial-Religious Folo, 249
Racism, 200
Rain, 164
Ratings, 130
Recipiency, 232
Recital, 8

Record Keeping, 230
Records, 231
Reds-Braves, 199
Reduce, 192
Register, 31
Reject, 148
Religion, 122
Rent, 211
Reorganized, 209
Reports, 163
Requirements, 117
Restricted, 30
Rumor, 21
Runner, 198
Rural, 191

Safe, 22
Santa, 78
School Board, 222
Selection, 191
Shares, 212
Sharing, 211
Shoplifting, 31
Shoppers, 234
Shotgun, 61
Slay, 239
Smokers, 142
Solitary, 85
Spectator, 205
Speed, 163
Spring, 3
Statistics, 117
Sterile, 95
Sting, 88
Stocks, 208
Styles, 123
Subsidy, 103
Sunshine, 242
Superintendent, 18
Survey, 211
Suspension React, 123
Swimmer, 168

Teaching, 150
Three Dead, 162
Tippers, 13
Top Twenty, 157
Tourism, 209
Trade, 198
Trail, 192
Trees, 3
Trial (1), 52
Trial (2), 53
Trip, 52
Truck, 163
Tsouprake, 168
TV Viewing, 40
Twins, 86

Union, 122
Unobtrusive, 103
Unsafe, 63
Urban, 191

Various, 3
Verification, 18
Vigilant, 232
Vouchers, 235
Vox Populi, 30

Waiter, 78
Weather, 7
Wedding, 11
Wind, 6

Youthful, 192

Zoning, 234
Zoo, 6

## Class Discussion

Agenda, 259
Analysis, Bids, 55
Banner, 185
Cities (3), 236
Con Artist, 244
Direct, 24
Disclosure, 177
Dumb-Down, 259
Educated Journalists, 109
Family Court, 194
Feedback (2), 166
Figures, 42
Fly-Participant, 133
Front-Page Play, 32
Guidelines, 252
Harassment, 194
Indefensible, 151
Interests, 104
Jargon, 216
Johns (2), 252
Lists, 119
Millionaires, 206
Names, 245
New News, 98
Passive, 159
Profile, 125
Pseudo-Events, 98
Puff, 216
Purpose, 66
Red, 208
Reds and Howard, 206
Reporters, 104
Second Day, 66
Seeing, 159
Syracuse, 74
Time, 90
Top Five, 83
Traits, 16
TV News, 91
Wasteland Revisited, 91

## DB/CAR

Amendment, 237
Books, 16
Census, 75
Chart, 152
Cheating, 133
Cities (1), 33
Colleges, 24
Contraceptive, 119
Costs, 160
Heroes, 259
Holocaust (1), 110
Income, 236
Judges, 237
Mothers, 56
Offenders, 84
Opposites, 260
Ponytail, 245
Priesthood, 125
Rape, 196
Readers, 91
RSI, 99
Safe Sex, 253
Scorecard (1), (2), 260
SLAPP, 196
STD (2), 56
Stolen, 166
Tactile, 104

## Fix It

Attribution, 26
Basic Budget, 238
Count 'Em, 133
Driver Check, 186
Fact Checking, 99

Handguns, 186
Leads, 67
Leave or Delete, 253
Match 'Em, 217
More Trademarks, 119
Prepositions, 125
Scrambled, 59
Tighten, Adjust, 187
To the Point, 152
Trademarks, 105
Usage (1), 50
Usage (2), 76
Who-Whom, 84

## Home Assignments

AIDS, 176
Analysis, Cemetery, 55
Bicycle Trip, 15
Brush-Back, 15
Choices, 90
Components, 24
Compute, 109
Contribution, 258
Disparity, 244
Dispute, 14
Drive, 14
Farrakhan, 131
Fog, 74
Gas, 15
Graduates, 206
Graffiti, 194
Guns, 14
High-Low, 216
Holes, 185
Layers, 98
Leads, 65
Mail, 14
Observe, 104
Oops, 151
Policy, 252
Readable, 165
Scapegoat, 124
Shooting, 14
Sources, 118
STD (1), 41
STD (3), 65
Taxes, 14
Technical, 32
Tennis, 15
Writer, 83

## Projects, Campus

Altruism, 150
Auditing the Campus, 165
Bias (1), 23
Binges, 192
Campus Crime, 184
Cheating, 73
Coverage, 205
Crime Count, 184
Dating, 130
Diet, 31
Educated, 83
Evaluation, 96
Gender, 117
Incidents, 123
Interfaith, 73
Involvement, 13
Ivory Tower, 89
Live In (1), (2), 103
Market Basket, 213
Marriage, 63
Omission, 258
Plans, 13
Policy, 184
Population, 90
Racial, 123
Ratings, 158
Recruit, 73
Remedial, 58
Requirements, 175

Right-Left, 235
Schedule, 243
Segregated, 258
Smokers, 176
Spending, 40
Tatters, 53
Tension, 108
Unwed, 108
Voters, 251
Weight, 40

## Projects: Community

Aged, 97
Arms, 124
At Risk, 90
Bias, 23
Big Dough, 98
Bodies, 41
Bottlenecks, 74
Broke, 215
Broken, 63
Career, 13
Car Theft, 185
Channel One, 243
College Plans, 23
Concern, 54
Deadbeat Dads, 109
DWI, 151
Eating, 31
Efficiency, 185
Environment, 165
Execution, 193
Feedback (1), 165
Firearms, 188
Fitness, 205
Gay-Lesbian, 97
Inhale, 131
Mail, 151
NAEP, 176
Omission, 258
Outdoors, 32
Polite, 53
Prayer, 13
Purchase, 159
Satisfaction, 130
Schoolhouse, 83
Scores, 63
Sex Education (1), 251
Status, 235
Sweet Stuff, 117
White Collar, 193

## Skill Drills

Abused and Misused Words, 5
Arithmetic, 43
Auditing Your Emotions, 160
Business and Labor Terms, 216
Court Terms, 196
Ethical, 260
Famous Works, 110
Grammar, Punctuation and Style, 4
Guidelines, 25
Identify, 25
Lead Choice, 66
Libel and Privacy, 245
Necessities, 58
Police Vocabulary, 186
Property Assessments, 237
References, 43
Simplifying, 67
Spelling, 4
Sports Vocabulary, 206
Tightening the Lead, 75
What's Next, 119

## Tests

Case, 167
Define, 254
Error Identification, 99
Punctuation, 111
Spelling, 84

Subject-Verb Agreement, 126
Troublesome, 238
Usage, 197

## What's Wrong
Arson, 246
Backache, 16

Escapee, 105
Hopped Up, 161
Jilted, 26
Look Again, 218
Prizewinner, 179
*The New York Times* Bloopers, 50
Vote, 133
Wet, 92

Winner, 33

## You Decide
Anti-Gay, 179
Case Studies, 262
Claims, 161
Enhancement, 33

Gangs, 76
Holocaust (2), 112
Johns (1), 105
No English, 207
Rapper, 254
Restrictions, 153
Sex Education (2), 264
Term Paper, 60

Index **279**